The Personal Art

ALSO BY PETER ROBINSON

Poetry

Overdrawn Account
This Other Life
Entertaining Fates
Lost and Found
About Time Too
Selected Poems 1976–2001
Ghost Characters
The Look of Goodbye
The Returning Sky
Buried Music
Collected Poems 1976–2016
Ravishing Europa
Bonjour Mr Inshaw

Prose & Interviews

Untitled Deeds
Talk about Poetry: Conversations on the Art
Spirits of the Stair: Selected Aphorisms
Foreigners, Drunks and Babies: Eleven Stories
The Draft Will
September in the Rain
The Constitutionals

Translations

The Great Friend and Other Translated Poems
Selected Poetry and Prose of Vittorio Sereni
The Greener Meadow: Selected Poems of Luciano Erba
Poems by Antonia Pozzi

Criticism

In the Circumstances: About Poems and Poets
Poetry, Poets, Readers: Making Things Happen
Twentieth Century Poetry: Selves and Situations
Poetry & Translation: The Art of the Impossible
The Sound Sense of Poetry
Poetry & Money: A Speculation

The Personal Art

Essays, Reviews & Memoirs

Peter Robinson

Shearsman Books

First published in the United Kingdom in 2021 by
Shearsman Books Ltd
PO Box 4239
Swindon
SN3 9FN

Shearsman Books Ltd Registered Office
30–31 St. James Place, Mangotsfield, Bristol BS16 9JB
(this address not for correspondence)

ISBN 978-1-84861-743-8

CONTENTS

PREFACE

The Personal Art is a selection from my critical writings on modern and contemporary poetry produced over the last forty years, to which I have added a section of memoirs connected with a life that turned to such writing, as well as a few occasional pieces on my own poetry. Almost all of these pieces first appeared in other places. I am grateful to the editors and publishers of the volumes for their prompting, encouraged revisions, general support, and for permission to reprint here. Details of first publication can be found in a note at the end of the volume. The writings chosen have been organised into five sections. The first collects essays, articles, and essay-length reviews on some of the older twentieth-century British poets who most engaged me when young, arranged according to the chronology of the writers' works. The second contains a gathering of articles and reviews of twentieth-century American poetry, the third gathers writings about other British poets who emerged in the 1960s and 1970s, some of them associated with what's called Cambridge School, which I encountered when first studying there, and with the British Poetry Revival. The fourth does the same for poetry from the island of Ireland, and from other Anglophone poetries. The final one is a gathering of occasional memoir pieces.

For one reason or another, I have never had to earn a living as a reviewer of books, and have, for the most part, been able to choose what to spend time thinking about and writing on. Naturally, a number of these pieces were produced because I accepted invitations to write on the book by the journal concerned. Others happened because I wanted to express gratitude or indebtedness to, interest in, and affection for, the writers concerned. The book's opening item, 'The Personal Art', is an expanded version of an essay written in response to an invitation to produce an account of my own poetry for the *PN Review*. I have placed it at the beginning to give it salience as a title piece – one that briefly sketches some of the concerns engaged with over the years. What unites the writings gathered here is an involvement with the nature of poetry, its forms of subjectivity, the minutiae of its techniques and how they can work to make experience, of selves and their relations with others, complexly intelligible. This is why I have adopted *The Personal Art* as the title for the collection, always remembering that the personal has meaning within implied and addressed cultural and social conditions that require and assume the existence of other persons (represented, referred to, implied or addressed) and their personal lives – for the personal is, after all, what we have in common.

Peter Robinson

still one need not fail

to wish poetry well
where intellect is habitual –
glad that the Muses have a home and swans –
that legend can be factual;
happy that Art, admired in general,
is always actually personal.

Marianne Moore, 'In the Public Garden'

ONE

THE PERSONAL ART

'Où sont des morts les phrases familières,
L'art personnel, les âmes singulières?'

These *ubi sunt* lines from Paul Valéry's 'Le cimetière marin' ponder the
fate of homely phrases once used by the dead, their personal gift, and
their individual souls. I have taken literally the second of his three terms
as a title for this brief essay about poems in relation to privacy and the
marketplace. Let me introduce the issues with a perhaps trivial example.
My second book, *This Other Life* (1988), contains a poem about setting
off to visit a friend in hospital and failing to reach her, thanks to a
rainstorm, before visiting hours ended. 'Depending on the Weather' first
appeared in a magazine with a slightly different opening to its fourth
verse. 'Ten years on now, you have had two children, / complications' is
a revision of 'you have had two hernias. / And children'. The later version
is an improvement – I hope you'll agree – and the poem's dedicatee was
not sorry to see the disappearance of that word 'hernias'.

It was not, I'm afraid, in consideration of her sensitivities that I made
the alterations, but rather in response to the publisher's. That clumsy
end-stopped line in the earlier version, and its gratuitously reversing the
sequence of my friend's bodily pains, are good enough reasons for the
change. However, if my publisher also objected to the poor technique,
he chose nevertheless to express his criticism as a consideration for a
reader's imaginative and moral delicacy. I had been too personal. Still,
a bit of me continues to worry over the artful and half-disembodied
vagueness of 'complications', which could prompt ideas ranging from
various birthing difficulties, to the notion that having kids complicates
life. I'm similarly slightly regretful about the loss of the particular reason
for my friend's being in hospital.

The case of the 'two hernias' is perhaps a small instance of what
Elizabeth Bishop in a letter described as her 'George Washington
handicap – I can't tell a lie even for art'. If not exactly lying in the
revised version, I could accuse myself of being economical with the
truth. However, I did make the change with some tardy consideration
for another of Bishop's artistic principles: tact and discretion, especially
about experiences not one's own. The publication of a biography, letters,
and recollections has made it abundantly clear how autobiographical

Bishop's poetry is, while equally showing what art she deployed to present this often anguished material with reticent good manners and 'the joking voice'. The truth of her poems, then, depended not on the handicap of an inability to lie, but had to be achieved despite it.

George Oppen differently emphasised the problem when writing to Charles Tomlinson on 5 May 1963: 'Not, perhaps I should add, that I take truthfulness to be a social virtue. I think very probably it is not. But I think it is poetic: I think really nothing else is.' If social and poetic values are to be considered distinct, it may be the task of some writing to keep them in touch with each other. One of the assumptions, here, is that poems are balancing acts: they have a truthful eye on their subjects, on the people involved, and on the demands of language and form; but they also take into account the minds of other people, such as editors, publishers, perhaps reviewers, and most of all, possible readers. Poetry begins in private lives, and is frequently about a private life too. If it reaches the public domain, it does so with the aid of, largely though not exclusively, the marketplace.

Though I'm going to emphasise the intimate and personal in this essay, what I have to say is not an embattled reiteration of Pound's 'a tawdry cheapness / Shall outlast our days', or his affront at the debasement of values 'Decreed in the market-place.' It is, rather, the exploration of a dilemma faced by any poet who finds that poems don't grow if they don't grow out of direct personal experience, and therefore always begin in autobiography, yet who also believes that this personal experience only has literary value if it is transformed by art into an example of something other than the merely personal, as well as a communication between people. How and to what extent the personal experience must lose its particular savour, if it must, so as to become such a communication and an art object in the public domain is another context for the balancing acts involved in poetic composition. While the poet and a language make this communication possible, it is publishers, postal services, bookshops, libraries, and most of all readers who make it happen. Though poems are usually written in private, the poet's creative solitude is populated with the memory of words and voices. While these include a vast array of other poems, songs, and writings, they are also made up of family, friends, acquaintances, public figures, and the critical utterances that have gone into producing literary self-awareness or conscience. Just as Wittgenstein was at pains to demonstrate that there could be no such thing as a private language, so the poet's composing privacy can only be understood as a communal affair.

Similarly, what we consider events in private life or personal experience are frequently particular examples of all too common happenings. Robert Creeley has suggested that it is 'the personal which makes the common in so far as it recognises the existence of the many in the one.' *This Other Life* has a set of eight poems about the aftermath of a young woman's rape in Italy during September 1975. One of the many differences between being raped and being made love to is that, while the latter is an intimate form of social recognition, the former denies and assails the socialised privacy and individuality of its victims. That the rape that occasioned my poems was witnessed at gunpoint adds to what might be called the false public character of the event. When the rapist was brought to trial and the victims called as witnesses, this public aspect was, to that extent, socially recognised. Yet such a subject, one that appears all too regularly in papers and on television as news, is not readily accommodated. Talk of it causes embarrassment, spoils conversations. To be raped, in this sense, is to have been subjected to an experience that is simultaneously an isolating private pain (not to be communicated) and a painfully public fact (happening with other people present, then retold to a policeman, a solicitor, and finally in a court of law).

My attempt in those poems written between 1979 and 1985 was, it seems now, to renegotiate those terms 'private' and 'public', expressing tactfully what cannot usually be said, and so making a recognition of what had happened, while simultaneously restoring to the painfully public retellings a measure of intimacy and warmth that was differently denied in each case. W. H. Auden's epigraph to *The Orators* is one slogan for this poetic project: 'Private faces in public places / Are wiser and nicer / Than public faces in private places.' In my first book, *Overdrawn Account* (1980), a sequence of poems called 'The Benefit Forms' had tried a similar stylistic revaluing of unemployment and welfare state provision, experiences that occurred before the rape but were made into poems after it. More riskily, I was on similarly shifting private-public grounds when composing the poems of an infidelity and in 'Confetti', about another couple's marriage breaking up, in *Entertaining Fates* (1992).

Borrowing from Adrian Stokes' writings on art, I convinced myself that this aesthetic re-shaping of the private and public were forms of reparation. My book of criticism, *In the Circumstances* (1992), was an attempt to justify what Paul Muldoon in a recent poem has described as 'that daft urge to make amends / when it's far too late'. Ian Sansom once underlined the fact that I 'seem torn between the idea that poetry has a duty to make amends and the belief that such an ambition is misplaced'. This is fair, but the apparent contradiction disappears if the 'reparation' I claimed could be found in and through composing poems is described as the emblem of an intimate understanding which has been damaged, denied, or destroyed. I would suggest that 'A September Night' seeks to be such an emblem, even when it appears in its last line ('I'd just make amends') to doubt what Muldoon calls 'that daft urge'. Even 'Depending on the Weather' could be read in this light as an attempt to convey a feeling frustrated by a storm.

This is one reason why the poems I write tend to be lyric dialogues, actual or implicit, with addressees in the second person singular, or which oscillate between second and third persons. In poems such as those about the rape, like 'Cleaning', the change of pronoun dramatises, at the level of the poem's speaking voice, a shortening of the distance that has been extended by a violation of the two people's privacy. My efforts had partly been encouraged by Frank O'Hara's 'Personism: A Manifesto', and especially the passage where he describes writing a poem for someone he was in love with on August 27, 1959, and 'While I was writing it I realised that if I wanted to I could use the telephone instead of writing the poem'. Works that attempt to foster intimacy by their tone and address are not the equivalents of private phone calls or letters, especially when they most resemble them. The fact that a poem is written, rather than a call made, suggests that the purpose is not, or not only, to establish an understanding 'between the poet and the person'.

Some of my poems, written to be read by the people involved and by others unknown, try to bring into a public space the poetic equivalent of an intimacy which was, for whatever reason, lacking in the human occasion from which it arose. Apostrophes in poems are addresses to absent persons, and readers are 'overhearing' what may seem to have the mysteriousness of half a private telephone conversation. Yet these readers are not overhearing anything they are not meant to hear, and the other half of the conversation does not exist. The 'half' in the poem is designed to reveal all that the reader, strictly, needs.

Despite the fact that intimate poems apparently between just two people may resemble the vastly influential 'confessional' poem, this lyric dialogue style cannot afford to dramatise much the narrating poet figure. When Robert Lowell hears his 'ill-spirit sob in each blood cell, /

as if my hand were at its throat… / I myself am hell', his written up lines cast the experiencing self into an attention-claiming posture. Later, in the painful sonnet 'Reading Myself', he links his phrase making to a lack: 'I memorised the tricks to set the river on fire – / somehow never wrote something to go back to.' Yet just such a going back over things is at the heart of poetry's work and its capacity to endure. Placed between two or more people, a lyric dialogue poem is wary of upstaging the others involved; it is not then centred on one individual's problems or shocking experiences, and does not even partially confess, but is offered to the other addressed and the reader as a poetic recompense for an intimate understanding that is only too frequently not there in life.

Vittorio Sereni thought that 'one doesn't read a poem, one lives with it', and his emphasis points to an intimacy that is there in the relationships that people who need poetry build up with the work of poets that, as we say, they care for. No one ever said it was easy living with someone, and the same can be said for living with a poem. What's more, if you need this experience of long-term relationship with texts, it's likely you will seek out works that give pleasure and satisfaction over a long period; you might like things to be difficult from time to time; and you will not be convinced by poems which are ready to give their all on first acquaintance. If living with a work brings greater familiarity, it is as if the poem has also got to know the reader better: greater familiarity with a literary text is a form of self-knowledge. The intimate understanding produced by this living with a poem is an equivalent of, though by no means the same as, the intimacy with an experience, other people, a language and at least one literary culture, which produced the work.

Living with a poem, as with someone, means being involved in a process. The writing we'd prefer not to live without is, as W. S. Graham wrote, 'brought to life by the reader and takes part in the reader's change'. Finding such life-given, life-giving works involves considerable experiment and reconsideration. The poems I need are often not the ones I thought I wanted. Given the ideas about lyrical intimacy sketched above, it may not come as a surprise that I find myself returning to writing which was not intended only for immediate publication, but which seems to have some prior work to do, and which is full of the purpose to communicate, though not, apparently, to me: many of Shakespeare's 'sugared sonnets among his private friends', are like this, though it has not prevented them from remaining in print for a number of centuries. This preference for intimate works will not justify writing only for an amicable province of one's own creation. The intimate tone and seemingly private subjects I have been speaking up for are, after all, not quite what they seem: they are there to help in the constructive re-composition of damaging occasions, not to confess faults, even when moral considerations and the admission of error or an expression of regret are part of what has gone into the poem.

To achieve the aim of placing in a public space poetic equivalents of intimate understandings that were missing from life, a poet needs readers, that's to say, some being attended to, and this involves a certain amount of literary 'success'. The required degree and type of this phenomenon will vary from poet to poet. Likely to hinder or thwart its achievement is a lot of personality marketing: this is because the writing of the poems and their being read needs processes of deepening acquaintance and self-knowledge; you cannot properly get to know someone, including yourself, if presented from the first with a decided commodity. I wonder if I am alone in finding myself quite frequently put off reading a book of poems by the guff on the back. This is not only because the claims being made are frequently hard to sustain, but also, far from characterizing the poetry, they paradoxically make all the poets sound the same. Similarly, the poet who comes to believe his or her identity as presented for the purposes of market share targeting risks being condemned to a life of self-parody.

This 'identity' has little to do with the 'art personnel' of Valéry's lines. There, you remember, the poet is meditating on what has happened to dead people's familiar turns of phrase, their personal talent, their individual souls. Human interactions have become fixed, if not erased, by death; processes of growth have ceased. In 'Concerning *Le Cimetière marin*', Valéry describes a compositional attitude in which the poet nourishes 'doubts, scruples, and regrets – so that a work perpetually resumed and recast gradually takes on the secret importance of an exercise in self-reform.' As if responding to Rilke's appeal at the end of his 'Archäischer Torso Apollos' that 'Du mußt dein Leben ändern' [You must change your life], Valéry suggests that it can be achieved through prolonged creative work, while Sereni's idea of the reader living with a poem indicates that this labour of self-reform need not be confined to the realm of the poet's efforts. After all, one prerequisite for writing and revising well is a reader's keen eye and ear for a poem's complexes of meaning and sound. It is in the processes of such sustained co-existence that I would begin to understand Richard Wollheim's idea that 'Art is, in Wittgenstein's sense, a form of life.'

The personal art I have been defending is to be achieved through vital relationships – with language, experience, other people, and between readers. After all, the poet is just another reader once a poem is finished. During the summer of 1974, I worked as a security guard at a factory in Speke. When on nights, the job involved making hourly trips around the various clocking points on the premises. To pass the time on my rounds and scare away the dark, I would speak poems out loud. As a result, I still have off by heart snatches of Charles Olson's 'The Twist' and Elaine Feinstein's translation of Tsvetayeva's 'Poem of the End'. For me, such a repeated saying of poems is the key experience of this personal art. 'We must try to live!' as Valéry urges in his final verse, but just listen how that exclamation springs up from the sound of the noun and verb in the preceding phase, 'The wind lifts!': 'Le vent se lève! ... Il faut tenter de vivre!'

BASIL BUNTING: WE'LL ENAMEL HIM!

Writing to Dorothy Pound in September 1965, Basil Bunting called his long poem 'Briggflatts' 'the best thing I have done by miles'. Without it, his oeuvre, which now has a trajectory with a high point of arrival, would appear more like a handful of variously ambitious longer poems, a number of perfectly turned lyrics, a little group of satirical squibs, and some experiments in translation. His masterpiece was first published in *Poetry* (Chicago) in January 1966. The magazine had supported Bunting since it accepted 'Villon', the first of his longer poems, in 1930 – and continues to do so in that Don Share, currently in charge, is the editor of this complete, annotated edition of the British poet's work. Deirdre and Stuart Montgomery's Fulcrum Press published *Briggflatts* in book form the month after its magazine appearance. These near simultaneous publications on both sides of the Atlantic are the crowning moment in a writing life that had been beset by difficulties, and repeatedly interrupted by circumstances both personal and political, that, despite its many achievements, leaves his oeuvre rather like a range of eroded hillocks and foothills when compared with 'the Alps' – as Bunting described it in 'On the fly-leaf of Pound's "Cantos"'.

Yet Bunting would insist that he had come to his sense of poetry before encountering the example of Ezra Pound, and his view of the art contributed to placing the bar for successful work consistently higher than Pound would set it. 'DICHTEN = CONDENSARE' is the definition of poetry attributed to Bunting in the *ABC of Reading*. 'Dichten', meaning 'to seal, to caulk, to make tight, to write poems', is made equivalent to the Italian for 'to thicken'. To write poetry, then, is to give density to linguistic texture. Bunting is also famous for edited down sonnets by Shakespeare, removing the reiterative baroque of his sugared style – as if they would have been better written by Hemingway. This places his practice firmly in the tradition of modernism's dislike of ornamental flourish and recursive explication.

'Adjectives drain nouns' is among the poet's sayings that have been absorbed into routine creative writing advice, but Bunting also thought that articles did so as well. Taking his cue from the adaptation of Fenollosa on the Chinese Character, his work manifests a belief that greater concretion and immediacy would be achieved by reducing to a minimum the articles and other determiners, dealing out directly the frequently monosyllabic nouns and verbs, like hard gems with as little in the way of setting as possible. One can sense the benefit of such a strategy at its best at the beginning of 'Briggflatts' where there are just four definite articles and no indefinite ones in the first eleven lines. Yet it is a mannerist mode and reaches an almost self-parodic *nec plus ultra* in the late poem 'At Briggflatts meetinghouse', which begins: 'Boasts time mocks cumber Rome. Wren / set up his own monument'. This poem has two definite articles and one indefinite one in a total of twelve lines. Its opening appears made of three verbs and three nouns, two of them proper names, though two of the verbs might be plural nouns, hence the curious feeling of being pummelled by barely construable syllables, the reader's consciousness like the stone on which the mason times his mallet in the first movement of 'Briggflatts' with its 'lark, mallet, / becks, flocks / and axe knocks'.

This is his signature style, which comes to its great fruition in the poem in five parts with a coda that he called his 'autobiography'. Reading through Share's gathering of all his surviving poems, including two schoolboy compositions made at Leighton Park in Reading, is to see how a coherently tight-lipped aphoristic style ('Blame / stays the same') could emerge from variously successful experiments in longer 'sonata' form (usually three or four contrasting movements – the most satisfying, for my money, being the early classic 'Villon' and 'Aus dem Zweiten Reich', while 'Loquitur' and ' The Spoils' also contain finely achieved passages). The taut, sometimes brutally direct, style of his occasional lyrics – in which the Poundian satirical squib is usually the least successful of his modes – are frequently fully achieved, and there are two very fine ballads, 'Gin the Goodwife Stint' and 'The Complaint of the Morpethshire Farmer', which show Bunting's lifelong love of Wordsworth, a commitment sharply separating him from the tastes of his mentor who had jeered at the British poet in his 'Homage to Sextus Propertius' – the poem of Pound's that most impressed Bunting.

There are a good number of beautifully finessed lyrics, from 'Weeping oaks grieve…' of 1924 to 'Now we've no hope of going back' first published in 1980. Alongside these are the free adaptations mainly from Latin and Persian, though preeminent among them is 'Chomei at Toyama', made by rendering as verse an Italian translation of *Hojoki*, a Japanese prose classic written by Kamo no Chomei (1155–1215) in the vicinity of Kyoto three years before his death. As Pound's stylistic originations would often be tagged to a polemical point about what the scholars had failed to understand, so Bunting's Chomei is rendered tendentiously as one who loses faith in his Buddhist beliefs ('My tongue / clacked a few prayers', it ends) – though this is to emphasise only one of the possible interpretations of the original – while the translation's attractively concrete renderings manifest a cleaving to the material world even in its transitory nature, not, perhaps, wholly at one with the Buddha's teachings ('Swirl sleeping in the waterfall! / 'On motionless pools scum appearing / disappearing!' it opens).

Bunting's publishing career also contrasts dramatically with Pound's assiduousness as regards print. His work was first gathered in a privately funded booklet, *Redimiculum Matellarum* (1930), printed in Milan, soon unobtainable. An attempt to interest T. S. Eliot in a typescript called *Caveat Emptor* later in the 1930s came to nothing (Eliot seems not to have warmed to Bunting's work, and his being implicated in 'Attis: Or, Something Missing', a sonata about cult-religion-inspired castration, is not likely to have helped). The *Poems 1950* collection of his work, published at Pound's instigation by the Gleaners Press in Texas, was not proof-read by the poet and contained an intemperate introduction by Dallam Flynn, its editor – which is believed to have prevented the book's issuing in this country by Faber, because Bunting is said to have refused to let it appear without the introduction, though Share reports Eliot as believing it 'too Poundian'.

As a result, the obscurity of the poet's works in the late 1950s is now perhaps difficult to conceive. In 'Debt to Mr Bunting', Roy Fisher reports his becoming aware of this writer's existence when, at their first meeting, Gail Turnbull showed him 'The Orotava Road' and 'The Wells of Lycopolis' – which Turnbull had written out from a borrowed copy of the Galveston edition, and was passing around samizdat fashion. Without the efforts of Fulcrum in the mid-1960s, achieved in collaboration with the intervention of a young Tom Pickard in the poet's life, Bunting could have remained little more than a second-generation modernist rumour. Thanks to that moment of international fame, his work was to remain in print, as the presses that issued it fell, with Fulcrum, then Oxford, and on to Bloodaxe – who made a deal with New Directions for an American edition, which is perhaps where the poet might have been all along. Only now, some thirty years after his death, and half a century since Eliot's, Bunting's works finally find themselves between the covers of a book from Faber & Faber.

A labour of love, Don Share's edition does Bunting's work all the justice that could be asked for it. It is a byproduct of the Editorial Institute at Boston University, founded by Geoffrey Hill and Christopher Ricks. Share's volume places itself in the tradition of John Haffenden's Empson (2001), Archie Burnett's Larkin (2012), and appears on the heels of Ricks and McCue's Eliot (2015). In such eminent editorial company, it thoroughly holds its own, and is largely free of occasional qualms expressed in reviews of those works. Empson left behind a similarly slim *Collected Poems*, so Haffenden's provides the model for an annotated edition in which the entries on the individual poems are a marvel of contextual reconstruction and reader first aid. The same is true of Share's Bunting, though Haffenden has the advantage that Empson's eccentric intellectualism allows for explications that are not available to a Bunting scholar since the construction of his poems is musical and conceptually implicit. The addition of uncollected work to the oeuvre is less overwhelming than Burnett's Larkin, for there are only a couple of limericks, and the presentation of uncollected work such as 'They Say Etna' is essential to an understanding of Bunting's trajectory, not a dilution of it. Finally, the listing of textual allusions is light and largely plausible.

There are ironies. The poet who composed a mordant squib addressed '*To a Poet who advised me to preserve / my fragments and false starts*' now has a twenty-four-page section of his works pointedly named by his editor 'Fragments and False Starts'. In this 671-page book's primary text extent of 271 pages, the poet only collected some 150 of them in his lifetime. Bunting is now also the subject of a 618-page biography, *A Strong Song Tows Us* (2013) by Richard Burton – whose author dutifully cites Bunting's own five-word version, 'Minor poet, not conspicuously dishonest', which nonetheless manages to frame a confession in the implication of its second phrase. Bunting has now also posthumously experienced the attribution to his work of scholarly-style allusiveness. In 'Attis: Or, Something Missing', he renders Dante's 'l'farem di smalto' as '*we'll enamel him!*' – though, since it's Medusa who'll do this, the sense will be 'turn to stone'. To instance a source for the translation (which has dictionary support), Share recalls Andrew Marvell's 'He gave us this eternal spring, / Which here enamels everything' in 'Bermudas'. Yet if this is a one-word allusion, it is a non-significance-starting one. What's more, despite the theme of persecuted nonconformity, neither Marvell nor this poem deserves a mention in the collection edited by Peter Makin, *Basil Bunting on Poetry* (1999).

The poet wrote of his masterpiece that the 'sound of the words spoken aloud is itself the meaning'. Share's edition gives us a fresh opportunity to speak the poems aloud and properly hear their meanings. 'Name and date / split in soft slate / a few months obliterate' is how the first movement of 'Briggflatts' concludes. The words of Bunting's poems were not cut in soft slate, petrified as stonemason's marble, or enamelled by a Medusa-muse. They were written in notebooks and typed on paper. It is through the multiplication of copies and the reprinting of reliable editions that literary works survive. Don Share has provided a canonical Basil Bunting in a thoroughly convincing and usable edition. He has done his poet, these poems, and their readers, an invaluable service.

F. T. PRINCE:
'DELIVERED UP TO FICTION'

For someone born in 1912 the Second World War, its preludes and aftermaths, broke upon life, not as for those born a few years later, with the start of maturity but as an interruption of what had already begun. F. T. Prince reflects in 'Memoirs in Oxford' how 1931 was just the beginning, which 'only made it worse / For those beginning absolutely – / The sense of everything acutely / Set going in reverse.' 'Walks In Rome' finds him remembering 'the post-war post / strength and decision' but, unlike the figure in his 'Afterword on Rupert Brooke', able to 'grow old, eat dirt and be satisfied.' The late 1940s are described as 'not post the sense of wasted and dull old self-division.' By 1939 Prince had published a first volume of poems, a volume that opens with the extraordinarily accomplished 'An Epistle to a Patron.' It might have been freely adapted from Leonardo's letter to Ludovico Sforza, with glances at Pound's Malatesta Cantos and Adrian Stokes: by the end, the poem has become a fictive address to the tyrannical reader, closing 'I have simply hope, and I submit me / To your judgement which will be just.'

It is a poem that fits the description of himself given in 'Not a *Paris Review* Interview' where a beginner in 'The Twenties, anywhere, / Had at once to be aware / Of the Moderns and their kin.' In the list of poets that follows there is no mention of W. H. Auden, who had decisively altered the landscape into which Prince entered between his beginnings in the 1920s and his début volume *Poems* (1938). This lateness is perhaps a clue to the entire oeuvre, which shows a need 'to be aware' and a sense, perhaps, of never quite being in step with the times. The independence thus demonstrated is among Prince's strengths, and he has commanded a discerning though smallish audience. In 'Finis Coronat Opus' he wryly notes: 'Think, how in databanks one snoozes / Safe in the bosom of the Muses / With Larkins, Harrisons and Hugheses.' Prince's second volume takes its title from the classic World War II poem 'Soldiers Bathing' of 1942, but the book did not appear until 1954, a year before Larkin's *The Less Deceived*. The landscape was about to be altered again.

A reason offered for Prince's difficulty in 'Not a *Paris Review* Interview' concerns his relations with those tyrannical readers, enquiring if one could 'See the persons and occasions / In long pieces as evasions?' Though the answer offered is a defence of art as made object not confession, Prince's *Collected Poems 1935–1992* has its share of apparently more direct pieces. Although 'Soldiers Bathing' takes in 'The idea of Michelangelo's cartoon' and 'Another Florentine, Pollaiuolo', becoming a meditation on Christian acceptance of suffering, it is spoken as by the poet himself. Near its opening the poem notes, 'I watch the freedom of a band / Of soldiers who belong to me' and moves through first-person announcements such as 'I see', 'I remember', 'I think', 'I mean', and 'I feel', to 'I watch a streak of red that might have issued from Christ's breast.' The poem's directly spoken formality contributes much to its appeal. There is a more guarded researcher's voice ('We see the difficulty draw him on') from within the Modernist dream of history which first appears in 'Strafford' from *The Doors of Stone*. It is a poem that recalls Geoffrey Hill more than once, speaking of 'that "lost business" in the North' or how he 'Forgives the axe his coming stroke'. Indeed, the entire volume, with its poem 'Campanella' and evocations of imprisonment, frustrated love, and devotion, may have exerted an influence upon the composition of Hill's *King Log* poems. John Ashbery would then be not the only 'strong' poet to have learned from Prince.

A candour similar to that in 'Soldiers Bathing' is also to be found in the two reminiscence poems, 'Memoirs in Oxford' and 'Walks in Rome', where Prince finds himself confronting his earlier self-confusions and appreciates how works which seem accounts of the poet's life are also ones where, as he notes in the early 'To a Friend on his Marriage', 'My passion for the gay and grand / Deliver[s] you up to fiction.' A consciousness of literary reflexivity informs these autobiographical poems. For Prince, the shaping structures of fiction carry over into poetry. In 'Memoirs in Oxford' he observes:

And English and French novelists
   Once dwelt on home as preparation
Through good plain love. If asked 'For what?'
They might have said at least 'Why not
   To live again in our narration?'

Such living again is, of course, never the same as living was. 'Walks in Rome' considers Prince's past by pondering what Stendhal, from whom he draws the title, would have made of the poet's life: 'Yet the novel for him / was about youth – though I / did not die young'. What links both works, and appears to be among Prince's main concerns, is desire, religious or secular, and in both cases he canvases in his poems the responses of acceptance and rejection, as well as of love's difficulties and frustrations. 'Memoirs in Oxford' concludes with an invocation of the atheist Shelley's rebellious passions, his 'verse that spurns the crowd, / Breaks from the wreck of empires, wars…' and sees it in religious terms, before the skilful diminuendo of the poem's close:

> It would be like a hymn, a creed;
>   Yet I began with no such aim,
> But looked for meaning in the past,
> Youth and frustration, and at last
>   This was the way it came.

Prince has taken his five-line stanza from Shelley's *Peter Bell the Third* and it is apt that the poem should close on Shelley, coming itself as it does from 'the wreck of empires, wars…'. The combination of indirection and candour in these poems which contain the distillation of what 'Walks in Rome' calls 'my half-century and more / of debate' on 'those two conundrums, faith / and human passion' was and is inspiring. In the same poem, Prince describes himself as an obsessive craftsman: 'Not to be satisfied but lingering / Cutting, cancelling, rubbing, fingering –', yet he frequently returns to the truth that a work of art has to fish from unconscious levels. In 'Not a *Paris Review* Interview' he avers that what 'conscious will can bring /May or may not help him / Through what is really *dreamt*.' His earlier 'The Old Age of Michelangelo' had drawn out what the implications of this dream might be, for 'the dream stirs in the stone' and

> If I could clutch you in the claws of dream,
> And take you up with me in loneliness
> To the roof-tree, angle of heaven, vault
> Of exquisite pale buffeted glare:
> I should gain or regain
> The heaven of that high passion, pallor, innocence
> – I should gain or regain
> The sole pure love, and fence it with my wings.

What this indicates is that the relations of conscious will and surrender to inspiration are not only at the heart of writing poetry, but also crucial to experiences of love and religious aspiration. Prince's poems are, frequently, not only meditations upon the interaction of these forces, but themselves demonstrate the conundrum in art of being able to do what you want by doing precisely what you can't help but doing. It is the indissoluble interdependence of these forces in Prince's work that makes it so reliable, and has made it so for others.

The poet writes that with 'Walks in Rome' the 'verse is based on the line-lengths established in *The Yüan Chên Variations*'. The note on the latter poem acknowledges Arthur Waley, yet its imaginative reconstruction of friendship between the two Chinese poets Po Chü-i and Yüan Chên is a part of twentieth-century English and American poetry's fascination with an antique aesthetic East, also found, definitively, in Pound's *Cathay* and Bunting's 'Chomei at Toyama'. There is a distinctly autumnal feel about this impressive poem, and not only from its opening:

> Eight times the autumn weather
> has drenched with rain
> those grasses that wave
> green on your grave.

Prince's own unease about what is achieved in a life of writing, which 'Finis Coronat Opus' describes as a sense 'That nothing done or won excuses / The hobbled life, the sprains and bruises', perhaps appears delivered up to fiction in the memory of an ancient poet's friend, whose 'flame is dumb, / and from his brush / no new songs will come.' The final poem in Prince's second collected edition is called 'Last Poem'; regretfully, I suppose, we should take Prince at his word. He will 'wait for, yet a while hence, / My own silence.' F. T. Prince concludes his 'Not a *Paris Review* Interview' with the thought that 'There need be nothing / But a personal spring / To wind us up and keep us going.' His spring may now be winding down, but it remains a pleasure to re-read these poems, whether of transformed autobiography, curious research, or personified voices. And what does it matter when, in the words of the early poem 'Chaka', 'at last there will be something to be said / That I have made my own'?

W. S. GRAHAM:
'A CHANGED OTHER PERSON'

Clive Wilmer's poem 'W. S. Graham Reading' describes the poet in old age at Heffers bookshop, Cambridge, unable to fix on a single work from his *Collected Poems 1942–1977* (1979) which he wanted to read: 'as if to surrender to a single instance / of language / was to surrender.' It was an embarrassing moment for the event's organisers. The poet either drunk or badly hung-over, the reading stalled, the small crowd's patience no more than could be expected:

Then: 'Read any one of them,' somebody cried:
'they're all marvellous!'
    And we beheld a marvel:
an Archangel
    a little damaged
igniting the dark firmament with speech.

I can vouch for the documentary accuracy of Wilmer's poem. I was there. But I confess it wasn't me who called out that unsolicited testimonial, and confess too that I neither think Graham and his work quite deserving of Coleridge's 'damaged archangel' epithet, nor that 'they're all marvellous' is the true story of his poetry. Matthew Francis begins his editor's Introduction to the recently published *New Collected Poems* (Faber and Faber, pp. 381): 'Admirers of W. S. Graham have long felt that his *Collected Poems* is due for revision'. He is certainly a poet whose work deserves to be available in full, or at least rather more than the 250-page selection that he assembled himself. There's always a question, though, about what 'in full' might entail. Francis notes that 'The present collection makes no claim to be a *Complete Poems*, but I believe it does contain his best and most representative work.'

A loaded contrast with Philip Larkin, whose *The Less Deceived* (1955) was published in the same year as Graham's *The Nightfishing*, has dogged criticism over the last twenty years or so. Douglas Dunn rightly insists on the petty irrelevance of any such needing to choose between them in his Foreword to the volume: 'There are different kinds of poetry and they are all indispensable.' The organisation of Francis's *New Collected Poems* is, though, unlikely to cause the controversy that Anthony Thwaite's Larkin *Collected Poems* (1988) did. Francis restores the integrity of Graham's individual collections. The poet failed to collect his first composed – thought second published – book, *The Seven Journeys* (1944), and he cut poems from his first three acknowledged collections. His editor brings these back into print. He also dispenses with Graham's eccentric method of producing a Contents list by numbering the poems collected and merely noting the names of the individual books from which they are taken as an afterthought. Nevertheless, the qualm remains. Graham, for whatever reason, thought the ones he excluded weren't as 'marvellous' as those he put back into print.

At the other end of his oeuvre there are three broad categories of out-take. First, there are poems that Graham published but didn't collect, and which were released in a small press *Uncollected Poems* (1991), plus one from a back issue of *Stand* included in *Selected Poems* (1996). Secondly, we find unpublished poems that were rescued from notebooks sold for a monthly maintenance cheque to Robin Skelton in Canada and which appeared in *Aimed at Nobody* (1993). Then, thirdly, there are various others gathered from letters and manuscripts by Francis, including '*from* With the Dulle Griet in Canada' – an ambitious, but troubled, late attempt at a long poem connected with his 1973 reading tour. Dunn notes in his Foreword that the 'repetition of "language" and communication as obsessive, unfinished subjects can at times feel overdone.' Graham being a poet with a handful of obsessive themes, the later poems he didn't collect do tend to be variations on matters handled in pieces that he did.

Take, for example, 'Falling into the Sea' (first published 1977) and drawn from *Uncollected Poems*. It's an advice poem about how to enjoy drowning ('Breathing water is easy / If you put your mind to it') and ends:

What has happened to you?

You have arrived on the sea
Floor and a lady comes out
From the Great Kelp Wood
And gives you some scones and a cup
Of tea and asks you
If you come here often.

I'm not sure what's happened to 'you', but what's happened to the poem is that it's descended from the disturbingly unreal to the merely whimsical. In the official canon of 103 poems that Graham collected, this drowning obsession is well represented, in 'Three Poems of Drowning', for instance, from *The White Threshold* (1949), a collection whose title announces the centrality of the topic. In 'The Nightfishing', it is crossed with the language theme. Alluding to T. S. Eliot's allusion to *The Tempest*, Graham makes the metamorphoses of literary drowning ('pearled behind my eyes') into an analogy for the processes of self-change experienced in and through language use:

> So I spoke and died.
> So within the dead
> Of night and the dead
> Of all my life those
> Words died and awoke.

We speak and that moment of life dies and we are already other people, but the words, especially if they are printed, awake into a form of permanence. The deeper oddity of this metaphor, though, is that if poetic language is like the salt water of the sea, then poets on the job are simultaneously both in and out of their element – and if poetic language is one version of ordinary language use, then so are we all.

Graham's poetry began to appear during the Second World War, and, as in 'Many without Elegy' or 'Men Sign the Sea', among the first drownings that concern it are those of combatant sailors and flyers. This is not always evident in the early work because it is wedded to the widely noticed turn dark-wards in the language of high modernism during the course of the 1930s – a turn led by writers with loyalties to the Celtic traditions in the British Isles. I'm thinking of Dylan Thomas's youthful fame, but more of *Finnegans Wake* (1939), a work that Graham clearly knew. He quotes from the 'A hundred cares, a tithe of troubles and is there one who understands me?' passage at the book's close in 'Notes on a Poetry of Release' (1946), and his correspondence is frequently imitative of its nonce and portmanteau words. Joyce's final work, written in Paris during the hey-day of the Surrealists, attempts a synthetic unification of human history and consciousness. It's clearest paradox, one which it foreshadows for subsequent experiments, is that the 'everybody' who comes in it is not quite understandable by anyone. The Apocalyptic movement in 1940s British poetry looks like a response to the acknowledged failure of the 1930 Oxford group to direct the course of events with a social activist plain style. Instead, taking a leaf from the Surrealist book, the poets would tap into the obscure archetypes of a common unconscious so as to get back, behind the scenes, their access to a shared relevance which had been cut off through cultural division and global conflict on a directly-addressed level. There is, thus, much that is both heroic and quixotic about 1940s poetry in Britain; and its aims and purposes could be more sympathetically understood. Yet the equally understandable post-war backlash from it, foreshadowed in Australia's Ern Malley Affair, seems to have left us in a perpetually reactive oscillation between ever more parodic versions of Philip Drunk and Philip Sober.

The importance of W. S. Graham's later style is that it points to one possible way beyond that blocked oscillation. Criticism has tended to date his later style from *Malcolm Mooney's Land* (1971), but there are clear signs of it in poems such as 'Since All my Steps Taken' and 'Listen. Put on Morning' which open *The White Threshold* (1949) and it is fully formed in the 'Three Letters' that conclude the volume. The 'word-drunk' 1940s style was achieved by jamming together clusters of unusual adjective-noun pairings in long lines and capacious stanzas, as in 'I am the frosty prophet of a grasshopping summer' – the last line of a final fifteen-line verse from 'The Sixth Journey'. The art of Dylan Thomas lay predominantly in his ability to sustain a strong rhythmic pulse through the heavy traffic of stressed syllables. Graham's early work has a less clear pulse; at times, as in 'Explanation of a Map', its reading momentum can be clogged: 'I cast, before peace grips my world's stoked womb, / High my bled ground.' He alleviated this weakness, as here in 'The Hill of Intrusion', by shortening his lines: 'The ear sings better / Than any sound / It hears on earth / Or waters perfect.' Shorter lines require far more concentration on unstressed monosyllables to maintain a rhythmic poise, and this simultaneously strengthens the auditory inevitability of the poetry by thinning out the adjectival traffic.

Graham had been concerned with the poet's cultural isolation from the beginning. His great insight was that this theme could be given an acute focus by locating it in the problems of specific, intimate exchanges. Once again this starts much earlier than is assumed by the superficial divide of the publishing gap between his 1955 and 1971 volumes. It has been clearly located by the time of the 'Three Letters' of

1948, dedicated to his recently dead mother, and the series of 'Letters' that follow 'The Nightfishing' itself. What this produces is poetry whose themes are recognizably those of mid-century high modernism. Illuminating comparisons can be made with issues of isolation and communication in the theatre of Samuel Beckett and of Harold Pinter – one of Graham's long-term sustainers. The intimacy of address in these and later poems to his parents, artist friends, and, above all, to his wife, make his work more profoundly communal than is assumed in superficial comparisons with the much-advertised poetic responsibility of 1950s social realism.

Yet Graham's achievement came at quite a high price. He may not have been on the archangelic level of Coleridge, but he did subscribe to a romantic theory of art and damage. In an unused section from 'The Dark Dialogues' published in *Aimed at Nobody*, we can read:

> I hope I do not write
> Only for those few
> Others like myself
> Poets maimed for the job.

Fairly inert syllabics, these; and they do no more than voice the reasonable fear that he is too much of a poet's poet. He needn't have worried, though. It's practically a definition of a good poet that she or he is, and will survive the reputation of being, a poet's poet. Margaret Blackwood and Robin Skelton, the editors of *Aimed at Nobody*, provided this poem with a title in square brackets. The poems from this collection with titles that are Graham's own tend to be of a higher quality with a greater degree of finish. The poet liked this 'mained for the job' idea enough to repeat it in correspondence. He may have decided to let that bit of poetry stay unpublished in his lifetime because the phrase had found a far more definitive and moving formulation in 'The Thermal Stair', an elegy for the painter Peter Lanyon who had died in a 1964 gliding accident:

> The poet or painter steers his life to maim
>
> Himself somehow for the job. His job is Love
> Imagined into words or paint to make
> An object that will stand and will not move.

But like the problem of whether it can be martyrdom and not merely suicide if heretical believers put themselves in the way of persecution, there must be an issue about the exact situations in which an artist 'steers his life to maim / Himself'. Graham's line ending leaves momentarily open the possibility that it won't be only 'Himself' that is getting maimed in life. There's a lesson to be learnt from the way in which Joyce himself, researching the themes of *Exiles* and *Ulysses*, encouraged the platonic enthusiasm of Roberto Prezioso for Nora Barnacle in 1912–13, stimulating his own jealousy to the extent of publicly humiliating Prezioso. Graham's letters and poems to the painter Roger Hilton reveal him intimately involved with both self-inflicted and collateral damage, while distinctly robust in his awareness of how it needs to be fended off and creatively survived: 'All this virile anger and destruction. Why not somehow say it through your paintings' or 'Why don't you try to … make yourself paint from 8 in the morning to 12 midday. Something must be superimposed on the illness of being alive.'

You could, though, suspect Graham of putting a brave front on a maimed life with the measure of control and aim in that word 'steer'. Maybe the romantic creator just messes up his life and then claims that it was all planned so as to produce 'love' in 'art'. Yeats may write that 'The intellect of man is forced to choose / Perfection of the life, or of the work', so as to lament consequences of the choice made. Yet there is no such dilemma. You can't guarantee that you will get the one by neglecting the other, and you may well muck up your life anyway by thinking in such crudely contrasted terms. This is one of the reasons why Henry James's story 'The Lesson of the Master' could be advising us not to take guidance about how to live from people who recommend we devote ourselves solely to art. Yet even James in this story appears to entertain the flattering and possibly deluded notion that such devotion will bring the rewards that 'compromising' by also living a life will deny. But that way sadness lies.

Another of the divide-and-rule conceptual traps in contemporary culture is that separating the sheep of supposedly private relations between poets and readers, from the goats of projected public roles for writers intervening in public debates at moments of national and international crisis. The latter of these, curiously congruent with 1950s ideas of poetic responsibility, has been claimed for vanguard writing which might take as its model a Milton or Mayakovsky (both painfully defeated, as it happens, in their public careers). The former is then marginalised as socially quietistic. Again, though, Graham's work shows how false this dichotomy may be. 'Notes on a Poetry of Release' is focused on the intimate action of poetry in its placement between writer and reader: 'The poem is not a handing out of the same packet to everyone, as it is not a thrown-down heap of words for us to choose the bonniest. The poem is the replying chord to the reader. It is the reader's involuntary reply.' Or again: 'The meaning of a poem is itself, not less a comma. But then to each man it comes into new life. It is brought to life by the reader and takes part in the reader's change.' As Rilke put it in 'Archäischer Torso Apollos', 'Du mußt dein Leben ändern' [You must change your life]; and the fourth of Roy Fisher's 'Handsworth Liberties' concludes that 'in the crowd of exchanges / we can change'. In poetry, as in everything else, the public and the private are neither distinct nor separable cultural spaces. 'About the Stuff', an *Aimed at Nobody* poem from 1968, addresses itself to the 'lens of language' with which a boy might go out to start a fire in summer, but

> Who wants to set the whole hill-side
> Braken foxgloves and playing vixens
> On fire? No, only it is I want
> To disturb the paper, to burn a sense
> Of a changed other person in
> On to the white of this public skin.

We can hear Graham working to effect that change in the discovered rhyme of 'vixens' and 'sense', or in the stressing of the preposition 'in' at a line-ending, one of three such parts of speech in a row, so as to effect the stanza's close. That local torque applied to spoken talk's stress-patterns is what the poet does to 'burn a sense / Of a changed other person'. W. S. Graham's 1946 manifesto concludes by inviting us to 'endure the sudden affection of the language.' We should take him at his word.

'AS WALLPAPER PEELS FROM A WALL': DONALD DAVIE

Our influences are like parents: we don't exactly choose them and often only come to recognise the truth of the affinity after many years. No doubt there is burden and anxiety, especially when we seem to have let them down, but also an ineradicable fondness, even when it is they who seem to have let us down. It is to Robert Wells that I owe, initially, Donald Davie; in the spring of 1972 he encouraged me to attend the lecture 'Eliot in One Poet's Life' and to stay on for the poetry reading. Yeats's remarking that 'We make out of the quarrel with others, rhetoric, but of the quarrel with ourselves, poetry' dents an idea for a phrase's sake. The others with whom we quarrel are too much parts of ourselves. This may helpfully be remembered when reading Davie's polemics or considering his distinctions. The issues addressed are usually substantial and urgent, but they are rarely considered independently of the self that is addressing them; and, needless to say, those others on the receiving end of Davie's quarrels at least in part with himself may often have every right to feel indignant or exasperated, hurt, or all three. Nevertheless, self-contradictory divisions in Davie have contributed to the insightful excitements of his criticism, deriving as they so often do from his arguing and judging with alternatives: Symbolist or Augustan, carver or modeller, free or metred verse… Yet even when such distinctions are conceptually plausible, it is only too possible for poets, singing amid uncertainty, to straddle his categories.

So it has been for 'words' and 'things'. The early poem 'Among Artisans' Houses' turns upon the relation between an observation of circumscribed habitations threatened with disappearance, and meanings of the word 'civility'. There is some matching between the word and the scene viewed, but no perfect fit:

And if civility is gone,
As we assume it is, the moulds
Of commonwealth all broken down,
Then how explain that this still holds,
The strong though cramped and cramping tone
Of mutual respect, that cries
Out of these small civilities?

Here, as in Davie's first critical book, 'discussion of diction becomes discussion of the poet's place in the national community, or, under modern conditions (where true community exists only in pockets), his place in the state.' Davie, seeming here to oppose the removal of poets from the city, has stated that 'essay and poem were equivalent and almost interchangeable attempts to grapple with the one same reality.' His metaphor implies hand-to-hand combat between two separated entities: the post-war reality, and his writing. A detachment between these two also indicates that the reality is perceived independently of efforts to grapple with it. In *These the Companions*, Davie remarks that he has been enabled 'time and again to declare myself a man *pour qui le monde visible existe*.' Yet he has also written: 'If I am so literary myself that I sometimes despair of breaking through a cocoon of words to a reality outside them, that is above all my mother's doing. And I am grateful, mostly…'. Davie, if taken at his word, can 'sometimes despair' and, almost simultaneously, feel 'grateful, mostly' about this 'cocoon of words'. Yet, despite the gratitude, an isolation within language provided some of the torments for 'the man going mad inside me', the man 'In the Stopping Train' who asks: 'Jonquil is a sweet word. / Is it a flowering bush?'

This is the same man who had pointed out in *Ezra Pound: Poet as Sculptor* a set of allegiances in Pound's preferring in Canto LXXXII the 'things' of Ford Madox Ford to the 'words' of Yeats:

> and for all that old Ford's conversation was better,
> consisting in *res* non *verba*,
>   despite William's anecdotes, in that Fordie
>   never dented an idea for a phrase's sake
> and had more humanitas

Ideas can also be things if you imagine them as 'never dented' like the bodywork of a careful driver's car. In following Adrian Stokes's early preference for sculpture over modelling, for the carving artist, Davie was emphasizing the moral and cultural value of a care for things. In manifesting a respect for the medium, a sculptor is understood to be acknowledging the 'reality outside':

> It seems clear that we should range with them [carvers] that
> way of dealing with words which regards them, as Pound says,
> as 'consequences of things'; and with the other … the way of

the modeller, that symbolist way with words which regards things, in the last analysis, as the consequences of the words that name them.

This is not the sculptor as portrayed in Thomas Hardy's *The Well-Beloved*, whose proclivity is to project into the stone an image of the loved object, reproducing the effect of a phantom visitation that he has perceived flitting about in the features of a series of women. Stokes's later development, one not warmed to by Davie, was to appreciate an interactive complexity of giving and receiving in processes of making and experiencing art. Davie's insistence on the moral value of carving suggests a resistance to the modeller, the part of himself in a 'cocoon of words'.

His 1957 note on 'With the Grain' announces that 'I have little appetite, only profound admiration, for sensuous fullness and immediacy; I have not the poet's need of concreteness.' Faced with the example of Charles Tomlinson's art, Davie admitted that 'I mistook my English empiricism for the poet's concreteness'. The poet Davie would have liked his words to be nearer the world of things than his temperament would seem to allow, and the conditional moods of his verbs in 'With the Grain' itself bespeak a need and a desire:

> Under that cliff we should say, my dear,
>   Not what we mean, but what
> The words would mean. We should speak,
>   As carpenters work,
> With the grain of our words. We should utter
>   Unceasingly the hue of love
> Safe from the battery of changeable light.

Davie adopts a perception from Stokes's *Colour and Form* and applies it to the languages of poetry and domestic love, where a contrast between hue and tone is matched against a difference between saying what we mean and saying what the words would mean. In his lecture 'The Art Lesson', Richard Wollheim cites Wittgenstein's criticism of these alternatives (defined as 1. We mean what our words mean; and 2. Our words mean what we mean) and offers an apt analogy to show what the two ideas have in common:

Both views treat language as though it could be broken down or analysed into innumerable ordered pairs of elements, each pair consisting of a word and its meaning – rather like, for instance, the way in which the married population of a country, or at any rate of a monogamous country, could be analysed without remainder into many many couples, each couple consisting of a husband and his wife.

Davie's association of 'what / The words would mean' with carvers supposes that a respect for the natures of words would be equivalent to a respect for the world of things 'undeniably out there' and with a similar respect for others' differences – an escape, perhaps, from the 'unsmoothed resentment' of domestic quarrels obliquely alluded to earlier in 'With the Grain'.

The poet as sculptor's orientation towards words and things promises an awareness of what Tomlinson, reviewing the *New Lines* anthology, had called 'the vital continuum outside'. Where then is the material for making a poem to be found? For the stone carver of 'To a Brother in the Mystery':

> The medium is its own
> Thing, and not all a medium, but the stuff
> Of mountains: cruel, obdurate, and rough.

Yet the medium of a native language is not substantially other than us, like stone, not fully and undeniably out there. Unlike the relation of sculptor to stone, poets are inside the medium simultaneously with its being inside them: they have been formed by the language composed into form. Words are as difficult as selves, bespeaking us as we speak them. This does not mean that poets cannot, like carvers, respect their medium. Nor does it mean that the 'equable light' of 'With the Grain' is inconceivable. Rather, the phrase suggests a generosity and openness to the words' various natures as we use them, a detachment from the compulsiveness of unreflecting outbursts, which is compatible with the deployment of words to shape our meanings within and through the meanings of the words themselves. Davie's 'equable light' may be taken as a phrase indicating morally valuable qualities in a poet's relation to words, and one which depends upon an understanding of the independent existence and 'otherness' of words, yet within a musical continuum of our speaking them.

Wollheim's analogy challenges the assumption of 'perfect match' between words and meanings, and, implicitly, between words and things. The word 'post', for example, cannot have a perfect match, like an ideal marriage, with letters delivered by mail, because it is simultaneously consorting with wooden stakes in the ground, positions where soldiers stand, jobs in companies or institutions, and so on. Nevertheless, the belief that words can and do embody sensuous experience has vivified much of Davie's best poetry. His translation of a Pasternak original from *My Sister Life* in 'The God of Details' may stand as an emblem:

> Come rain down words as does
> The garden its dried-peel, amber,
> Distractedly, profusely,
> Yet sparsely, and yet sparsely.
> No need to gloss the reason
> Why thus punctiliously
> In madder and in lemon
> Leafage precipitates...

After another verse of such invocation, the stanzas form a series of questions about who made this profusion: 'You ask, who stablishes / That asters taste, and peonies, / Agonies come September?' The final stanza opens by answering: 'The omnipotent God of details, / The omnipotent God of love ...'. In this poem the interweaving of sounds, as in 'asters taste' or 'peonies / Agonies', offers not a match but an equivalence analogically relating words and things. The entire poem cross-grains evocations of fecund process with delineated particulars. 'Excellence is sparse', the next poem, 'Ezra Pound in Pisa', reaffirms; but 'The God of Details' has supposed that excellence is also 'Sluicing', empowered by a 'sexual spark'. The combined influence of Pasternak and Pound issued Davie into a self-excelling encounter with the world's body as it may be analogically structured in the textures of poetic phrasing: 'Can it be the arum asks / Alms from the morass?'

In 1974, looking into *The Shires*, I found 'Essex', where such binding textures standing for a natural plentitude are supplanted by the flat statement of a dissociation:

Names and things named don't match
Ever. This is not
A plethora of language,
But language's condition;

Sooner or later the whole
Cloth of the language peels off
As wallpaper peels from a wall,
However it 'hangs together'.

Davie admits into his Essex of the mind 'hope, / Disappointment, fatuous shocks' and alludes to, without addressing, his 'unfinished business / There with my own failures'. The language of a mind's experiences in a place has blotted out the world of things or stymied the language which might make what is 'undeniably out there' visible. It seemed then as if Davie had become like the housewife in 'Back of Affluence', who, for different reasons, misses nature's appearing to confirm Pound's idea of the ideogram:

And what she
Could have seen, she had not
The ease of heart to see:
The sun like a Chinese brush
Writing in delicate shadow
'Tree' on a framehouse front;
The handsomely carpentered boards
Fanned across, splayed over
With a serene springing.

This is perhaps why, in 'Essex', Davie mentions a visual artist when confessing that 'Constable's country merits / Better'. In his memoirs he reports the conversation of a friend and abstract painter who could 'declare confidently and with eloquence on many occasions, that painting was a way of analysing the natural world'. 'In this', Davie concludes, 'he was at one with John Constable'. In 'Essex' it is as if the 'Manoeuvring, kingmaking' experiences of the career academic and literary politician have thwarted the poet.

Our influences are like parents: we don't exactly choose them. Davie's poem had prompted a memory of my father's mother's house in

Rusholme, Manchester, a house by then demolished and my grandmother dead. 'Essex' may be disappointingly about disappointment, but it is matched by the poverty of this would-be objectivist piece called 'Language's Condition', written in December 1974. It begins by reporting that Davie, in a poem –

> likens language
> to wallpaper,
> strips peeling
> off a wall.
> In that house,
> my grandma's,
> the feel of it
> was fragile
> as biscuit
> might well
> crumble under packaging.
> Lacking a subject to share
> inarticulable despair will do,
> as behind the rhyme scheme
> plaster cracks,
> brick and mortar start to go.

In a recent foreword, Davie has summarised a view of poetry's groundlessness to which he is opposed: 'Since poetry itself has no secure basis in human experience, so (they say) whatever at any given time is declared to be basic to it can be shown to be on the contrary conditioned by historical time…'. Where Davie has wanted to have something solid beneath it, in 'Language's Condition', taking a cue from the chapter on Roy Fisher in *Thomas Hardy and British Poetry*, I suggest that the 'basis' may be collapsing behind the 'poetry'. This was, of course, merely to reverse the direction of the grain. I needed to appreciate that while names and things named don't perfectly match, the relation between a natural language and the world in which those who speak it pursue their lives does not feel, and so, for a poet at least, is not merely arbitrary. It may be that poetry has no 'secure basis' in human experience, but there can still be reciprocity between the activity of making poems and actions in the world because various vocabularies and cultural processes are shared by both spheres. If there is no epistemological link that will ground the values of words in a poem upon the facts of the world's things, there are still practices of encouraging and commiserating, of remembrance and repair, for example, which can make a valuable shape in words by evoking a no longer existent and speechless thing, practices which are themselves secured on acts of faith in doubt. Davie has himself credited something similar in 'Or, Solitude': 'The metaphysicality / Of poetry, how I need it!' Yet such metaphysicality is a 'basic' which is necessarily 'conditioned by historical time', for 'Only through time time is conquered', and to accept that is to be where we cannot help being. We are in our element.

I came back to that memory and Davie's poem almost ten years later, after my attention had been drawn to some other words of T. S. Eliot's: 'Poetry 'is capable of saving us,' he says; it is like saying that the wall-paper will save us when the walls have crumbled.' Poetry cannot save us in the Christian sense in which Eliot is meaning the word 'save'. Yet there is the awkward syntactic fidelity of such poems as Davie's 'Housekeeping', in which a Wordsworthian mother ('She toiled, my father a baby, through the hard / Fellside winters, to Barnsley') is heard in memory collecting blackberries:

> How the sound carries! Whatever the dried-out, lank
> Sticks of poor trees could say of the slow slag stealing
> More berries than we did, I hear her still down the bank
> Slide, knickers in evidence, laughing, modestly squealing.

The delayed verb 'Slide', for example, or the assonantal chiming of 'Clement time brings in its / Amnesties, Aunt Em' from 'Abbeyforde', or the recent '1945' where a pastoral West Country is found 'In women's arms, oh you who crossed the line!' instance how we can keep verbal faith with the things of our history and that what is saved, as in Hardy's 'Under the Waterfall', remains precariously through historical time in the memories of people. It took a while to find the true significance of my father's mother's wallpaper:

> In the house where my father was born and grew
> – tattered lace flapping from a broken window
> in its dereliction – wallpaper was fragile
> as I brushed against it; then
> anaglypta, the word is, hung on while

brick or plaster, whatever the thing was,
gave to my touch: like digestive biscuit
crumbled under packaging.

Everyone has to start somewhere and be pointed in a direction. Without
the peculiar and specific combination of word and thing that constitutes
another person none of us would be able to begin or continue. Here I
would like to end by simply expressing my gratitude to Donald Davie.

THOM GUNN'S
SENSE OF THE MOVEMENT

Thom Gunn was a little over two-and-a-half when, on 27 April 1932, Hart Crane jumped off the stern of the *Orizaba* into the Gulf of Mexico. Yet with that leap, tensions in his art were already emblematically forming. Yvor Winters, one of Crane's correspondents and in 1927 an admiring reviewer of *The White Building*, is said to have felt confirmed in his mature style and rigorous critical principles by this suicide. Yet Winters' neo-classicism, which deplored the notion of a self-destructive orphic responsiveness, conceals the contribution to Crane's career made by the conflicts in his parents' failed marriage, the social exacerbations of his sexual orientation, and the compulsions of his period life-style. Crane's fate could be attributed to a nihilism supposed in his aesthetics and 'the danger that he may develop a sentimental leniency towards his vices and become wholly their victim, instead of understanding them and eliminating them.' You could be forgiven for thinking this sentence from Winters' 1930 review of *The Bridge* referred to more than Crane's verse-vices. Gunn found himself uneasily responding to Winters' ever more tendentious exclusivities some twenty-three years later.

At Donald Hall's suggestion, he went in 1954 to Palo Alto, California, to study with Winters. Their first meeting, according to Gunn's memoir 'On a Drying Hill', has the retrospective air of 'high comedy'. The jejune English poet mentions 'Hart Crane and Robert Lowell, two recent discoveries of mine' at which Winters 'grunted.' Gunn also mentions how he later heard details from Winters' 1927 and 1930 reviews at first hand: 'Crane's line about the mammoth turtles, for instance, had remained for him a touchstone of the alive bright image through over twenty-five years' and 'Crane's words to the Medicine-man in 'The Dance' – 'Lie to us' – he found especially reprehensible.' Gunn notes, however, that the informality of creative writing classes allowed Winters to 'cite the virtues of poems by people he would seem to have largely repudiated in print – Crane, Frost, Williams'; while, in a chapter of *Allusion to the Poets* (2002), Christopher Ricks shows how such inconsistencies extended to echoes in Winters' own verse. When, in 1956, the American asks Gunn to call him Arthur, the British poet's response also has a note of ironic comedy: 'I felt as if I were a partner in some doomed love affair'; and during the following decade the Dear John letter of critical banishment duly arrived in response to a sheaf of poems. 'He was a man of great personal warmth', Gunn recalls in 'My Life Up to Now', 'with a deeper love for poetry than I had ever met in anybody else. The love was behind his increasingly strict conception of what a poem should and should not be.'

In 'On a Drying Hill', Gunn reports Allen Tate's comment that 'Winters made the mistake of judging people by their poetry' and in the earlier memoir notes of his young self: 'it already seemed to me that his conception of a poem was too rigid'. He offers Dylan Thomas's 'The force that through the green fuse drives the flower' as 'good poetry' excluded by Winters' definitions. On 9 November 1953, the day Thomas died, Gunn left a note for Karl Miller: 'This is a black day for English poetry.' Not all the Movement poets would see it in quite those terms. That Gunn identified Winters's definition of poetry with his attitudes to life is underlined when he writes that his critical 'rigidity seemed to be the result of what I can only call an increasing distaste for the particulars of existence.' Crane experienced that stiffening and distaste as it was forming in Winters' review of *The Bridge*. He prefigured Gunn's point with a joke in a letter to Isidor Schneider on 8 June 1930: 'Poets should defer alluding to the sea... until Mr. Winters has got an invitation for a cruise!' One of those 'particulars of existence' may well have been why Gunn was in America – to be with Mike Kitay, the dedicatee of 'The Inherited Estate', placed after 'To Yvor Winters, 1955' in *A Sense of Movement* (1957).

Back in England 1955 also saw the publication of both Philip Larkin's *The Less Deceived* and Donald Davie's *Brides of Reason*. The Movement, in so far as it existed, had arrived. Gunn was included in the *New Lines* anthology (1956); Charles Tomlinson was rejected from it. Yet a comparison of two poems concerned with Shelley's death by drowning – Gunn's 'Lerici' from *Fighting Terms* (1954) and Tomlinson's 'Tramontana at Lerici' from *Seeing is Believing* (1958) – reveals that it's the latter's 'air / Unfit for politicians and romantics' which more closely resembles the fastidious aesthetics of a Wintersian restraint than Gunn's 'Others make gestures with arms open wide'. Tomlinson wrote a critical review of the *New Lines* anthology from which he had been excluded. This made, to the hasty eye, Gunn a Movement poet and Tomlinson, a student of Davie's at Cambridge, not one. From just such haphazard circumstances the confused and confusing clichés of literary history are forged. Similarly, in Larkin's *Selected Letters*, both one to Richard and Patsy Murphy on 8 July 1957 and another to Robert Conquest on 2 May 1974 contain references back to Hart Crane as a Jazz Age music- and booze-lover whose ability to write poetry is contrasted with Larkin's usual drought. He doesn't appear to have known about Crane's fearing his inspiration had dried up, fears which may have contributed to that suicidal leap from the *Orizaba*'s deck.

The specificities of poets' lives, aesthetic experiences, and creative condensations are so much more complex than the gang-lands of literary journalism. Gunn noted decisively in 'My Life Up to Now': 'It was around the time of the original publication of this book, 1954, or perhaps a little earlier, that I first heard of something called the Movement. To my surprise, I also learned that I was a member of it.' The poet acknowledges some loosely-defined formal tendencies and a rational self-consciousness of style that his early work might have seemed to share with that of the variously different Larkin, Davie, Amis, Jennings, Wain, and MacInnes. Still he concludes: 'The whole business looks now like a lot of categorizing foolishness.' Doubtless; yet there *are* reasons for Davie's book being called *Brides of Reason* – ones not unconnected with the fact that a volume of criticism published in 1947 by Winters is called *In Defence of Reason*.

Gunn's 'To Yvor Winters, 1955' could be mistaken for an oath of allegiance, especially if you overlook the delicate implications of its first sentence: 'I leave you in your garden.' Most of the poem then composes, like the following lines from towards its close, a homage-like synopsis of Wintersian aesthetics in the style of the master:

> But sitting in the dusk – though shapes combine,
> Vague mass replacing edge and flickering line,
> You keep both Rule and Energy in view,
> Much power in each, most in the balanced two:
> Ferocity existing in the fence
> Built by an exercised intelligence.

The poem's opening farewell is expressed so plainly and briefly it might have been meant to be overlooked. Certainly Winters didn't dwell on that line – his comment on receiving the poem being that 'he hoped he was worthy of it.' In the second verse, Gunn scouts the temptations to 'renounce … empire over thought and speech' or to deny 'the discriminating brain' and, as might be expected, steps back from both: 'we have to live / In a half-world, not ours nor history's, / And learn the false from half-true premisses.' But the poet and critic echoing in Gunn's poem at this point is not so much Winters, the experience-denying advocate of Christian poems whose faith he couldn't share, as the proud-to-be-atheist William Empson of 'This Last Pain':

> Imagine, then, by miracle, with me,
> (Ambiguous gifts, as what gods give must be)
>   What could not possibly be there,
>   And learn a style from a despair.

The dusk in 'To Yvor Winters, 1955' has been 'Filling the human with his own despair'. Gunn may be recalling Winters' story 'The Brink of Darkness', but he also remembers a poem that conjures a style – a means for conducting oneself through life – out of an absence of grounds for its existence. Empson's outlook is a thorough antidote to the experiential impoverishment of the Winters aesthetic. He embraced varieties of both verbal and sexual ambiguity, and he saw the need to maintain balances between the contrary pulls of axiomatic wisdoms – often with the aid of devices such as the repeated lines of the villanelle.

Was the title of Gunn's 1957 book crafty or misjudged? To have the word *Movement* so prominently displayed on your book jacket might again look like confirmation of your being on the side in the news. But a glance inside the book makes it clear that the opening line of 'To Yvor Winters, 1955' also gives Gunn's sense of moving. The first poem is 'On the Move', located in California, with the unattributed (and later cut) epigraph '*Man, you gotta Go.*' His book underlines from the outset that his view of what the word 'movement' means has little to do with the 'rappel à l'ordre' being staged by some English people born around 1920. Gunn published *Fighting Terms* so soon after coming down from Cambridge that you could be forgiven for thinking he was referring to university terms; and it's partly because he was such an early starter as a prominently published poet that he would qualify for The Movement pigeon-hole at all. Born in the year of the Wall Street Crash, Gunn is three years younger than Allen Ginsberg, whose 'Howl' was written in San Francisco during that same year of 1955; he is just one year younger than Andy Warhol. They look like members of the same generation if you recall that *A Sense of Movement* contains 'Elvis Presley' with its slogan: 'He turns revolt into a style'; and Warhol did nothing if not exemplify Gunn's phrase – in, for instance, his *Elvis* screen-prints of 1963–4.

None of these differences was lost on Davie, who, in a 1972 review 'The Rhetoric of Emotion', found himself able to admire Gunn's 'Street Song' style but hardly his revolt:

> when Gunn in another poem in *Moly* presents the spiel of a San Francisco drug-pusher in a form strikingly reminiscent of Herrick's 'Cherry Ripe' or Dowland's 'Fine Knacks for Ladies', what can he be implying, if not that this traffic, which has called up so much agitated emotion for and against, is no more sensational than the trade that was plied by many a Jacobean Autolycus? On grounds of private morality, of personal hygiene and civic order, we may or may not agree with him; but that is another question.

Here Davie puts his life-style differences with Gunn to one side since his fellow expatriate provides him with so ready an example of what formally he would profess. Again in 'To Thom Gunn in Los Altos, California' from *In the Stopping Train* (1977), Davie alludes to 'The Geysers' from *Jack Straw's Castle* (1976) to mark the distance between them: 'Nothing rhymes with this / Lethal indifference that you plumbed to even / Once in a bath-house in Sonoma County.' The inclusion in the same poem of a reference to Winters' 'The Slow Pacific Swell' reveals Davie to have been accommodating a measured admiration for Gunn's supposed extremities within the reiterated terms of that reason-versus-experience debate.

Gunn himself noted of *Moly* (1971) that 'Metre seemed to be the proper form for the LSD-related poems, though at first I didn't understand why.' The suggestion he makes is less challenging than are Davie's: 'Thomas Mann, speaking about how he wrote *Doctor Faustus*, tells of "filtering" the character of the genius composer through the more limited but thus more precise consciousness of the bourgeois narrator. I was perhaps doing something like Mann.' But how is a metred or stanzaic poetry that could shape Pushkin's *Evgeny Onegin*, or Vikram Seth's Californian remake *The Golden Gate* (1986), more limited than the so-called open forms? When have 'more limited' minds been 'more precise'? Analytical philosophers don't tend to be mediocrities. Such false analogies between limited consciousness and formal constraint also default into absurdities such as that Fulke Greville, first Lord Brooke (whom Gunn has anthologised), was bourgeois – or that Schoenberg wrote 12-tone music on mind-expanding chemicals. Gunn speaks enthusiastically of LSD-trips, both good and bad, as means for self-discovery and understanding. However, this may be to confuse means with end. There were people who did not achieve self-clarity through the use of the drug. Perhaps the enlightenment came from thinking and reflecting on your mind-expanding experiences, not on the experiences in themselves. Gunn's regular forms may have been such a process's poetic-technical equivalent.

The poet began writing in a sententious classicising code when in Britain the blackmailer's charter was still on the statute books. In 'Remembering the 'Thirties', first published in 1953, Davie places Auden and Isherwood for 'this coy / Insistence on the quizzical, their craze / For showing Hector was a mother's boy'; and Larkin in 'Naturally the Foundation will Bear Your Expenses' makes his 1961 poem's speaker an unpatriotic pansy on poppy day – off 'To greet Professor Lal / (He once knew Morgan Forster), / My contact and my pal.' Gunn's appearances in Larkin's *Selected Letters* include a compliment to Robert Conquest on 20 Feb 1962: 'I liked your Gunn limerick. What a genius that man has for making an ass of himself.' Then, to the same recipient on 21 Sept, there's a nudge-nudge about his sexuality: 'old Feel-Of-Stands Gunn.' In the November of the year Gunn published 'The Feel of Hands' in *My Sad Captains* (1961), Larkin wrote those lines from 'Broadcast' about Maeve Brennan's 'hands, tiny in all that air, applauding.' 'The Wound' is the first poem in Gunn's first book and it opens his *Collected Poems* (1993); it's an allegorised account of 'sharing even Helen's joy' and 'growing up... / As... that stubborn boy'; in which 'my bed / Became Achilles' tent'. Larkin's erection joke, and the fact that 'The Wound' should be an account of problems related to the poet's sexual orientation, strongly suggest the conditions from which Gunn was emerging – and the distance he and Anglo-American culture would travel in reaching his award-winning seventh collection *The Man with Night Sweats* (1992).

In the *Collected Poems*, Gunn provides a note of apology for his poem 'In Santa Maria del Popolo': 'I am not sure where I read this account of Caravaggio's death. I later found that it is not the accepted one.' The poem's context also includes assumptions – ones qualified in Catherine Puglisi's *Caravaggio* (1998) – about the painter's sexual tastes:

No Ananias croons a mystery yet,
Casting the pain out under name of sin.
The painter saw what was, an alternate
Candour and secrecy inside the skin.
He painted, elsewhere, that firm insolent
Young whore in Venus' clothes, those pudgy cheats,
Those sharpers; and was strangled, as things went,
For money, by one such picked off the streets.

We're to take it, surely, that the man who fled Rome after killing
Ranuccio Tomassoni on 28 May 1606 in a duel was strangled by a
pudgy cheat who might also have been a picked-up whore, rather than
by an insolent girl dressed as Venus. Gunn may be alluding discreetly
to speculations about St Paul's sexuality in the 'alternate / Candour
and secrecy inside the skin', or to such implications in the vigorously
realistic painter's rendition of the fallen man's flesh. Certainly, Saul
appears to be embracing nothing but a light-source, and the Biblical
text has a voice asking why a policy of persecution is being pursued.
In Gunn's final couplet, the St Paul of Caravaggio's road-to-Damascus
painting has indeed 'the large gesture of solitary man' who is 'Resisting,
by embracing, nothingness.' In his 1930 review, Winters had accused
Whitman and his followers of regarding 'annihilation, complete
negation, as the only good'; so 'these poets, and Mr. Crane as well, are
headed precisely for nowhere'. Gunn's continuing debate with Winters
can be heard in that parenthetical addition: 'Resisting, by embracing'.

In *The Life of Metrical and Free Verse in Twentieth-Century Poetry*
(1997), Jon Silkin cites the line 'I heard you wake up from the same
bad dream' in 'Lament' from Gunn's 1992 collection and observes that
'Under the pressure of grief the language … breaks down the metre
so that there are – to my ear – no stress syllables and only two final
durational ones. One must count the syllables to perceive the prosodic
structure.' Here is the passage:

In hope still, courteous still, but tired and thin,
You tried to stay the man that you had been,
Treating each symptom as a mere mishap
Without import. But then the spinal tap.
It brought a hard headache, and when night came
I heard you wake up from the same bad dream

Every half-hour with the same short cry
Of mild outrage, before immediately
Slipping into the nightmare once again
Empty of content but the drip of pain.

There are problems in Silkin's account: one is his technical analysis of
the line; another his description of relations between a presumed state
of feeling 'the pressure of grief', an art medium 'the language', and a
formal resource 'the metre'. Gunn's line is a decasyllabic pentameter
with notional stresses on 'heard', 'wake', 'from', 'same', and 'dream'.
That's its metre. Its intonational shape ruffles this underlying pattern
by insinuating a tetrametric structure with the four feet as perhaps
an iamb, two anapaests, and a spondee. The combination of these
two gives a further shape with three points of stressed-pitched focus
('heard', 'wake up', and 'same bad dream'), a lengthening sequence of
syllable groups in which the pitch level rises through the two verbs to
climax on the rise and fall of the elongated syllable in 'dream'. Thus the
line's main point of attention is the other person's 'same bad dream';
it is more interested in 'you wake up' than in 'I heard', and it is more
interested in 'heard' than in 'I'.

Silkin argues that Gunn 'has learned to evacuate the ego' by teaching
himself 'to cooperate with free verse, with the result that the metricality,
with or without rhyme, is not permitted to dictate to experience.'
Silkin's terms here hark back to the polarities in Winters' criticism of
verse and syntax for courting unreason and chaos, and the retort that
he and his followers are shying away from experience with their closed
forms. Yet Silkin's 'not permitted to dictate' suggests a counter-diktat on
the part of those who should 'cooperate with free verse'. So here again
feeling and experience are aligned with the 'free', and dubious control
management strategies with the 'metrical'. Gunn notes in his essay on
H.D., Marianne Moore, and Mina Loy, that 'hardness, softness, and
derivative terms used in literary criticism look back to an obviously
sexual origin'. I would add that none of these tendentious dualisms
derived from sexual stereotyping is likely to be helpful or experientially
convincing. What is the 'feeling' in a poem except a reading of 'the
language'? What is the 'pressure' except, in large part, a 'rhythm' which,
whether metred or not, only exists in so far as it is the words of a unique
poem's lines. Gunn doesn't 'evacuate his ego'; he places an 'I' pronoun
in the first foot of an iamb so that it is pronounced unstressed with the

reduced vowel sound. Such details are suffused with the thinking and feeling, the ethics and aesthetics of the narrated moment, and their consequences are as relevant for 'free' verse as for poetry in a metre.

The experience of visiting a man dying of AIDS has precious little to do with reading a poem about visiting such a man. What little the reading does have in common with the visiting is generated by the poem's technique and not by the experience. The 'pressure of grief' that Silkin detects must be heard (and he must have heard it) in reading the poem, not as something pressing on the poem from outside. Fuller understanding of text creates context. I don't exactly disagree with Silkin's notions about the poet and his ego, notions borrowed from a comment of Gunn's on Christopher Isherwood's style; but it's presuming too much to attribute his poem's meanings and effects to anything other than the techniques of language that Gunn employs. In 'Lament' he has a first person singular pronoun that narrates the events of the 'courteous' man's last days without drawing discourteous attention to itself, and this is expertly done by means of the metre and rhythm of his lines. 'Henry VIII's court was a much more dangerous place than a singles bar in San Francisco', Gunn writes in his review of the *New Oxford Book of Sixteenth Century Verse*. He could as equally have learned the technical-ethical principles manifest in 'Lament' from the stoic formality of his beloved renaissance courtier-poets composing farewells when fortune's wheel has turned fatally against them.

His recent elegy 'To Donald Davie in Heaven', collected in *Boss Cupid* (2000), begins with a reported change of mind: 'I was reading Auden – But I thought / you didn't like Auden, I said. / Well, I've been reading him again, / and I like him better now, you said.' Gunn then admires the older poet for 'your ability to regroup / without cynicism'. It's something that Yvor Winters, despite all his inconsistencies of precept and practice, seems never to have been able to do. In the 1959 essay 'Remembering the Movement', Davie was not only 'regrouping / without cynicism' but also looking back in 'anger – with myself as well as with others'. Among the things he criticises is 'the insularity', and not only one of national literatures or literary aesthetics, 'which has ready its well-documented and conclusive sneer at Colette and Marianne Moore, Cocteau and Gide and Hart Crane.'

GEOFFREY HILL:
TOILING THROUGH TIME

1

Geoffrey Hill has long been engaged by what he has called 'the Endurance of Poets.' The title of four poems about what some poets have had to bear and how they have lived on after themselves sees its respective artists pitted against religious and political persecution. Hill has also written about the working conditions of oppressed labourers, such as the woman with 'a face hare-lipped by the searing wire' in *Mercian Hymns* XXV. In his second volume of critical writings, *The Enemy's Country: Words, Contexture, and Other Circumstances of Language* (Oxford University Press, 1991), he addresses himself to the working conditions that certain poets have endured. Who are the enemy, and where is the country? Hill's main enemies are the aristocratic amateurs and literary patrons of earlier centuries, who now appear to have been replaced by reviewers, editors, anthologists, and minor poets. Yet Hill's concerns go beyond the politics of Grubstreet to the 'cose del mondo' of Machiavelli and the ethics of government. Further, he repeatedly uses the word 'world' in a religiously derogatory sense ('the sordid brokerage of this world'), by which the enemy's country becomes everywhere, and the just city of philosophers, poets, or divines, is 'Any where, anywhere, / Out of the world!'

Dr Johnson is cited on *Of Dramatick Poesie*: 'the author proves his right of judgement, by his power of performance.' 'Proves' can mean 'tests in practice' as well as 'removes doubts about.' Hill's Clark Lectures were memorably powerful performances: grim demonstrations of the intelligence 'at bay' tinctured with a theatrical staging of the same condition. Reading the scrupulously presented texts, it is possible to feel that while his power of performance, with its ambiguous character of finely-tuned, sustained concentration and melodramatic debating, tests in practice Hill's right of judgement, it does not remove doubts about the foundation of his right or the reliability of judgements. Each of the four lectures is a sustained, concentrated performance, replete with learning and observation. One such observation is Hill's comment on the form of the 'Envoi (1919)': '"Rhythm" here is not easily separated from metrical subterfuge; it is not absolute but relative, reminiscent, an adjunct to something else; and that something else is not entirely divorced from "blague".' The poem's rhythmical form, then, is an invocation of an equivocal attachment to English metres; it fondly recalls and smartly places them.

Hill's judgement is proved by his supporting references to Pound's concept of an 'absolute rhythm' for purposes of contrast, and to his idea of 'blague,' that's to say, a stylish mockery of the obtuse. It is also proved by Hill's capacities as a practitioner in the field of poetic rhythm, by his ability to say with confidence that 'in the second stanza of "Envoi (1919)" the nine irregular lines are six regular pentameters in disguise.' However, Hill's formula here is slightly inexact. Of the nine lines, there are pentameters, and, of these, 'Red overwrought with orange and all made' is a skilfully irregular decasyllabic line in which the first two and the final three syllables take stresses. There is little regular about the stresses in this line, except in so far as such irregularities are a part of the form's vitality, a thing Pound well knew. Nor is there any disguise. There are further problems: Hill does not ask if there is definitely such a thing as 'absolute rhythm' – beyond what he describes as the 'urgent and poignant… claims to absolute judgement which Pound from time to time puts forward on behalf of poets and poetry.' It is possible that all rhythm, being in time, is 'not absolute but relative,' and highly likely that all rhythm is 'reminiscent' in its relations to natural language and poetic culture. What's more, Hill's prose here is a problem: 'not easily separated from… an adjunct to something else; and that something else is not entirely divorced from…'. The sentence seems to contain a qualified statement about how 'Rhythm' is related to 'blague.' Both of the key concepts are in philosopher's scare-marks, either to indicate the special status of these words in Poundian lore, or to mock such special status, or both. The articulation of these ambiguously hedged concepts includes two mysterious 'somethings' and two adverbially qualified negations of distinctions. The sentence appears an exemplary performance of sustained precision in the guise of an evasive and pompous circumlocution, or vice versa.

Hill's power of performance partly derives from his being known as a poet. This is made clear on the book jacket, and it is unlikely that the poet himself had nothing to do with what he has elsewhere described as 'customary witless encomia' (*TLS*, 27 Dec 1991): 'He is the most powerful living poet,' 'Hill is so very powerful,' 'poetry sounds with more authority,' 'the commanding note is unmistakable.' The echoing tones here (power, authority, command) are in tune with a theme of the four lectures, namely, the status of the poet. 'It is necessary, and necessarily chastening,' Hill observes, 'to have to return upon the undeniable fact that neither Wotton nor his biographer Walton show themselves over-concerned with questions of poetic authority and status.' Hill is concerned with such questions because he is aggrieved by the ways in which social power and status interfere with what, for him, is the proper judgement of values. The 'Unhappy Circumstances' of his first lecture are frequently found in relations between poets and patrons:

> The tone of seventeenth-century dedications strongly suggests that those who possess 'instrumentall' power are to be credited with 'natural power' as a perquisite of status ('the secret working of God, which men call Good Luck') and that those who do not are liable to find their 'naturall' power slighted or denied.

This means that aristocrats are sometimes called geniuses by geniuses because the latter need the support of the socially powerful, and that geniuses are sometimes called or made to be drudges because they do not have the status or financial security to claim the title 'genius' as if it were a birthright.

This observation about what poets have been obliged to endure is founded on Hobbes's distinction between natural and instrumental power. Hill notes that the 'root of the matter is perhaps to be found in Hobbes's distinction.' Leaving aside the question of whether a 'root' can be a 'distinction', I take up Hill's 'perhaps' because the distinction may be unworkable. Natural power is 'Faculties of Body, or Mind' such as 'extraordinary Strength, Forme, Prudence, Arts, Eloquence, liberality, Nobility,' while instrumental power is 'Riches, Reputation, Friends, and the secret working of God, which men call Good Luck.' Hill asserts that 'mixed feelings, then as now, about the nature and quality of "genius" arise from the complex system of brokerage and bargaining between reciprocating groups of "haves" and "have nots".' A reason why 'genius' is in inverted commas here may be that nowadays the word is rarely used in discussing the things poets make, and only occasionally appears in the evaluation of poets as social entities, as reputations. Even if some do worry about 'the nature and quality of "genius",' I don't believe Hobbes's distinction would be helpful to them, since some of the qualities it separates under the headings of natural and instrumental powers are uneasily located in their pigeon-holes. Is the ability to foster and maintain a friendship not a natural power? Has prudence nothing to do with the maintaining of instrumental powers? Do riches have no influence on the development of natural powers? Is not luck inescapably involved in both categories?

How simple matters would be if all poets were embittered, downtrodden outsiders, and all the aristocrats wealthy, pitiful amateurs. The lives and works of George Herbert and T. S. Eliot complicate the first case, while those of Sir Philip Sidney and Lord Byron do the same for the second. Hill's schemas of 'haves' and 'have nots' are not as crude as the first proposition, but his qualifications distance him less than might be necessary from such patterns:

> The Rt. Hon. H. H. Asquith, in his presidential address to the English Association in 1919, offers himself as a 'somewhat threadbare amateur' yet pronounces magisterially on what he calls 'the sovereign quality of Style.' 'Style,' which is 'incommunicable, almost indefinable, never mistakable,' is epitomised for Mr Asquith by Wotton's 'incomparable lines "On his Mistress, the Queen of Bohemia".'

Hill himself gives a reading of some lines from the poem, and finds Wotton 'a minor poet' because 'his "intrinsecal Familiarity" with what men do is not immersed in, is not infused by, the practice of an uncommon alertness to the common practices of speech.' Wotton, a skilful statesman, a person with instrumental powers as well as natural ones, is being judged by a commoner, of no great social standing, and Hill makes the point that his own academic and poetic rectitude is at odds with the grace of Wotton's poem: 'A style at once so ingenuous and so ingenious appears, indeed, to have taken certain pre-emptive measures against this kind of clownish truculence.' Perhaps 'pre-emptive measures' is a little self-important, as 'clownish truculence' an exaggerated characterisation of Hill's 'diffident caveat.' Here the lecturer is putting on a powerful theatrical performance in an academically reconstructed arena of status and power. Yet Sir Henry Wotton need not have considered it necessary in writing that poem to pre-empt the judgements of a university man. Nevertheless, Wotton's 'comely verse' is to be judged, as aristocratic amateurism, a cut above the one-time prime minister H. H. Asquith: 'Just so, one infers from Mr Asquith's presidential style the solecism that would be committed if one were to so take him at his word ("threadbare amateur") as to treat with scorn his trifling and patronizing "reflections".'

Though, as Hill points out, *All for Love* was written *con amore*, Dryden was in no sense an amateur, and I imagine that the busy college teacher and poet identified with the earlier writer's circumstances. Hill notes that 'Dryden shows that he is not unaware of the extent to which "a flood of Little businesses, which yet are necessary to … Subsistence" imposes a ceaseless attrition upon this intimate creative selfhood.' He returns to familiar vocabulary when focusing on the power of Dryden's craftsmanship to overcome his drudgery: 'It is a matter of angry pride with him to redeem the circumstances of the second by exercising the skill and judgement of the first.' Something of Hill's own dilemmas may be sensed in the unlikelihood that the 'angry' can 'redeem.' Dryden had felt 'curb'd in his Genius, lyable to be misconstrued in all I write,' but Hill rises to affirm that very genius in a remarkable performance at the end of his second lecture. Commenting on the Preface to *All for Love*, he finds 'a cursory formal nod in the direction of "compleasance," the obligatory, accommodation of critical opinion and of the rabble of one's so-called peers.'

This sentence was first addressed to a large lecture room full of Hill's fellow academics, some poets, critics, numbers of students, various clergymen, and assorted other members of the public, that's to say, 'the rabble of one's so-called peers.' Dryden's Preface also has a sense of occasion; it is 'the moment when genius will step forward and declare itself.' So 'the author proves his right of judgement, by his power of performance.' How do the so-called peers attempt to judge whether they are in the presence of 'genius' or being presented with a forward-stepping imposture? Hill concludes that 'When the tuning and hefting "concurre",' which is to say when the writing is finished, 'we know it, it is self-evident. To this extent we may say that Emerson is vindicated in his grand claim: "Instantly we know whose words are loaded with life, and whose not".'

Needless to say, we know that Mr Asquith's words are not loaded with life; but, wait a minute, didn't he say that 'the Sovereign quality of Style… is incommunicable, almost indefinable, never mistakable'? What is it that proves Hill's right to announce that when the chosen words 'concurre,' 'it is self-evident,' and yet does not prove Asquith's right to announce that 'the Sovereign quality of Style' is 'never mistakable'? Are we thrown back onto Hill's being a hard working professional who has written poetry, so that when he says it's 'self-evident' he's talking from experience, whereas Asquith is a self-confessed 'threadbare amateur'? As far as the poet is concerned this is an appeal that may not be made, for as Hill notes, 'with every new work the true poet reverts to' the condition of 'a genuine apprentice, a potential master' and adds that for this reason a poet 'cannot have a "career" but as a lifelong apprentice-master he may well compose more than one masterpiece.' This is well put and true, but it means that poets never reach a state of absolute judgement or knowledge from experience, denied to others, which would allow them to claim that 'we know it.' Even if they know it about their own works, which may perhaps come right 'with a click like a closing box,' they only know it from time to time, between which they revert to being apprentices. Should they think a poem is right, prudent poets are like Jane Austen, whose 'invincible distrust of her own judgement induced her to withhold her works from the public, till time and many perusals had satisfied her that the charm of recent composition had dissolved.'

The qualities of a style or the concurrence of words in an attuned poem are never self-evidently or unmistakably anything. Both Asquith and Hill appear mistaken in their exaggerated 'claims to absolute judgement.' Such claims 'which Pound from time to time puts forward on behalf of poets and poetry' are 'the more urgent and poignant' because they cannot be proved. Works of art can be accurately described and can have qualities and values attributed to them; readers and listeners can be convinced by or come to agree which such accounts, but this reaching of conviction or agreement involves a process of critical appreciation and understanding; it is not given in a sudden revelation to the few. If Asquith was 'trifling and patronizing' when he elaborated his foolish phrases about style, Hill appeared offensively assured of his superior judgement when he composed the lecture's closing sentences.

Similarly, given the lecturer's 'intelligence at bay,' a man before 'the rabble of one's so-called peers,' it might be fair to ask who 'we' are in 'we know it, it is self-evident.' Hill has a tetchy note about the complacent use of first-person plurals. He is objecting to some sentences by Professors Bradbury and Bigsby in the General Editors' Preface to the 'Contemporary Writers' series:

> '*Our*' time must here mean '*your* time made placable to our cultural scenario.' If they truly, meant 'our time' they would have to take account of e.g. *my* time. Margaret Drabble and

John Le Carré do not figure among the most important writers of my time, but my scepticism, and the views of those who might share my scepticism, are effectively excluded from consideration by being included in the complacent locution.

Hill's objection to the appropriative strategies of some well-placed literature promoters is just. Yet his emphasis on '*my* time' and 'my scepticism' may appear tainted with a wounded *amour-propre*. The editors of a series of populist handbooks cannot take into account everyone's time, so that 'our time' cannot mean literally, never mind truly, what it says.

Bradbury, and Bigsby are two of the enemies in *The Enemy's Country*. In the course of his book Hill cites some advice about the value of having enemies: 'We benefit, according to Plutarch, from being reviled and traduced by those who hate us, for by such harsh means one comes to know oneself.' To be 'at bay' also has its advantages: 'If it were not for the darkness and the enemies' torches the beauty of factive *virtù* would not shine out so in defiance of that circumstance...'. In the final lecture, on Pound's 'Envoi (1919),' Hill describes the anthologies edited by Jessie B. Rittenhouse which were made up of now forgotten poets who were writing at the same time as Pound and shared some of his period tastes for the promoters of early music and Japonisme. Miss Rittenhouse also reviewed badly Pound's *Lustra ... with Earlier Poems*, and Hill concludes 'While not claiming that "Go, dumb-born book" stands as a direct riposte to the prejudicate opinions of the *Bookman* review, one may fairly regard it as a poem "at bay," confronting not only the fragile appeal but also the heavy proscriptions of the Rittenhouse ethos.' A consequence of such arguments might be that the geniuses may be grateful for the minor writers who allow their art to be distinguished by making it distinguishable from the encompassing gloom.

This is what Dryden might seem to be doing when he allows that John Oldham, who died at the age of thirty, had already produced 'generous fruits' which 'Still shew'd a quickness' while, he adds, 'maturing time / But mellows what we write to the dull sweets of Rime.' Hill points out that the '"We" is again concessionary' and shows how this voluntary and gracious condescension is taking place in a context of compleasance whereby patrons are praised for qualities they do not have. He suggests that by recognizing the element of being agreeable even within the intense personal note of Dryden's poem readers may allow that Dryden is not 'fearing his own inevitable decline into mellifluous etiolation.' Being agreeable is the sullying price that Hill does not intend to pay, so that towards the end of the same chapter on 'Dryden's Prize-Song' he announces that 'Style is a seamless contexture of energy and order which, time after time, the effete and the crass somehow contrive to part between them; either paying tremulous lip-service to the "incomparable" and the "incommunicable" or else toadying to some current notion of the demotic.' Dryden condescends voluntarily; he shows in the decorum of his poem a magnanimity. Yet Hill does not leave it there. The poet is working in the enemy's country, and when he 'has been "provok'd" into magnanimity we should not, in justice, underrate the cost of that.'

If Hill has felt affinities with Dryden's circumstances, he also wholeheartedly admires George Herbert's conduct as a poet and clergyman. Elsewhere he praises 'Herbert's "singular Dexterity" in administering reproof with gentleness' and two reasons for behaving with such consideration towards those who by our judgement we take to be our inferiors are that 'Thou shalt love thy neighbour as thyself' and 'Ye have heard that it hath been said, Thou shalt love thy neighbour, and hate thine enemy. But I say unto you, Love your enemies…' For those who feel the need to define their good qualities by contrasting them with others' characteristics or who need to conceive of themselves as 'at bay,' surrounded by a rabble of their inferiors, it is as well to recall that this difference from others is what they depend on, and in loving their enemies as themselves they may be able to overcome the enemy within, that image of others' weaknesses which they fear to find in themselves. Let poets, like everyone else, be on guard against their need for enemies.

2

In his new Preface to *Brand*, Geoffrey Hill recalls Sir Peter Hall's suggesting he try a metre shorter than the tetrameter: 'The best gifts one person can make to another, in this field of endeavour, are technical details; it is the precise detail, of word or rhythm, which carries the ethical burden; it is technique, rightly understood, which provides the true point of departure for inspiration.' Describing the poet's art, Hill underlines the need for technique to be 'rightly understood'; however, when pointing towards the poet's achievements, he emphasises the immanence of value in what's created. If his version is 'sound', he notes, 'the soundness will be self-evident within the textures of the verse.' But to whom? A consequence of Hill's account is that 'the textures of the verse' must also be 'rightly understood', which cannot mean just taken as the poet assumed they should be. *Canaan*, Hill's first new poetry for over a decade, is demanding of readers who are independently able to appreciate how a poem's structure contributes to its 'soundness'.

The 'Tribute to Geoffrey Hill' issue of *Agenda* contains a review by the poet of T. S. Eliot's *The Varieties of Metaphysical Poetry*, his Clark Lectures. 'Dividing Legacies' turns its criticism on a distinction between 'pitch' and 'tone':

> It was the pitch of *Prufrock and Other Observations* that disturbed and alienated readers; it was the tone of *Four Quartets* which assuaged and consoled them. That is to say, Eliot's poetry declines over thirty years from pitch into tone...

Leaving aside whether the movement from 'disturbed and alienated' to 'assuaged and consoled' is necessarily a decline, or just avant-garde cant, I doubt that pitch and tone can be so conveniently separated. Hill exemplifies what he takes these words to mean: 'In "The Love Song of J. Alfred Prufrock" (1910–11) the distinction between I, me, my, we, us, our, you, your, his, her, they, them, one, it, its, is a proper distinction in pitch; in 'Little Gidding' (1942) communication is by tone'. He quotes six lines, including 'You are not here to verify...' and 'You are here to kneel...' then asks, 'How is the repeated "you" to be understood?'

It is convenient that he doesn't cite the next line and a half, with its pitch distinction between 'They' and 'you': 'And what the dead had no speech for, when living, / They can tell you, being dead'. Since it is 'the dead' who are the focal subject of the line and a half, the pitch of 'They' is higher than that of 'you', and the pitch contour of 'They can tell you' is a double trochaic wave. The 'Little Gidding' lines echo this from 'The Love Song of J. Alfred Prufrock': '"I am Lazarus, come from the dead, / Come back to tell you all, I shall tell you all" –'. Is Eliot's decline evident in the pitching of 'I shall tell you' and 'They can tell you'? A difficulty with Hill's comparison of the 1910–11 poem with that of 1942 is that he doesn't compare like with like. 'Prufrock' is praised without quotation for its use of pronouns. 'Little Gidding' is criticised for its use of one pronoun in a brief passage. In the 'familiar compound ghost' section of the same poem, Eliot deploys these pitch-distinct pronouns: his, I, we, *you*, myself, he, they, my, you, them, your, our, us, me.

When, in 'Prufrock', the 'Streets that follow like a tedious argument / Of insidious intent' are 'To lead you to an overwhelming question …', Hill's second interrogation of the 'you', in the lines from 'Little Gidding', equally applies: 'Is it the modern second person singular or second person plural; or is it the emphatic demotic substitute for what the *OED* terms a "quite toneless, proclitic or enclitic, use of 'one'"?' This 'you' is also used for a form of self-address, as Hill's third and final question indicates: 'Is Eliot instructing himself, self-confessor or self-penitent, taking upon himself penitentially the burden of common trespass, or is he haranguing the uninitiated, some indeterminate other – or others – caught trespassing on his spiritual property?' The 'you' in line 10 of 'Prufrock' is indeterminately sustained between the three possibilities Hill gives in his second question, just as is the 'You' in the 'Little Gidding' example. What is different are the contextual implications of the indeterminacy.

Does the opening of 'Prufrock' have no tone? Hill's criticism of Eliot's 'success' takes tone to be a tactful selection of content and style to suit an audience. But 'Pitch is highness or lowness of tone' and 'tone' is the way something is said. Thus 'tone' characterises phrases and sentences, while 'pitch' informs single syllables, such as pronouns. The composition of 'pitch' over words and lines in a poem, its 'pitch contour', produces 'tone'. What is wrong with those lines from 'Little Gidding' is not a decline from 'pitch' into 'tone', but a conflictual indeterminacy of its 'you' pronoun. Eliot is attempting to combine a self-critical spiritual pilgrimage with some criticism of, and help for, a common predicament, but, as Hill points out, the ambiguous pronoun is revealing his divided aims, not combining them. The same pronoun's indeterminacies are attuned in 'Prufrock' where there is no poet speaking in his own voice and no immediate context outside the poem to which it refers, though the *Inferno* epigraph and the volume's dedication to the dead Jean Verdenal supply further frames of implication. But it is the history 'Now and in England' of 'Little Gidding' that troubles its ambiguous 'you', as Hill's third question eloquently attests. This is a failure of 'tone', and one in which he, for the sake of his intransigence, needs to find that Eliot so dubiously succeeds.

One of Hill's tones comes into relief when lines from 'Concerning Inheritance' are compared with the anecdote to which a note tells us they allude. Empson recalls a lecture of Bertrand Russell's in which

> He brought out a coin, and the business about 'me seeing my
> penny' was gone through with some new twist... Then some-
> body at the back of the room began to laugh, and it turned
> out that what he had got was half-a-crown. I thought it a very
> neat symbol of the Whig aristocrat and his democratic views;
> the actual value of his coin was a thing he would not have
> considered it polite to notice.

The 'neat symbol' understands vulnerable inconsistencies in the
philosopher's position, telling them in a language as far from literary
mandarin as Empson could get it. With its 'prize apologists' (denigrated
by 'prize'), its could-be oxymoron 'plebeian nobleness', and its 'servitors'
(Oxford undergraduates supported by college funds in return for menial
duties), Hill's poem rises above Empsonian talk to accuse and intercede:

> as to prize apologists
> for plebeian nobleness, who would have found it hard
> telling one servitor from another, who spun
> half-crowns to enlightenment – *I take this penny* –
> grant inequity from afar to be in equity's covenant...

As Schoenberg's *Sprechstimme* underlines, speaking 'pitch' should not be
confused with a singer's 'concert pitch' or 'perfect pitch'. Hill composes
pointedly with the context-defined sounds of a natural language, but
is inclined to treat them as a keyboard of absolute-defined values.
He would use a high style to attune important abstract concepts like
'equity', but such a mode has traditionally gone along with elevated
social position; his vertical pitch-tone range is fitted against a class
ladder. Disparaging Eliot's tone by inspecting the pitch, Hill declares
himself indifferent to a reader's response unless it be one of disturbance
and alienation. The danger for Hill's poems is that their lofty kneeling
doesn't grippingly trouble and confuse, but just repels.

Peter McDonald, reviewing the new work in *Thumbscrew*, outlines the
supposed distinction between 'pitch' and 'tone', then accommodatingly
observes 'This will seem recondite enough', but 'when poetry is routinely
assessed in terms of its tone, the awkward, niggling, unresting insistence
on verbal pitch will seem beside the point, and ... this *is* the point.' Yet

if there is no clear distinction, I doubt there is any such point. 'Pitch' and 'tone' are not a Punch and Judy of aesthetico-moral alternatives, bashing each other in the seaside booth of a sad poetic culture. 'To the High Court of Parliament' and 'Churchill's Funeral', McDonald tells us, achieve a 'pitch of intense and unsparing scrutiny on the idiom of prevailing prejudice and unintelligence'. 'De Jure Belli Ac Pacis', he notes, 'subjects contemporary commercial greed and cultural amnesia to a similarly exacting weight of scrutiny'. What Hill objects to is how and by whom suffering is remembered, as in the executed member of a German resistance group whose death 'serves / to consecrate the liberties of Maastricht', or in a Hollywood Holocaust film: 'so let the rights / be speculation... *Schindler!*' For long-time readers of Hill, this is familiar enemy country.

Writers on the poet, anxious to match his pitch, can catch themselves on his words, as here in the third section of 'Canaan', with 'unsparing scrutiny':

> Iniquity passes
> and rectitude.
> They do not spare
> the sucking child nor are they
> sparing with trumpets.

Hill is so unsparing with such turnings upon individual words, such pitched battles, that it can be felt as a routine, one deflecting the poem's intelligence from a gruesome though familiar fact about war into a faint echo of Alun Lewis's grim 1945 title, adapted from Job: *Ha! Ha! among the Trumpets*. Of Hill's phrase describing the executed anti-Hitler plotter, von Haeften's 'high-strung / martyred resistance', Lachlan Mackinnon wrote in the *TLS* : 'The play on "high-strung", though, with its reference to piano-wire, makes one wonder how completely the poet is in control'. Hill's control of the words is beyond doubt. But has he imagined how others may hear them? Would it disturb him that his pitch-dark phrase sounds viciously clever?

In the first part of 'Churchill's Funeral' wounded soldiers are returning to what may be blitzed railway stations 'under the dim roofs / of smoke-stained glass':

as if by some
miraculous draft
of enforced journeys
their peace were made

strange homecoming
into sleep, blighties,
and untouched people
among the maimed...

These lines glance at the miraculous draft of fishes, punning the while
on a military draft; they move from 'homecoming' to 'maimed' by way
of a 'blighty' (a wound serious enough to require repatriation, regarded
as 'lucky' if not maiming). Though 'untouched' may suggest 'not
suffering from shell-shock', its play on 'unwounded' and 'unmoved'
rings false. Among the wounded there may be military personnel and
civilians who have not sustained injuries, but it's unsparingly hard on
the unscathed to be associated by this ambiguity with the unfeeling. Is
this another pun too far?

The poem's pitch contour absorbs these flickering senses of 'draft'
and 'untouched' into a cadence for the worn-out soldiers: 'the men
hefting / their accoutrements / of webbed tin...' In the last verse,

nobilmente it
rises from silence,
the grand tune, and goes
something like this.

The pitching of the 'it' is poised, neither as stressed as the trochaic verb
at the start of the next line, nor as weak as the final syllable of the Italian
musical instruction. The pronoun's placing at the end of the line also
gives focus, raising its pitch above what it would be if relegated to the
position of a weak syllable at the start of the following line. This tune
first 'rises' and then 'goes' (it fades), or 'goes / something like this' (it is
hummed), or, combined, it fades away with more or less the following
melody. The pitch of individual items, syntactically unfolding and
arranged in two-stress syllabics (4/5/5/4 pattern), produces a falling
pitch contour over stanzas, and generates a weary, muted tone.

This opening section, and most of 'Churchill's Funeral', is among the best writing in *Canaan*, lament and anger checking each other. The first of the 'Dark-land' poems is in a bitter key. Of 'Aspiring Grantham / rises above itself', Mackinnon notes: 'If the first two lines are not a joke about Lady Thatcher, they are remarkably clumsy.' But they immediately become a tease about Anglican spires: 'Tall churches wade the fen / on their stilts of glass.' Hill's wit may be maladroit, but his pointing a finger at Maggie merely for climbing 'above her station' is inadequate. Alan Wall, in the *Agenda* tribute, was moved to remark: 'Well, so perhaps at times does Bromsgrove, and through the same educational system that elevated Margaret Roberts'. Denis Thatcher's money, among various phenomena, had a hand later.

A distrust of the poem's implied attitudes is supported by flaws in the ethics of its technique. The opening quatrain tricks the reader with a 'joke' which is never statedly at Mrs T's expense. Similarly, in 'Cambridge lies dark, and dead', the second adjective appears to qualify the place:

> Cambridge lies dark, and dead

> predestined Elstow
> where Bunyan struck his fear –
> flint creed, tinder of wrath –
> to flagrant mercies.

Wrong again: the second adjective refers forward to 'Elstow'. In verse two, Ely appears 'beset / by winds of straw-burning'. Is the poem imagining that Bunyan's wrath will set fire to a Thatcher's materials? If the political barb is blunt, the insinuations about the university town where the poet once worked are sly ('lies' must be a pun) and, in the case of 'dead', no sooner invited than withdrawn.

'Algabal' takes its title from the name of an 1892 collection by Stefan George, which, according to E. C. Mason, 'aesthetically idealises a cruel, power-mad conquer'. Stauffenberg, who appears in the poem, carried the bomb in the July 1944 attempt on Hitler's life, and was (Alan Bullock notes) 'a favourite of Stefan George, the poet'. Hill's first verse pitches into George: 'Rhine-rentier, / contemptuous bankrupt, / you placed sacraments / in the hands of receivers.' He died in 1933, the year in which the Nazis came to power and Walter Benjamin, whose influential concept of 'aura' derives from the poet, wrote: 'If ever God has smitten a prophet by fulfilling his prophecies, then this is the case with George'.

'Contempt is in order', Hill's poem continues, and wishes that the Hitler plot had succeeded: 'Almost, for Childe Stauffenberg, / it fell so'. Though Stauffenberg, a youth of noble birth, also *to the Dark Tower came*, 'Childe' sounds a touch fey, and is made more so by the change of direction in the next three lines: 'but this was tragedy / botched, unimagined, // within that circle.' Here, 'circle' is savoured: it can refer to the George clique of writers and critics, the group of July plotters, and a *girone* of Hell. Among the German poet's works is a translation of Dante. If this all smells of the study, so has much of Hill's work. In 'Algabal', though, his well-researched lines are not sustained (as they usually are in *Péguy*) by a strong rhythmic pulse or by rhyme; broken and short-breathed, their stylistic devices are all the more exposed. George's desk 'is a pure altar', where sacrifices are made: 'not / for the coarse earthen things / to bleed their spirit' (the failed plotters, for example); 'but for a vital / scintillant atrophy, / a trophy / of the ageless champion.' Hill's ending relies on that 'atrophy, a trophy' discovery, but such impetus as the poem still has is dissipated in its own technical self-congratulation.

The 'you' pronoun is more tenderly deployed in 'Pisgah', speaking to a familiar ghost in a garden:

> This half-puzzled, awkward surprise is yours;
> you cannot hear me or quite make me out.
> Formalities preserve us:
>   perhaps I too am a shade.

'Pisgah' is among the book's more likeable pieces, far from the rancour and religiosity on evidence in too much of *Canaan*. Hill addresses our MPs, all of them, in the last 'To the High Court of Parliament', its closing poem: 'You: as by custom unillumined / masters of servile counsel.' The pronoun is contrasted with '"thy" high lamp' which presides 'over against us'. Both 'You' and 'thy' are partially detached from horizontal syntactic movement and vertically pitched up by means of the colon and inverted commas. If you find the tone hectoring, look at the pitch. In 'Pisgah' the steadied cadence of the pentameter and the imaginable occasion of speech absorb and render affecting even the stylistic tic in 'Formalities preserve us'. *Canaan* is not a book that could be accused of capitulating to a consensus, but it may be caught in the snare of its poet's *amour propre*. If there is a danger that 'tone' can degenerate into a fake assumption of 'common humanity', there is an opposite danger that 'pitch' will be etiolated by assuming a posture of isolate disdain. Could it be that the 'tone' flaws found in the later works of T. S. Eliot are mirrored in the 'pitch' flaws of later Geoffrey Hill?

3

It is little more than two years since Geoffrey Hill published *Canaan*. Not since *Mercian Hymns* (1971) followed so quickly on the heels of *King Log* (1968) has the poet been as prolific. His new book-length poem evokes the *Trionfi* of Petrarch in its cover design, its title, and in the text itself:

> *Vergine bella,* as you
> are well aware, I here follow
> Petrarch, who was your follower,
> a sinner devoted to your service.

Readers who expect Hill's language to be densely burnished, and will perhaps be at ease with the poem's familiar latinate mariolatry, may be surprised by the subsequent simplicity of these lines. The section's apostrophe to the BVM acknowledges that 'One cannot purchase / the goodwill of your arduously simple faith' like setting up 'a small convenience store / established by aloof, hardworking Muslims'. Hill's almost-identification with the 'aloof, hardworking' people of another religion, maintains its own laborious distance in the 'One cannot purchase… faith / as one would acquire a… shop'. This self-evident observation has not prevented wealthy Christians from investing for eternity, sponsoring centuries of European culture into the bargain, as Hill's poem registers: 'Donors are permitted / to give of themselves, with saints and martyrs, / kneeling at the altarpiece's edge'. Addressing the Virgin, *The Triumph of Love* petitions to be received as such a gift:

> I ask that you acknowledge the work
> as being contributive to your high praise,

     even if no-one else shall be reconciled
     to a final understanding of it in that light.

These lines suspect that the culture into which it is published will not be able to take the poem as such, and not only because too many are not Christians: 'The rule is clear enough: last / alleluias *forte*, followed by indifferent / coffee and fellowship.' Does the line-end-isolated adjective qualify both nouns? Hill's practising co-religionists are either routinely nice people who drink unpleasant coffee, or, hearing the zeugma, hypocrites who can't make coffee either.

  A model for the poem's numbered sections of varying lengths may be the sequences by Antonio Machado, who is praised in *The Triumph of Love* for putting 'his own voice to slow-drawn induration'. It was Machado's Abel Martín and Juan de Mairena, among others, who served as prompts for the imaginary writer Sebastian Arrurruz of *King Log;* here too, there are signs of a framed text that would institutionalise the separation between composing poet and enunciating subject. This critical distance is repeatedly underlined by the interventions in square brackets of a meddlesome fictive editor, who officiously inserts information, even daring comment on the state of the text. The 'GREAT WORKE' of which its Nehemiah 6:3 epigraph speaks and from which the writer 'CAN NOT COME DOWN' (for 'WHY SHOULD THE WORKE CEASE, WHILEST I LEAVE IT, AND COME DOWNE TO YOU?') is not then just Geoffrey Hill's *The Triumph of Love*, but one that doubles up as the text of a projected old poet with distant detractors who, despite the epigraph, betrays himself into descending to his critics' imagined level. Putting words in their mouths, this projection states, with smartly miscalculated justice, that 'It's self-evident he can't / keep up a fiction, even for twenty lines'.

  Though his earlier, scrupulously impersonal work bespoke its maker from the recesses of a dramatised lyric speech, *The Triumph of Love* gives of its author with bluntly intrusive references to Hill's situation as man and poet. The Christian faithful are quizzed for a suspected residual anti-semitism:

     But what strange guild is this
     that practises daily
     synchronised genuflection and takes pride
     in hazing my Jewish wife?

Elsewhere, the poem ventriloquises some literary types chatting about the author photograph on the jacket for *The Lords of Limit*: 'How would you define his body-language? / Stoic consensuality? Sceptic paranoia?' Much of the work is taken up with stooping to worse *ad hominems* than those to which even malicious reviews or critical essays usually descend: 'Rancorous, narcissistic old sod – what / makes him go on?' Thus, this buffeted and buffeting poem does not read as a hermetically-sealed monodrama, or portrait of a martyr poet à la Charles Péguy; its framing devices are self-consciously riddled with lines which purport to be in more or less *propria persona*. The resulting disturbed fiction is not unlike Pound's *Mauberley*, where author and character overlap in what one hopes is an absurdly exaggerated self-portraiture. It thus demonstrates the self-ruination involved in seeking amid the deafening noise of spite to preserve a measure of dignity even when such efforts serve further to bemire.

The Shakespeare of Sonnet 24 knew the poet to be a lowly trader at work in his 'bosom's shop' – the heart being both 'artist's studio and retail outlet' as one editor felicitously glosses it. Yet where in Hill's English period the poet's words demonstrated how high-sounding language would be ensnared in base motives, and was emblematically impacted with such trip-ups, now a spaciously discursive style (recalling *Four Quartets* in its mockery of '*senex / sapiens*' or 'the wisdom reserved for old age') deploys a barrage of mistakes, errata slips, envious calumnies and the like from which it would remain loftily aloof, however compulsively driven to 'COME DOWNE':

> Extraordinary how *N.* and *N.* contrive
> to run their depilators off the great turbine –
> the raw voltage would flay them. Such
> intimate buzzing and smooth toiletry,
> mingled with a few squeals, may yet
> draw blood from bloodless Stockholm. *Mea culpa*,
> I am too much moved by hate –
> pardon ma'am? – add greed, self-pity, sick
> scrupulosity, frequent fetal regression, *and*
> a twisted libido? Oh yes – much
> better out than in. *Morosa*
> *delectatio* was his expression, that Irish
> professor of rhetoric – forget his name.

Forget my own name next *in hac*
lacrimarum valle.

On one of the other occasions when the bounty of that explosives
expert Nobel, nowhere mentioned by name, ruffles the poem, the writer
concerned is noted: '[Internal / evidence identifies the late / Eugenio
Montale as the undoubted / subject of this address. – ED] The poem's
ancillary figure, who editorially parenthesises yet more as the sequence
continues, sees no need to point out who might these phoneys be, for
whom the poem later seems to intercede: 'Bless, / of your charity, for
your orator's sake, / worthless *N.* and *N.* now Swedish millionaires.'
Does loving thine enemies require the Christian to maintain those who
are to be loved as enemies? Certainly 'worthless' is chary of being over-
charitable: 'I / write for the dead; *N.*, *N.*, for the living / dead'– a jocose
enjambment the poem naturally recognises, by continuing: 'No joke,
though...'

While, beyond the sphere of shop-talk's higher and lower gossip,
it's not possible to identify these two wealthy scribblers, 'that Irish /
professor of rhetoric' is unmistakably Seamus Heaney. The 'forget his
name' can be short hand for 'I forget...' or an imperative, a quibble
made clear by the reapplication of the phrase to the poet figure himself.
Nor does *The Triumph of Love* give reasons (outside the self-inflicted
sins listed) for this attack, beyond Heaney's worldly success and use of
a Latin tag to label its poet's involved melancholic brooding. It is hard
not to feel, then, that the sequence is, for better or worse, a bruised and
self-bruising scuffle in the top poets' yard – what *The Triumph* itself
admits is: 'thirty / vicarious rounds of bare-knuckle.' For other literary-
critical enemies, the poem employs pseudonyms: Croker, MacSikker,
and Séan O'Shem (read, presumably: shorn of shame), who seem like
the Englishman, Scotsman, and Irishman of a schoolboy joke. A grimly
slapstick, scholarly humour is frequently deployed, as in the bemoaned
but aptly inept evaluation of that earlier Shem's *Finnegans Wake* as a
'dead end'.

The Triumph of Love is an exemplary study in ruination. It returns
again to Europe's war wreckage in its stylish evocation of a Blitzed
Coventry ('flame-shadow bronzing the nocturnal / cloud-base of her
now legendary dust') and to *Daniel* for its painfully acute image of
Bomber Harris's 'whirlwind': ('in Leipzig, out of the sevenfold / fiery
furnace?') Most centrally exploded, though, appears to be its poet's

sense of himself. The sequence opens in Offa territory, with a one-line image ('Sun-blazed, over Romsley, a livid rain-scarp') and announces that 'Guilts were incurred in that place', guilts that are questioningly glossed as 'self-molestation of the child-soul'. Having found its author's own young self wanting, the poem does not stint on the shortcomings of contemporary youth, who are berated for being culpably unaware of others' pain, death and grief:

> By what right did Keyes, or my cousin's
> Lancaster, or the trapped below-decks watch
> of Peter's clangorous old destroyer-escort,
> serve to enfranchise these strange children
> pitiless in their ignorance and contempt?

The exhortation to judge not that ye be not judged is mere prudence if taken to mean that you can hedge on the Judgment Day by keeping your counsel; rather, it warns that judging words constitute judgments of those delivering them. Of this, and its consequences, *The Triumph of Love* provides eloquently self-aware illustration.

Hill's poem is approached through the triumphal arch of a title-page design adapted from a 16th-century translation of Fraunces Petrarcke. The hardback has a jacket whose framing devices form a contrast with the parodic self-denigration of its own staged position-jockeying. There is a pre-publication canonisation by Harold Bloom: 'a great and difficult moral, cognitive, and aesthetic achievement – "a sad and angry consolation" almost beyond measure'; a blurb that calls it 'a masterpiece in the forgotten mode of *laus et vituperatio*'; and five further plea-bargaining quotes (methinks it doth protest too much) singling out Hill's poetry as 'the finest' or 'the major achievement'. To reach such heights, the *Wall Street Journal* notes, 'the ascent is steep, the view austerely sublime', and the *Boston Globe* places his oeuvre, not with English-language writers, but 'the work of Mandelstam and Montale' – two Ms whose posthumously published poetry wouldn't persuade me to bracket them together.

A sorry, elegiac light plays over Hill's poem's eloquently-sketched '*moral landscape*', its:

> conglomerate, metamorphic rock-
> strata, in which particular grace,

individual love, decency, endurance,
are traceable across the faults.

'But leave it now, leave it', the verse urges, rising to beseech or, more
frequently, dragging itself down to writhe like Sebastian as yet another
exaggerated critical barb strikes – but not home. In the light of the
jacket encomia, a reviewer may be left speechless, further *laus,* let alone
balanced or limiting judgment, appearing invidious or otiose. So, in its
much-wounded, lonely superiority, let *The Triumph of Love* stand as an
example to us all.

                                    4

If it's not baroque, why fix it? This poor joke appears in the dialogue
of Walt Disney's *Beauty and the Beast.* The pun on which it turns also
provides Geoffrey Hill with the opening for section V of his latest book,
The Orchards of Syon (2002): 'Baroque says nothing broken, though to
break / off labours the point, / and it judders and all.' The line-break
at the word 'break' does indeed labour the point. Even if you like self-
referential formalism, you might find this self-mockery too knowing
for your taste, while, if you don't happen to appreciate its tacit assertion
of an importance that merits the mock, you'll find, if you care to
persevere, much arch word-play that's likely to irritate. *The Orchards of
Syon* is as replete as ever with over-wrought passages of what some have
praised to the skies, and others would prefer not to touch. Many of his
poem's sections have set-piece landscape evocations which will be to the
taste of those who like Hill's bordering-on-the-parnassian word music;
almost all of them have their tags from poetry in other languages, their
cryptic references to persons and texts, the gleanings of a lifetime's
reading, parodic malapropisms, and staged misrememberings which
loudly signal themselves as jokes.

   The Orchards of Syon is composed of seventy-two twenty-four line
sections of unrhymed verse mostly in four or five stress meters. The
blurb's reference to 'a blank-verse meditation' is not quite accurate,
but Hill's more recent book-covers have tended to traffic with the
slap-dash marketplace that their contents have deigned to despise.
The sales-pitch on a new volume of his work is now usually at sorry
odds with the poet's reflections on his poetry's worth in interviews or

in the text itself. Nor should it surprise anyone, least of all the poet and his supporters, that Hill's work has prompted strong, equivocal, and contrary responses – it being so contrarily ironic in its semantic structures. It seems unlikely that he is either as bad as his detractors would have it, or as overwhelmingly great as his blurb choruses would have us believe. Yet the critical situation remains caught between cheap denigration and praise beyond measure. I take it that Hill's poetry is of value and cultural importance. My interest is in reflecting a little on its underlying trajectory, on how the oeuvre has changed with the publication of his four recent volumes, and on why responses to the work remain sharply divided.

His poetry as a whole can be read as a meditation on the bodies of work and human bodies of other poets. The impersonality that Hill used to insist on, but has now repudiated, used to give these meditations an air of scholarly objectivity – yet only an air, for they were simultaneously transposed reflections on his own situation, even when the comparison was a contrast. In 'What's Become of Wystan?' Philip Larkin diagnoses Auden's loss when he moves to America by noting how 'His immediate reaction was to take a header into literature.' But Hill's volumes, with the possible exception of *Mercian Hymns*, have always had their head in literature, their complement of poems about poets and, indeed, *The Mystery of the Charity of Charles Péguy* published in 1983 is a *nec plus ultra* of this habitual strain. In the last three books, *Pisan Cantos* fashion, we are offered meditations not on one writer's fate, unless it be Hill's own, but the coopting of various valorised figures and tags from their writings. Here some of his sources and touchstones are attributed to a capitalised Leopardi, Ronsard, Pavese, Coleridge, Hopkins, Watts, Dante, Char… Recent attempts to argue that Hill is not difficult seem misjudged. To feel at home in his work and to have sampled something of his sources might well require the lifetime of study that he has brought to its composition. Yet familiarity with his materials can also produce a certain alienation, since they appear so appropriatively deployed. Each new volume has its roster of poets newly welcomed into the fold. In section V, for instance, comes the first appearance of the French poet André Frénaud, whose *Il n'y a pas de paradis* (1962) is an intriguing source for what his blurb calls 'Hill's Paradiso'.

The problem with having Larkin set up the issue of literary reference is that he has an oversimplified 'life on the one hand, literature on the other' outlook which means that almost *any* overt references to other writers will be plenty, no, more than enough. The issue, then, is not whether Hill should have the right to be so thoroughly poetry-loving in his work, but, rather, what results this produces. It's more than possible to have doubts not about the fact that Hill includes various references and evocations of other poets, but about the ways in which he goes about doing it, and especially now in his self-exposing, later vein. So has Hill's espousal of overt self-dramatisation – his version of the confessional, as it almost is – been good for his perpetual recourse to the lives and works of other poets? Where there used to be an air of scholarly selflessness in his poems about Mandelstam or Robert Desnos, now there is the more than tacit admission that his allusions to other poets' predicaments and ways of conducting themselves are, as they also were, forms of self-projection. The now evident benefits in writing poems by an apocryphal poet like the Sebastian Arrurruz of *King Log* were that we encountered neither flailing subjectivity, however dramatised, nor the shadowy appropriation of others' actual fates.

Hill has long been an equivocal admirer of Ezra Pound in some of his literary manifestations, and in *The Orchards of Syon* he has adopted a version of the pally references to the dead, including people with whom the poet was not on familiar terms, scattered throughout *The Cantos*. Take, for instance, Hill's section LIII:

Sensual intellectualism now the rage
no longer, dead Ingeborg, lost
surrogate in the lion's mouth, *nella*
Bocca di Leone. If we could
recommence this, what would I have to say?
The first one and a bit lines might hold,
perhaps, for a good kick- or jump-start,
like getting this short story off the ground.
I think I prefer you without makeup
as I suspect Celan did also.
I'm less sure of the plump Italian; he
loved young Jewish women – Irma Brandeis,
Dora Markus – but moved on, to Opera,
which could have brought you together. So where,
then, might we have met? Monteverdi's *La*
bufera e altro? Il buffo e altro? The Storm
Flah-Flah is where I would endeavour,

> now, to transport you in imagination:
> *ad ulteriorem ripam*, the refuelling
> autumns of Goldengrove; all this despite
> Dis's archaic hold, plus evidence
> that you were mishandled by death's angel
> yourself; or even that this *Cantilena*
> is not a flying-boat.

To start at the bottom, a '*Cantilena*' is a kind of keening lament, while 'Catalina' is the name given by the British to a Consolidated Model 28 P. B. Y. flying-boat that was designed in 1933 and saw service throughout the Second World War – its great moment being the spotting of the *Bismark* in a gap of fog when the German battleship had temporarily evaded the pursuing fleet's radar. What is this arch slip-of-the-mind doing as the close to a passage that has no sooner begun than it calls up 'dead Ingeborg'? This person appears on two other occasions in the poem, in each case referred to like this. Readers who don't know as much about twentieth-century European literature as Hill may be at a loss. Who is she, and why is she being referred to in so familiar a way? She's Ingeborg Bachmann (1926–1973) and she had a brief affair with Celan (1920–1970), who escapes being referred to in the passage as 'dead Paul', while as far as the text knows she never met 'the plump Italian' who escapes being referred to as 'dead Eugenio' by not being named at all. He is Eugenio Montale (1891–1981). *La bufera e altro* (1957) is the name of his third book of poems. Jonathan Galassi renders it, slightly over-colloquially, as *The Storm, Etc.* It's not an opera by Monteverdi; but notice that poet and composer, as in examples from Freud's *The Psychopathology of Everyday Life*, share a first syllable of their surnames. Bachmann might conceivably have met Montale, because the Italian poet worked as an opera critic for the *Corriere della Sera* and the Austrian poet wrote the libretto for Hans Werner Henze's *Der Junge Lord* (1964). Henze, born in the same year as his librettist, also had a relationship with Bachmann.

There are photographs of the Austrian poet wearing a lot of bright-coloured lipstick, and some others of her without it. She also had herself photographed in front of a sculpture of a lion's mouth in Rome, I believe – hence, perhaps, Hill's '*nella Bocca di Leone*' phrase, rendered as 'in the lion's mouth'. It was the name of the street where she lived. Though Celan's poem 'Corona' is said to be a tribute to their romantic friendship, whether he liked her with or without lipstick is an opinion he may have taken with him to the grave. Hill's doubt about Montale's view of the question comes from his remembering the last lines to the first part of 'Dora Markus', which, in Galassi's explaining translation, read: 'maybe what saves you is an amulet / you keep with your lipstick, powder, file: / a white ivory / mouse; and so you live!' Montale didn't exactly love Dora Markus because he never met her. His poem was given this title because his friend Bobby Balzen sent a photograph of her legs and teased him with the possibility of composing a poem to her. Both Dora Markus and Ingeborg Bachmann were from the south Austrian province of Carinthia. Doubtless, Hill knows this – just as he knows that Montale did love Irma Brandeis, an American Italianist with whom he wanted to emigrate to America in 1939 but couldn't. Montale didn't exactly move on to Opera, since he had trained as a singer before devoting himself to poetry, but not to worry. Perhaps it comments on the trajectory of his oeuvre.

'Dead Ingeborg' then becomes the object of Hill's tender imaginative care: he would like to transport her back from the underworld to his paradisal landscape in England. 'Goldengrove', a leitmotif of the poem, is from Hopkins's 'Spring and Fall'. He will do this despite the God of the underworld (Dis), and despite the agonizing facts of Bachmann's death (she was badly burned in bed either in a smoking accident, or perhaps a suicide attempt) in which she may well be described as having been 'mishandled' – and despite the confusion about the lament and the flying boat. Why all these tenuous associations? Why are we invited to wonder about whether Celan, or Montale (if he had met Bachmann) would have preferred her with or without makeup? The poet's second wife, Alice Goodman, a young Jewish American opera librettist whom he met in 1980s Cambridge, and with whom he emigrated to America, used to wear a great deal of bright red lipstick. And the flying boat? It was built in America, and used among other things for air-sea rescue missions by British flyers. Perhaps if the poet had a flying boat and not merely a lament, he could better transport Bachmann in imagination to the other bank – *ad ulteriorem ripam*, whether that be across the Atlantic to Goldengrove or across the waters of Lethe. Hill's work will find its exegetical editors sooner rather than later. Someone will, doubtless, come up with a better account for the flying boat than these freewheeling speculations, or the idea that 'Catalina' for *'Cantilena'* like 'Montale for 'Monteverdi' are staged Freudian enactments of old age's memory playing tricks with the poet. The density of Hill's compacting work means that each of his poem's seventy-two sections can be read in this puzzling sort of fashion.

Humour is a funny thing. Some of its varieties are close to a ritualised humiliation. Hill claims to have been influenced by Hylda Baker and Frankie Howerd, but sometimes his effects seem nearer to a Norman Wisdom getting up to be knocked down again, or a Tony Hancock facing an audience that is not finding the routines funny: 'Laugh, damn you!' as part LXI of *The Orchards of Syon* has it. Hill has long been teaching us 'not to look down / So much upon the damned' ('Ovid in the Third Reich'), and to 'strive / to recognise the damned among your friends' ('Annunciations'). He has equally been teaching us to hear the real force and atrocity in colloquial speech. Here, like a cornered comic with a bad scriptwriter, one of his voices turns upon the unsmiling audience – and literally damns it to Hell.

In his *Paris Review* interview, Hill describes as 'humorless' those critics who took parts of *The Triumph of Love* as ghastly bits of grandly self-humiliating vitriol, rather than tragi-comic stagings of the same thing: 'two or three of the harshest critics… seem not to notice what I might call a very strong element of autobiographical comedy, or even clownishness.' Later he adds:

> The author is perfectly aware of the grotesque difference between his own resentments and the plight of millions, between the claims that he makes for himself and the several holocausts of his age. The whole structure of the sequence, particularly the way the phrases are shaped, the way certain allusions are made to Laurel and Hardy, and comic papers is an acknowledgement of this monstrous inequality; and to read it in any other way seems to me to reveal humorlessness, and an inability to listen.

But what if you are a practised reader of the author's verse and you hear these differences of claim, you hear the clownish jocularity, the repartee and such like, but still you ask yourself what could bring such a scrupulous poet to think for a minute that such autobiographical comedy could be made out of so many grotesque juxtapositions? How could they not detract from his proudly angry vituperation against the cultural amnesia of his times? Because the poet has decided to make fun of himself doesn't mean he's given up performing, or very much seeming to perform, his self-appointed task of scourge and satirist.

Roberto Benigni's *La vita e bella* didn't, in my view, wholly get away with its concentration-camp joking, but its author doesn't simultaneously accuse his audience of superficiality and indifference. A question about Hill's late poems might be whether the slapstick enlivens and facilitates the cultural criticism, or whether the jokery vitiates it by revealing a misjudgement in the entire strategy.

Humour does indeed come in many forms. It is certainly possible to find the likes of Wisdom, Hancock, and Howerd, or Cleese for that matter, merely painful to watch without having to accept that you have no sense of humour at all. One response to Hill's late books that hasn't been canvassed much, to my knowledge, is that they are painful in just this sense. When someone slips on a banana skin, especially one put there by the person himself to be slipped up on, some may laugh and others will not. What's more, comedians can't resort to bullying the audience about their lack of humour if people aren't getting or enjoying the joke. Neither can poets. Charlie Chaplin makes some of us laugh too, though *The Great Dictator* is by no means his best work; and he makes us laugh partly because the resourceful tramp often wins out against the odds. But that's not Hill's kind of happy ending, and – despite the book's being vaunted as his 'Paradiso' – his poetic face seems no less set in a worse-than-Keatonesque mask. In part LXVIII of *The Orchards of Syon* one of its voices announces '*Ce n'est pas drôle*', while in the final part LXXII comes the suggestion 'Stop / trying to amuse with such gleeful sorrow.' Whoever says that, and to whom, it sounds like a good idea.

CHARLES TOMLINSON
IN THE DEEP NORTH

For a poet it may not seem rare to be present at the inspiration of a poem, but there have only been one or perhaps two occasions where I was there at the conception of someone else's. In September 1992, Charles Tomlinson was invited by the British Council to attend their contemporary poetry seminar at Hakone, a spa resort between Tokyo and Fuji City. The poet's wife Brenda accompanied him, and the senior administrator at the Council in Tokyo, Yoshiko Asano, organised their visit to Japan – including trips south to Kyoto and north to Sendai. She is the dedicatee of a five-poem sequence called 'Zipangu', Marco Polo's name for the country, which would first appear in *PN Review 91* (May–June 1993) and then in *Jubilation*, published by Oxford University Press in 1995. The first of the poems, 'The Pines at Hakone', combines responses from the lakeside hotel there with a visit to the Yasukuni Shine to the war dead in Tokyo. The second and third, 'Heron' and 'Shugakuin Garden', evoke the Kamogawa river flowing through Kyoto, and the imperial garden in the summer palace below Mount Hiei, while the final one, 'Epilogue', rounds off the sequence by recalling that Marco Polo had mentioned the country he heard called 'Zipangu' but never visited it. Though I am familiar with all the places that inspired Tomlinson's sequence, it is the fourth, 'Yamadera', with whose occasioning I was involved. Yoshiko Asano is graciously acknowledged in Tomlinson's dedication, though she is not addressed and does not otherwise figure in any of the poems.

I had started teaching at Tohoku University, Sendai, in April 1991, and was happy to collaborate in arranging for British poets and academics to visit us for talks and readings at our Department. Charles and Brenda were to stay for two days, the second to be given over to sightseeing. There are only a few places suitable for day trips from Sendai, most of them associated with Bashō's famous travel journal in haiku poetry and prose called *Oku no Hosomichi*, deriving from his visit to the region from the late spring of 1689. The most famous spot, which is said to have reduced Bashō to gasps of admiration for its beauty, is Matsushima – the bay with thousands of small pine-topped islands along the coast north of Sendai. Hiraizumi, site of a famous battle, is the furthest and most arduous day-trip of the three, inspiring 'Natsu kusa ya / tsuwamono-domo ga / yume no ato ('Ah summer grasses / are all that's left / of warriors' dreams', as adapted by Donald Davie in 'An Oriental Visitor'). We decided to take the poet and his wife to Yamadera where Bashō also wrote a famous haiku, one cited entire in Tomlinson's poem deriving from our visit. The name of the place means 'Mountain [Yama] temple [dera]', and it takes about an hour to reach by train.

The travellers for that day out were Professor Zenzo Suzuki, who specialises in eighteenth-century literature and was then the Head of Department, Yasushi Saito, the most senior graduate student and Department Assistant, Charles, Brenda, and myself. We met at Sendai Station, found our way to the platform, and then had a short wait for the local stropping train. Three of the things we talked about come clearly back to mind. The first of these was the title of Bashō's most famous manuscript, and how it may be translated. *Oku* is the noun for 'interior' or 'inside' or 'in back'. It is followed by the possessive particle *no* – 'interior's'. *Hoso* means 'narrow' and *michi* means 'path' or 'way': *Interior's narrow-way*. The Tohoku (north-eastern) region of Japan was, in 1689, regarded as an obscure and dangerous rural area, far from the centres of culture in Edo, feudal Tokyo, and Kyoto. There are various attempts at this title in English, *Back Roads to Far Towns* being the American poet Cid Corman's memorable one; but by far the most famous, which we discussed at the station, is *The Narrow Road to the Deep North*, the Penguin translation by Nobuyuki Yuasa (1966) – now near idiomatic, thanks in part to Edward Bond's 1968 play.

This part of our conversation is reported on in Tomlinson's 'Yamadera':

> it will rain soon – in time
> for our arrival
> by this narrow way
> to the deep north,
> though 'deep', they say,
> is a mistranslation
> of the title of Bashō's book,
> and 'far' would be more accurate
> 'though less poetic,' they add.

There may be a number of explanations for the poem's slight slip over Yuasa's title, for Tomlinson alludes to it here as 'this narrow way / to the deep north', referring to the local railway line into the mountains, which comes back again towards the poem's end, and 'way' prepares for the casual double rhyme on 'they say' two lines later. He footnotes the reference as follows: 'The title of Bashō's travel book, *The Narrow Way to the Deep North*, is the translation (or invention) of Nobuyuki Yuasa (Penguin Books, 1965).' The date of publication is usually given as a year later, and for *Way* read *Road*. One explanation for this reference, 'more accurate / than mere accuracy' as 'Yamadera' also puts it, might be the chance of that rhyme with 'they say' – while another may be that our conversation included discussion of the more literal translation of *michi* as 'way' and that this memory of our observations had overwritten Yuasa's word choice.

Whether the Penguin edition's title is a 'translation (or invention)' is to raise the issue we might also have been discussing, and one resolution of it would be to assert that it is both. The word *Oku* has the same Chinese character that appears in 'okusan', one of the Japanese words for 'wife' – which might be rendered with the old north-country colloquialism 'her indoors'. Yuasa's opting to translate it with the adjective 'deep' is, I think, a stroke of genius, and his addition of 'north' to produce a noun-phrase justifiably explanatory. It sounds from Tomlinson's lines as if I had also recalled Cid Corman's rendition of it as 'far', though the American poet's 'towns', also there to produce a workable noun-phrase, is as much an addition. So, as I say, the poet's ear for rhymes might have been what insinuated 'way' into the texture of Tomlinson's 'Yamadera' and been misremembered back into Yuasa's rendering of Bashō's title. The word also rhymes with 'they', of course, and that double rhyme is the means used to conflate into an economical pronoun Professor Suzuki, Yasushi Saito, and myself – and thus to evoke our casual chat, gossip, or reiteration of commonplaces, while, in any case, it was most likely me who uttered that shorthand observation that in this case 'deep' is more 'poetic' than 'far'.

A second topic of conversation, there at the station, was the haiku that Bashō composed at Yamadera: 'Shizukasa ya / iwa ni shimi-iru / semi no koe', which might be rendered as 'What quietness / penetrating rock / cicada's voice'. Japanese doesn't have a universal system of singulars and plurals, so that the 'semi' could be many cicadas or only one. As a result Toshiharu Oseko translates 'semi no koe' as 'The voices of cicadas' in *Bashō's Haiku* (Tokyo: Urawa-shi, 1990), while Yuasa has 'A cicada's voice alone'. Puzzled about how native speakers hear and interpret the last phrase of the haiku, I asked my colleagues whether they thought that there had been only one cicada or many, and put the answer received from Zenzo Suzuki into the first stanza of a poem that, unaware of Tomlinson's, I would draft two months later in Sendai and finish in March 1993 in Parma, Italy. It was accepted for publication that April and made its first magazine appearance in *Stand* some six months after 'Zipangu' had appeared in *PN Review*:

> On the platform at Sendai
> waiting brought up this example:
> were there one or more voices
> in his cicada verses,
> silence penetrating rock
> at a local mountain temple?
> 'They're plural,' you'd reply.

This poem of mine – later published in *Lost and Found* (Carcanet, 1997) – is called 'Deep North' and has for epigraph this same haiku in a version which tries to preserve an un-decided-ness about the number of the cicadas and (my own prompting confusion) whether it is the sound, or the silence, or both, that forms the subject of the verb 'to penetrate': 'What silence / penetrating rock / the voice of the cicada'. Tomlinson puts another version, which also preserves the number ambiguity but, quite rightly, not the verb's subject, into 'Yamadera':

> Our rail-track way
> is a smooth ascent
> through turning maples
> into cooling autumn air,
> *the faint aroma of snow in it.*
> It was here he wrote –
> but would not write today –
> *the shriek of the cicada*
> *penetrates*
> *the heart of the rock.*
> He came, then, in heat.

Tomlinson's seasonal description I find acutely evocative. Yet one of the difficulties for translators of haiku is that in the originals of such short poems, as in the interpretation of the number of cicadas, the implicit cultural associations, including allusions to the seasons and earlier poems in both the Japanese and Chinese poetic canons, play a large part in a reader's response. Such cultural associations are the first things to fall away from a translation into another language, and the very shortness of haiku leaves the translator with little space to compensate for such losses.

Though Tomlinson's only, and tacit, allusion to our conversation about the number of cicadas may appear in the tact of his translating its last line with his first '*the shriek of the cicada*', where 'the cicada' can figure a numberless generality, he does include a more sustained allusion to a third topic we discussed, namely what Bashō was doing making that journey through the Tohoku district which began in the spring of 1689 and went on for more than two and a half years. Professor Suzuki would like to insist, with something of a twinkle in his eye, that Bashō's purpose in travelling through a part of the country governed during the Edo period by the Date clan was not only the composition of haiku poetry and narrative prose, but the undertaking of espionage on behalf of the Shogun in Edo. We had been taking this possibility half-seriously boarding the train for Yamadera. Tomlinson brings it into his account of our return:

> They say he came as a spy
> (the villages are passing in reverse order now),
> that there was more to it than met the eye,
> calling on abbots and warriors,
> to sniff out plots before they occurred.
> There is no doubt, some say,
> others that it is absurd
> to speculate now.

And here they are, speculating, as that 'They say' suggests, yet once more. Tomlinson's way of building this into his poem maintains a wary distance and keeps his travelling companions undifferentiated in that third person plural: so that a reader might casually wonder who these 'they', these 'some' and these 'others' are, for, unlike Wordsworth's 'I wandered lonely as a cloud', Tomlinson's travelling companions are not effaced in composition, but they are located, as it were, in the margins, left or right, of the lineation. My poem occasioned by the same day out was prompted by Zenzo Suzuki's retirement Festschrift, so when poetry and spying comes into its second verse, there is again this single, though also unnamed, interlocutor:

> And were close readers
> of the English graveyard school
> code-breakers redeployed
> once hostilities had ended?
> I wondered was it true,
> your half-serious theory
> that Bashō was a government spy?

Sometime earlier Professor Suzuki had suggested I read William H. Epstein's 'Counter-Intelligence: Cold War Criticism and Eighteenth-Century Studies', which makes a suggestive argument relating the practice of close reading and disclosure of encoded material in New Critical accounts of Thomas Gray's 'Elegy in a Country Churchyard' to the espionage experience of many eighteenth-century literature scholars from the same generation as James Jesus Angleton, Italophile student of English Literature, who had photographed Ezra Pound on the roof of the poet's apartment in Rapallo in 1938 – and would later become the obsessively mole-hunting head of the CIA. The spy-catching that has entangled Matsuo Bashō in its webs appears, as Tomlinson's poem notes, not to be something that can now be resolved – although recent research appears to suggest that while the poet may not have been a spy, there is evidence pointing to his follower on the journey, Kawai Sora, who kept a more factually accurate diary, being a government inspector tasked with reporting on any unrest in the Date clan's territories.

These days Yamadera has become a touristic pilgrimage site and there are dusty, well-worn paths with stairs for the visitors to climb. On the way up to the viewing platform at the top, we stopped to catch our breaths, and talked a little about the series of wooden stakes inscribed with Chinese characters that were leaning against the rocks beside the shrines. Tomlinson's poem refers to this conversation from our ascent:

> On the way down
> we see once again

what arrested our upward climb –
stones to the miscarried,
and prayer-wheels
to wish the unborn
a reincarnation in a human form.

The account of this conversation about Japanese mortality customs in 'Deep North' is rather different, since the part of it I remembered and put into a third verse has it that the inscribed wooden stakes are not gravestones, but signs representing prayers for the dead who are given new death-names when they die:

Wood stakes at Yamadera
were memorials for their dead
with new names to fend off terror
at death, you might have said
staring at rice fields and roof-shapes
from the highest viewing platform –
inspiration for a visiting poet.

That 'visiting poet' phrase might also appear to be concealing a plurality behind its singular – silently evoking not only Bashō and Sora in late spring 1689, but also Tomlinson and the author of those lines in autumn 1992.

Charles was indeed inspired by that prospect in Japan's northern central mountain chain. His account of the viewing platform at the top of the mountain forms the central and most expansive passage in 'Yamadera':

He came, then, in heat.
The climb up the mountain face
which is the temple
must have cost him sweat,
his feet on the thousand steps
that lead past the door of each shrine
up to the look-out where
you can take in the entire valley,
echoing, this afternoon,
with shot on shot

from a whole army
of automatic scarecrows.

Perhaps all four visiting poets were on duty, or on the lookout, when
visiting Yamadera – though I had not expected to write anything on
or about our day out, and did not take writing materials with me.
Tomlinson, on the other hand, let slip just how much of a professional
poet he was when, on the return train journey to Sendai, he took a
small red-lined notebook from his raincoat pocket and began jotting
down details in biro, things such as the names of village stations we
were passing through. He must have been sufficiently struck by the
experience of visiting the mountain temple and place where Bashō
wrote his haiku (deeply engraved into a large rock at its foot) to feel
that some possibly usable verifying detail might not go amiss.

The notes Charles took were subsequently built into his poem's
opening lines:

> You go by the local line:
> schoolchildren keep getting off the train,
> returning to those villages
> beneath vertical mountains.
> Kunagane: conical hills
> beyond the little station;
> Sakunami: the sky is darkening
> and so are the trees;
> it will rain soon – in time [...]

So there we were, sitting on the train returning, and in the presence of a
poet gathering material for what must have been an inspiring moment.
I had never seen anyone doing that before, and, not counting myself,
haven't since. It was a surprise to see a poet so intent on the possibility
of turning our experience directly into art, and that doubtless had an
influence on my later thinking in response to the Festschrift prompt
that there might be a poem in what had evidently been an occasion for
Charles – though as I say unaware, at the time, that he had made a part
of his 'Zipangu' sequence out of our day trip.

So, in context, that 'inspiration for a visiting poet' line of mine has
the inspiringly senior figure of Charles Tomlinson first and foremost
tacitly in mind, making a contrast with the slower and less fluent poet

who was also there and is inscribed in the opening of my final verse:

> But I would be obliged to wait,
> let sound sink into stone.
> A noise of gunfire, I supposed,
> uncovered thoughts of someone
> dead ten years, but no less hurt
> at warfare and war's echoes.
> It was just a birdscarer's report.

While coming down the mountain, Charles and I had talked a little about translating Italian poetry. He was preparing for publication his versions of the Parmese poet Attilio Bertolucci's work, which would appear from Bloodaxe Books in 1994, and we also mentioned Vittorio Sereni, a friend of Bertolucci's since the 1930s, whose Anvil Press *Selected Poems* of 1990, in translations by Marcus Perryman and myself, Tomlinson had warmly welcomed in the *Independent*. What Tomlinson's poem calls the sound of 'a whole army / of automatic scarecrows' had reminded me of a passage in Sereni's poem 'Un posto di vacanza' ('A Holiday Place'), in which peacetime phenomena can't help starting traumatic memories of wartime violence: 'and in '51 a rare outboard's whine upriver / was subtly alarming still'. I even mentioned to Charles that the birdscarers, as I call them, would have been 'alarming' for Sereni – and that remark of mine might be the explanation for the buried metaphor and its implications in his 'whole army / of automatic scarecrows'.

So the 'someone' in my final verse is another unnamed figure, the poet Sereni recalled by that as-if-espionage 'report' of what seemed like gunfire – but wasn't. In his 2007 book-length discussion of Wordsworth's 'The Solitary Reaper', *Field Notes: 'The Solitary Reaper' and Others*, J. H. Prynne observes: 'a strong commitment to write women back into the world from which they have been marginalised comes into conflict with the traditional gender role of the working male poet as the active comptroller, even as implicit oppressor of women almost invisible (though not here inaudible) in their relegation to archaic tasks' and Prynne concludes that this 'young Highland Lass is the counterpart to Dorothy, equally disappearing because the male poet must do his masculine poetic work, alone'. Both poems I have cited and discussed here, inspired by that day out to Yamadera in 1992, are vulnerable to these same strictures. Brenda Tomlinson, the poet's lifelong companion and someone to whom he was evidently devoted, is as written out of 'Yamadera', and 'Deep North' too, for that matter, as Dorothy is from the encounter with those daffodils that produced 'I wandered lonely as a cloud'. Yet, though this issue of poetry and gender is an urgent one, these poems are as reticent about the names and presences of the other male persons there too, and only able to indicate who contributed what by their words. For the practice of poetry, lyric poetry especially, as it has shaped us and we, to the best of our abilities, have shaped it, rarely has the space, or angle of approach, to lose focus and momentum in filling out the details of who said what, and who is being referred to at this or that point in the work.

The one exception to this, here, is the role played by the dedication to Yoshiko Asano at the head of Charles Tomlinson's 'Zipangu' sequence as a whole. She might be thought, in a sense, to represent the 'onlie begetter' of these five poems, in that as a local representative of the British Council she was the point of contact for Tomlinson's visit to Japan, and will have done her best to make sure, in collaboration with the likes of me, that the poet and his wife were comfortably and safely looked after during their stay. What Prynne notices, and so sharply focuses in his sustained commentary on Wordsworth's poem, is – in that work's economy with the truth of its occasion – one of the great contexts for perpetual dilemma in the composition of poems, formed out of obligations to a poem's structures of feeling and form and to its prompting occasion, as well as to the interests and attention-economies of readers.

In this light, Charles Tomlinson's 'they say', his 'some say' and his 'others' in 'Yamadera' are valiant efforts by the poet to reference, at lines' left and right margins, yet without dissipating rhythmical focus or direction of travel, the presence of those prompting, provident voices that day on the platforms, trains, and mountain. Our poems, it would seem, and much literary art besides, have to be written on a 'need to know' basis that requires the effacement of such facts as the presence of Dorothy and her companionship when composing on 'the bliss of solitude'. Yet these same compulsions to give priority to the structures of form and feeling that shape such poems insinuate a nagging desire – one to which, since we are all 'poor passing facts', I have tried to respond here, so as – as Robert Lowell has it in 'Epilogue' from *Day by Day* – 'to give / each' her or his 'living name.'

GAEL TURNBULL:
GRACE ABOUNDING

Gael Turnbull's position in micro-histories of twentieth-century British poetry was already secure long before his death in 2004. Some bare facts of his early biography, a life split between childhood and youth in both northern Britain and Canada, then a working life divided between North Ontario, the Worcester in the English midlands, and Ventura, California, uniquely placed and displaced him to be a conduit by which not only could he introduce hidden American poets such as Edward Dorn to British readers in the 1950s, but also to help publish work by younger British poets in locations such as Cid Corman's *Origin*, edited far beyond these isles. Looking back, the phase Turnbull helped to occasion and sustain with his *Migrant* magazine and Migrant Press publications looks like a hey-day for Anglo-American poetic relations, a fairly short-lived moment of mutual influence with various and broadly-speaking beneficial effects on both sides of the Atlantic. One of its beneficiaries, the poet Roy Fisher, echoes Charles Tomlinson's 'I owe everything to Gael!' in his eloquent note on the back of this book's jacket – and to some it will seem a pity that Turnbull's crucial and exemplary role was not more fully and publicly acknowledged before his sudden death at the age of seventy-six.

What is by no means as certain is the position his poetry occupies in the choir of poets born between the century's two largest wars and who began to emerge, if that's quite the word, towards the end of the decade that had been journalistically commandeered in the name of a loose grouping of slightly older poets whose grip on the machinery of reputation and status-making decidedly exceeded the scope (though not necessarily the memorability of individual performances) demonstrated by their now completed poetic oeuvres. Whether there was a 'conspiracy' to obscure writers like Turnbull, or Matthew Mead and Christopher Middleton (to name but two others), would be difficult exactly to prove; but the fact remains that Turnbull found himself obliged, and perhaps also temperamentally inclined, to publish – with a sustained determination – homeopathically in, for the most part, out of the way places, short runs, and with a care not matched by anything in their public reception.

For some of his near contemporaries, poets such as Fisher and Edwin Morgan, this method of publication did not exclude periodic collection in more visible trade editions, ones that received notices eventually building into an intermittent but fairly robust public profile. Turnbull's Cape Goliard books, *A Trampoline* (1968) and *Scantlings* (1970), or his Anvil Press *A Gathering of Poems 1950 to 1980* (1983) did not result in any such visible up-take. Leaving aside whatever disappointment or sense of injustice as might have left their traces here (and there are sardonic later poems such as 'With Thanks and Homage to That Critic', 'The Poetry Reading Poem', and 'National Poetry Day' that suggest it may have rankled), this state of affairs left the poet's widow and those immediately concerned about the posthumous fate of his work with 41 more or less fugitive publications, multiple and revised appearances of the same poems, and not much idea from the poet himself about how he would have drawn it all together.

With the assistance of Jill Turnbull and in association with Mariscat Press, Tony Frazer of Shearsman Books has admirably and conscientiously edited *There are Words: Collected Poems*, a volume worthy of its author's lifelong dedication to the art. The use of a running head to indicate the published source and date of poems on the page we are reading is a satisfying chronological solution to the issue of where poems should appear – in that it represents the publishing history with as little editorial intervention as possible in the circumstances. Some such decisions have had to be made, and poems that were revised appear in their original places, but in their later manifestations, and with notes to indicated provenances – a sensible compromise. It is possible to prefer the earlier versions, as I do in the case of 'The Borders Revisited', where the magazine version can be read among the samples from issues of *Perfect Bound* on the *Jacket* #20 website. This Shearsman edition is not a Complete Poems; but it is an essential addition to the bookshelves of anyone seriously interested in twentieth-century poetry in English, an elegantly presented reader's edition of most of the work, and with a fine jacket illustration by the artist John Christie, with whom the poet had collaborated in a 1990 Circle Press publication.

Turnbull was an ever-exploratory, variously motivated poet whose work emerged in a large variety of forms all equally valued. If you like poetry of almost any sort there will be things here to move, instruct, inspire, entertain, and delight. Here are the closing lines to 'John Bunyan: of Grace':

cling to that
relief and shelter
burden from me
sweetness in it
drops of honey
ease to speak
O now I know
such overflowing
all the goodness
such abundance
scarcely bear it
so out of measure
even to utter

Jill Turnbull writes in her Introduction that the poet would sometimes describe himself as a 're-arranger of words'. In the composition of this poem, 'most of the phrases and images', the author notes, are from John Bunyan's spiritual autobiography *Grace Abounding*. The phrases have then been placed together with a Zukofsky-like care to elicit an 'overflowing' mimetic music (notice how 'so out of measure' slightly disrupts the expected pattern), one that dramatises the emergence, as if from nowhere, of that sweet sense of goodness. The access of grace is also indicated to be a painful experience undergone, and the analogous element of discontinuity separating the phrases, even as the unpunctuated enjambments draw them together, helps prevent this quality of feeling in the movement of the poem from being detached and projected as a status claim that would nullify the goodness being attested.

Turnbull's poetry has an extraordinary range. Among the early poems are renditions of Nordic saga materials, social-realist poems such as 'Industrial Valley' subtitled 'Northern England' or 'Lumber Camp Railway' reporting on experiences in North Ontario, brief lyrics with an Objectivist flavour, elegantly crafted prose poems, and a few pieces – 'Now That April's Here' (1957), for instance – which express a dislike of formalist exercises and associate them with reactionary cultural politics: 'Put the Great back in Great Britain. / Write a letter to *The Times*. / Lots of fun with Billy Butlin. / It's a poem if it rhymes.' Later work adds to this variety some longer series and sequences, sometimes produced by self-generating processes, yet shorter aphorism-like poems, and Turnbull's own variation on the found poem, in his case one in

which the materials gathered from a particular source text can be reconfigured into a poem of the author's own construction but without any
author-generated words. As he grew older, Turnbull allowed himself to
speak more intimately and personally, though never with a confessional
purpose. His poetry regularly returns to near the bone experiences from
his life in the medical profession; so there are problems and pains, but
they are from the doctor's casebook, or so it seems, and the doctor views
them as calmly as he can, sometimes with the chill of a real life story
documented for our admiration or our warning. Though a writer with
a distinctive timbre and coherent sound, his contribution was more in
the field of creative and verbal possibility than in the exploration of sensibility or identity. Turnbull's variety will allow him to rhyme, though
not with exclusionary rigidity, to use standard-issue meters if required,
as well as a vast range of cadences and speech phrasings. His work has
the capaciousness and grace to eschew as little as possible.

In a sampling of remarks from print and notebooks appended in
a 1992 'Some Afterwords', Turnbull wrote: 'the form of a poem must
be of positive use – and it may be that it functions more in the making
than in the result'. Read next to René Char's *Feuillets d'Hypnos* no. 98,
this observation could indicate a limit in Turnbull's sense of poetic
technique. Char noted of 'La ligne de vol du poème' that 'Elle devrait
être *sensible* à chacun.' [The poem's line of flight. Everyone must be able
to feel it.] For Char the 'positive use' that the poem must amount to
cannot merely function 'more in the making than in the result'; rather,
the form of what's made is its aerial trajectory, and this has to be as
present to the reader of the results as to the poet in the process of its
construction. Thus, rhymes may help poets find what their work needs
to say (as in the 'trouver' root of the word 'troubadour'), but their role
will be to structure and space the formation of meaning, sense, and
feeling in the reader – and that same reader will, at least subliminally, be
appreciating this added value in her or his own processes of discovery.

Turnbull's poetry is practically never without imaginative verbal
interest, and there is a perpetual delight in words to be experienced
here; but I do feel that this pleasure is at times more displayed in the
construction of the work than sensed and so, in effect, found by the fully
participating reader. This is most evident in poems that are generated
by the substitution of lexical items in set syntactical structures, as here
in 'Homage to Jean Tinguely', the Swiss kinetic artist (1925–1991):

a wishing of untangling
an unravelling of mangling
a tingling of insistence
a jingling of persistence
a tracery of mingling
a simplicity of jangling

The tribute play with the name is highly skilled and so is the ability to produce right-sounding but unpredictable variations – yet some of that verbal energy is sapped for me by the indefinite articles, the Latin genitives, and the 'jangling' remnants of inflected word-ends. The entire 24-line exercise is perhaps more self-delighting than illuminating. Yet the piece is also a generous tribute to a fellow artist, and this *Collected Poems* contains a fair leavening of such works.

Turnbull also writes in his 'Some Afterwords' about the relation between the sounds of a self in a poem and the one that made it. 'The poem', he writes, 'must speak for itself'. I do know what he means, but of course poems can never do that; they have to be spoken by people, including the ones that made them. He adds that most persons 'are curious about other people and in our response to a poem we often experience, even intensely, something that is akin to what is called in other contexts "personality".' He then added: 'Yet other experience tells us that this connection is not straightforward, that the poem in which we may take delight or which we may find engaging, may be written by someone we find unpleasant or tedious.' This is doubtless true; though we should distinguish between the personality that we would find tedious over dinner, and the personality that might be found tedious in the work itself. This would be another area which allows for legitimate differences of 'fit' between reader and work: some will doubtless find Swinburne's poetry less 'unpleasant or tedious' than others, but who would be sanguine enough to suggest that its character had no connection with its author's?

Turnbull's poetry, on the whole, gives an overwhelming impression of unguarded access, for better and worse, to its maker's mind. This is precisely how Fisher, who knew the man for almost half a century, put it in his jacket blurb: 'Of all my lost friends he is the least dead. The unique pace of his mind, sometimes troubled, always curious, seems still to be keeping us company somewhere just out of reach.' For this reader, who only met him two or three times in the company of others, the 'pace of his mind' is the side-effect of a style – one which has almost no time for the mannerisms of poetic 'personality' at all, a style which is like listening to a radio so perfectly tuned that there is never the crackle of any interference, and no jamming signals from old Albania either:

> I think you must have written them on postcards, your poems,
>   like something one sends home while visiting abroad;

> or like woodcuts that one finds in an old book in the attic and
>   stares at on a rainy day, forgetting supper, forgetting to
>   switch on the light;

> but not antique, though out of time, each fixed in its moment,
>   like sycamore seeds spiralling down that never seem to
>   reach the grass.

These are lines from his 'Homage to Jean Follain', the French *intimiste* poet (1903–1971). For this tribute, Turnbull deploys an unmannered, plain-speaking prose, with carefully chiselled phrasing, a style that doesn't imitate Follain's short-lined lyrics but does pay homage to his quiet tones and undemonstrative timbre. The writer of such tributes also comes across as no poet's poet, but one who likes poetry, and there is a heartening generosity to this, as if from a gone world, even to the extent of that slightly antique-sounding 'one finds'. But the poem itself is 'not antique, though out of time' and 'fixed', by means of those well judged and cadenced prose phrases, 'in its moment' too.

     This sustained limpidity does make the occasional social interference noise stand out more sore-thumb fashion when it does occur, as in the lines from 'Now That April's Here' quoted earlier. The signature limpidity is unnervingly present in most of Turnbull's poems, even the occasional five-finger exercises. Here, though, and for a final example, are the opening nine lines of his twenty-page chef-d'oeuvre 'Residues: Down the Sluice of Time':

> glitter of what's far off
> flash of the unseen
> casting back the light
>   pulse of the stars – and the dark
>   consumes our sight – in a shuttered room,

a candle flickers – and her eyes ignite
to rekindle
at source
the first fire –

There is no irony, precious little defensive obliquity, a complete absence of 'cool' or self-regarding fashion in the display of the text, and no psychological difficulties to be addressed as regards the world being presented. He keeps his eye on the object, as it were, but that attention issues longer works such as this into materials of great unpredictability, deployed with a skilful tonal switching, though one which maintains an aesthetic and formal dimension through the practices of lungs, heart, mind, and ear, rarely allowing the work to disperse in the sprawling outer suburbs of the programmatic long poem, that chimerical holy grail about as rare a promoter of good work as the white whale of the great American novel.

Being bereft of a readership, or even the idea of one, can be a painful problem for a poet; and in this case it's all the more a shame because Turnbull's range of experimental styles doesn't at any point make him less a social and sociable writer. His works are never rebarbatively defended against reader access, or other forms of absorption into the cultural bloodstream practised by those who, in all good faith, believe that they are contributing to political or cultural resistance movements by being barely intelligible. Though some of his works have been faintly marred by the culture of neglect in which they were obliged to find their way into the light, nevertheless, through the poet's generosity of spirit and verbal grace they did make it far enough to be collected in this admirable publication – and a well deserved posthumous gratitude is surely better than no gratitude at all.

ROY FISHER THROUGH THE YEARS

1

When does a tension become a contradiction? Or when does a contra-diction cease to generate vital quandaries and instead negate itself? Can such negations authenticate and set free? Or do they cancel out? These questions are prompted by the new, somewhat chronological reordering of Roy Fisher's writings in *Poems 1955–1980*, which brings back into print most (though not all, as advertised) of Fisher's published poetry and prose between those dates. A tension is referred to in the book's 'blurb': 'Roy Fisher's work is a unique mixture in British post-war poetry of English "provincialism" of subject-matter with internationalism of style and aesthetics.' It is characterised, as John Ash writes in the *Atlantic Review*, by a tension between 'the traditions of English empiricism on the one hand and the perceptual experimentation and formal artifice of European modernism on the other'. There is indeed a tension between Fisher's English 'provincialism' and international modernism; but, just as the former 'ism must be dressed up between inverted commas, so its tensed opposite might be dressed down as 'international'. This is not because the sources for Fisher's methods are actually confined to England, far from it; these sources do, nonetheless, retain a recherché, distant glamour. An early poem, 'Leaving July', collected for the first time, describes how

> Low crippled clouds drag on a naked sky
> over night leaves that point
> ravines of darkest green down steeply
> from the pale plateau of glaucous twilight;
>
> the sky flattens on the land and gazes
> back up into itself with rainwater eyes
> out of blue rutted sockets on a builder's site.

The word glaucous, 'of dull greyish green or blue', shows the stamp of its country of origin through the botanical meaning 'covered with bloom as of grapes', the produce of Mediterranean Latin and Greek. A recent usage associates it with France and modernism in England by means of the title to 'Yeux Glauques' in Pound's *Hugh Selwyn Mauberley*.

Travelling by the lines 'Thin like brook-water, / With a vacant gaze', Fisher drops it off in the English provinces where 'rainwater eyes' gaze 'out of blue rutted sockets on a builder's site'.

Tensing the local and the European allowed Fisher, at first, to present a context – the local – without being obliged to use the language familiarly associated with or attached to it. 'Toyland', another early piece, and a poem that could be cited to endorse Fisher's English 'provincialism' of subject-matter, shows him chafing against the obligation to stick with the words that are predicated by the context, words received that fit and seem fitting: 'I might by exception see an ambulance or the fire brigade / Or even, if the chance came round, street musicians (singing and playing).' Here the brackets are a cough around stating the obvious: the point where the 'formality', about which the poem divagates, becomes just a formality. Inversely, this tension is a scheme for importing words that will retain their foreign local colour, as in 'glaucous' above, without bringing with them their locality or context. Fisher's Europe is that of the stay-at-home pressing his nose to a travel-agent window; his different modernisms, various forms of impure diction.

The obligations of context – where a word is located – may bespeak further senses of relation. For if it is the potential to become 'just a formality' that puts the copula at risk, composing informally within a context can release some of the density of the habitual and familiar, a density thinned by constant recognition. But the refusal of predication or the avoidance of syntactic obligations, rather than necessarily thwarting mere habituation, may render the work down into only inert bits, frustrated pieces. The poem 'At No Distance' hovers precariously on this precipice. In the earlier collage of prose and poetry, *City*, Fisher uses relative clauses to indicate the distances in a family that are disclosed through war. His poem 'The Entertainment of War', disparaged for its unchallenging familiarity by the poet himself in *19 Poems and an Interview* (1975), is nonetheless an early essay in Russian Formalism's *priem ostrannenija*, 'the device of making it strange', which was discussed by Donald Davie in *Thomas Hardy and British Poetry* with regard to more overtly defamiliarising works such as 'As He Came Near Death' and 'Three Ceremonial Poems'. In 'The Entertainment of War', the strangeness is integral to the events, so that despite the conventional narrative mode, the habitual life of the family is distorted, giving fresh density to habit, through the bombing:

When I saw it, the house was blown clean by blast and care:
Relations had already torn out the new fireplaces;
My cousin's pencils lasted me several years.

Vacuuming is imaginatively enmeshed with sudden, quick death in the ambivalences of 'blown clean', occasioning the 'blast' unexpectedly and aptly followed by 'care'. The relations have picked the corpse of the house to the bone, and the poet as a boy is closely involved in the sharing out of distant relatives' property:

These were marginal people I had met only rarely
And the end of the whole household meant that no grief was seen;
Never have people seemed so absent from their own deaths.

The concluding prose paragraphs of *City*, in the 1968 revised version, combine a familiarity which is not contemptuous, because properly distant, and a separateness that is not just one thing after another, because syntactically related:

I have often felt myself to be vicious, in living so much by the eye, yet among so many people. I can be afraid that the egg of light through which I see these bodies may present itself as a keyhole. Yet I can find no sadism in the way I see them now. They are warm-fleshed, yet their shapes have the miniscule, remote morality of some mediaeval woodcut of the Expulsion: an eternally startled Adam, a permanently bemused Eve. I see them as homunculi, moving privately each in a softly lit fruit in a nocturnal tree. I can consider without scorn or envy the wellfound bedrooms I pass, walnut and rose-pink, altars of tidy, dark-haired women, bare-necked, wifely. Even in these I can see order.

The paragraph has to skirt being touching, in a weak sense, so as to remotely touch on the private lives of 'so many people' in a city. Not only does it see order, but constructs it generously. The 'well-found' bedrooms are built on sound foundations, and in the separate, yet interrelated, points of attention through which the syntax moves the poet not only finds them successfully, he finds them in good health.

The releases and unexpectedness that occur in Fisher's writing on human and domestic relations have a necessary obliquity and a distance that could free the poet in *City* from what he has called, in discussing the somewhat later poem 'For Realism': 'the entailments of [things] in ordinary reality', while still describing: 'a place which was real to me, a place with family association'. This release from context, from what might be called the over-determination of a familial landscape, may have been a necessity for Fisher – and the contrary need to remain in context is also evidenced above. Yet the aesthetic allegiances Fisher took on proved, with *City* in the first place, peculiarly suited to what was occurring in that landscape. 'On one of the steep slopes that rise towards the centre of the city all of the buildings have been destroyed within the past year', *City* begins, and later:

> The new city is bred out of a hard will, but as it appears, it shows itself a little ingratiating, a place of arcades, passages, easy ascent, good light. The eyes twinkle, beseech and veil themselves; the full, hard mouth, the broad jaw – these are no longer made visible to all.

By the time international modernism in architecture reached the English provincial cities it was already approximately half a century old. When Fisher, in *City*, creates a tension between a prose style to describe, among other things, the minutiae of the older Victorian city and a poetry of half-anxious refrains, he effects an overall heterogeneity of styles in the work which represents a sponsoring tension in the city itself. So, for example, his modernism in 'Lullaby and Exhortation for the Unwilling Hero' includes an allusion to one thirty-year-old archetype for the style, T. S. Eliot's *The Waste Land*. 'What are the roots that clutch, what branches grow / Out of this stony rubbish?' is scaled down and secularly reformulated as 'What steps descend, what rails conduct?' – the borrowed lines of a provincial city's shopping precinct. But the prose quoted above holds the figure in a densely equivocal stance that embraces nostalgia for the Victorian 'full, hard mouth', an architecture that dwarfed the city's inhabitants, and an equally qualified enchantment with the glassy modern style – a semi-transparent illusion, half concealing a hard will. And the quiet, almost disinterested tone of *City* keeps these ambivalences tensed. A decade or so later that tense poise has become a blunted sarcasm at the discrepancy between the

international modernist provincial architecture and a 'social realism',
the latter term in this case synonymous with social disillusion as here in
'Artists, Providers, Places to Go':

> The little figures in the architect's drawing
> the sleep of reason begets
> little figures.
>
> Nose the car up through the ramps
> into a bay, and leave it,
> keys in the dash by regulation –
> cost-effective:
> come back and find it gone,
> you got free parking.

'Seven Attempted Moves', from some five years earlier, with its
concluding 'Confinement, / shortness of breath. / Only a state of mind.
/ And / Statues of it built everywhere', can still gasp sceptically, without
sounding so down in the mouth.

The precariousness of Fisher's vital discontinuities founded on
the potentially contradictory need for a freed, freeing diction and the
obligations of contextual or local necessity can be felt in two transitional
poems, 'Suppose – ' and 'Continuity': the latter being the first poem
Fisher wrote after a two-year silence from approximately 1968 to 1970.
'Suppose – ', which begins: 'Suppose that once in a while / It still works,
just as it used to', goes on to doubt the strength of 'realistic' notation
by following 'Curtained from street flashes / By afternoon clatter, / A
crowd of faces and feet', with the shrugging gesture: 'That sort of thing';
and equally doubts the value of Fisher's '1905 Modernist' sources,
before summoning up the confidence to conclude:

> Why Alexandr Blok, the beautiful,
> Dealt out humbug,
> Still made sense –

'Continuity' acknowledges itself islanded in the familiar without
urgency: 'Purpose? No purpose. Apparitions? None'. Yet in essaying a
mild description it effects an unemphatic analogy for the difficulty the
poet has in swimming beyond the forms he has made in time:

> The fish-trap gives the water form,
> Minimal form, drawn on the current unattended,
> The lure and the check. So much free water.

A poetic agnosticism sensible in 'Minimal form', or the lines 'The old flat arrangement, / Dry track of half a voice' and 'Just enough light to ask questions by' from 'Suppose – ', has employed the 'realism' that is 'only common sense' to doubt aesthetic freedoms and set the freedom from a habituated contextual necessity, which aesthetic sophistication may confer, to run down localised notation. These two poems succeed by living dangerously near the edge where tensed contraries cancel each other out.

Roy Fisher's work in the 1970s shows the tensed contraries in gestures of conflict which only occasionally result in the vital quandaries noted above. '107 Poems' and 'In The Wall' could be cited as among such exceptions. 'The Only Image' begins with a tiny observation ('Salts work their way / to the outside of a plant pot / and dry white') and concludes:

> I can
> compare what I like to the salts,
> to the pot, if there's a pot,
> to the winter if there's a winter.
>
> The salts I can compare
> to anything there is.
> Anything.

John Ash notes that 'it is a wry comment on the absolute arbitrariness and wilfulness of imagination. It records a realist's defeat'. Such an apt account has two crucial weaknesses, however, weaknesses inherent in the poem. First, 'the absolute arbitrariness and wilfulness of imagination' is a formula that does not distinguish between the many forms of mental activity that relate things, ranging perhaps from pure delusion to clear intuition. The imaginative freedom to relate the disparate in an unstable, variable or effaced context is what the poem evidently asserts, but in doing so it has as little to say as John Ash about what exactly is to be compared to what and why; that is, nothing about how one connectedness, or one abutted disconnectedness, may be preferred to another; nothing about just, necessary relations. If it is the imagination which discloses such relations, and syntax – in however attenuated a form – which bears them, then it is merely the illusion of choice that is substituted for a functional relation when the imaginable is multiplied to infinity. Secondly, if 'The Only Image' records 'a realist's defeat', it is a pyrrhic victory for the imagination. 'Realism' inflicts terrible losses on imagination in 'The salts I can compare / to anything there is'. For 'anything there is' places the poem's consciousness back in this strictly limited context: a rigid world of atomistically perceived things. Here an implicit contradiction cancels itself to nothing.

A similar cancelling occurs in 'Handsworth Liberties'. *Poems 1955–1980* includes a condensed, revised version of Fisher's note on *The Thing About Joe Sullivan* (1978) for the Poetry Book Society Bulletin. It indicates that this cancelling out is pressed on the writer by an inner necessity, from which the sequence arises, but which is effaced in the composition. The note describes how 'a gratuitous visual impression, always of some actual but quite inconsequential location – a street corner or suburban-industrial vista – near my home' would attach itself to a particular piece of music and be recalled each time the music was heard. 'At length I decided that these visual memories had persisted for so long in laying claim to my attention that I would round on them and put them to work … Writing the poems did not banish the images, but they came to seem less intrusive.' In the earlier version of this note the last sentence read: 'I still experience the images, but they have been subjected to a genial exorcism.' Exorcising the intrusive, these poems are a relief from phantasmagoria (a Poundian term describing the visual imaginations of poets for whom 'whole countrysides, stretches of hill and forest travel with them'). The eighth poem finds relief by projecting a residual context in which the art of 'making strange' is extended to include perception without memory:

> At the end of the familiar,
> throwing away the end
> of the first energy, regardless;
> nothing for getting home with –

The poem acknowledges what is restricting about this peculiar receptivity to things without recognition or recall: the effacement of those social habituations that make a return home possible. But the contradictions proliferate here too, for if 'nothing has a history', as the poem notes, there can be no such place as 'home'. Concluding, the poem gestures at its lost connections: 'Getting home – getting home somehow, / late, late and small.' Fended off by that 'somehow' is the contextual density of the 'late and small' child's-eye-view of a familial landscape compounded of the strange and those family ties that facilitate return. But the poem is not a child's-eye-view. Its aesthetic formulations are those of a poet with a history of his own styles in mind. The programmatic tone of the writing seeks to reconstruct by abstract statement the supposed disconnectedness of the wandering child's landscape, without the tonal burden of the situation that is alluded to in 'late and small'.

The abstracted calm in 'Handsworth Liberties' may exorcise the intrusive imagery, but it does not produce that sense of intrusiveness for the reader. The gripping, compelling quality of the imagery – as it is described in the note – has been replaced by pale annotations of context without obligation, without the necessary contingency of the familiar, but rather with occasional lists of familiar things: 'a laundry – / brick, laurels, a cokeheap / across from the cemetery gate – / a printing works and a small / cycle factory; hard tennis courts'. Fisher's note on the poems explains their lack of intrusion as a preferred state of affairs. While the sceptic in Fisher can find that the tension between the provincial and the international modernist serves as a way of doubting both, or can find his poems crippled by such doubts ('In The Black Country' makes self-mockery from the tentativeness of 'Suppose –'), the aesthetician can use the contradicting possibilities of his old tension to rule out what he no longer wants to have to be burdened with in poems. The discontinuities that created a spacious ground for tensed quandaries may serve him as a way out of his poems' inner necessity, leaving the reader with a neutral gesture – 'late and small'.

'Style', dedicated to Michael Hamburger, is a programme note to this aesthetic. It refuses the sense that style effects 'intricacies of self and sign' or 'the language of one's time / and class. The languages / of my times and classes' and prefers to

> reach the air
> as a version by my friend Michael.
> He knows good Englishes.
> And he knows the language
> language gets my poems out of.

The poem prefers what may well have already been preferred. 'The Least', a poem from the early seventies, seems to have been inspired by Paul Celan's 'Ein Auge, Offen', and Hamburger's versions of Celan's 'Heimkehr' and 'Unten' may have contributed to the orientation of poem eight in 'Handsworth Liberties':

> Led home into oblivion
> the sociable talk of
> our slow eyes
>
> Led home, syllable after syllable ...

In his Introduction to *Paul Celan: Poems*, Hamburger notes the German poet's recognition that he could not treat his extreme loss of context and of family, through war and annihilation, 'directly, realistically', yet also: 'Very few of his German readers, for instance, could possibly be expected to know that Mapesbury Road – the title of another late poem – is a street in North West London where Celan used to visit a surviving relative, his father's sister, who is addressed in the poem'. The attenuated distance between context and aesthetic gesture in Celan's work bares a pressure of experience, in experience's near effacement, that goes to authenticate the gesture. Yet when Fisher prefers to weaken or distance context by writing 'the language / language gets my poems out of', a neutral version of Celan's straitened utterance, thus using Hamburger's often exemplary translatorese as a way of 'getting his poems out of' (which can also mean 'avoiding') a language bearing and betraying familiar ties, the liberties he takes have not that authenticating urgency in Celan which derives one of its sources from negation and effacement. The contradictions of context and diction are employed to evade by a cancelling negation the quandaries that they had begun by releasing. In adopting the language of translation, inevitably an English somewhat remote from its own or the original language's context, Fisher imports words without the burdensome entailments of their localities. Such an absence of burden in words is the very condition of work against which Hamburger's and indeed all translations to different degrees must struggle: conditions that necessitate translators' introductions. Fisher's 'A note on the Handsworth Liberties' serves a similar function, alluding to a distant or hardly to be felt context from which the poems rise. It is a gesture of responsibility, as he might be implying in 'Wonders of

Obligation' when he writes that the 'things we make up out of language / turn into common property. / To feel responsible / I put my poor footprint back in' – or this would be one way to read them.

2

A reader familiar with Roy Fisher's publishing history might imagine his contract for this new edition containing a rider that the book has to be distinctly different from his three earlier 'collected poems' volumes. Certainly Fisher has come up with a gathering of work that is his most complete to date (though by no means a Complete Poems) and one characteristically non-definitively open-ended. The words 'collected' or 'complete' are nowhere to be seen. The book's main title, *The Long and the Short of It*, alludes in one of its meanings to the literal fact that the volume contains all his longer works (his two Oxford collected volumes did not include 'The Cut Pages') as well as the vast majority of his shorter, short, and very short pieces. Fisher's work ranges from the five-line joke poem called 'Epic' to the short epic called 'A Furnace'. The book is by no means a complete Fisher, because it pointedly excludes a number of poems that have previously been collected ('Occasional Poem', on the death of John Berryman, or 'To the Supposed Dancer') and other possible candidates for inclusion that have been published in pamphlets or magazines ('Three Early Pieces', 'Abraham Darby's Bridge'). It also steers clear of any approach to the fairly large body of early, uncollected poems – such as the elegant 'The Lemon Bride' – cited and discussed by James Keery in his chapter from *The Thing about Roy Fisher: Critical Studies* (2000). The book collects for the first time a few early poems that had got away ('Kingsbury Mill'), the completed text of 'The Dow Low Drop', which had appeared in abbreviated form in the 1996 Bloodaxe *New and Selected Poems*, and quite a number of shorter, occasional, or elegiac poems written during the last decade or so.

The book is not as reliable as it might have been, containing an unhappy peppering of minor misprints and typos; and Fisher had long ago issued a statement on such textual slippage in 'Irreversible': 'The *Atlantic Review* misspelled Kokoschka. / In three weeks he was dead.' This book's 'fine cracks', which by no means diminish the importance of its publication, are further sign that for the poet it is not one of those graveyards of performance described in 'Five Morning Poems from

a Picture by Manet' as 'splinters of fact stuck in the earth's fat rind.'
The poet notes in the Acknowledgements that 'These poems no more
amount to a biography than I do' and thus 'an arrangement that seemed
chronological' would be 'false'. This effectively damns the two Oxford
volumes (1980 and 1988) to falsity, for some such rough arrangement
– with the exception of 'The Ship's Orchestra', put at the back in an
appendix – appeared to have been tried there. In *The Long and the Short
of It* 'nothing of the kind is attempted', and the resulting rearrangement
of his works will provide an intriguingly coherent deployment of texts
both for Fisher's long-time readers and those fortunate people who,
coming upon his work for the first time, can encounter its uniqueness
afresh. For the chronically chronologically minded, Fisher has added
dates of composition after titles in the Index (though the mysterious
dates '0000' after 'City' and 'Interiors with Various Figures' must – for
the time being – stand as either collapses in the face of a too complex
chronology, dada jokes, or merely production slip-ups). Fisher kindly
acknowledges my 'help in the preparation of this book'; for the record,
my contribution involved no more than an acted-upon suggestion
about what to do with the poems that didn't evidently fall into generic
categories, plus a few pleas for inclusions, in some cases of which the
poems' defence council was overruled by the presiding judge.

Even for those who know Fisher's work well, this book offers
revealing and refreshing encounters and conjunctions. The texts have
been ordered into nine sections, of which five could be described
as 'generic'. The first contains long works such as 'City', 'The Ship's
Orchestra', 'The Cut Pages', and 'A Furnace'. The third is made up
of comedy poems like 'A Modern Story' about poetry competitions,
'Paraphrases' about the weird epistolary life of a poet with an
international reputation and no books in print, or 'The Poetry Promise'
about keeping the customer satisfied in these market-driven days, or
'The Nation' – written before the institution in the UK of a 'National
Poetry Day', but a perfectly judged mockery *avant la lettre* of such
superficially populist, culturally retrograde antics. The fifth gathers
poems dedicated to other writers and artists for festschrifts, memorials,
or from no occasional prompting, such as 'Staffordshire Red' (for
Geoffrey Hill), 'Emblem' (for Lorine Niedecker) and 'Songs from the
Camel's Coffin' (for Gael Turnbull), its title borrowed from Turnbull's
own 'For a Jazz Pianist', in which he describes '(a camel's coffin?)' as 'a
black / and polished upright / slotted box'. The final section of Fisher's

poem records his arrival in the USA for a visit that included a reading event at Notre Dame (where he was photographed playing one such camel's coffin, a photo subsequently printed in a university yearbook, captioned in the manner of 'Irreversible' as a picture of John Cage):

> Born in the middle of the island and never leaving it
> in fifty years, then startled
> on stepping down to the battered tarmac of O'Hare
> to discover that the air above it,
> the entire medium of elsewhere,
> wasn't as I'd guessed it would have to be, a heavy
> yellowish fluid tending towards glass,
> towards mica. Why in all that time
> had nobody said?
> I'll never be sure, that's for certain.

Such lines as these casually instance Fisher's uniqueness – his ability to preserve a remarkable freshness in his encounters with the world, which we can then encounter too, refreshing our sense of the lived. This is not exactly a Russian formalist 'making strange', because to Fisher the thing, in this case the air above O'Hare, is strange anyway. Fisher's art is about processing experience without lessening its strangeness. It is about *keeping* it strange – and this has required his never being 'sure' and 'that's for certain.' Section VII of his book is devoted to the sequences and series of shorter writings, the 'Interiors with Various Figures', the 'Texts for a Film' about Birmingham that Tom Pickard produced, the 'Seven Attempted Moves', 'The Six Deliberate Acts', 'Five Morning Poems from a Picture by Manet', the four poems 'To the Memory of Wyndham Lewis', or the 'Three Ceremonial Poems'. Last of these generic groups, section VIII, is given over to collaborations with artists – such as 'Correspondence' with Tom Phillips, 'Also' with Derek Greaves, and the many others with Ronald King. Missing from this section though is 'Cultures', a collaboration with King (helpfully described by Ralph Pite in his chapter from *The Thing about Roy Fisher*) but one whose arrangement defies publication in a book of this kind.

While these five sections are the volume's reinforced structure, built upon the grounds of compositional habits and preferences, the other four sections – gatherings of poems that don't fit any of those generic categories – are, as far as the organisation is concerned, the book's most revealing. These mid- or short-length poems tracking individual moments of inspiration contain borderline overlaps with other sections. 'The Thing about Joe Sullivan' might be thought Fisher's most dedicated poem, in that it expresses an overwhelming fascination with the psychology and aesthetics, and indeed ethics, of this white Chicagoan jazz pianist's style; but it doesn't appear in section V, presumably, because these two musicians – Fisher has also worked as a semi-professional jazz pianist – were not personally acquainted. Similarly, 'One World', a poem reporting on an early teaching experience with a remedial class at a school and reflecting on the unlikelihood that such pupils could have come to be readers of little magazines, might have appeared in the comedies section – since it was first published in one of the pamphlets of such work issued by the late Richard Caddel's Pig Press. Yet its account of teaching a class of severely underprivileged children is not, properly read, a joke at all. So the fascination of these more apparently ad-hoc sections lies in their prompting a reader to think about how and why specific works have found their way into each of these four and, further, why individual texts found there have become neighbours.

Section VI, for instance, appears to be made up of poems that variously address without satire Fisher's evolving awareness of his own aesthetics. Born in 1930, and not in 1885 or thereabouts, Fisher, though willing to give interviews, has felt no inclination to write manifestos, whether group or personal, or indeed to establish his 'poetics' by means of academic, critical, or hortatory prose – and especially not before the fact of having written attempts at pieces of literary art. Thus, 'For Realism', 'A Poem Not a Picture', 'The Lesson in Composition', 'Of the Empirical Self and for Me', or 'From an English Sensibility' come together with other relevant pieces to define, however obliquely and inconclusively, what Fisher has thought and felt he has been up to all these years. Nor does this section, since it is the occasional work of decades, pretend to offer a single, coherent aesthetic position. No sooner have we read the close of 'For Realism' ('A realism / tries to record, before they're gone, / what silver filth these drains have run'), than we encounter the six-line epigram 'It is Writing' which ends: 'I mistrust the poem in its hour of success, / a thing capable of being / tempted by ethics into the wonderful.' It is hard to believe that the latter, from 1974, has not been placed thus on the same page as a tacit comment on the former, written in 1965, and made a moral meal of by Donald Davie in the chapter 'Roy Fisher: An Appreciation' from

Thomas Hardy and British Poetry (1973).

But why, then, asks the doubter, isn't 'The Thing about Joe Sullivan', with its tacit ethical-aesthetic commentary, or 'The Memorial Fountain' with its 'thirty-five-year-old-man, / poet, / by temper, realist, / watching a fountain' – why are these poems in section V, and not alongside 'For Realism' or the 'Lesson in Composition'? One pragmatic reason is that the various mid-length poems must not be lined up by overt or obvious similarities. If you put 'For Realism' next to 'The Memorial Fountain', for instance, you allow a misleading statement to form, one which appears to imply that Fisher is, despite appearances to the contrary, really a realist. So, in these sections, there is un-simplifying variation and contrast too; and there is conscious avoidance of any chronology (even the generic works are shuffled so as to display pointed-ness but not evident thematic or biographical continuity. This is surely why the first section begins with 'Wonders of Obligation', that classic account of Fisher's reluctantly associative art 'We know that hereabouts / comes into being / the malted-milk brickwork' and its – understated for the most part – cultural values: 'The things we make out of language / turn into common property. / To feel responsible / I put my poor footprint back in.'

Fisher, 'unsure … for certain', has stated in an interview that there is still such a thing as 'honest scepticism'. He said it in the hey-day of that post-modern scepticism which, since it multiplies doubt to infinity, haplessly drops scepticism out of the equation – allowing its proponents to flourish mechanical rejections of justifiable assertion (about what truth is, for instance) that in practice leaves everything precisely as it was. Honest scepticism, I take it, means allowing doubt its place in an understanding of the world, both natural and human. Doubt then functions as a means to further apprehension and understanding, not as a device for short-circuiting any such gains. Fisher has never believed, as Charles Tomlinson emblematically did with the title of his second collection, that 'seeing is believing'. He too has been, as he put it in 'City', a poet who lived 'so much by the eye', but he did so to address the processes by which the world takes shape around us, breaking up, and reconfiguring its solidities, altering the angles of sight, or focal length, so as to access a knowledge of change and evolution. 'A Furnace' proceeds by enacting the life of energies, powers, forms, or evidences not only to access knowledge of change, but to assist it. Fisher's scepticism about poetry with a moral attached has found its role in defining his field of operations, since on its right flank were the social moralists of the 1950s, Philip Larkin, Kingsley Amis and Davie, with, nearby, in the Tomlinson of the 1960s and 1970s, an epistemological moralist of international distinction.

However, to live outside the law you must be honest; and Fisher's scepticism means that he is not without beliefs about aesthetic, literary, poetic, and therefore social and political conduct – beliefs that might be identified in the differences between overtly propagated rules of behaviour with a social flavour, and complexes of learned practices about relations with others that, for one thing, would be betrayed by imposing them on others, by boasting about holding them, or by announcing that you have just acted in accord with them. In 'The Lesson in Composition', Fisher writes of how 'Whatever I start from / I go for the laws of its evolution, / de-socializing art, diffusing it / through the rest till there's no escaping it.' This is a prosaic poem responding to the oppressive social demand that the marketplace has, mysteriously, imposed on poetry over the last few decades. I say 'mysteriously' because you would have thought that the marketplace has so little real use for poetry, it not making much money for anyone, that it could have been left in peace. The thorough marginalisation of the art some time before the rise of our current version of market economics should have found it well positioned to resist such demands. Yet such is the power of ideology that poetry's more socially adaptive operators have felt compelled to sing from the same stock-exchange hymn-sheet. Fisher's poem approaches its end by describing the British version of this problem. 'Art talks', he writes,

> of its own processes, or talks about the rest
> in terms of the processes of art; or stunts itself
> to talk about the rest in the rest's own terms
> of crisis and false report – entertainment,
> that worldliness that sticks to me
> so much I get sent outside
> when the work wants to start.
>
> I'm old enough to want to be prosaic;
> I shall have my way.

Art offers its benefits to individuals and, through them, to the society at large, only if it is allowed to follow its processes without the imposition of formulated social demands – whether they are promulgated by a national union of writers, or as a requirement from publishers and their allies in newspapers and award bodies to address the immediate interests of imagined consumers. Fisher's scepticism about identity and the idea of the discontinuous self, the role of body sensations, of ontology in epistemology can also be related – paradoxically it might seem – to Jazz and the life of the performer.

Yet this is not pop music. Fisher became interested in his music at a point just before the moment when it was to be pushed aside. He has, as a consequence of that marginalisation, accompanied distinguished American performers on their tours of the British provinces. This is slightly different from the kinds of relation to an audience of readers that many writers will take for granted. The latter is slower, more cumulative, based upon two separated activities that take place within the privacy of the writer's or reader's conscious minds – and one that is only supported, or sometimes even hindered, by encounters with the poet in performance. The musician who performs on a nightly basis needs an internalised sense of what a good performance will be that pays only marginal attention to what the audience may or may not have thought. Fisher is thus complexly placed both to understand the way in which art is necessarily a matter of presenting its products to informed people who appreciate that art, and of knowing how to preserve the autonomy of the performer from audience demands that can in so many ways prove to be art's ruination.

The doubt about being able to know ourselves, a first step on the road to such self-knowledge as may be granted us, naturally extends in honest sceptics to the knowledge of others. The limited access al-lowed to the rest of the world then requires a process of acquaintance, a repeated returning to and reconsidering of phenomena. One limit in Fisher's work is the locating of experience in shared relationships be-tween people. The works that might seem at first most to qualify such a statement ('Interiors with Various Figures' and 'The Ship's Orches-tra') only tend on closer acquaintance with their unique strangeness to reinforce it. This limit might seem to be escaped from by the comedy poems of section III. Comedy requires a relation to constituencies and social groups. The poet's relative lack of ease with such situations of identification and provision, may account for some of the weaknesses in that section. 'Sets', for instance, was inspired by the quarrels between various groups and sub-groups of poets about who precisely should control the UK Poetry Society. Beyond the more 'committed' inner circles of such writers and their support teams it might be expected to reverberate with rather less force:

> If you take a poem
> you must take another
> and another
> till you have a poet.
>
> And if you take a poet
> you'll take another, and so on,
> till finally you get
> a civilisation: or just
> the dirtiest brawl you ever saw –
> the choice isn't yours.

What saves this from being a faded joke about a shrunken corner of a lost world, is the crispness and clarity not only of the writing, but also of the double disappointment it dramatises through, for example, the workings of unobtrusive rhymes: 'poet ... get', 'so on ... civilisation', and 'saw ... yours'. Equally, the way that 'or just' breaks up the resolving rhymed close on the word 'civilisation' is a perfectly judged ruffling of high-minded high hopes. So the poem first describes a process that we who admire and enjoy this art have all experienced – the growth of a learned and then fed fascination that can access some of the finest productions of highly sensitised minds, and then marks a precipitous slide into isolation, conflict, and the total loss of anything like art or control. Many of Fisher's poems dedicated to other poets could be called counteractive moves in this cultural destruction of poetry and the conditions for its best production. 'You Should Have Been There', written for Peter Riley in 2000, is exemplary in its acknowledgement of just how essential imaginative collaboration is in this most personal, and often most isolate, of arts: 'you should have been there / to make two of our sort / too many for the territory / I'd split the shift with you', he proposes, 'while the broad- / bodied waitress in black with an ominous eye / stalks by'.

Roy Fisher's is, then, a poetry of scepticism, one that included a healthy scepticism of poetry. It has been protected from the cancelling to nothing of moralised minimalism – by accepting a need to grow loquacious and to address with ever greater reach the implications and ramifications of its congenial, not to say congenital, modes first intuited through exposure via Gael Turnbull to American writers such as W. C. Williams, Denise Levertov, and Cid Corman in the late 1950s and early 1960s. This is what Fisher's lesser known, and by some less appreciated, work of the 1980s and 1990s has been about. In 'A Furnace' and elsewhere his 'honest scepticism' has tacitly defined a complex social and political agnosticism – addressing, for instance, the survival of ancient religious modes for giving significance to mortal processes, while criticizing established religion's expropriation of death, and the role of the dead in our lives. Since the end of the 1970s, Fisher has published work that takes carefully calibrated steps in the direction of the social, while simultaneously keeping the time's overweening social demands in their place. He has indeed put his 'poor footprint back in'. The first part of 'Texts for a Film' (1991) begins 'Birmingham's what I think with' and over more than fifty years this poet has found evolving means for turning that thought into art. I first encountered his poetry on a library shelf some thirty-five ago. If not quite 'what I think with', Roy Fisher's work has nonetheless contributed substantially to what and how I think – and, *al que quiere!* (to those who desire), it can do the same.

TWO

ELIZABETH BISHOP:
'EXACT AS HORROR'

In a letter to John Taylor on 27 February 1818 Keats offered the axiom that 'if Poetry comes not as naturally as the Leaves to a tree, it had better not come at all.' Elizabeth Bishop saw it differently. 'Writing poetry is an unnatural act,' she wrote in a prose fragment printed here, and 'It takes great skill to make it seem natural… Most of the poet's energies are really directed towards this goal: to convince himself.' One sadness clinging to *Edgar Allan Poe & the Juke-box*, this invaluable gathering of unpublished materials, is not so much in the story it shadows of her difficult life, its lost relatives, friends, and lovers ('the art of losing isn't hard to master'), but in the record it presents of her various failures to convince herself that the work underway, at whatever stage, the candidate poem, 'is really an inevitable, *only* natural way of behaving under the circumstances.' Despite her lifelong devotion to the art of poetry, both Bishop's authorised oeuvre and her other writings would suggest that she was by no means easily convinced. An aphoristic note dated c. 1937 finds her describing poetry as 'air transportation (in its present state)' and concludes: 'Some poems ascend for a period of time, then come down again; we have a great many stranded planes.' Alice Quinn's labour of love, with its fascinatingly detailed notes, appendix, and facsimile reproductions is a long exemplification of the lines from William Empson's villanelle 'Missing Dates' about how 'It is the poems you have lost, the ills / From missing dates, at which the heart expires.'

That 'you' appearing for the first time at line 16 in Empson's poem appears to be echoed in Dylan Thomas's equally famous villanelle with the same irrupting pronoun: 'And you, my father.' Bishop had written to May Swenson on 4 November 1956: 'I've tried for years to do a villanelle, I like them so much, but without much luck – like Thomas's – *Do not go gentle into that good night*.' Twenty years later, she does the very same thing at the same line in 'One Art' with 'Even losing you I shan't have lied.' These three villanelles variously focus down, by means of that new pronominal note, on personal issues of breaking or broken relationship as they approach a completing close. Bishop's parenthetical '(*Write it!*)' draws attention to the poem's completion as a resolving achievement of emotional equilibrium, of attachment and detachment

– absorbing into the texture of her poem an implication that 'the art of losing' would inevitably include the poems you couldn't get, or get right. Bishop's villanelle is then also about the risk of 'losing' poems because the crisis feeling out of which they grow swamps the will required to complete them. The circumstances in which the poem might be made to seem the only natural thing overwhelm the poet's energies in their efforts to achieve a workable balance between the evocation of crisis and its purposeful shaping – emblematised in this case by the completion of the villanelle form itself.

'One Art' is not an uncollected poem; but Quinn most helpfully reproduces the sixteen preserved draft sheets in her appendix. Reading these prompts the thought that composing a poem requires the writer to establish a relationship (one of trusting possibility, of purpose and potential) with the words being shaped; and it's this sense of potential relationship which releases the ability to add, subtract, rephrase, reorder, develop and curtail that may be involved in completing the work. Equally, completing a poem means establishing and settling that sense of possibility, that potential for action, change, growth, and development, as a trustworthy structure that readers can use to activate such relationship-building skills in and for themselves. Notwithstanding the overwhelming evidence of the poet's need to nurture and sustain relationships *through* writing in Robert Giroux's edition of Bishop's *One Art: Selected Letters*, Quinn's book evidences the poet's faltering and at best partial success to establish them *in* these writings and in the endlessly difficult processes of poetic and literary composition. A fragmentary passage towards the close of 'Homesickness,' which never got beyond a handwritten sketch of materials with a couple of indicated rhymes, might stand as an epigraph for many of these painfully thwarted pieces: 'It was too late – for what, she did not know. – / already – , remote, / irrepair*able* (rhyme)   irreparable.' If the experience approached here proved too remote for reparation (the draft is subtitled '1900'), only too soon the candidate poem would prove so as well.

One of Bishop's gifts lay in being able economically to describe the look of things. Quinn opens her introduction by noting some of the stray materials contained in the Vassar archive from which she has drawn the texts collected here: 'Begonias ghostly in a galvanised bucket' is one. Yet this only goes to show that creative writing, and poetry especially, is not exactly or accurately described as descriptive or description. Such stabs at vivid notation as that phrase about the begonias in a bucket have to be activated, turned into purposeful evocations, by means of an occasioning difficulty. One of Bishop's best poems, 'The Bight,' a piece that gets along by means of some seaboard scene-painting in which, enviably perhaps, 'birds soar / on impalpable drafts,' has to work into that stalking-horse procedure signs of an urgent stock-taking purpose – one signalled by its subtitle '[*On my birthday*].' The poet herself was only too sceptically aware of her descriptive abilities and to what they could lead: whether calling herself 'a minor female Wordsworth', denigrating '"our beautiful old silver" school of female writing', or noting the boredom of nothing to do but 'registering their flora / their fauna, their geography' in the 'infinities / of islands' nightmare from 'Crusoe in England.' She knew what it was like to have sets of descriptive fragments in the notebooks, but nothing resembling a verb to join those bits together.

The frontispiece to Quinn's book shows a hand-written completed draft of the title poem. Though its first sentence is promisingly confident ('Easily through the darkened room / the juke-box burns; the music falls'), the rest of the first stanza sidles to a close without the satisfaction of a main verb:

> *Starlight, La Conga*, all the dance-halls
> in the block of honkey-tonks,
> cavities in our waning moon,
> strung with bottles and blue lights
> and silvered coconuts and conches.

Alongside this stanza Bishop has written 'blue as gas, / blue as the pupil / of a blind man's eye'. Are these words for use in a subsequent but never-written draft? Quinn notes a link between this blind man's eye and that of the narrator's neighbour in Poe's 'The Tell-Tale Heart.' She doesn't connect them to the lines in 'The Bight' where 'the water… doesn't wet anything, / the color of the gas flame turned as low as possible. / One can smell it turning to gas; if one were Baudelaire / one could probably hear it turning to marimba music.' Could 'The Bight' be a poem that sublimates, intimating without dwelling on, some of the bitter matter that 'Edgar Allan Poe & the Juke-Box' too directly tries to address? The associations of water, gas, Baudelaire and marimba music might hint that this hangover-like poem has some such material behind its 'awful but cheerful' seaside clutter.

In the frontispiece facsimile 'Edgar Allan Poe & the Juke-Box' has been firmly struck through with a heavy diagonal line. The reasons why poets put lines through apparently completed work are many and various, ranging from momentary pique, through temporary self-doubt or creative depression, exhausted self-disgust, all the way to definitive critical rejection of the draft from further consideration. I'm going to explore the idea that Bishop deleted the poem because she came to view its concluding speculations as tentatively forced and muddled:

> Poe said that poetry was *exact*.
> But pleasures are mechanical
> and know beforehand what they want
> and know exactly what they want.
> Do they obtain that single effect
> that can be calculated like alcohol
> or like the response to the nickel?
> – how long does the music burn?
> like poetry, or all your horror
> half as exact as horror here?

This is a troubled and troubling attempt to address the relations between poetry, alcohol, and sexual compulsion. It appears to want at least partially to contradict Poe, but goes only so far as obliquely to question him. This concluding verse may well be responding to the passage in 'The Philosophy of Composition' where Poe describes his writing of 'The Raven' – an attempt to show that 'not one point in its composition is referrible either to accident or intuition' and that 'the work proceeded, step by step, to its completion with the precision and rigid consequence of a mathematical problem.' Thomas Hardy, a cunning poet himself, described Poe's account as 'a fiction,' and Fernando Pessoa, who imitated and translated the author, thought Poe deluded. Quinn's extensive and somewhat rambling note does mention 'The Philosophy of Composition' in passing, but not the notorious account of 'The Raven' – though she does cite a passage by Baudelaire on Poe's obsession with 'the adjustment of means to effect.' When the inventor of the detective story describes poetry as exact, by reflecting on such calculated causal links, he makes the poet an equivalent of his own Auguste Dupin, whose imaginative leaps of association are presented to readers as analytical deductions. Poetry is not 'exact' in this way, however *attuned* its parts, because the *effects* of a work of art can never be exactly correlated to its means. There is no strictly causal relationship between the promptings embedded in the work and anyone's possible responses to them at any time.

Nor are pleasures 'mechanical.' You can't know in advance, for sure, what will give you pleasure. You can only assume and hope. The mechanical causal relationship between the nickel being put in the jukebox and the music selected being played – though that word 'selected' interrupts any strictly mechanical link – is by no means the same as the even more associative relationship between the music and the selector's variably unpredictable pleasure in hearing it ('the appetite may sicken,' as Shakespeare noted), to say nothing of the varieties of possible responses by other listeners to the same song. The effects of alcohol can be predicted, with varying degrees of skill and capacity to act on the self-perceived evidence, but they can't be calculated exactly, as can be commonly noticed when we stand up from a table or go outside and find ourselves more tipsy than we thought. Bishop is not likely to have been good at such calculations either, given her documented problems with lost weekends.

'Edgar Allan Poe & the Juke-Box' takes place in one of those honky-tonks, where people are drinking hard, playing the music, and then engaging in some casual sexual groping which the poem doesn't detail. Quinn's note does, however, refer us to manuscript materials that mention 'the full and final degradation of our love.' Those appear to be its exact horrors, far more specific (though not specified) than Poe's pseudo-scientific creations of mystery and imagination – as, for example, in 'The Murders in the Rue Morgue', where the horrific events aren't murders, or even crimes, since the Ourang-Outang that is revealed to have killed the victims can't be attributed with legal intent. Bishop's poem evades its subject, questions but fails to address its theme, and appears unable either to reflect on, or benefit from analysis, of the relationships, or lack of them, between its suggestively associated materials. Her need to understand and also detach herself from the poem's subjects is only too clear, but so too is her apparent failure to do either. That's why I think she may have put a line through it.

What is the difference between the sadness sticking to many of these poems and drafts, and Bishop's authorised poems? Urges, drives, and compulsions are what may motivate the writing of poetry, and may be made into its subject-matter; but her completed poems manifest ways in which these energies are transformed into objects pleasingly useful to others. Sexual compulsion, alcoholism, grief, loss, depression or despair may seem to occasion art, but they are as likely to be its dispersers too. Bishop's uncompleted poems have the air of works in which the compulsive will, afflicted by what it seeks to represent, cannot extricate itself to the point at which it may be able to observe itself in art as a form of life. The world, which includes others' representations of it, can thus only too easily overwhelm the will in poets' efforts to achieve a workable balance between circumstantial description and purposive shaping. The poet is prompted to acknowledge the mass of surrounding objects, the 'silvered coconuts and conches,' but then to resist them or to put them in their place by the action of verbs and the agencies not only of inanimate subjects but human pronouns – sentient presences implied by exclamatory, or vocative, verbal behaviour. Bishop's poems that either don't wholly work or don't get finished show ways in which what Coleridge called the 'shaping spirit of imagination' may be differently stymied by situations that are also crises of description, or collapses in the face of the overwhelmingly quotidian, or the burdens of maintaining control without defences and supports. Bishop's attempt at an 'Aubade and Elegy' for her friend Lota de Macedo Soares, who had committed suicide in New York in 1967, is the most painful example of such collapses: 'No coffee can wake you no coffee can wake you no coffee / No revolution can catch your attention / You are bored with us all. It is true we were ['were' deleted] boring.'

Quite a number of the pieces presented in this collection have human relationships, or their failures, as themes or occasioning subjects. One of the most successful, 'It is marvellous to wake up together...', has been in circulation since Lorrie Goldensohn published it in 1992. This was the poem that led me to hope that Bishop's uncollected verse would be the equivalent of a new book by an over-scrupulous poet who, it now seems, proved only rarely self-deceived about her own writings. Here is the middle verse of three:

> An electrical storm is coming or moving away;
> It is the prickling air that wakes us up.
> If lightning struck the house now, it would run
> From the four blue china balls on top
> Down the roof and down the rods all around us,
> And we imagine dreamily

> How the whole house caught in a bird-cage of lightning
> Would be quite delightful rather than frightening;

Bishop's reasons for not publishing this completed, though untitled, poem are also not known. Did the poem depend too much on a personal relationship? It cannot have been held back because she feared the exposure of her sexuality; the gender of the bedmate is not revealed in the first-person plural pronoun. Perhaps she came to think the association between the electrical storm, and the electrocuting-electrifying power of love to transform the world risked the charge of sentimentality? Is there whimsical falsity in the poem's central metaphorical relationship? Whatever it was, the unpublished poem remained carefully preserved – and, strictly speaking, so it remains.

Quinn, or her publisher, made the decision to present some of the material included in this volume as facsimile only. The contents inform us that 'It is marvellous to wake up together …' is on page 44. However, the book designer seems to have added the style-feature that facsimile pages don't have page numbers. The only way of finding page 44 is to realise that it must be the 'illustration' between pages 43 and 45. This is a particularly bad decision for 'In a Room,' a poem covering two facing pages in facsimile, and one that has no orientating page numbers in sight when you attempt to decipher the holograph-annotated but un-transcribed text. This also leaves students or critics who would like to quote the facsimile-only poems with the task of editing a text (in the verse cited above I have not transcribed the first use of the word as 'lightening' – with the 'e' deleted by hand). Still chasing 'It is marvellous to wake up together…', you look across to read the transcribed text, the poem published from the surviving typescript – and feel justified in doing so because this is the policy elsewhere (with 'The Traveller to Rome' on pages 74 and 75 for example). But on page 45 the text is a different one called 'Florida Deserta.' Where is 'It is marvellous to wake up together…'? By the time you've worked out that the low-resolution reproduction of the creased typescript is all you are going to get a degree of trust in the relationship sustained by the book has evaporated.

Something similar is true if you try to track the note to the same poem. Quinn's annotations are keyed by a marginal page number and a title in quotation marks, but not picked out in italics or capitals or larger type. If the notes go on for more than two facing pages, as they often fascinatingly do, then readers must flick about to orient themselves with more of their time and attention lost. Continuous running heads signalling which poem or page is being annotated would have been more helpful. The effect of this decision is to strand the notes in their own evident absorption with Bishop, her life, contacts, and writings. Once found, the note on 'It is marvellous to wake up together...' begins with four brief paragraphs listing its two extant copies, noting the minor variants between them, reporting on Goldensohn's finding and printing the poem, then giving some biographical context: was it written at Key West or earlier? Is the other person Marjorie Stevens or Louise Crane? (It's probably the former). Then follow two pages of interesting, but loosely associated, researches that inform us, for instance, how 'Bishop has numerous entries in her notebooks about rain (see the note for "After the Rain").' Here the editor's weakly focused associations of topics underlines the triviality of description without occasion. Her book contains no index of titles. So you head back to the contents pages and run your finger down until you find 'After the Rain' on page 55. Then you do more flicking to locate the note, then read more associative citations of descriptions of rain. Later in the note you come across: 'In Bishop's poem "Rain Towards Morning," the conjunction of birdcage and bedroom occurs, too, along with "an unexpected kiss".' That's all. There's no page reference for this work; so, momentarily at a loss, you head back to Quinn's contents page – where you don't find it. Is the title a variant of some other draft? No, it's one of her published works, the subtitled second of 'Four Poems', and can be found on page 77 of *The Complete Poems 1927–1979*. That fact might have graced Quinn's text. Sadly, her annotations frequently unravel into not so much notes for the poems, as, rather, typeset collections of loosely associated material accumulated while working in the archives.

Edgar Allan Poe & the Juke-box is thus an important but slightly bungled hotchpotch. Quinn's appendix with the unpublished prose materials and the manuscripts of 'One Art' also contains two pieces of verse. The fragmentary 'Ungracious Poem' is placed there because the editor admits in a footnote that she 'could not determine where to place it chronologically in the volume proper.' The completed 'Verdigris' is 'included with reference to the prose fragment "Villanelle" because it is a villanelle.' No explanation is given for why it is not in the volume proper, besides the reported fact that 'Bishop did not consider it successful.' Yet she also sent it to *The New Yorker*, and had it rejected in January 1950 on a split decision. Given the other works that Bishop neither thought successful nor completed enough to send out, the relegation of this poem to the appendix is a puzzle.

One question addressed by a number of the volume's reviewers was whether publication of these texts would harm Bishop's reputation. That seems a dated anxiety, because the mere existence of the book implies a reputation that can sustain the interest in these occasionally trifling and often painfully aborted works. The question might have been whether the moment was right for the presentation of this work, and whether a commercial publisher could cope with what this publication abundantly reveals was required. *Edgar Allan Poe & the Juke-box* is a partial assemblage of some five separable items. One of them is a poetry collection, perfectly suited for inclusion as an appendix of a future *Complete Poems*, of works both uncollected and unpublished (perhaps the book's subtitle is not quite correct in opting for the former term). It would include the Edgar Allan Poe title poem, 'It is marvellous to wake up together...', and a fairly large number of others, some of them featured in newspapers and journals to advertise the existence of the book, such as 'Syllables' and 'Apartment in Leme.' This collection of more or less completed poems would have been valuable and enjoyable as a book in its own right. As a collection, it might have better suited a title like the one chosen, not wholly inexplicably, for this more various and apparently authoritative gathering. These completed poems, though ones not thoroughly convincing to their author, form the most satisfying part of Quinn's volume.

Then there is a specialist publication, containing more than Quinn includes, of Bishop's definitely uncompleted drafts, fragments, false starts and tailings off, her notes for unwritten poems, and related matter. I have attended a power point illustrated lecture by Barbara Page of Vassar College that included material not published here. This work might prove so complex and tangled as to require a database publication. Then, as sampled by the 'One Art' drafts in facsimile, there is the equivalent of a Cornell Bishop in which her various authorial collections, plus the unpublished or uncollected but completed poems, receive the honour accorded to William Wordsworth and W. B. Yeats – fully transcribed texts of manuscript materials with complete editorial apparatus. Further, there are the uncollected review essay and memoir drafts gathered in the ragbag appendix, which could form some of the materials for an enlarged complete prose. Finally, there are Quinn's annotations, which constitute both a useful draft of core matter for editorial work on the above volumes – as well as the extensive, but under-organised raw material for Quinn's own as yet unwritten, but broadly sketched book on the poet at work.

Do Bishop's writings have sufficient standing to sustain such industry? There's room for disagreement here. A commercial publisher would likely only contemplate undertaking a definitive *Complete Poems* and a companion prose volume. Very probably Elizabeth Bishop's reputation is here to stay; but the decisions and work required to present the full corpus of completed poems, both authorised and not, in variorum, as well as unravelling the mass of drafts and fragments, will require many more years yet. In the meantime, Alice Quinn's *Edgar Allan Poe & the Juke-box* must surely provide hours of incalculable pleasure through which her readers, like the John Ashbery on the jacket for whom 'there can never be enough of her writing', may work on their own relationships with more of her – second- and third-best, maybe, but nonetheless fascinating – words.

ROBINSON'S REPLY
TO WELDON KEES

The most moving moment in James Reidel's grippingly well-told biography *Vanished Act: The Life and Art of Weldon Kees* is, for me, when a fourteen-year-old girl at Preservation Hall, Bourbon Street, in 1962 exclaims 'Daddy, it's Weldon Kees!' But when she looks again for the person who had been kind to her as a friend's young daughter: 'the man and his companion were gone.' I was introduced to Kees in 1978; it was an ordinary meeting with an author – through his work. A student left a message with an attributed snatch of verse on it: 'He might awake to hear the news at ten, / Which will be shocking, moderately.' I took the quotation from 'Robinson at Home' personally and went to the library. What I found left a list of questions for which James Reidel's long-awaited biography provides some answers. A later meeting with Kees occurred during 1989 or 90, in the pages of the *TLS*, where I read 'Looking for Weldon Kees' by Simon Armitage. It ends with the borrowed phrase: 'I thought I made out Robinson ahead of me.' Armitage's gumshoe pastiche about trying to find a copy of Kees's out-of-print 1962 *Collected Poems* (rev. ed. 1975) resulted in the Faber 1993 reprint – which, the ff website implies, is out of print once more. They should follow Nebraska's lead and issue a third edition of this volume by, in Donald Justice's words, 'an important poet, among the three or four best of his generation.'

One of the many useful services Reidel's well-researched biography performs is to make clear that when Armitage describes how Kees 'locked both doors / of his Tudor Ford / and took one small step / off the face of the planet' he's got the wrong make of car. It was a 1954 Plymouth. The Tudor Ford belonged to the Lowell of 'Skunk Hour'. Lowell is from Kees's generation, and there's an unwanted irony in this car from the signature confessional poem having strayed into one about the poet from Beatrice, Nebraska. David Wojahn in his new introduction to the poems asserts that they have 'little in common with what came to be the prevailing poetic concerns of the coming decade.' Kees disappeared on Monday 18 July 1955. The following year saw the publication of both *Life Studies* and Allen Ginsberg's *Howl* – at whose first reading Kees is reported, apocryphally, to have been present. What those two successful public poets have in common is that, however vocal their criticisms of American policy, they demonstrate patriotic commitments to the ideal well-being of their Republic. Wojahn draws attention to Justice's also describing Kees as 'one of the bitterest poets in history' and adds: 'the world has seen figures who are arguably far more bitter (Philip Larkin comes to mind).' Yet Larkin, who shared a passion for New Orleans jazz, projects a parodic English malaise. Kees's may lie in disillusionment with the culture to which Lowell and Ginsberg devoted so much of their poetic energies.

While poets as different as Rexroth and Lowell found themselves in jail for conscientious objection during World War Two, Kees just wanted to avoid the draft. Mind you, his memorably sarcastic review of Rukeyser's instant war poem, *Wake Island* ('There's one thing you can say about Muriel: she's not lazy') conceals the hours and the stress that Kees put into his commentary for the Paramount Newsreel film of the fighting on Iwo Jima. Some years later, where Lowell was maniacally siding with the un-American activities committees by denouncing Elizabeth Ames at Yaddo, and Malcolm Cowley was organizing her defence, Kees opposed the politicised smear campaign but was not willing to support her wholeheartedly because he couldn't overlook her organisational limitations. Even so, there's no shilly-shallying about his occasionally explicit beliefs: 'Look, Mr. Dondero, art is not a weapon, no matter how insistently you, the Nazis, and the Communists maintain that it is. Persons desiring to make weapons do not become artists' (*The Nation* 5 Oct 1949); and Kees's friend Anton Myers reports that Weldon delivered 'the merited rebuke of all time' to Mark Rothko who 'said he didn't feel anything when he saw the films of the Nazi death camps'. After 'a shocked little silence', Kees is reported to have said: 'What you mean, Mark, is that you're a moral dwarf.'

Though filled with illuminating detail, Reidel's book does include the odd inaccuracy. In 1941, Kees is trying to interest New Directions in a selection of Beddoes' poems 'taken from *Death's Jest Book* and other works in the four-volume Edmund Gosse edition of 1849'. This would have been precocious of Gosse, who was born in that year; his two two-volume editions of Beddoes' works were published in 1890 and, posthumously, in 1928. There's also some poor copy editing here and there. When Kees decides to call his Lincoln Zephyr 'Tiresias', Reidel belabours this family joke about a poor old androgynous car that has 'foresuffered all' as also 'a nod to the surrealism of Appolinaire'.

That's presumably the Apollinaire – also missing from the index – who foreshadowed the birth of André Breton's movement with his *Les Mamelles de Tirésias*. T. S. Eliot's poem is referred to in different places as *The Four Quartets* and, correctly, *Four Quartets*, while within a few lines Kees's New York gallery-owner is rightly called 'Pollack' and then confused with the action-painter and spelled 'Pollock'. Reidel's book will, I hope, have the chance to be as perfect as a second edition.

At a 1943 cocktail party in New York, Kees runs into the poet George Barker who he describes in a letter to Norris Getty as 'better than his poems' and a 'Noel Coward type of fairy'. Reidel confirms this by adding that Kees found him 'more likeable than other member of the "third sex".' Just how many illegitimate children would Barker have had to father to fend off such a misidentification? But perhaps that's why the Mid-Westerner liked the Englishman: he was more or less straight. In youth, Kees is described as the sort of handsome, svelte, and well-groomed man who would get taken by cruising gays to be one of their kind. His homophobia had a defensive cast. Though it doesn't follow that all homophobics are in denial about their sexuality, such a shadow is thrown across Reidel's biography. He identifies no male partners for Kees, but quotes his alcoholic and recently divorced wife as having said that when he disappeared it was to shack up with a man. Yet she also wrote three years later to the Conrad Aikens asserting that she always assumed he jumped off the bridge. In Bourbon Street, Kees was sighted, if he was sighted, escorting a blonde. The moody, lonesome poet is described as having a secret wound. But Reidel offers no solid evidence for the gay-angle, and mentions in his essay that Getty was a 'masculine' homosexual. It seems unlikely that Kees will be posthumously out-ed.

Armitage's poem also says 'There was too much water under the Golden Gate / since the day that dude became overrated'. On this topic, Reidel keeps pretty quiet. Despite its subtitle, his is not a thoroughly critical biography. The devoted and enormously knowledgeable editor of Kees's *Reviews and Essays, 1936–55* (1988) and his novel *Fall Quarter* (1990) is not going to give his author a panning such as you can read on Amazon: 'this hybrid novel by Kees and Reidel is grossly deficient as either humor or satire'. Nor does he handle his subject's setbacks with the cool appraisal of Robert E. Knoll, editor of the 1986 book *Weldon Kees and the Midcentury Generation: Letters 1935–1955*, which Nebraska has just reissued in paperback. On Knopf's rejection of *Fall Quarter* in 1942, Knoll notes that 'the judgements are understandable' and explains: 'Kees's talent was essentially imagistic, in that he captured the tone of a moment and the atmosphere of a single occasion in short forms – poems, sketches, brief narratives.' Yet when he adds that Kees 'concerned himself with the interior life, the response of a single person to a private world', we can hear the author of 'Weldon Kees: Solipsist as Poet' setting out his stall. Knoll's volume of Kees's letters and Reidel's biography present a person with a limitless interest in the goings-on of an anything but private world. Once more, the subject matter of Kees's bitterness may be being underplayed.

What Reidel's approach indicates is that Kees can still seem a cause to be championed. Dana Gioia contributes a useful piece to Siedell's volume on 'The Cult of Weldon Kees'. Gioia notes that it was predominantly poets who advanced Kees's reputation, rather than academic critics whose agendas he sees as more and more removed from those of the writers. 'A cult is a religious community', he observes, 'built around devotion to a single deity'. The note is struck when Armitage begins his gumshoe piece: 'I'd heard it said by Michael Hofmann / that *Collected Poems* would blow my head off'. In the *LRB* for 23 May 2003, Hofmann lists 'the dominant period voices' as 'Gunn, Kees, Plath, Larkin, Hamilton, Lowell, Muldoon, Reid'. This is one of those self-fulfilling DIY traditions that some poets go in for – exaggerated, even if the poet Hugo Williams does like him, in calling Kees one of the dominant late '50s or early '60s voices. Isn't that just the sort of evaluation Weldon might have liked to hear, but didn't, in 1955? When a Los Angeles pianist catches his name and says: 'Oh yeah, you're the author of *The Last Man* and *The Fall of the Magicians*', Kees adds in the letter reporting it: 'This is God's truth.' Wojahn asks: 'Is Weldon Kees a major poet?' 'He is surely a significant one', comes the measured reply. Kees's four Robinson poems and two handfuls of others will likely be his passport to immortality. Still, in his essay 'The Silent Film of Weldon Kees', Reidel is less protective of his poet, writing that when *Poems 1947–1954* came out 'poetry had become a sideshow for Kees.' He adds that a late review comparing his work to various films pointed to 'how poetry had defeated Kees.' When the polyartist (as B. H. Friedman defines him) disappeared, he walked out on a somewhat under-achieved and intermittent poetic oeuvre collaged from scraps of influences. The third part of his late poem 'The Hourglass' has: 'yet only in this way / Is Being shifted and transformed. / Once out of time...' That's 'Burnt Norton' – varied with a dash of Sartre or Heidegger. Reidel notes that both Kafka and Céline have characters called Robinson. One likely prompt may have come from Rimbaud's 'Roman' in which 'Le cœur fou Robinsonne à travers les romans'. 'Aspects of Robinson' ends with his 'His sad and usual heart, dry as a winter leaf.' If Kees did get his 'sad ... heart' from Rimbaud's 'mad heart', he exemplified an influence thoroughly digested. It's the crucial difference.

In his biography, Reidel charts a careful course between over-protecting Kees and turning his book into six chapters of partial failures with a prologue and epilogue to round them out. Still, he can't avoid telling the story which Wojahn succinctly describes as that of 'a restless, agitated soul always on the lookout for the Big Score – which invariably eludes him.' Kees begins as a short-story writer and achieves publication in little magazines, but never produces a collection in his lifetime; he attempts a novel or three, but they fail to find publishers. In the meantime, he's getting somewhere with poems, going from magazine successes to anthology appearances, to a small press collection, *The Last Man*, and then a trade second book that sells quite well. But the firm is taken over, and *The Fall of the Magicians* falls out of print. The subsequent efforts to publish a third collection with a New York commercial house get nowhere slowly, and his final poetry publication, *Poems 1947–1954*, appears once again from a small press on the West Coast. This is not such an unusual or bad track record for a poet between the ages of 25 and 40, but it was neither good enough for Kees – who is described as never getting over the failure to place his third book with a prominent firm. Nor was it enough, apparently, for the parents of an only child.

While not getting his third book published, Kees becomes an abstract painter and does well enough to have a gallery, three one-man shows, and to have people admire and occasionally buy his work. Yet, once again, they don't quite admire it enough. His friend Clement Greenberg doesn't roll the log in *The Nation* at the crucial moment. Kees is among the 'Irascibles' who publicly criticise the Metropolitan Museum's selection policy in 1950. However, he doesn't get included in the group photograph of New York School painters taken on 24 November and published in *Life* on 15 January 1951 – according to Irving Sandler's essay in *Weldon Kees and the Arts at Mid-Century*, though the caption says it was taken on 1 January 1950. Mind you, neither was Hans Hofmann. Kees said he wouldn't have wanted to be included, even if he'd not been out of town. Then, having not quite made it in New York, and dissipated his energies in manic impresario roles at Provincetown during 1949, he heads for the Coast and there tries to break into the music business as a writer of lyrics for jazz numbers, comedy, and torch songs. So he finds himself on the uncool side of what – according to Roy Fisher – Larkin used to call the Be-bop barrier, and too clever by half to pen the decade's mindless pop lyrics. He makes experimental movies, writes an existentialist play, acts in vaudeville sketches, does radio talk-shows about films, collaborates on various social-anthropology projects – and neglects either to paint many more of his nearly successful abstractions, or to compose sheaves of his way-above-average poems. Kees had defended his painting venture by saying that 'Shifting from one to the other I don't get into the periods of absolute sterility that are often experienced by writers who just write, or painters who just paint.' When beginning this phase he describes himself as 'embarking, though, on a lot of new departures'. That's the Kees problem in a nutshell – too many departures, not enough arrivals: 'The mirror from Mexico, stuck to the wall, / Reflects nothing at all.'

One function that might have been performed by Siedell's collection of essays is to offer an overview for this plethora of activities. How good a painter was Kees? How good a pianist was he? What is truly distinctive about his poetry and short fiction? How good an art critic was he? Unfortunately, such questions are not directly addressed in these casually edited, uneven pieces. For me, only the chapters by Gioia and Reidel wholly rewarded with fresh information or insight the time they took to read. The failure of the book's various art critics to give a nuanced evaluation of Kees's painting – such as the T. J. Clark of *Farewell to an Idea: Episodes in the History of Modernism* (1999) might have done – was particularly disappointing. Friedman can do little more than admit: 'In short, considerable art historical work, work of the most rudimentary sort, remains to be done on Kees's *oeuvre.*' Dana Gioia's point about divergences between poets and critics is underlined by the manner of Nicholas Spenser's 'Late Modernism and the Minor Literature of Weldon Kees's Poetry':

> Unable to abandon the modernist belief in the referentiality of the symbol, yet aware of the impossibility of identifying the symbol's meaning, Kees voices a desolate late modernism through Robinson. Correspondingly, Robinson's subjectivity hovers between the deterritorialized schizophrenic dissolution

of postmodernism and the reterritorialized paranoic terrorism of modernism.

Robinson's reply to this is that while Kees had problems that may have driven him to suicide, this cannot have been among them. Though it's not impossible to make a simulacrum of sense from Spencer's academic junk-speak, the attribution of inability and awareness to the poet that then merely 'voices' a vague period mood is itself both 'late' and 'desolate'. Here's Kees describing work on 'Aspects of Robinson': 'about half way through the writing of the first draft of it, I began worrying about the possibility of its turning chi-chi and pure New Yorker; and my attempt to avoid that quality set up a lot of odd divisions and strategies'. The Robinson poems will likely last because they demonstrate such invention in managing cultural awareness, and, again, a concrete feel for their subject's situations – strategically divided from the 'chi-chi and pure New Yorker'. The italicised quotation – or slight misquotation, actually – in 'Relation to Robinson' ('*And then a day as huge as yesterday in pairs / Unrolled its horror on my face / Until it blocked –*') is from Emily Dickinson's 'The first Day's Night had come –'. The poem is dated 1862 in the R. W. Franklin edition. It might be intriguing to follow up the contribution of that Civil War period, fear-of-madness piece to a work which Spencer says shows 'the presence of schizophrenic postmodernism's ontological dominant'.

Despite his ending the biography with the 1962 sighting of Kees in New Orleans, Reidel is firmly decided on the 1955 Mexico or suicide question. He's sure Kees jumped off the Golden Gate. In a sense, this is the practical option. It saves the biographer from having to follow Ambrose Bierce south of the border in the dangerously vain hope of finding any trace of his subject. What's more, even if Kees didn't jump into the water, what he did do was walk away from being the Weldon Kees whose story we have been following. Reidel gives no evidence for the existence of poems, paintings, songs, or other artefacts, left behind by the same man working under another name. Kees runs out of genres in which not quite to succeed enough for the figure he needed to cut. Wojahn, whose pre-publication praise is cited on the jacket of Reidel's biography, notes that the 'reasons for Kees's apparent suicide aren't entirely clear'. Was it character? Upbringing? Fate? Sex-life? Money-problems? Mid-century American society to blame? Reidel gives circumstantial accounts of implied answers to most of the possibilities.

In this, his policy of much more sympathetic description than analysis is successful, at least up to a point.

Discussing the break-through composition of 'Robinson', the biographer has this to say about what may have prompted the poem and its fellows:

> He had not, however, set aside the intriguing philosophical problems his unwritten novel posed about the impossibility of understanding another human being and the contrast between an expected personality and the real one, which is not real in the first place, but simply a construct.

Kees had written that his young scholar character 'has seen and heard too much and knows that the task of fully discovering and understanding another human being – at least this one – is an impossibility.' While suggestive in a dashed off synopsis for a novel Kees may never have intended to write, this is hardly a promising philosophy for a biographer – even one who may be identifying with Kees's scholar in pursuit of a missing poet. If we accept Reidel's first 'impossibility' idea, there's no reason to stop at 'another human being'. It's impossible to understand oneself as well. Then, no sooner has the biographer typed the word 'real', then he thinks better of it and opts for 'simply a construct' – though there's not much that's simple about constructing a personality. Then again, given that we are all impossible to understand anyway, isn't that exactly why we go about forming understandings of ourselves and of others? Wojahn writes that Robinson is both 'Kees's alter ego' and 'epitomizes the conformity of the 1950s' as well as 'the decade's inherent sense of dread.' Did Kees invent Robinson so as to split off some parts of himself he didn't like, pretending thus that they weren't him, or did he do the same thing so as to understand and manage better those parts? Reidel's biography avoids the snare of attempting a speculatively psychological portrait of Kees, allowing, instead, circumstances and events to draw a picture of his life. In this sense, the philosophy of impossibility saves his biography from one shortcoming, but perhaps pitches it towards another.

The almost complete absence of comment on Kees's sixteen-year marriage leaves a great void at the heart of the book. Why did his wife Ann not want to have children? Why did Kees write the chilling 'For my Daughter' ('These speculations sour in the sun. / I have no daughter. I desire none')? Spencer answers that by suggesting it had been written as 'an expression of reflexive celebration, or at least relief, at its own lack of extra-textual reference.' But in negations reference doesn't fail when there turns out to be no referent. Did the Keeses ever have doubts about their decision? From the mention of a diaphragm just before their breakup it seems Ann didn't. Yet there are a couple of stray indications of it on Kees's part in his behaviour towards Pauline Kael's young daughter, for instance, in 1955. Some friends of Ann and Weldon seem to have taken the poet's wife for a nonentity, and in his biography Reidel doesn't have much to add. Yet on the only occasion when her husband is described as having the occasion to be unfaithful, the biographer remarks: 'Kees was not the kind of man to discuss whether or not his encounter with Mary McCarthy had continued after the diner episode.' Nor does he give any sustained explanation for Ann's descent into chronic alcoholism. He does imply that they may have married so Kees could signal he was not gay to the cruisers. Shouldn't a false and provincial marriage have unravelled as soon as they reached New York, if not before? The couple did separate for some months when Kees first went there, but whether this was a break-up with a make-up, or an agreed plan, isn't wholly clear. Though Reidel gives barely any explanation for why they were together so long in the biography, his film essay notes that 'Ann complemented Kees' and 'Only to the perceptive did the knowing looks that Ann gave Kees when he dominated cocktail party talk suggest the symbiosis of their relationship.' When they divorced, just a year before the Golden Gate disappearance, Reidel sees it as a relief. His subject is once again making the smart move. Yet Kees falls into a year of depression, stimulant-produced sleeplessness, under-eating, impresario project forming, and two less than satisfactory brief affairs. The biographer doesn't tell us what became of the woman with whom the poet spent the majority of his adult life. There's more that might be known here, and more to understand.

The four Robinson poems construct the pathology of a character from his habits and purchases. In the near absence of nature and community, he is an urban artefact, an alienated statistic – hence the humdrum name – created by the choices made while furnishing a room, shopping for clothes, or passing the time. This is not a human being to understand; it's a 'personality' to interpret through a criticism of his socially sanctioned tastes. Yet Robinson, wishfully perhaps, always appears to escape his definitions. Kees was early onto this culturally perceptive and also self-defining theme. 'Robinson at Home' and 'Aspects of Robinson' appeared in all but subsequent issues of the *New Yorker*. Reidel comments that this 'elated Kees, but success also warned him away from writing more. He told his friend Charles Addams that there was a 'law of diminishing returns more exacting on poetry' and so 'Robinson would have to be put away for now.' Kees was only to write one more – 'Relating to Robinson' – and this reluctance to dilute on the poet's part has drawn imitators to fill a gap that may not be there. Along with 'Looking for Weldon Kees', a poem that also features the poet's best-known character, Armitage included six more Robinson poems in his 1992 collection *Kid*. Three further additions to the corporate corpus can be found in Antony Dunn's 2002 collection *Flying Fish*, including 'Robinson's Revenge' – where the game turns sour: *'My great grandfather did for Weldon Kees… and I'll know which day to check the obits / for Armitage'*. Even if the law of diminishing returns can bring in its revenges, these homages to the parent-creations still wittily contribute to guaranteeing their afterlife.

Wojahn concludes that Kees's 'poetry has won readers more loyal than those supposedly claimed by many major poets' and 'We have every reason to expect that such will continue to be the case.' Did the Lowell who wrote 'For the Union Dead' recall Kees's 'Travels in North America' with its passage on Los Alamos and its 'cars that look a little more like fish each year'? I wonder if the Elizabeth Bishop, future author of 'In the Waiting Room', whom Kees describes as 'a very nice person' after their one meeting, remembered his poem 'Aunt Elizabeth' in which its subject is 'Imprisoned by *National Geographics*'? And I can't help asking myself if that voracious thief Bob Dylan didn't pick up a copy of *Collected Poems* now and then in the '60s and '70s. Kees's 'The Situation Clarified' is the portrait of a librarian who gyrates 'Through all the latest books' and appears to be killed by someone who gives his name 'As Jones. "Jones is my name," he said.' The last line of 'June 1940' reads 'An idiot wind is blowing'. In 'Relating to Robinson' we hear that 'From an uncurtained second-storey room, a radio / Was playing *There's a Small Hotel*', and in the same poem its narrator is 'Running in sweat / To reach the docks'. Yet whether these are sources for 'Ballad of a Thin Man', 'Idiot Wind', and 'Simple Twist of Fate' is likely to be yet one more of the unanswerable questions that float around the name of Weldon Kees.

'THE SPACES BETWEEN':
JEAN VALENTINE

Though momentarily concealed by the placing of her *New Poems* first, followed by earlier volumes in chronological order, the crucial development in Jean Valentine's poetry as revealed by *Door in the Mountain: New and Collected Poems 1965–2003* (2004) occurs between the publication of her debut *Dream Barker* (1965) and her second, *Pilgrims*, in 1969. Valentine's first book contains Lowell-style lyrics involving family members, key life experiences, and loco-descriptive occasions. There is even one called 'Asleep over Lines from Willa Cather' whose sustained phrasings explore the edges of consciousness and dream – a transit-zone that would never be far from her poetry. 'Tired of London', from the same book, revises its allusion to Dr Johnson's saying about world-weariness to the thought that if an American woman is tired of London she may not yet be tired of love:

> This way love's conversation, the body and mind of it, goes
> On after love: we shall come to call this love,
> And this roar in our ears which before long
> We become, we shall call our song.

The writing is eloquently formal, and slightly gawky, combining a gesture at natural exploration of feeling, with an uneasily rhetorical insistence on closure. The enjambment is energetically veering – all winningly characteristic of a poet's early work. These poems give the reader time to settle in and explore the experiences being narrated, as in 'Sunset at Wellfleet': 'A spit of sky, awash with Venetian gold / Hangs over the Congregational bell-tower, where / Last night the Northern Lights sifted their fire, / Shot through with the airless dark, romantic and cold.' Traces of Lowell and patches of Bishop tell of influences to outgrow, while the sentence's closing rhyme is a little too squarely predictable – though not so obvious as in this couplet from 'Cambridge by Night': 'Every public place in this city / Is a sideshow of souls sword-swallowing pity'. That is the sound of her juvenilia crying out to be left behind.

In the years between those two 1960s books, Valentine abandons the full dramatizing of personal narratives showing a little too much indebtedness to the mid-century so-called 'confessional' styles. My favourite among these earlier pieces is 'New York April 27, 1962' whose last verse has a wonderfully improvised formality:

> No-one forgot my birthday. Twenty-eight.
> How shall we celebrate?
> Fetch my blanket, dearest, there's something in the air,
> Dark, quick, quicksilver, dark eyes, brown hair,
> Bringing all the presents: someone is coming late:
> The babies cry, the bell rings in thin air.

Instead of such orchestrations she heads towards a sparer, shorter-lined, notational poetry of imagistic hints and guesses, one that bears a resemblance to the revived objectivism of the later sixties and seventies. On her way to this particular vanishing point, she produces poems that might constitute a best of both worlds, poems which have a poised formality but also an uncluttered precision of phrasing and cadence. The eight-line poem 'Night' from *Pilgrims* is attractively such a one:

> From this night on God let me eat
> like that blind child on the train
> touching her yogurt as I'd touch a spiderweb
> the first morning in the country – sky red –
>
> holding the carton and spoon to her mouth
> with all her eyeless body, and then
> orientally resting, the whole time smiling
> a little to one side of straight ahead.

This is not only an *ars poetica* but also an epigram about how to live. The momentary ambiguity of the first line is resolved in the better direction; the brief interpolation 'red sky', which would be a warning, plus the informal 'and then' nevertheless collaborate to effect the poem's life resolve, which, in its more precarious improvisation performs precisely what the last line says.

The distance Valentine travels from her debut work might be shown by her elegy for Robert Lowell, a poem called 'Working' from *The Messenger* (1979), written in a sketchy style some way beyond the art school title of Lowell's breakthrough book: 'A ladder of stuff:

soft, gray, / broken oar, a feather, / a shoe, a child's pencil case; / light drawing us / to light, / day speaking to day…' Those flickering allusions to Lowell's last book seem slightly too sure of the reader's fellow-feeling, a little under-worked. If her mature style rather recalls George Oppen's or, even more, Lorine Niedecker's poems, her materials are not theirs, for she sticks with an intimately personal and psychologised range of themes despite the switch in means for addressing them. Valentine stays with her 'dream' inspirations, expecting the levels of consciousness touched in sleep to offer truths not vouchsafed to waking life, as in 'Barrie's Dream, the Wild Geese' from *The River at Wolf* (1992):

> 'I dreamed about Elizabeth Bishop
> and Robert Lowell – an old Penguin book
> of Bishop's poetry – a thick china cup
> and a thick china sugar bowl, square,
> cream-colored, school stuff.
>   And Lowell was there,
> he was talking, and talking to us,
> he was saying, "She is the best –"
> The the geese flew over,
> and he stopped talking. Everyone stopped talking,
> because of the geese.'
>   The sound of their wings!
> Oars rowing, laborious, wood against wood: it was
> a continuing thought, no, it was a labor,
> how to accept your lover's love. Who could do it alone?
> Under our radiant sleep they were bearing us all night long.

This offers a full mix of what's good, and not so good, about Valentine's mature poetry: the received wisdom concerning literary reputations and the poetic canon, the intimacy of range without the chill of a thoroughly autonomous viewpoint, the way that the truth of dream is reinforced by the privileged authority of natural event, and the slightly corny message about love and others' love – which is then somehow resolved by the way the geese, or the dead poets, are supporting us. We can, of course, hope that this will be so, can hope that saying makes it so; but, like a cartoon character over the edge of a cliff, the poem treads an air of unsupported fine feeling.

As the advance towards minimalism continues, and the inwardness
stays dominant, there are poems that flicker on the threshold of communication, ones in which too much is implicit, as here in 'The Blind
Stirring of Love' from *The Cradle of the Real Life* (2000):

> I rub my hands my cheeks
> with oil   my breasts
> I bathe my genitals, my feet
> leaf and bark
>
> redden my mouth to
> draw down your mouth
> and all along
> you have been inside me
>   streaming
> unforsakenness…

The trouble with this is that it flirts with the language of body parts and
love so as to assert an abstractly good thought about the psychology of
love. We are not, I think, meant to take 'and all along / you have been
inside me' literally – so as to avoid the thought that she has drifted off
into dreaming a poem during sex. Here are all the dangers of the puritan
minimalist lyric – its bare honesty is too pure for its own good, and from
physical detail to neologistic close there leaks a sorry embarrassment.

Such weakness in her poetry might be indicated by its restive anno-
tation – as if she had never quite found a thoroughly distinctive style.
'Letter', from the *New Poems* section, begins well, but soon starts to
insist on its thematic significance with dabs of attitudinizing gesture:

> The hornet holds on to the curtain, winter
> sleep. Rubs her legs. Climbs the curtain.
> Behind her the cedars sleep lightly,
>
> like guests. But I am the guest.
> The ghost cars climb the ghost highway. Even my hand
> over the page adds to the 'room tone': the little
>
> constant wind. The effort of becoming. These words
> *are* my life…

Does an italics-supported enjambment like 'These words /*are* my life'
aid a reader's identification, or prevent it? The careful self-consciousness
in such writing can reassure; but it may also be off-putting in its insistent
fussiness. Valentine's effort has been to get the delicacy of her poetry to
resonate in the gaps between the said and the not-said – which is one
reason why both Adrienne Rich and Fanny Howe, offering plaudits
for the jacket, settle on the word 'spaces' to catch what characterises
her style. This territory has long been, and is likely to continue to be, a
testing ground for competing ideas about what it means for poetry to
be reader-friendly. Do we invite readers into the poem by giving them
lots of space in which to engage in a constructive reading, or by inviting
them to activate a structure that is fully in place in the text?

I suspect this is another of the false distinctions that has been po-
larizing poetry over the last decades. It's false because in both cases
readers have to do the same thing. The question is rather in the kinds
of relationship and balancing invited between all poetry's imaginative
blanks and verbal promptings. Jean Valentine's trajectory is of interest
not least because she renegotiates this balancing of means, producing as
she does, some well built texts at every stage:

> Basho spent the first thirty years of his life
> apprenticing; four years alone in a small hut
> on the outskirts of Tokyo;
> the last ten years
> walking. Walking here
>
> today I saw him, Basho, at the far edge of the field;
> and you alongside him; your steps,
> his long black and white steps stirring up
> red mica dust to drift across the new day's light, and the heat.

Here at the close of 'Birthday Letter from South Carolina', in *Home.
Deep. Blue* (1989), Valentine identifies herself with Japan's great old
man mad about poetry. She too has done her fair share of apprentic-
ing and walking, noticing as she does such haiku-like details as that so
elegantly caught in the poem's final two lines. There may appear to be
more searching than finding in the course of this new and collected poems, more trial and error than thoroughly convincing achievement. Yet
the best of her travelling through the door in her mountain constitutes
a moving and valuable contribution to this dauntingly difficult art.

FRIENDLY EXCHANGES:
ANNE STEVENSON

Festschrifts for poets suffer from generic problems. The composed-for-the-volume gift-poem is often under-occasioned and lovey-dovey; the one without a dedication can seem to be along for the ride. With *The Way You Say the World*, John Lucas and Matt Simpson have assembled an enjoyable tribute to Anne Stevenson on her 70th Birthday that mostly avoids such pitfalls. There are some greeting-card verses, true; and some of the successful pieces, Jamie McKendrick's 'Right of Way' or Dennis O'Driscoll's 'Classic Days' for example, would grace volumes dedicated to any poet. Mairi MacInnes's 'Anne's Poem', though, is exemplary in its use of her own material in a context provided by the dedicatee, while registering anxiety about such homages: 'What could I say to you? The facts / brought on a fit of grief? Not so.' It ends: 'the past, Anne, changed through you – its hurt, / its flowers and fruit, its cold banalities.' MacInnes's last two words clinch this as rather more than a warm feeling for a birthday.

Preferring not to register the inevitable costs and prices of the subject's achievements, essays in poets' festschrifts can be dully complimentary. Lucas's sustained study of Stevenson's style avoids this by the inclusion of illuminating comparisons with other poets and by implying a firm sense of what is less well done in her oeuvre. Most of the prose here earns its keep, in particular Emily Grosholz's introductory study, Margot Waddell's psychoanalytical divagations on Stevenson's 'A Surprise on the First Day of School', and John Greening's close reading of 'Arioso Dolente'. Another likeable thing about *The Way You Say the World*, a tribute itself to Stevenson's ecumenism, is that Tom Leonard rubs shoulders with Dana Gioia; Gael Turnbull is one contributor from Clive Wilmer; Lee Harwood's next to Seamus Heaney, Peter Redgrove before Deryn Rees-Jones. Such volumes serve the purpose of inter-generational and sometimes inter-factional solidarity above and beyond the sums of their parts.

Jeremy Hooker discusses Stevenson's Welsh connections and, as if to underline his point, the most sustained and attractive new work in *A Report from the Border: New and Rescued Poems* is the 'from Cwm Nantcol' section. Stevenson's poems have the air of thought-experiments. In his piece, Greening notes that her strength lies in the 'determination to sustain a thought, an intuition to its very end.' But since there's no end of brooding on things, poems – like thoughts – must be brought to suitable pauses. Stevenson's are occasionally pushed too far. In one of the rescued poems, 'Branch Line', twenty-seven lines of well-written evocation close first with *'Meaningless life,* I'm reading in the TLS, / *a nexus of competing purposes…'* But if life is such a nexus, it must be filled with human meaning. Stevenson goes on: 'God is impossible. / Life is impossible. / But here it is.' 'You're impossible!' a philosopher might exclaim to her husband – though not in the sense that he couldn't conceivably exist. The final line's pronoun restricts it to contradicting only the second of Stevenson's two grandiose propositions. Yet however improbable or unlikely God's existence might be, you'd have to be the Almighty to know he was impossible; while the mere fact of being able to announce life's impossible means you are living it. Hooker justifiably sees Stevenson as a religious poet in the Puritan tradition. But in 'Branch Line' description is not revelation; it's an involving lead-up to some wincing bits of higher chit-chat.

Stevenson can also write poems with a thought too few. 'Questionable' is about a woman who, when she says 'I seem to be hungry', also 'knew she meant / Oh, to be thirty years younger, / lying with his head in my lap…' The man with his 'charming accent' suggests they get something to eat: 'So Nudeln mit Pfifferling had to do. / Maybe what his eyes said was innocent. / Maybe it was not. She never knew.' Yet what the woman says invites the thought that we can never be sure what a body sensation means. Registering this would have increased the questionableness all round, while the man's response could then have either been an understanding or a misunderstanding, of her or of himself.

Emily Grosholz notes that 'Stevenson's methods are often Copernican, forcing us to entertain two perspectives at once'. Though no poem can or should force a reader to do anything, Stevenson's title piece, 'A Report from the Border', is an effective example of her placing conflicting viewpoints within the space of lyric. 'Wars in peacetime don't behave like wars', it begins, going on to vocalise in italics arguments that oblige the less well-off to accept a status quo: *'Making money out of making money / Helps us help you.'* Then comes the telling close: 'This from the party of useful words. From the other, / Hunger's stare, / Drowned crops, charred hopes, fear, stupor, prayer / And literature.' A similarly dialogic style, balancing even-handedness with an assurance that the better case had better get the last word, animates a poem about her parents. 'A Marriage' presents her dying mother speaking of the future to her father, the philosopher and author of *Ethics and Language* (1944) and *Facts and Values* (1963). 'When my mother knew why her treatment wasn't working, / She said to my father, trying not to detonate her news, / 'Steve, you must marry again. When I'm gone, who's going / To tell you to put your trousers on before your shoes?' Like many poems about poets' parents, this is a tacit account of the author's creative identity: 'They couldn't imagine the future that I am seeing, / For all his philosophy and all her common sense.' Stevenson has combined imagining with the wittily contrasted attributes of father and mother. Imagination, philosophy, and common sense: it's not a bad description of Anne's poems – frequently both down-to-earth and unobtrusively profound.

JOHN ASHBERY:
'AS MY WAY IS'

Through 'a gauze-curtained window giving directly onto the sidewalk of West Fifty-third Street', John Ashbery once looked out of a major retrospective to where 'unexpected light from the street and the veiled backdrop of traffic and passers-by produce one of those subtle dislocations of everyday life that are at the heart of de Chirico's art.' The Italian painter combines in the cityscapes of his 'metaphysical' period three features dear to Ashbery – the mundane, the imaginary, and the distinctly individual: 'if the symbolic meaning of recurring images like the bananas, clocks, gloves and artichokes remains unknown, they are obviously repositories of deeply personal feelings and experiences', he wrote. That glimpse of West Fifty-third Street seems one such apparently arbitrary confrontation, an occasion when meaning starts to stir. Glancing back at the world as if it were a picture when you're reviewing an art exhibition, such truant attention is one of poetry's mainsprings. Ashbery's 'The Instruction Manual' takes as its starting point a similar truancy:

> As I sit looking out of a window of the building
> I wish I did not have to write the instruction manual on the uses of
> a new metal.
> I look down into the street and see people, each walking with an
> inner peace,
> And envy them – they are so far away from me!
> Not one of them has to worry about getting out this manual on
> schedule.
> And, as my way is, I begin to dream, resting my elbows on the desk
> and leaning out of the window a little,
> Of dim Guadalajara! City of rose-colored flowers!
> City I wanted most to see, and most did not see, in Mexico!

Poetry, then, is what you shouldn't be doing: dreaming, for instance, as in Joseph Cornell's 'hotel' boxes which re-create not 'the country itself but the impression we have of it before going out there'. Chance encounters in which meaning starts to stir are perhaps intersections of mundane fact, an imaginary perspective, and some barely hinted-at repositories of feeling and experience. Willing them to happen probably fails because the perspective feels contrived and the repositories remain closed. It's like 'Trying to avoid / Ideas', as in 'What is Poetry', but we 'Go back to them as to a wife, leaving / The mistress we desire?' The title of that poem is in the interrogative form, but without a question mark. No answer to its possible question would be likely to satisfy, and the poem's final line is tentativeness itself. 'It might give us – what? – some flowers soon?'

One morning in *Flow Chart*, the speaker is in the library, his 'brain getting chafed / as everything in the reading room took on an unreal, sombre aspect', until he stops working on 'some dumb theory' and gets out into the streetscape which 'always looked refreshingly right, as though scene-painters had been at work, and then, /at such moments, it was truly a pleasure to walk along, surprised yet not too surprised / by every new, dimpled vista.' But too quickly these days 'some dumb theory' comes along to make a programme or procedure out of just sauntering along. Such programming turns poetry and the other arts into a form of perversion, 'perversion in the only meaningful sense of the term', as Adam Phillips defines it in *On Kissing, Tickling, a Being Bored*, 'knowing too exactly what one wants, the disavowal of contingency, omniscience as the cheating of time; the mother who, because she knows what's best for us, has nothing to offer.' The beautiful early poem 'Some Trees' moves by accepting circumstantial gifts, living attentively in time, patient to have whatever repertoire is on offer reveal itself, so that

> you and I
> Are suddenly what the trees try
>
> To tell us we are:
> That their merely being there
> Means something; that soon
> We may touch, love, explain.

This repertoire of various responses is drawn from us by recognizing and enjoying our own limits, 'glad not to have invented / Such comeliness', and it will answer to the variety of the situation in which 'we are surrounded' by 'A canvas on which emerges / A chorus of smiles, a winter morning.'

Similarly, 'A Blessing in Disguise' seems a love poem addressed to life itself, the preferred plural 'you' containing and using, among its multitudes, the lyrical 'I' addressing it:

> You see,
> You hold me up to the light in a way
>
> I should never have expected, or suspected, perhaps
> Because you always tell me I am you,
> And right. The great spruces loom.
> I am yours to die with, to desire.

After all, there is no knowing life itself, except in the many lives which have lived, or are living, or will shortly live it– and only these by way of a single, temporary consciousness. Ashbery's poetry frequently appears such a blessing in disguise, composed in a style that catches those rare moments when our difficulties disappear, not because we have answers to the great questions, but because the questions themselves seem to have been spirited away.

About eight years ago, reviewing a show by the English expatriate Trevor Winkfield, Ashbery observed:

> the notion that it's OK to like any kind of art as long as it's good of its kind has gradually gained credence, while the equally heretical one that art may, under certain circumstances, be pleasurable and still not flunk out now looms in the sky above the art world like a giant cartoon light bulb, signifying 'Idea!'

Such notions are perpetually present for some, while for others culture seems only intelligible if formulated in terms of sentences which assert that if so-and-so is right, then what's-his-name must be wrong, or in which there are two types of poets: those who believe that there are two types of poets and those who don't. Yet for each of us the way contingency presents itself is differently experienced and others' solutions, however helpful as examples, will never exactly serve. Any poem that is 'good of its kind' must also be *sui generis*, unrepeatable. Ashbery has said, 'The more you like a poet, the less you ought to write like him, because what you were liking in him is a uniqueness.'

The very idea of having fixed principles about what poetry is, or should be, substitutes an illusion of time-cheating omniscience for a readiness to accept contingency's offerings. Making art requires a repertoire of possible responses to each unexpected, unsuspected situation that occurs, and the ability to respond instinctively to unforeseen problems contributes to that sense of relief and surprise which greets the appearance of a new work. As Ashbery writes in 'Self-Portrait in a Convex Mirror', it is 'never the things / We set out to accomplish and wanted so desperately / To see come into being', because such willed efforts are inevitably just more of the same, de Chirico's 'sad attempts to recapture the magic of the "metaphysical" paintings', for example. People who need art are looking for that surprise and relief which not only makes life more liveable, but creates something lasting out of how it was lived:

> Is there anything
> To be serious about beyond this otherness
> That gets included in the most ordinary
> Forms of daily activity, changing everything
> Slightly and profoundly, and tearing the matter
> Of creation, any creation, not just artistic creation
> Out of our hands, to install it in some monstrous, near
> Peak, too close to ignore, too far
> For one to intervene?

Parmigianino, the starting point for that poem, is elsewhere described as putting 'his craftsmanship at the service of a sense of the mystery behind physical appearances, which makes him a precursor of de Chirico himself'. Yet what is perhaps most moving about Parmigianino's self-portrait is that this mystery is achieved solely by means of unusual perspective. The mysterious, in this sense, is what ordinarily surrounds us, waiting to be seen in that way. In 'Summer' from *The Double Dream of Spring* (a book title borrowed from a de Chirico canvas), 'Summer involves going down as a steep flight of steps / To a narrow ledge over the water.' There, at the heart of the mystery we confront the mere fact of existing at all: 'the face / Resembles yours, the one reflected in the water.'

Jane Freilicher is said to be 'one of those artists like Chardin, Cézanne or Giacometti who, unlike Delacroix or Gauguin, find everything they need close at hand'. Ashbery's poetry in its truant attentions appears to combine both types, as here in 'And Ut Pictura Poesis Is Her Name' where the attention shifts from still life objects, through memories, to a homely version of Eliot's reflections on diction in *Little Gidding*, which are first exemplified from the immediate surroundings, then by way of a de Chirico-like image and a decidedly exotic, far-fetched sound:

> Now,
> About what to put in your poem-painting:
> Flowers are always nice, particularly delphinium.
> Names of boys you once knew and their sleds,
> Skyrockets are good – do they still exist?
> There are a lot of other things of the same quality
> As those I've mentioned. Now one must
> Find a few important words, and a lot of low-keyed,
> Dull-sounding ones. She approached me
> About buying her desk. Suddenly the street was
> Bananas and the clangor of Japanese instruments.

In reply to Helen Vendler's suggestion that this poem doesn't 'create the artifact', Ashbery justified its ending ('understanding / May begin, and in doing so be undone') by commenting: 'that to me is the way understanding comes about'. What might at first seem a personal defence, an 'as my way is', turns out quietly to assert a view of human understanding itself. Even in the tentativeness with which he suggests that *his* way of growing in knowledge and experience may also be *the* way, Ashbery shows what de Chirico in one of his titles called 'The Uncertainty of the Poet' – which is only the rare, wide gaze of someone unwilling to pin him or herself to a few facts and opinions, an outlook at least as old as Keats's. Freilicher's paintings, Ashbery notes, 'struck me at first as tentative, a quality I have since come to admire and consider one of her strengths, having concluded that most good things are tentative, or should be if they aren't'. His last clause, with its (for him) unusual 'should', reminds us that understanding and acceptance of diversity have their own discreet ethics.

Ashbery has been regarded as a practitioner of the fictive for its own sake, but those 'subtle dislocations' with which I began may have a different end. Criticizing painters who improve nature to heighten realism, he remarks, 'Jane's long career has been one attempt to correct this misguided, even blasphemous, state of affairs; to let things, finally, be.' Here, the word 'blasphemous' hints that those ethics of tentativeness are in contact with a faith in creation and, perhaps, beyond. It is not only as artists that we don't know where we are going; but, looking back, the choices made sometimes seem to have pointed down the best direction, perhaps the best possible, because the only one there was. The poems written come to seem sketches for some larger project begun a long while back that you live in hope of viewing with equanimity, as here in the third of *Three Poems*:

> We are trying with mortal hands to paint a landscape which would be a faithful reproduction of the exquisite and terrible scene that stretches around us. No longer is there any question of adjusting a better light on things, to show them ideally as they may never have existed, of taking them out from under the sun to place them in the clean light that meditation surrounds them with. Youth and happiness, the glory of first love – all are viewed naturally now, with all their blemishes and imperfections.

Part of the contingency which it would be perverse to disavow, Ashbery's work has become another fact in the world, something 'too close to ignore, too far / For one to intervene'; it has its own recalcitrant otherness, its uniqueness, to sustain it through the long ordeals of appropriation or neglect. And what is this uniqueness for? To send us back towards the 'exquisite and terrible scene' where, sometimes, 'there are ice-cream parlours to go to / And the pavement is a nice, bluish slate-gray', where 'People laugh a lot' and, grateful to John Ashbery for his gift, it would be good to reply in the words of that poem's title, 'Thank You for Not Co-operating'.

TED BERRIGAN:
NO APOLOGIES AND NO PRIZES

John Ashbery wrote a review of Ted Berrigan's *The Sonnets* in 1968. The piece had been 'commissioned and set up in type by *The New York Times Book Review* but not printed.' Available now in Ashbery's *Selected Prose* edited by Eugene Richie (Ann Arbor: University of Michigan Press, 2004), it ends like this:

> There are no apologies to be made for ugly lines and no prizes to be handed out for good ones: that would be like smashing your window or pinning a blue ribbon on it because you like or dislike the view. It is the aesthetic of 'It's what's happening, baby,' and as we all slide mindlessly towards total media mix, there is still time to notice, in reading Mr. Berrigan, that the poetry is there.

Now it's not unknown for the rich and powerful to do more than smash windows or pin ribbons on them because of the view. They employ landscape gardeners, or, as in Robert Lowell's 'Skunk Hour', they buy up the real estate opposite and let it fall. But pop art, in its hey-day, was more interested in re-landscaping art, in letting its older structures fall, than in converting the slice-of-life out the window into the picturesque. Almost forty years after Ashbery wrote those words, though, here in the resoundingly white-noisy silence of 'total media mix', where we're obliged to remain mindful despite the endless slide, Berrigan's *Collected Poems* are back as reports from one of those old twentieth-century scenes when things used to be happening, baby, and people used to use that funny put-down vocative 'baby'. How well have these 663 text pages of apparently instant reports on experience worn? Can the immediate be a joy forever?

Ted Berrigan (1934–1983) was a second generation, a 'school of' artist. But wait a minute, back in 1970, when Ron Padgett and David Shapiro edited *An Anthology of New York Poets* (Vintage), which includes sixteen of his poems, they could write in their Preface that 'It would be facile as well as misleading to see these poets as forming a 'School,' to pass them off as a literary movement. Like water off a duck's back, such abstractions roll back into nothingness.' But even ducks' backs ain't what they used to be. In her Introduction, Alice Notley writes that 'Ted is often characterised as "second-generation New York School." That label, with its "second-generation," seems to preclude innovation. Ted's career as a poet, after his earliest, sentimental poems, begins in the innovation of *The Sonnets*.' Though she intends to outmanœuvre one perfectly false implication of his label (Rembrandt *is* better than his teachers), she more or less allows it to stand. Yet even here Berrigan's innovation shows in another seeming divergence from antecedents – as if the volume itself were a title-page misprint for *Berryman's Sonnets* (1967).

Among the back jacket commendations on *The Collected Poems*, we find Ashbery himself allowing that 'Ted Berrigan was a leader of the New York School; his crazy energy embodied that movement and the city itself.' It would be worth taking Ashbery at his word; it may well require a second generation, or a shoal of followers, to form a school. The people who, willy-nilly, serve as primary exemplars may not have known that this is what they were doing as they worked in their semi-obscurity. That must surely be the case for Edwin Denby, something of a Douanier Rousseau among the Cubists; and how could Frank O'Hara, the author of 'Personism: A Manifesto', imagine that he was laying out the principles for a 'we all do this, we all do that' style which, three or four generations of imitators later, shows up in little magazines just about anywhere? Second-generation, 'school of' artists signal allegiances in their style as first generation artists cannot; and just as Jesus didn't live long enough to become a Christian (only occasioning the name by dying on a cross), so Frank O'Hara may never have belonged to the New York School.

The timelessly immortal opening to his elegy 'The Day Lady Died' – 'It's 12:20 in New York a Friday / three days after Bastille day, yes / it is 1959' – might even be an allusion to the Rogers and Hart standard 'I Didn't Know What Time It Was', as covered by Billie Holiday on *All or Nothing at All*. The song tells about how your love has set me to rights, so that 'I'm wise / I know what time it is now'; and it's perhaps not completely fanciful to imagine that this is the song that 'she whispered … along the keyboard / to Mal Waldron and everyone and I stopped breathing'. In its best outing, the device of beginning a poem with the time of day looks to be a highly contextualised and pointed piece of writing. O'Hara had prefigured the device in 'A Step Away from Them' three years earlier ('it is 12:40 of / a Thursday'), and he may have prized open the floodgates by repeating it in the 'It is 12:10 in New York and I am wondering' of 'Adieu to Norman, Bonjour to Joan and Jean-Paul' (also 1959). Still, looking at the similarities and differences between one of O'Hara's 'I do this, I do that' poems, and a Berrigan homage to the mode, I couldn't help wondering if a personal manner can become the template for a tradition.

In his comedy poem 'Paraphrases', Roy Fisher includes a letter from a bizarrely devoted fan: 'Dear Mr Fisher I am now / so certain I am you that it is obvious to me / that the collection of poems I am currently working on must be / *your own next book!*' In Berrigan's *The Sonnets* the speaking clock becomes such a tic that you could fear he had become O'Hara:

> It's 8:54 a.m. in Brooklyn it's the 28th of July and
> it's probably 8:54 in Manhattan but I'm
> in Brooklyn I'm eating English muffins and drinking
> pepsi and I'm thinking of how Brooklyn is New
> York city too how odd I usually think of it as
> something all its own…

The fact that sonnet XXXVI is subtitled 'after Frank O'Hara' relieves us, a little, of fears for such an identity crisis, but even so the cravenness of the imitation is in danger of not being a compliment to the originator, but rather a destruction of it in the 'play on that the appetite may sicken and so die' manner: 'It's 8:30 p.m. in New York and I've been running around all day / old come-all-ye's streel into the streets. Yes, it is now, / How Much Longer Shall I Be Able To Inhabit The Divine' – which manages to get both of the great New York mentor figures in the space of three lines. Here is a sampling from the 'synchronise your watches' mode: 'Dear Margie, hello. It is 5:15 a.m.'; 'it is 3:17 a.m. in New York city, yes, it is / 1962, it is the year of parrot fever'. In the later collection *Many Happy Returns* (1969), you find: 'It is 12:10 in New York. In Houston / it is 2 p.m.'; 'I wake up 11:30 back aching from soft bed'; 'It is 7:53 Friday morning in the Universe'; 'At 6:30 woke Sandy / fucked til 7'; 'It's 5:03 a.m. on the 11th July this morning' – these last three from works with the title 'Personal Poem', also borrowed from O'Hara, though sometimes given a # number to distinguish them from their neighbours. These citations can be found between pages 29 and 117. The last poem in the book, 'Grace After a Meal' (another O'Hara echo there!), ends 'It is 5:23 a.m., and the sun / is coming', it's in the 'Early Uncollected Poems' section; while one of Berrigan's 'Last Poems', 'Don Quixote & Sancho Panza', includes the line '253 lbs later, it is May, 1983.' This apparently documentary device is, of course, an aesthetic conundrum all of its own: after all, it's either very rarely or never the time the poem says it is when you read it, and is unlikely to have been even as the poet wrote it, never mind when it was collected in a volume, or reprinted. The device, while seeming to deny its reality, only goes to underline the timeless perpetual present of the poetic text; and yet that perpetual present, in Berrigan's case as in everyone else's, also has the irreducible flavour of its particular moment – back when sex and drugs and rock-and-roll were a lifestyle revolution and even poetry could hitch a ride to the party.

Yet there is innovation, or at least variation, in Berrigan's use of the big clock device. When O'Hara tells you what time it was, it's a form of *cinéma vérité*, and you take it as, at least conventionally, true. To all intents and purposes it is 12:20 when he says it is, and that tunes the reader right into his slice of lunch. When Berrigan does it in *The Sonnets* there's a fair chance the same line, or a slight variation on it, will crop up a few pages later. The reportage element has been subsumed into the themes and variations of a colloquially musical poetry making, Berrigan's idea perhaps of how to get his sonnets to be a sequence of sorts. 'Dear Margie, hello. It is 5:15 a.m.' – or a riff on the same phrase – appears at least six times, twice in the poem where it first appears. The desire to be always a-making of poetry comes over as one of this book's overriding compulsions, a kind of perpetual note-taking, and it seems to absorb everything and anything in a life obsessed with poetry and poets. Nor does it appear to be the lonely business it is for many a poet, either. Numerous of Berrigan's poems are collaborations, *Memorial Day* with Anne Waldman, for instance. The O'Hara-style title was Berrigan's idea. His poems are also forever naming names and addressing themselves to friends and acquaintances. It's an unusually sociable kind of lyric gesture, and in that too effects a variation on the O'Hara's address-book mode, rather than simply an attempt to duplicate it. In his *All Poets Welcome: The Lower East Side Poetry Scene of the 1960s* (University of California Press, 2003), Daniel Kane's first chapter is called 'Community through Poetry'. For those conscious of the fact that communities are only such because they exclude people, Alice Notley has gracefully provided a Glossary of Names to ease reader-stress connected with the field full of folk mentioned in these poems. Unfortunately, the notes are frequently too minimal – '**Tom Raworth** (**1938–**) British poet' – to be worth the effort of looking them up, or, if you do, to make you feel any more at home. Introducing the Hawks at the Albert Hall in 1966, Bob Dylan described his musicians as 'poets … all poets.' Given that one of them was an excellent drummer, Dylan's honorific wouldn't be far wrong for most of Berrigan's named friends and interlocutors.

His familiarity with O'Hara's poetry and apparently comfortable failure to get away from it are everywhere in sight. 'American Express', while quite different in its formal conventions from 'Joe's Jacket', depends upon the idea of a borrowed coat for its friendly occasion:

> Cold rosy dawn in New York City
> not for me
> in Ron's furlined Jim Bridger
> (coat)
> that I borrowed two years ago
> had cleaned
> but never returned, Thank god!
> On 6th Street
> Lunch poems burn
> a hole in my pocket

There he goes again with a nod towards the close of 'A Step Away From Them': 'My heart is in my / pocket, it is Poems by Pierre Reverdy.' O'Hara's hero worship crops up here as elsewhere in his literary name-dropping, and the expressed liking for other poets' work becomes a device that Berrigan imitates too. In 'American Express' Ron Padgett's borrowed coat is hymned just as Joe LeSueur's jacket had been before it; and as exemplified here, second generation writing can be so much more self-consciously stylish than its source texts – Berrigan's close having all the returning poise of an 'in the manner of' work which travels with a fair idea of exactly where its next poetic meal is coming from:

> The mist of May
> is on the gloaming
> & all the clouds
> are halted, still
> fleecey

> & filled
> with holes.
> They are alight with borrowed warmth,
> just like me.

It's difficult not to feel that this charmingly poised close is indebted to yet a third O'Hara poem, the one called 'Cambridge', with its generous tribute to the warmth that you can get from someone else's art. O'Hara is 'Just like Pasternak', but 'lacking the Master's inspiration, I may freeze to death / before I can get out into the white rain. I could have left / the window closed last night? But that's where health / comes from! His breath from the Urals, drawing me into flame...' Berrigan's hero worship of O'Hara has its source in his master's own name-dropping literari- and artiness. The elegant circularity of 'American Express', like a serpent eating its own tail, or like the close of 'In Memory of my Feelings', is never far away: and this is another aspect of Berrigan's 'second generation' poetry.

Like a good deal of pop art, Berrigan was a recycling artist, one more on the lines of the utterly eclectic Robert Rauschenberg in his combines than the artfully painterly Jasper Johns. Berrigan could be a junk poet (though amphetamine pills seem to have been his drug of choice), a junk poet in his recycling of others' fragmented broken lines, their ways of entering a poem; and as we have seen with his keeping-an-eye-on-the-time device he, doing unto himself as he would unto others, also recycles his own lines. In the fourth of *The Sonnets*, it's a rendering of the first line from Rilke's early poem 'Herbsttag' that provides this one's opening:

> Lord, it is time. Summer was very great.
> All sweetly spoke to her of me
> about your feet, so delicate, and yet double E!!
> And high upon the Brooklyn Bridge alone,
> to breathe an old woman slop oatmeal,
> loveliness that longs for butterfly! There is no pad
> as you lope across the trails and bosky dells
> I often think sweet and sour pork'
> shoe repair, and scary. In cities,
> I strain to gather my absurdities
> He buckled on his gun, the one
> Poised like Nijinsky

at every hand, my critic
and when I stand and clank it gives me shoes

The inescapable risk in making collages of this sort lies in the jagged whole proving less than the sum of its discontinuous parts. Daniel Kane's *All Poets Welcome* has an entire section devoted to collaboration, appropriation, and anonymity in second-generation New York School poets. He quotes from Ron Padgett on appropriation: 'It did challenge that notion of the solitary author sweating it out. Using other people's lines means you have a bigger toolbox to work with. It doesn't mean you're going to make better or worse art. You just have more possibilities.' Yet in the poem above, and in Berrigan's very large oeuvre as a whole, there is nevertheless an '*arte povera*' effect, as if the more possibilities of thieving from everyone and anyone including yourself (thieving from yourself: an innovative concept) produce as its presumably unintended side-effect a desperate shortage feeling, a snatching at whatever is at hand. Yet this may also be one source of the poetry's true expressiveness – the experience of an unforeseen poverty at the heart of endless possibility. The effect can be found on almost any page, as here, for instance, in insults thrown at him during 'After Peire Vidal, & Myself': 'Alone, & / In Pain, in Limbo, is where you live   in your little cloud-9 home   Ted! / Pitiful!' It's possible, too, that the expressiveness of so much Berrigan collected together, and edited in this canonical fashion, serves to reveal his poetry as the sustained expression of a problem bravely masquerading as its solution.

The work of epigones can also demonstrate a dearly bought freedom to be different in a reminiscent way, as in this attractive middle-period poem called 'Old-fashioned Air', a poem dedicated to '**Lee Crabtree (1942–1973)**: Musician, member of the rock band The Fugs.' It's a sure sign that a situation comedy is reaching its sell-by date when to keep it going the scriptwriters do the same jokes in different countries; but humming the New York talk and strolling the walk across the pond gives a curious charm to this piece occasioned by the academic year that Berrigan spent teaching at the University of Essex (1973–74), where he made contact with a large number of writers, including Douglas Oliver who later moved to New York, becoming Alice Notley's husband after Berrigan's death. This year in England left a distinct mark on a group of poets who variously folded the New York mode into British 1970s styles. 'Old-fashioned Air' shows how it could be done:

> I'm living in Battersea, July,
> 1973, not sleeping, reading
> Jet noise throbs building fading
> Into baby talking, no, 'speechifying'
> 'Ah wob chuk sh 'guh!' Gee.

Perhaps the poem's air is 'Old-fashioned' not only because it's situated in the old world, but because it uses capital letters at the beginning of each line, and has a thread of rhyming around the same sound, the second vowel in its lengthened pronunciation, the sound of the dedicatee's first name, echoing through most of it:

> There's a famous power station I can't see
> Up the street. Across there is
> Battersea Park
> I walked across this morning toward
> A truly gorgeous radiant flush;
> Sun; fumes of the Battersea
> Power Station; London air;
> I walk down long avenues of trees
> That leant not gracefully
> Over the concrete walk. Wet green lawn
> Opened spaciously
> Out on either side of me. I saw
> A great flock of geese taking this morning walk
> Unhurriedly.
> I didn't hurry either, Lee.

As can be heard in these lines, it is to Berrigan, among others, that we are indebted for the bright idea that O'Hara's 'I do this, I do that' mode could be both heterosexualised and domesticated. The old-fashioned sound of the piece, its more reflective and faintly melancholic air, partly derives from its being an 'I did this, I did that' poem – sign, as it would prove, of ways in which this particular American style of the moment could not quite be exported without having its energies metamorphosed, *Ambassadors*-fashion, by the differently embedded life of the old world, as can be heard in some of John James's poems in *Striking the Pavilion of Zero* (1975). 'Old-fashioned Air' continues:

I stopped & watched them walk back up toward
& down into their lake,
Smoked a Senior Service on a bench
As they swam past me in a long dumb graceful cluttered line,
Then, taking my time, I found my way
Out of that park;
A Gate that was locked. I jumped the fence.
From there I picked up the *London Times*, came home,
Anselm awake in his bed, Alice
Sleeping in mine: I changed
A diaper, read a small poem I'd had
In mind, then thought to write this line:
'Now is Monday morning so, that's a garbage truck I hear,
    not bells'
And we are back where we started from, Lee, you
    & me, alive & well!

The affection expressed is distinctly attractive. Nevertheless, the change of sexual orientation in the private-made-public style brings with it consequences. O'Hara's poetry might be seen as an outing of the complexly private into the social space of New York. As well as metaphorically oblique sex poems ('Twin spheres full of fur and noise'), O'Hara has his higher devotions ('I worry about this because I / love you'), his thoroughly articulated anxieties (There was / something I had to do. But what?'), and, above all, a piercing solitude ('loneliness, / … drifting into my ears off Sendai in the snow') sensed within the gregariously sociable: 'I drink to smother my sensitivity for a while so I won't stare away / I drink to kill the fear of boredom, the mounting panic of it'. The relative cultural non-location of a gay man in the 1950s and early 1960s, even in the New York art scene, makes O'Hara's sexuality more smartly allusive and even momentarily elusive, thanks to his many poems devoted to women writers and painters with whom he was particularly close.

Berrigan's can suffer, particularly in the earlier work, from an almost meaningless sexual bravado ('fucked til 7'); for at approximately the same moment, heterosexual counter-culture was still inflected, if at times ironically, with stereotype gender roles. You can catch the tang of this world well lost in the repartee between Berrigan and Waldman at the opening of their reading from *Memorial Day* available on the CD that comes with *All Poets Welcome*. Berrigan's sexual clock punching has not worn well: 'Last time I counted I think / It was about / 50 / * / The number of people, / I mean' (*Train Ride*, 1971). Later, the love poetry for his wife can be as soft as this piece dated July 11, 1982: 'Dear Alice, / The reason I love / you so much is be- / cause you're very / beautiful & kind. I / also appreciate your / intelligence, though what / 'intelligence' is I'm not / sure, & your wit, which / resembles nothing I've / ever thought about. / Your loving husband, / Ted Berrigan'. I suppose there's barely such a thing now as a text that shouldn't be published; but this tender message made me wonder. Only the signature suggests it might not be merely personal, and vulnerably so even in that charmed circle – for like O'Hara in his manifesto, while typing it the tender poet and evidently loving husband could have known that 'if I wanted to I could use the telephone instead of writing the poem.' Not knowing him personally either, a reader might equally suspect some 'protesting too much'.

A part of Berrigan's work also suffers from the instant datedness in poetry not of objects but of media and consumer culture: 'Mister Robert Dylan doesn't feel well today / That's bad'. Nor can such personal writing always avoid sounding like notes from an increasingly unlovely life, made so by the addiction that was fuelling what Ashbery called his 'crazy energy', and the need to make a living as no more nor less than a poet. This required an increasingly peripatetic life away from New York in creative writing residencies and the like. Mark Ford, an anthologist of Berrigan's work (*New York Poets II: Edwin Denby to Bernadette Mayer*, Carcanet 2006), in interview once made that old 'why should I care?' remark about others' experience in poetry ('I can't bear poems about grandfathers, or fishing expeditions, or what it's like to move into a new house'); yet his attitude could be thought as relevant for some of Berrigan's more personal jottings as it might be for works in the provincially anecdotal veins. Poetry sings out from an endlessly shifting no-man's-land between the naff and the cool – too much of the former and it's condemned to trivial irrelevance, too much of the latter and it's self-censored by yet another version of correctness and period agenda. But if a poem's verbal arrangement gives pleasure, all sorts of risky non-cool materials may be accessed; and Berrigan is too haplessly open-mouthed and -eyed to be altogether street-wise:

> The days' usual aggressive
> > contrary beat
> > > now softly dropped

into a regular pace
        the head riding gently its personal place
where pistons feel like legs
        on feelings met like lace.
                Why,
take a walk, then,
        across this town. It's a pleasure
to meet one certain person you've been counting on
                to take your measure
who will smile, & love you, sweetly, at your leisure.

'Peace' in effect quotes its rhymes, as modern poets since Hardy have been doing, producing, after its own fashion, a piercingly second-hand sentiment – not unlike that in the borrowed imagery of pop art that is now some half a century old.

'Personism' was, of course, a mockery of poetic theory '-isms'. Yet it is the fate of a good joke to be repeated until the humour's been drained from it; and so it has been with O'Hara's version of poetry made with no more for technique, supposedly, than 'your nerve' from the circumstances of an unusually incident-filled everyday life. The curious contradiction of O'Hara and his school is that they were able to 'copyright' a manner of notation for the personal, which, like the individual fashions that everyone is wearing this season, half conceal the fact that everybody's personal is likely to be different. Berrigan's can't help being faintly mannered, because a quotation, and so less freshly insouciant; he also seems more vulnerably needy in relation to his friends. 'Last Poem' – neither his last, of course, nor the last in the book – courageously addresses such dependence at its close:

I grew tall & huge of frame, obviously possessed
Of a disconnected head, I had a perfect heart. The end
Came quickly & completely without pain, one quiet night as I
Was sitting, writing, next to you in bed, words chosen randomly
From a tired brain, it, like them, suitable, & fitting.
Let none regret my end who called me friend.

As 'Last Poem' also exemplifies, aside from the postcards, telegrams (like the one to Jack Kerouac: 'Bye-Bye Jack. / See you soon.'), half-jokes and stunts, there are the many standout poems, ones like the title piece to the 1982 gathering (posthumously published in 1988), 'A Certain Slant of Sunlight':

> In Africa the wine is cheap, and it is
> on St Mark's Place too, beneath a white moon.
> I'll go there tomorrow, dark bulk brooded
> against what is hurled down at me in my not hat
> which is weather: the tall pretty girl in the print dress
> under the fur collar of her cloth coat will be standing
> by the wire fence where the wild flowers grow not too tall
> her eyes will be deep brown and her hair styled 1941 American
>   will be too; but
> I'll be shattered by then
> But now I'm not and can also picture white clouds
> impossibly high in blue sky over small boy heartbroken
> to be dressed in black knickers, black coat, white shirt,
>   buster-brown collar, flowing black bow-tie
> her hand lightly fallen on his shoulder, faded sunlight falling
> across the picture, mother & son, 33 & 7, First Communion
>   Day, 1941 –
> I'll go out for a drink with one of my demons tonight
> they are dry in Colorado 1980 spring snow.

The art of such poems, and it is one that can be learned from an intensive reading of O'Hara, resides in beginning quite casually with an apparently random association of details (the drink in Africa and New York bearing a remote resemblance to 'the poets / in Ghana' and the 'bottle of Strega' from 'the PARK LANE / Liquor Store' in 'The Day Lady Died'), then, as in O'Hara's best, the casual details build to the discovery of a personal issue in their interconnected pictures, an issue that accesses the poem's piercingly true and unexpected emotion. 'A Certain Slant of Sunlight' was, perhaps, inspired by the poet's mother, Peggy Berrigan, becoming 'ill with lung cancer' – as suggested by this volume's useful six-page chronology of the poet's life and works. Alice Notley, with the poet's sons, Anselm and Edmund, have performed a great service to the poetry community by so tactfully and skilfully editing the oeuvre of a poet who, like the hero who so enabled these writings by his example, did not live to turn the pages of his *Collected Poems*.

BIG IDEAS:
JORIE GRAHAM AND CHARLES SIMIC

Jorie Graham and Charles Simic have things in common besides having won the Pulitzer Prize for poetry. Both have biographical and cultural ties with Europe: Simic was born in Yugoslavia in 1938 and emigrated at the age of 11; Graham spent part of her childhood in Italy, was educated at the Sorbonne, and grew up speaking three languages. Their work is ingrained with this transatlanticism: Graham's 'From the New World' and Simic's 'Two Dogs', for example, link the horrors of mid-century European history to an America with an eerie resemblance to Vladimir Nabokov's – that tacky, grim and dangerous campus novel cum road movie *avant la lettre*. Indeed, there are moments when Graham's work can seem like the unhappy love child of Lolita and Humbert:

> I went into the bathroom, locked the door.
> Stood in front of the mirrored wall –

> not so much to see in, not looking up at all in fact,
>   but to be held in it as by a gas,
> the thing which was me there in its chamber. Reader.

Graham has that Humbertian habit of grabbing the 'Reader' by the lapels with a palpably-designing direct address, and the allusion to a 'gas … chamber' in this toilet from 'From the New World' is not accidental. Simic, by contrast, can seem an alarming cross between John Shade, the American campus poet, and his 'friend' Charles Kimbote, the crazy alien – as here in 'Dream Avenue', where a strategic weirdness doesn't inoculate it against over-writing:

> You've no idea what city this is,
> What country? It could be a dream,
> But is it yours? You're nothing
> But a vague sense of loss,
> A piercing, heart-wrenching dread
> on an avenue with no name…

Both poets have been warmly noticed in *Soul Says: On Recent Poetry* (1995) by Helen Vendler: Jorie Graham's 'poetics leads to poems – the best in recent memory – on human self-division' and 'The next generation of political poets will need to be on their mettle if they want to surpass' Charles Simic. Each has an idiosyncratic style – set to leave its mark on the manners by which younger poets attempt to find ways forward.

Both are products of a cultural climate in which market niche identity reigns, one in which the thing a poet must have is an immediately recognizable signature style. Graham achieved it by abandoning the stuttering short-lined stanzas of her earliest books, *Hybrids of Plants and Ghosts* (1980) and *Erosion* (1983), opting rather for a long-lined, disjunctively accumulative manner – generating a rapturously desperate afflatus. Vendler's *The Breaking of Style: Hopkins, Heaney, Graham* (1995) devotes a lecture to this development in her work. Simic doesn't seem to have had a stylistic Road to Damascus. His best modes emerge from a repeating and refining through numerous collections: his poems rarely turn the page; he uses plain syntax, constructs light folk-song-like stanzas, and largely confines himself to a poor urban ambience. With both, the price to be paid for this achieved distinctiveness is met by individual poems – poems which can come out as barely distinguishable vehicles for a further batch of the niche product. The distinctiveness, then, characterises the poet, but not each individual poem. However, it may be that in the longer run the weakening of an oeuvre by a relentlessly signature style will reduce interest in the poet's distinctiveness too.

Vendler's case for Graham's poetry has been made often and strongly. The following lines form a characteristic end to the title piece from *The Errancy*:

> how long ago was it we said that? do you remember? –
> and now that you've remembered – and the distance we've
> traveled – and where we were, then – and
> how little we've found – aren't we tired? aren't we
> going to close the elaborate folder
> which holds the papers in their cocoon of possibility,
> the folder so pretty with its massive rose-blooms,
> oh perpetual bloom, dread fatigue, and drowsiness like leavening I
>   feel –

A poem grandly entitled 'The Guardian Angel of the Private Life' ends with a similar tiredness: '– before the credo, before the plan – / right at the homesickness – before this list you hold / in your exhausted hand. Oh put it down.' Indeed, by the finish of a Graham poem, it is possible to have been wearied by the mannerisms that Vendler positively describes as 'this typical flurry of injunctions, questions, and parenthetical interjections'. What's more, the enjambment with which 'The Errancy' comes to a stop produces an embarrassing collapse. To expose the first-person pronoun as a stressed syllable at the end of the line, attach it to the stressed verb 'feel' at the head of the next, then just end is to isolate the statement 'I / feel', like a teenage *cri de cœur*, from syntactic anchorage to its object ('drowsiness like leavening'); 'The Errancy' goes fatally astray at the point where a poem cannot afford to – its last line.

Graham's urgent meditations on the nature of 'History', 'Chaos', or 'Manifest Destiny' (three typical titles) and other such vast abstractions – which she scorns to go in fear of – need not, it seems, concern themselves with such 'fiddle'. Graham cites Marianne Moore in 'Motive Elusive', a ghastly rococo variation on the supposed ability of a child to block out the experience of 'the rape (ongoing) of the mother now' and her subsequent murder. That parenthesis, '(ongoing)', fails to register the imaginative cost in Graham's programmatic, acted-out immediacy. Her wincing pun in 'the fretwork of the small screams' pales before the wishful-thinking of the piece's close: 'do not fear for the child, / its gold is hid.' 'Motive Elusive' asks us to credit that the child's absorption in the flaking details of a wall in the same room as the sex crime will save it from the damage incurred while 'awaiting its orphanhood': 'you must / believe this – it can do – it can hold –', Graham badgeringly insists.

'Error is the heroic form of finding one's way – a purposeful wandering toward truth, a pilgrimage in which the heart's longing is guide', the blurb informs us, and the last of Graham's notes draws attention to her book's indebtedness to a critical theory about how 'Epic action begins with a gaze in the mirror', but requires a 'reformed narcissism' – a theory taking into account the etymologies of 'error' in 'wandering' (being a knight errant), and 'discourse' in running back and forth. The sublime drift of a Graham poem is to be understood, then, as a cross between action painting and quest narrative. However, 'In order to make a mistake [irre], a man must already judge in conformity with mankind,' notes Wittgenstein in *On Certainty* – and the knights of old were acting in complex relation with strenuous social and religious imperatives. We like to think we'll discover the new 'by trial and error', but serious erring requires implicitly accepted codes to violate (note the word 'pilgrimage' in that blurb).

What interests Vendler in 'Graham's recent work on models of history is that she avoids not only the classical and Christian models invoked by Yeats and others, but also the utopian models popular with socialist and feminist poets.' Yet, being a *fin-de-siècle* post-modern rhapsodist, Graham must allude to such models, as in 'The End of Progress Aubade' subtitled 'Eurydice to Orpheus'; Christianity too, in the form of myths and art works, is rarely far away – as when a note releases us from the need 'to recognise Piero della Francesca's "Resurrection" here' in 'Easter Morning Aubade'. The gestural progress of a Graham poem is frequently tagged to a big idea in the title so that readers can follow familiar associative tracks even while given the sensation of being at the critical edge of a paradigm supplied by theory.

Wittgenstein's brother Paul, the concert pianist, lost an arm during the Great War, and in *On Certainty* the philosopher has much to remark about the existence of hands. Graham takes up the business of a hand's being there at the opening of 'The Strangers', a passage picked out for exemplary use on her book jacket:

> The hand I placed on you, what if it
> didn't exist, where it began, shaking, the declension of
> your opening shirt, dusk postponed in each glazed and arctic
> button, pale reddish shirt – what if it doesn't
> exist – these fingers browsing the cotton surface, swimming in
>   the steadfast surface –
> what if there's no place it can exist
> this looking for a place to lie down in,
> to make a tiny civilisation –

The two strangers of the poem's title are involved in an erotic encounter by which, through just their own behaviour, or renewed belief in the existence of each other's body parts, they will be seeking a place to 'make a tiny civilisation'. Yet, if they don't already have something of a civilisation 'to lie down in', they won't have it in kit form to construct when they find the place. Civilisations are not the 'tiny' (a sentimentalizing diminutive) result of such acts; the acts, if successful, are signs of the civilisation.

Moreover, as her opening line implicitly acknowledges, if the hand really 'didn't exist', then the poem's speaker wouldn't be wondering about its existence. Graham's wandering lines might then count as heroic error, but they could also qualify as a confused pretext for something else. This is where the 'heart's longing' comes in, because their supposed worrying about the hand's existence is part of an intensely-fashioned love poem:

> is it the wingbeat itself it would cross through the
> envelope of flesh
> to get, this hand flat on you now, a badge, an x-ray,
> homing in, an hypothesis, monosyllabic,
> over the supple, gossipy, tin-can heart – unrelenting –
> to make you exist –

This 'make you exist' doesn't, presumably, mean 'bring you into being' – like God creating Adam with his index finger. The argument about the existence of the hand is the same for the body it touches: how can it be seriously doubted either by the one whose hand is doing the touching, or the other whose heart is being touched? Then, 'to make you exist –' must mean something like 'make you feel that you are really existing'. Vendler has written of 'the crucial intersection of the passional and the philosophical from which the poems radiate'; yet Graham's language here, while having a deep air, urges us to be profoundly moved by a touchy-feely moment in a bedding scene.

'Ideas make your hair stand up,' Charles Simic writes in his 'Notebooks, 1963–69', 'just as if you were to stick your finger in a socket.' He goes on to narrate a surely imaginary lovers' conversation between an admirer of Bishop Berkeley's *esse est percipi* and a follower of Doctor 'I refute it thus' Johnson:

> 'The external world,' she assures me, 'is the work of our sense organs.'
>
> 'Sweet Jesus! Does that mean our sweaty, naked bodies, being a part of the external world, are merely the work of our sense organs?'
>
> 'Not so loud, you fool,' she says as she pulls the covers up to her chin.
>
> 'Our sense organs themselves are the product of our sense organs.'

'In that case,' I say pulling off her covers, 'if I understand you correctly, we might not even be here!' But, she just glares at me and calls me stupid.

Simic's work also has its raft of abstractions, but his methods imply an awareness of Pound's advice to go in fear of them. 'An Address with Exclamation Points' begins 'I accuse History of gluttony; / Happiness of anorexia!' This too is characteristic, recalling the start to 'Department of Public Monuments': 'If Justice and Liberty / Can be raised to pedestals, / Why not History?' Neither appears in *Looking for Trouble*, but the book does contain 'Madonnas Touched Up with a Goatee': 'Most ancient Metaphysics, (poor Metaphysics!) / All decked up in imitation jewelry.' Its title signals the poet's familiarity with Duchamp's ploys for making visible the institutions of art by irreverent marginal incursions.

Simic's remorseless irony is a means for the simultaneous management of seriousness and an invulnerable detachment. One result of its ubiquity is that poems which deploy nearly contradictory ideas can seem chips off the same block. *Looking for Trouble* brings together selections from seven collections published between 1971 and 1982, then jumps to choices from Simic's two most recent American books, *Wedding from Hell* (1994) and *Walking the Black Cat* (1996). 'Midpoint', the last poem selected from *Austerities* (1982), plays with the idea (already tried out in the anecdote about the philosophizing lovers) that the world only exists when we perceive it: 'No sooner had I left A. / Than I started doubting its existence... B. at which I am destined / To arrive by and by / Doesn't exist now.' The speaker of the poem, being at its midpoint, marked by an asterisk, is neither here nor there. Indeed, having set out the poles of its dilemma, the poem finds little to do with them, closing thus: 'Knowing that on the day / Of my departure / It will vanish forever / Just as A. did.'

Two poems later, we've leapt twelve years and reached 'Late Arrival', the second piece in the selection from *Wedding from Hell*. It opens with a more familiar notion:

> The world was already there,
> Serene in its otherness.
> It only took you to arrive
> On the late afternoon train
> To where no one awaited you.

There's almost a memory of 'Midpoint' in the second verse's 'A town no one ever remembered / Because of its drabness', but not being remembered, here, doesn't mean ceasing to exist. Yet if this poem opens with a less horrid idea, one not making your hair stand on end, it moves to a more piercing close:

> It was then that you heard,
> As if for the very first time,
> The sound of your own footsteps
> Under a church clock
> Which had stopped just as you did
>
> Between two empty streets
> Aglow in the afternoon sunlight,
> Two modest stretches of infinity
> For you to wonder at
> Before resuming your walk.

This sentence, the second half of the poem, winningly makes its 'two empty streets' into 'Two modest stretches of infinity' without a flicker of overt irony, exclamation points, a show of profundity, or elaborate cool. The 'modest' disarms the 'infinity', which slips into the line's terminal position with no stagey capital letter. 'Late Arrival' sneaks up on the abstraction, takes it unawares, then leaves it behind in its perfectly-timed downbeat close.

In publishers' characteristic fashion, Simic's British house lets his readers know that their author has published another book with Faber, and is famously worth publishing because he has 13 titles to his credit in the USA (in fact he's released rather more). Among the ones they do list is a *Selected Poems 1963–1983*, yet this same volume was published in England in 1986 by Secker and Warburg thanks to the sponsorship of the Academy of American Poets and the generosity of Mr James A. Michener. The 'Selected Early' part of *Looking for Trouble* is more or less a choice from that selection, with the exception of the longer poem *White*, first published in 1980, which has undergone extensive and acknowledged revision. A chronological reading of his two Faber volumes and the unacknowledged *Selected Poems 1963–1983* – Simic's oeuvre as published in this country – reveals just how much more adept his work has become over the last decade and a half. There are good and memorable pieces throughout (the early 'enchanted objects' poems such as 'Fork', 'My Shoes', and 'Brooms', for example) but a far greater proportion that, like 'Midpoint', have a smart idea, some wittily surreal phrasing, and a deadpan delivery – but which get snagged on a lack of substantial development and an inertia of syntax and rhythm.

However, from *Unending Blues* to the recent *Walking the Black Cat*, Simic's collections have all contained poems that stand out from his routines thanks to their more focused specificity of detail, greater imaginative reach, or sustained narrative-like purposefulness. Thus, while 'A Letter' strikes a familiar note with its 'Dear philosophers, I get sad when I think. / Is it the same with you?', the much longer 'Shelley' describes the poet-to-be buying a second hand copy of the English romantic's works and reading them for the first time 'One rainy evening in New York City'. The opportunities for juxtapositions of the high-flown and the mundane are evident from this scenario, but Simic manages them in such a way that, as the poem develops, both begin to borrow colours from the other:

> The poet spoke of the everlasting universe
> Of things ... of gleams of a remoter world
> Which visit the soul in sleep...
> Of a desert peopled by storms alone...
>
> The streets were strewn with broken umbrellas
> Which looked like funereal kites
> This little Chinese girl might have made.

These 'broken umbrellas... like funereal kites' exemplify what Elizabeth Bishop described as 'the always-more-successful surrealism of everyday life' at its best; and Simic's can include the fearfully quotidian banalities of violence and cruelty, as in 'Two Dogs' where, Shade-and-Kimbote-like he is told an anecdote in the New Hampshire woods about an old American dog 'afraid of his own shadow', and remembers 'the Germans marching / Past our house in 1944.' Into this parade a 'little white dog' gets entangled, and the poem concludes: 'A kick made him fly as if he had wings. / That's what I keep seeing! / Night coming down. A dog with wings.'

'The Anniversary' begins by announcing that 'I'll walk the streets all day today / With my eyes closed.' It then builds a sequence of events for its speaker who passes by 'a matrimonial agency rarely frequented' where 'A bride will wait for me'. On to the scaffolding of 'a construction site, fifty stories up' goes the walker with shut eyes, 'arms spread wide to steady myself / With the wind gusting off the river':

> There's the Brooklyn Bridge
> Like an archer's quiver.
> There's the Bowery
> Where the dead are never buried.
>
> O unknown bride coming to rescue me,
> Walking on the narrow girder in your high-heeled shoes
> With your eyes tightly closed,
> The seagulls will snatch your veil
> Just as your gloved hand reaches for mine.

This is a teeteringly-balanced poem about hope and possibility, but also, for Simic's UK readers, a missed opportunity. Given the six blank pages at the back of *Looking for Trouble*, it would have been possible to allow his second Faber selection to close not with the joky, fragmented 'The Emperor' ('The Garden of Eden needs weeding, / And the soda machines don't work') – the penultimate piece in *Walking the Black Cat* – but with that collection's closing poem, 'The Anniversary'. We could have been tantalizingly left fifty stories up on that narrow girder with the speaker and his reaching bride, as in the last frames of an old cliff-hanger– eager to discover what will happen in the next instalment.

JAMES LASDUN:
EARLY RETIREMENT

James Lasdun's third book of poems, *Landscape with Chainsaw*, ends with an envoi called 'Happy the Man'. The title is a Horatian tag, taken perhaps from Dryden's rendering of Ode III, 29: 'Happy the Man, and happy he alone, / He, who can call his day his own', though it could equally come from the first words of Pope's 'Ode on Solitude' (as Stephen Burt suggested in his *TLS* review). Lasdun's verses begin on a not so happy note: 'Goodbye words; / my faltering muse's / unevenly burning flame / has sputtered out, and now like Diocletian / I'm taking early retirement.' The classical theme is maintained both with the allusion to the Roman emperor, and to the echo of an earlier pastoral version of 'retirement' in the contemporary idiom for a sometimes lucrative compromise with company shrinkage; and Lasdun's landscape in the second part of 'American Mountain' includes residua from just such business fortunes:

> abandoned houses – middle-income,
> cathedral-ceilinged, faux post-and-beam
> 'Woodstock Contemporaries'
> dotted along the creeks for IBM
>
> before they downsized; abandoned grist-mills; graveyards…

These lines, fretted with an irony about his retirement to where white-collar workers no longer retire, reveal much of the Lasdun flavour: there is some delicately inventive rhyming going on ('beam' and 'IBM'); there are internal assonances ('ceilinged' and 'along'); there's a deflationary enjambment ('IBM / before they downsized'); there's emphatic repetition ('abandoned houses… abandoned grist-mills'); alliteration ('grist-mills; graveyards') – all worked together with an off-hand, accumulative syntax and flexed rhythm. The *ubi sunt* theme is presented with a leavening of verbal pleasure; and while there are thoughts prompted here about how entrepreneurial economies work, this passage doesn't have the one thought too many which elbows the reader into lines of attitude-mongering – the blight of much contemporary poetry.

So, reaching 'Happy the Man' at the close of the book, readers have already encountered a number of strains which complicate any simple contrast between city and country. 'Either you clear your woods or they'll clear you –' as the chainsaw salesman puts it in 'Returning the Gift'. In Lasdun's book, nature appears not merely as it might be on an idealised Horatian farm, but red in tooth and claw as well. *Landscape with Chainsaw* closes its account like this:

> The dirt road
> dead-ends on wilderness;
> sometimes at night you can hear
> unearthly gabblings: Bear Mountain's coyotes
> closing in on a kill. Pure poetry.

The last two words of this final verse of 'Happy the Man' find a suggestive near-rhyme in 'coyotes' and 'poetry', but, looping back to the modest disclosure of the poem's opening ('Goodbye words; / my faltering muse's / unevenly burning flame') start an anxiety or two. The central three verses describe how as the writer is 'Homesteading' in the Catskill Mountains near Woodstock, Upstate New York, he'll remember how words were all he 'needed or anyway / wanted of the crack and grain / of real things'. Here he describes a taste for words which calls up an aspiration to the verbal self-sustenance associated with poésie pure: 'how in your loam they'd swell, split / and banner out into themselves...' But now, 'if I write, it'll be with a seed-drill'. There's a Heaneyesque flavour to this talk of seed-drills or 'the crack and grain / of' something or other. But is this a genuine retirement from poetry? Do we take him at his word and note the 'faltering', or do we brush it aside as a politely ingratiating goodbye for now?

Though somewhat concealed by the lavish design and generous space per poem that Norton have granted their author, *Landscape with Chainsaw* is a slimmer volume than *Woman Police Officer in Elevator* (1997). The book contains just twenty-four poems, one of which, 'The Backhoe', is reprinted from the previous collection. The legitimacy of this is that the new volume is not a collection so much as a coherent book thematically centred on the poet's life in 'retirement' with his wife and children, a theme foreshadowed in that earlier poem. As befits such a group of poems, there are a number of difficult matters interwoven and echoing from piece to piece. The one pointed up by the title is the conflict of man and nature symbolised by the chainsaw, but in 'Returning the Gift' this chainsaw becomes the occasion for an exploration of the poet's various identities-in-difference. Taking back the tool his wife has given him, the English poet encounters an Iron John of a backwoodsman who offers him some lessons in he-man-hood. The author's accent has given him away:

> British, right? I nod. That question here
> puts my guard up, like are you Jewish? did
> in England where it meant so you're a yid,
> at least to my hypersensitive ear,
>
> as British here means – but I'm being paranoid...

Paranoid or not, the central conflict that Lasdun's book explores is how it is that he has come to feel at home, to feel the pleasures of retirement, in a place where he of all people should be in a perpetual state of non-belonging. The poet, as described in this book, seems an ideal candidate for Nicolas Jenkins' new tradition of post-national, cosmopolitan writers (and Jenkins is the dedicatee of 'Returning the Gift'). This is plainly articulated in one of the book's most accomplished poems, the opening 'Locals':

> I envied them. To be local was to know
> which team to support: the local team;
> where to drop in for a pint with mates: the local;
> best of all to feel by birthright welcome
> anywhere; be everywhere a local ...

Thus 'Locals' addresses the true theme of finding yourself tempera-mentally and socially likely to be always on the outside looking in. But just as the last two lines of this stanza reach towards an unlikely sort of at-home-ness, so too the idea of a primary authenticity is made to look faintly foolish – as in 'the original prior claim' of those who were 'There, doubtless, in Eden before Adam / wiped them out and settled in with Eve.' But not according to the Old Testament or Milton's *Paradise Lost*, of course.

Lasdun's way with this dilemma is to dramatise the underlying paranoias, if that's what they are, in a lightly parodic and faintly ingratiating manner. This approach may itself be an aspect of the theme in modelling the behaviour of people who can't help feeling they are likely to be ostracised if they don't make themselves amenable. If they then feel at home, despite everything, there's a sudden mismatch between the ingrained 'outsider' psychology, the amenability, and the genial scene in which it's set. This too is likely to produce comedy, as in Lasdun's memorable encounter with the woman police officer in the elevator; his poetic persona is perfectly lucid and rational enough to see that the feelings which are putting him in a sweat don't have a leg to stand on, but his character's psychopathology of everyday life makes it impossible for him to disarm them and their being occasioned. Lasdun successfully revisits the title poem of his previous collection in 'Patrol Car: Bear Mountain' where this time it is the male authority figure of a policeman waiting in a parked vehicle that produces a 'whiff of the old id-slum'.

Landscape with Chainsaw even stretches to a Freudian joke and its relation to the unconscious: 'Later I invented my family's psychology: / Anglo, Super-Anglo and Yid.)' This is witty about his inherited inner conflicts, but it's also somehow slightly sad, like something that Woody Allen would have already used if he'd been British. And just as in the ever more unlikely exchanges with the man from the mall in 'Returning the Gift', so too you can suspect that the poetic persona's conflicts of reason and psychological panic are just slightly over-staged, which is what makes it feel faintly ingratiating. Other poems return to his Jewish identity theme in ways that make it far from a matter of simplistic identity politics. In the first place, Lasdun describes himself as from a comfortable, middle-class, assimilated background:

> 'We're not English' went the family saying.
> What were we then? We'd lopped
> our branch off the family tree:
> anglophone Russian-German apostate Jews
>
> mouthing Anglican hymns at church
> till we renounced that too...

Being told this about the poet makes it all the more difficult to feel that 'Deathmeadow Mountain', a poem about 'Celan's / meeting with Heidegger', manages more than to gloss (with the acknowledged aid of John Felstiner's book on the poet) Paul Celan's 'Todtnauberg' from *Lichtzwang* (1970) on that painfully indecisive encounter. 'Deathmeadow Mountain' renders the name of Heidegger's retreat which gave Celan's work its title, but in Lasdun's poem the two curiously linked kinds of identification (with a persecuted people, and with an authenticising philosophy of race and place) are related, but only by contrasting with, his evolving theme in the book – what it feels like to be at home somewhere when you don't have (and most likely don't want) the agonised relation to his chosen people that Celan explored, or the profoundly suspect philosophy of the woodland ways that Heidegger disastrously associated with Nazi views on Volk and Raum. This is the hinterland of deep conflict and damage against which Lasdun's retirement stages itself – as 'Woodstock' begins by underlining:

> Wudestoc: a clearing in the woods.
> Forty miles from the town itself;
> the name, as in Herzl's Judenstaat,
> less about place than disclosure –
> of a people, or an idea.

And it's as if Lasdun, a likely candidate for Jenkins' new cosmopolitan school of poets, can't quite shake off the less than useful notions of an authentic relation to a locality and a people, while knowing perfectly well that the ways in which local folk anywhere claim a primordial right so as to keep newcomers at bay has little to ground it in Europe if you go back far enough, and even less in America, where you don't have to go back very far at all. Lasdun's approach relies on a contrastive relation with these incompatible ideas so as to make his unusual at-home-ness feel distinctive. In 'Apostasy', for example, he revisits the sense of 'standing off' from cultures while being about to apply the book's thematic tool to one of his maples. *Landscape with Chainsaw* discloses a structural state of contradiction in its poems' outlook, but one which is almost nostalgically regarded, like a problem that has only just passed its sell-by date – some bitter-sweet food you were better not eating, but can't yet bring yourself to throw away.

Among Lasdun's other recurrent themes is the meeting of his European sensibility with an American milieu. The appealing 'A Tie-Dye T-Shirt', which first appeared in *The New Yorker*, opens: 'Home from prep school / in my short-trousered herringbone suit, / I counted hippies on the streets of Notting Hill.' This is audibly close to the opening syntactical gambit of Lowell's 'Memories of West Street and Lepke' (there's even the detail of the clothes the poet is wearing before the first person singular verb at the start of line three). Lasdun's schoolboy encounter with the hippies is of course a meeting with American counter-culture, as the contrast with the herringbone suit implies, and this occasions a memory of an earlier cultural encounter: 'I felt myself / in the presence of superior beings, / as Major Wynkoop said of the Cheyennes.' In the second and last verse, it's thirty years later on his property near Woodstock and the poet's daughter has made him such a T-shirt 'from one of the kits they sell / in the kitschy Tinker Street head-shops.' Here, a faintly Lowellesque note creeps in with the leap from 'kits' to 'kitschy' – like the summer millionaire from his L. L. Bean catalogue in 'Skunk Hour', or the 'Atlantic seaboard antique shop / pewter and plunder' in 'The Old Flame'. And, speaking of 'Skunk Hour', the appearance of the bear 'peering in for the trash / he's caught a whiff of' in the last verse of 'Property: The Bear' can't but recall that mother skunk and her children at 'the garbage pail'. In 'A Tie-Dye T-Shirt', though, when the poet puts on his daughter's present 'a strange / tremor of happiness goes through me' and, borrowing a bit of knights-move grammar from Paul Muldoon, 'I've half a mind to crack open / one of the spiked pods on this Jimson Weed', and 'hallucinate a week or two / in the psychedelic spring meadow'. Here, then, is a poem about achieving a certain present happiness and contentment by trading in the confessional 'herringbone' for the T-shirt's imaginative freedoms via that 'half a mind' colloquialism – a colloquialism with its discreet put-down for the 'stoned' generation as well. 'Woodstock', occasioned by the place and the rock festival, completes this move in a sustained stanzaic poem of Muldoonian autobiographical associativeness.

'A Tie-Dye T-Shirt' is appealing in its locating the author somewhat uneasily between the troubled but assured late-modern 'belonging' of a New Englander from a founding family and the post-modern cosmopolitanism of the most influential poet from the British Isles born in the 1950s. Though Lasdun has audibly learned from both these writers, in *Landscape with Chainsaw* he has his own style fully deployed:

> After the glassworks failed and the dairy farms,
> battened onto the shrapnel tracts
> clearcut for the furnace, failed in turn,
> and the last resort gave up its empty rooms
> to chipmunks and rattlesnakes, the facts

> dampened all but the simplest dreams:
> scraping a living; tending a bit of garden.
>
> I didn't think I'd like it but I did…

Here, once more, he skilfully builds up a syntactically-taut texture of description with associations of consonants and vowels, with unobtrusive rhymes and apt metres. What's more, he combines the rising curve of descriptive intensity with a natural drop into plain-talking assertion – one that avoids any trace of hapless bathos. 'Bluestone', of which this is the opening, is among a number of near perfect pieces to add to a personal selection of favourites.

In his *TLS* piece, Stephen Burt praises the longer poems like 'Returning the Gift' at the expense of others in the book: 'To compare these nicely balanced, seriocomic works to the brief, emblematic lyric poems Lasdun writes on the same subject ('Chainsaw I', 'Chainsaw II') is to see how thoroughly Lasdun's talents depend on his having a story to tell.' While it may be true that Lasdun can skilfully manage a narrative poem in stanzas, and evidently one or two of the book's shortest pieces reward with the minutiae of their technique in ways that Burt appears to have no taste for, I would contest his assumption that Lasdun needs a story so as go about his work. Some of his best pieces, both here and in his earlier books, are mid-length lyrics of circumstance and occasion that certainly sketch a situation, but stop short of a fully-fledged narrative. Take, for example, 'The Revenant', 'Curator', or 'The Recovery' from *Woman Police Officer in Elevator* and 'Locals', 'Van Maanan's Star', 'The Tie-Dye T-Shirt', or 'Bluestone' from *Landscape with Chainsaw*. Which is why it come as a bit of a surprise to find Lasdun seeming to have given this sort of thing up for the pure poetry of 'Blue Mountain's coyotes / closing in for the kill.' If he isn't joking (and a new poem called 'The Skaters' in the *LRB* suggests that he might have been) then it will certainly mean a loss for poetry. Still, James Lasdun is a writer with more than one string to his bow – a fact that Burt wants to minimise by denigrating other claims of his to our attention. But then if it's a story you want, his first novel, *The Horned Man*, is out this year from Norton. Poetry's loss, if 'Happy the Man' must be accepted as a true swansong, will more than likely be fiction's gain.

THINGS AS THEY ARE:
RAE ARMANTROUT

Working the vein she has developed in her previous volumes, Rae Armantrout's version of a late modernist minimalism continues to generate stylish poems of thoughtful reflectiveness. *Itself* is a beautifully produced book of three sections ('Itself', 'Membrane', 'Live Through'), suggesting progressively evolving concerns, the titles of individual poems frequently indicating associated meditations on related themes: 'Two and Two', 'Personhood', 'The Couple', 'End User', 'Houses', 'Home'... Though superficially disorientating in their extremely short lines, brief numbered sections, or parts separated by text-ornaments, or their rapid changes of topic focus, her poems are built on profoundly long-serving strategies.

Like so many of the pieces collected here, 'Geography' is built in three parts, a seventeenth-century religious sonnet at least in this respect, with a statement, a development, and a resolution:

> Touch each chakra
> in turn and say,
>
> 'Nothing shocks me.'

The energy points in what is called the subtle body, not the physical, already start thoughts about differences between entities in themselves, in their various other incarnations. So we start with a body and its self-identity, then its self-understanding, which involves attempts, material and spiritual, to become immune to the shocks wrought upon it by, for instance, 'Love and Death', as Bernard Spencer's 'Behaviour of Money' has it. The 'me' in quotation marks above is not the author exactly, not least because the opening imperative can be both self- and other-addressed. Then appear some seemingly routine shocks:

> Watching bombs fall
> on Syria,
>
> we feel serious,

occupied,

not preoccupied
as we were

previously.

'Syria' generates 'serious' as if the adjective from the noun; and this must tacitly be a standard criticism of self-importance in liberal consciences, when nothing is done, because we are merely watching. Here the drama of self-identity is recast in other ethical terms: we are 'preoccupied' in ordinary usage with our own troubles, and so are 'occupied' by those of others, though it is implied that we are also implicated in that occupation, a word with military associations:

'Makes me end
where I begun,'

wrote John Donne,

turning love
into geometry.

More than one Donne poem is implied, the thought triggered by her title 'Geography', for the metaphysical poet is a transit point linking it to 'geometry', words sharing an 'earth' prefix. Armantrout doesn't quite quote the final line of his 'Valediction Forbidding Mourning', because she divides its tetrameter at its mid-point, wittily finding her line-end where he had only marked a caesura. Donne's love poem is about a couple separating and yet, like splayed dividers, not separating. Armantrout finesses a rhyme on the poet's name and gives the three sections of her poem concealed, echoic end-chimes: 'me … previously … geometry.' The other poem of Donne's is 'On his Mistress Going to Bed' with its gendered geographies: 'O my America! my new-found-land, / My kingdom, safeliest when with one man mann'd'. Though not so sexualised, Armantrout's poem too is about self and other, each thing being itself, and yet all things being in processes of relationship with everything else – associated guiding ideas that inform a great range of occasions in the collection.

It's true of the poems' techniques as well, for they are lyrics by one person manned, and yet driven to find relationship with others, as does Donne's, whose analogies with discovery and colonisation remind us of how compromised our culture's senses of relationship with others can be – firmly underlined by the Syrian section of Armantrout's 'Geography'. Back in 1918, in his magazine *Nord-Sud,* Pierre Reverdy memorably formulated this key aspect of modern poetry in 'L'image', which he said 'ne peut naître d'une comparaison mais du rapprochement de deux réalités plus ou moins éloignées' and that the more 'les rapports des deux réalités rapprochées seront lointains et justes, plus l'image sera fort – plus elle aura de puissance émotive et de réalité poétique.' For modern poetry the comparison was taken to weaken by syntactic contamination the identities of the things compared, while, without some form of relevant connectedness poetry would relinquish any claim to sense making. The appeal of collaged realities, distant from each other yet aptly collocated, is that, like disjunctive metaphors, they suggest meanings without the deformation by authorial direction of the two entities. Armantrout's poetry remains firmly in this field and has had the skill to find new bottles for what often tastes like enjoyably familiar wines.

For even Reverdy was bringing fresh starkness to a much older poetic mode, as evidenced by Samuel Johnson's notorious characterisation of metaphysical wit, which may be 'considered as a kind of *discordia concors;* a combination of dissimilar images or discovery of occult resemblances in things apparently unlike.' In the metaphysical poets – and Johnson names Donne among them in his 'Life of Cowley' – 'most heterogeneous ideas are yoked by violence together; nature and art are ransacked for illustrations, comparisons, and allusions; their learning instructs and their subtlety surprises; but the reader commonly thinks his improvement dearly bought, and, though he sometimes admires, is seldom pleased.' Johnson contrasts such wit with poetry proper, but it has been the business of poetry over the last century to yoke wit and poetry, even by violence, together; and then to find ways in which it may also please readers. 'A Conceit', playing upon colloquial and literary uses of the word, is appropriately enough the second poem in Armantrout's *Itself.*

Nevertheless, a regrettable loss in such minimalist poetry is its formally renouncing expressions of critically un-alienated emotion. Her poetry references feeling, as in 'Watching bombs fall' 'we feel serious', but these lines don't attempt to embody how such an experience might

184 The Personal Art

physically compel. Her rhythm and line-endings are a structuring of thought and position, its thinking through by mental leaps (just such leaps as Reverdy's theory of the image requires for its functioning), a thinking that may carry with it implicated feelings, but not usually embodied or expressed ones. 'You' ends with the words 'not unhappy', again noting feeling rather than attempting to evoke it, while it begins with what might look like such an occasion: 'I discovered you at eleven, listening / to the Everly Brothers / singing 'Dream, Dream, Dream.' Citing a line from its lyric, though, her poem takes off into what feel like off-putting conceptualisations:

> Whenever I want you,
>
> longing puts distance
> between us
>
> and a supposed object –
>
> a space awash
> in possibility.

The way you talk about relationship changes the object of your reflections (the relationship), even at the moment you are attempting to say things about 'it'. The idea of a thing 'itself' might then be forever lost (to be found as 'possibility') in and by speech, pointing again at how Armantrout's poetry is one of microscopic linguistic scepticism.

So in 'Split', for instance, she articulates what looks like the opposite of her book title's identity condition. Here the interlocutors are a 'you' who again might be herself in part-selves, or might be others she is criticizing, for it is because 'you dodge / yourselves / by branching' that 'sights strike me / as' – at which the first section abruptly ends. The second and fourth then exemplify this seeing something as something else:

> A muscular gray cat
> trots
>
> along the top of
> the cinderblock wall

separating my couch
from the supermarket.

This resembles objectivist-style notation by a William Carlos Williams,
or other traditionally modernist way of reporting on things being what
they are – though likely to be changed, of course, on Wallace Stevens'
'blue guitar', or in the attribution of a use to the wall itself:

I take these
white streaks

of truck

glimpsed
between branches

to be blossoms.

The verbal actions in 'Split' are carefully discriminated: in the first 'sights
strike me', in the second the verbs are attributed to things, the lyrical
subject only referenced in the possession of the 'couch', while in the
third 'I take' and the object of perception is transformed ('In a Station
of the Metro' fashion) from an urban to a natural object. Armantrout
underlines such affinities when in 'Sponsor' she parodies the first part
of Stevens' 'Thirteen Ways of Looking at a Blackbird': 'Among twenty
brown hills / the only moving thing / was the Coca-Cola truck.' Ron
Silliman in his foreword to Armantrout's *Veil: New and Selected Poems*
(2001) suggests that 'The peculiar fate of the American world may be
that the most serious questions can only be posed through the vocabulary
of U.S. culture, which infantilises everything it touches.' While some
would put the 'Coca-Cola truck' in the poem as the figure for such a
serious question, others would because it enlivens the scene, and yet
others because it was there. 'Pop' ambiguities slither simultaneously in
all three directions.

A rationale for a minimalist technique, with its roots reaching back
into many traditions, is that it lays bare the means of its own poetic
action. Armantrout has adapted an entire repertoire of poetic techniques
to this end, including the words in philosophical scare marks, sudden
code switches, the dismembered poetic lines highlighting individual

words, and the foregrounding of meaning-bearing figures. Such strategies are based, I suspect, on equally deeply rooted suspicions of the arbitrariness of aesthetic imaginings, dangers in irrational feelings, and poetic trafficking with connections that lack rational justification – and now territory occupied by corporate desire-management. In her final poem, 'New Way', Armantrout may, or may not, have let a colloquial ambiguity get away from her when she writes: 'Just put words / down, one / after the last.' Even when they denigrate ('put … down') words, scrupulous poets are benefitting from their infinite flexibility and meaningfulness. 'We punch our secret / code onto the image', Armantrout asserts in the same poem, and this is what we do too attending to hers.

JOHN MATTHIAS:
SPEAKING PERSONALLY

'But still one need not fail', as Marianne Moore put it in her poem 'In
the Public Garden',

> to wish poetry well
> where intellect is habitual –
> glad that the Muses have a home and swans –
> that legend can be factual;
>   happy that Art, admired in general,
> is always actually personal.

And in that spirit I would like, here, to try and speak personally about
John Matthias's poetry, especially about a few of the poems in which he
himself speaks personally. Let me begin with some brief scene setting,
looking back over thirty years. In September 1976 my first-wife-to-be
found a tiny flat with bright yellow-painted walls, an attic conversion in
5b Herschel Road, just beyond Clare Hall in Cambridge, England. As
chance would have it, John Matthias, with his wife and daughters, came
to take up residence in Clare Hall at more or less the same time. I can't
recall how I heard there was an American poet staying in Cambridge;
but however I did, the name rang a bell, for in Spring 1975 I had found
a copy of his anthology, *23 Modern British Poets*, in a public library in
London and read much of its contents. Autumn 1976 was a time to
attempt new beginnings. I had co-edited the first issue of the magazine
Perfect Bound the previous summer, and John would give us 'After the
Death of Chekhov' for our second issue, a poem I'm especially fond
of and have written about elsewhere. That lyric is inscribed 'for Bob
Hass', and, as if to underline that poetry 'is always actually personal',
during the following year its dedicatee visited Cambridge, and together
we attended a lecture by the painter and art critic John Golding. In
those days I was trying to find a suitable and yet congenial direction
for doctoral research, attempting to paint and exhibit canvases in oils
and acrylics, and writing poems that would, a few of them, eventually
appear in early pamphlets and books. John will have been among the
first published poets I met and talked to at any length, certainly the

first American. He spoke of larger-than-life personages like his teacher John Berryman, of Yvor Winters, and Robert Bly. At some point he mentioned a forthcoming issue devoted to translation of the Leeds-based magazine *Poetry and Audience*, and suggested I try them – which is how three versions from Pierre Reverdy appeared in print. It was among my first publications in magazine outside student poetry circles, and for such reasons, among innumerable others then and later, I owe a personal debt of gratitude to the subject of this essay.

Introducing a talk which he calls a 'Self-Reading and a Reading of the Self', the poet cites Morris Dickstein asserting that

> a crisis of feeling is a consistent, unrecognised symptom of contemporary criticism itself. As our critical vocabularies have flourished on the analytic side, they have atrophied on the affective side. We have no accepted language in which to examine what really moves us in a writer.

However true this may be, it's possible to suspect that the phrase 'accepted language' locates its concern within institutional parameters where practitioners can feel that permission has been granted by means of an 'accepted language'. Speaking personally, after all, can only have value if it means something perpetually other than succumbing to the jargon of the schools, even should that be unimaginably revivified to include an affective one. This is like saying that it is more important to have people in the discipline, than to have the discipline in people.

Robert Archambeau begins his introduction to *Word Play Place* by locating a similar split in one mapping of American verse at the end of the twentieth century. He cites Alan Shapiro's sense that debate about the art 'does seem to divide itself roughly into two opposing aesthetic camps: one based on the lyric of subjective life, the other in the skepticism of the intellect'. This is not quite Marianne Moore in her public garden, finding that in the poetry she wishes well 'intellect is habitual', 'legend can be factual' and 'Art… is always actually personal.' Though arguing that Matthias in his practice is an 'integrative poet' whose work challenges such a divide, Archambeau underlines the division when he notes: 'if the lyric and epistolary side of his work receives less treatment in the present volume then the arcane and experimental side, it is not because the intimate and accessible poems are less important to Matthias's achievement… it is simply that the more abstruse poems require (and reward) a more extensive critical scrutiny.' Matthias, in this account, doesn't so much integrate the 'lyric' and the 'arcane' as switch from one side of the divide to the other, and the poet agrees:

> I've of course always written, and continue to write, poems of both kinds. In fact, the dialectic of my work seems to demand a poem of some simplicity and directness following completion of something oblique, allusive, and difficult. Even this year I followed 'Working Progress, Working Title,' perhaps the most experimental poem I've ever written, with 'Swell,' a poem about sitting in a fishing boat with my wife on Walloon Lake in Michigan.

Conceiving of 'both kinds' is distinct from thoroughly integrating the lyrical and the intellectually sceptical, in what might be the modernist holy grail of a non-dissociated sensibility. There is no end of evidence to support viewing Matthias's oeuvre as played across the tennis net of such a divide; though it is also possible to see how both types of poem are inflected with the characteristics of the other. Such inflections are, still, not the same thing as the poetry of an integrated sensibility – as that was fictively located before the English Civil War in T. S. Eliot's early criticism, another context in which 'legend can be factual' perhaps.

Dickstein's remarks, and Matthias's citing them, are a thread of the long romantic agony intensifying and etiolating itself in the dilemmas of modernism (and in the quandaries of literature as an academic subject developing contemporaneously). Such divisions, dilemmas and quandaries are likely to be implied in a collection of academic essays on a contemporary poet, where 'the more abstruse poems require (and reward) a more extensive critical scrutiny.' Matthias came to maturity as a poet with the immediate double inheritances of modernism and the confessionals; further, the confessional poet to whom he was closest is the John Berryman who did not have the means to survive at a distance from the academy. Berryman, like many another, had to maintain the Dickstein division within his working and imaginative life. Yet perhaps the first volume of ur-confessional poetry to win a prize and make a mark was Ezra Pound's *The Pisan Cantos*, winner of the Bollingen Prize in 1948, an award that Berryman defended, when John Matthias was seven years old. The defeat of his economic-cultural projects, and their delusive association with Mussolini's regime, are sustained in this part of his long poem by inflecting them with nostalgia, autobiography, and personal speaking: 'as no one else will carry a message, / say to La Cara: amo' or 'Tard, très tard je t'ai connue, la Tristesse, / I have been hard as youth sixty years'. Matthias's teachers and his educational progress led him to attempt (and the sustaining of life and family would required him) to maintain within an academic institution his evolving version of both personal and intellectually projecting strands.

Back in Cambridge in 1977, John also gave us the first part of the 'Stefan Batory' poems for *Perfect Bound*, the sequence about crossing the Atlantic on a Polish boat:

> To begin with a name –
> Katarsky –
>   To begin
> to leave with a name, Polish,
> for a Polish ship named
> for another, for Stefan Batory.
>   Name of Katarsky.
> Name of Stefan Batory.

We edited the magazine in a small student committee, and much to my embarrassment it was decided to pass on this submission. Yet in that decision there may lurk a larger issue about his work that will help focus poems I most admire and go back to for a renewal of bodily wellbeing, imaginative refreshment, reassurance, and intellectual stimulus – which is what, speaking personally, I haunt poetry for. The opening lines above are a bravura instance of an ability to draw recalcitrant materials, and especially polysyllabic proper names, into the sonic contours of a sustained poem. This capacity is at the heart of Matthias's oeuvre, and without it his achievement is unimaginable. Marjorie Perloff has commented on the 'nominalism' of nostalgic passages about European café society before the Great War in *The Pisan Cantos*:

> The seeming excess of Poundian names – the multiplication of restaurants, cafés, and those who people them – is thus offset by the recycling of a given unit in a context that changes its thrust in what is in fact a dense economy of meanings. The acute

awareness of difference is accompanied by the concomitant play of likeness – a linking of items that seem quite unrelated.

Proper names in poetry bring in history and knowledge of the world, helping, among other things, with the justification of a combined literary-scholarly approach, since the poem including history will require at least some learning on the part of the poet and reader. This is why Archambeau can occasion the work of his book in the side of Matthias's work that calls for explication. Yet, as in *The Pisan Cantos*, poetry replete with proper names in the culture of post-Romantic individualism shades off via arcane knowledge, or a highly individualised perspective on such knowledge, into a form of speaking personally. In a self-explication of his poem 'Kedging', Matthias has remarked: 'Although it's going to sound like name-dropping, a bit of family history may help to open up the poem.' Entire stretches of his large oeuvre are dependent upon this 'name-dropping' strategy, and upon his readers' accepting or coming to terms with it. 'After the Death of Chekhov' is no less challenging, beginning 'Anton Pavlovich has died / At Badenweiler, a spa'. Still, this is not as incantatory a 'name' poem as 'Stefan Batory', being written in short sentences and pitched at a spoken intimately personal level.

My own qualm with proper names in the soundscapes of poems is prompted not only because proper names function by means of historical, geographical, or literary bodies of knowledge more or less available to anonymous readers. The salience and oriented significance of such names are notionally fixed at a distance from the shifting drama of the poem's meanings which is not merely in the spaces of history, geography, and other information, but in the poet's shifting, usually implicit relations to those spaces. Further, this area of speaking personally sets up a reader-relationship with the language of a poem of a different order from that of the non-proper nouns. Other signs of my qualm might be that proper names look as if they refer to factual specificities, but turn out to be vaguely and yet prejudicially emotive concepts as when 'Ezra Pound and T. S. Eliot' show up in Bob Dylan's 'Desolation Row', or when someone says an experience is Kafkaesque. The much-loved Pierre Reverdy ('my heart is in my pocket') only rarely allowed a proper name into his poems, markedly at odds with the work of his great fan Frank O'Hara, who made his 'Personist' art from a Pollock-like splatter-drip of higher gossip coterie name-dropping.

One of the facts about my experience of art, one I have puzzled about long and hard, is that there are some works which lodge in the mind and come back hauntingly, while others run off its surfaces like the proverbial water off a duck's back. Further, I am not able to predict or determine which works will stick and which won't. Nor am I able to presume that if works don't stick this is a sign of something wrong with them, and not with me. I can also feel mildly resentful about these limits, and try to trick myself into appreciating work that doesn't initially stick, by, for instance, returning to it and looking again. Nevertheless, there are poems that give me the shivers when I first read them, and there are ones that don't. The poems I'm going to write about in this essay are by no means the only John Matthias poems I like but they are ones that have particularly registered, and stayed around in my mental landscape. Now, a natural assumption might be that the way to explore what makes the memorable ones memorable would be to speak personally, and engage in some sustained introspection. This might not be mistaken, since we are shaped by our experiences, and our experience of art, so that my taste is of interest to me precisely because it is mine. Yet there is accounting for taste. The one thing that distinguishes me from a bloke who doesn't know much about art but knows what he likes is that I can give reasons for *my* tastes, reasons intelligible in *your* terms. So you may not like what I like; but you can know and, I hope, appreciate why I like the things I do.

Richard Wollheim has a passage touching on issues related to how such a situation could be humanly possible in *Art and its Objects*, a book I was reading back at the time of those first meetings in mid-1970s Cambridge (scrawled in pencil on the half-title page of my copy I find 'John Matthias: 65898' – his phone number in Clare Hall):

> When we say *L'embarquement pour l'Île de Cythère*, or the second section of *En Blanc et Noir*, expresses a particular feeling, and we mean this intransitively, we are misunderstood if we are then asked 'What feeling?' Nevertheless, if someone tells us that to him the painting or the piece of music means nothing, there are many resources we have at our disposal for trying to get him to see what is expressed. In the case of the music, we could play it in a certain way, we could compare it with other music, we could appeal to the desolate circumstances of its composition, we could ask him to think why he should be blind to this

specific piece: in the case of the painting, we could read to him *A Prince of Court Painters*, pausing, say, on the sentence 'The evening will be a wet one', we could show him other paintings by Watteau, we could point to the fragility of the resolutions in the picture. It almost looks as though in such cases we can compensate for how little we are able to say by how much we are able to do. Art rests on the fact that deep feelings pattern themselves in a coherent way all over our life and behaviour.

What might be added to this, so as to prevent 'our life and behaviour' from being read off as cultural presumption is that there are aspects of life and behaviour in any society at all which can be understood as ways of acculturating core group survival needs – and these also pattern themselves coherently over the artefacts of a culture, so that you may not share those ways of expressing meanings, but you can appreciate why they do it that way. So I'm going to try and account for why the following poems work for me by describing the poems – for the meaning of a work of art is this interaction between an art object and a consciousness responding to it; and it's the describable specificity of the object which makes it possible for these meanings mutually to enrich those participating in cultural conversations. Describing the poems doesn't mean speaking any less personally; it means finding an organised set of materials that can be experienced by means of the senses in conjunction with a conceptualizing self-awareness, and then comparing and contrasting responses to those organised materials. Because 'deep feelings pattern themselves in a coherent way all over our life and behaviour', by describing the artistic patterning I offer an account of how outward criteria have been shaped for the expression of such deep feeling, and how the forms of those outward criteria have been read as meaningful. To understand even your own feelings you have to learn how to interpret the outward criteria to which you respond, the type of boy or girl to whom you find yourself attracted, for example.

John Matthias published his second collection, *Turns*, with Anvil Press in the UK, the year before his sabbatical in Cambridge, and I bought a copy in Heffers. There I found a poem memorable for the oblique expressiveness of its voice, one that lodged itself permanently in my memory, thanks in particular to its closing lines. The poem, in three sections, is called 'Survivors'. It goes straight into a voice speaking personally; though, aside from the fact that this voice is being quoted in Matthias's poem, it's not the poet's:

> A letter arrives in answer
> To mine – but six years late…
> 'John,' it says,
>   'Dear John …' and
> 'I remember absolutely nothing.
> What you say is probably
> All true; for me those
> Years are blank. I believe
> You when you say you knew
> Me then, that we were friends,
> And yet I don't remember you
> At all, or all those others
> Who had names, or anyone. You see,
>
> The fittest don't survive –
> It's the survivors.'

The momentarily poised, but swooping, and unstable line ends, the repetitions of 'All' like a musical theme, these set up the terms of this poem's musical ordering, and introduce a motif that will be returned to for the work's finale. The situation of the first part must be the American 1960s, perhaps some of the least forgotten years in the twentieth century, but here I imagine we are dealing with a Vietnam War veteran whose traumatic experiences have led to memory loss, or a victim of drug use that has had the same effects, or both and more. Matthias is receiving the friendship equivalent of a 'Dear John' letter. It is as if the failure of the person to remember has also annulled the validity or even existence of the writer, the other people, and their names. This impressively suggests that memories which aren't shared are not memories, as can happen to the very old when they recall factual happenings from their lives and are thought by their young carers to be suffering from senile dementia.

The next part of the poem relates the letter writer's mental damage to the relations between the sexes, a theme – the strength of supportive women – that runs as an undercurrent throughout Matthias's oeuvre, and one that has its own relationship, as I hope to show, with the American 1960s and beyond. Yet John does this by taking what, for the course of the second section, might seem like a skewed direction, making a sustained simile about how old women with their operated-on bodies and tradition-sustaining memories are survivors too:

> Like old women, burying their
> Husbands, burying their sons, lasting
> It out for years without their breasts
> Or wombs, with ancient eyes,
> Arthritic hands, and memories like
> Gorgeous ships they launch
> Despairingly to bring back all
> Their dead, and which, as if constructed
> By some clumsy sonneteer, betray them
> Instantly and sink without a trace.

The second part of the poem could itself seem to be sinking without at trace at this point. The unstable line-endings are sustained into this section, it is true; but here, more routinely, they stubbornly dramatise the 'keeping going' of the old women's bodies and minds. The poem also adverts to the possibility of its clumsiness by evoking the spectre of that bad sonneteer – and this is something that, again speaking personally, can never be banished from what's called the creative process, a process that often manifests itself as a stop-start series of qualms and dilemmas, the risk without which art cannot happen, one risk being that the work you are engaged in may not come off. The third section of 'Survivors' sets itself going by a reorientation, a form of self-correction, or invocation of another possibility, though one that preserves the gender distinction the second part is founded upon – a gender distinction with a significant period-flavour to which, as I say, like General Douglas MacArthur I shall return:

> Or women not so old –
>   but always
> Women, not the men who knock
> Their brains and bodies against
> Fatal obstacles & spit their blood
> On pillows & their hearts on sleeves
> At forty-five to die of being fit.

I've known a woman keep her watch
Beside a bed of botched ambition
Where her man lay down & took
Five years to die…

And though I drove one January night
Through freezing rain into Ohio –
And though I hurried,
Seeking the words of the dying –
All I found was a turning circle of women,
All I found was the lamentation of survivors.

Matthias drives into Ohio, his home state, to get back before relatives die, perhaps, so as to exchange last words with them, but all he finds is 'a turning circle', something automobiles have too. What the women are doing in this line is part of the poem's subliminal workings. Are they turning around the corpse? Are they turning away from the poet? Certainly, being a 'circle', they appear to exclude him from their lamentation, as if he were not one of the 'survivors', but a poet, standing outside so as to find and evoke. The poem also re-orientates itself by bringing in the first-person singular for the first time ('I've known …'), which then builds to the anaphora of 'And though I … / And though I … / All I … /All I …' So it might be thought that the poem is about finding the space to speak personally, to come back from the non-existence of someone else's amnesia. This isn't just or only self-assertion, but a poet's device for intensifying the sense of life, and death, being registered. The speaker doesn't get there in time, and what he finds once more gives the poem's title. The sudden flurry of ampersands in the third section perhaps indicates the influence of Berryman's dream song style. The narrative-like structuring of affects in 'Survivors', or, for that matter, the use of anaphora to build up closing tension, and the way that the poem ends on the word of its title, these are readable forms for the patterning of emotions around kinds of loss and disorientation that the poem thoroughly manifests by dramatizing them with incident, but not by overtly stating them. Yet Matthias has also made an art of telling, of spelling out, what his poem is about; and his success in this area, against the conventional wisdoms that 'less is more' and that you must 'show' and not 'tell', strikes me as both intriguing and worth responding to personally.

Acronyms can be funny things: I started reading 'C.P.R.' from Matthias's millennium collection, *Pages*, with the idea that it might be set on the Canadian Pacific Railway, as in Basil Bunting's 'Gin the Goodwife Stint': 'Twa pund emigrant / on a CPR packet.' But 'cardiopulmonary resuscitation' is what the poem's about. Notwithstanding that initially mistaken approach, it is a poem that has also stuck firmly in my personal anthology of Matthias's work:

> Poem after poem I've written to you, love,
> songs and foolish valentines,
> curt demanding notes, confused apologies and
>
> poems in the mind I dare not show you
> or write down, their praise
> of you so pornographic that they'd
>
> set the eye aflame or burn the hand
> that touched them.

The glimpse into the poet's erotic imagination here doesn't signal a 1960s lack of inhibitions, though the fact that he can bring it into the poem may well have a relation to that shift in the borderline between the public and private. Consider what paraphernalia of mythology and aesthetics Pound had to call upon so as to express ideas about heterosexuality in *The Cantos*. Rather, Matthias's allusion to his erotic fantasy life marks the limit to speaking personally in this poem that is being preserved – and this shows that, although the poem is addressed to his wife, it is also addressed to the anonymous 'us'. The poet is carefully locating the poem at the culturally and historically specific membrane between the private and the public, which, for poetry, is the place where it does some of its most important political work. He is carefully locating it so as, once again, to celebrate the strength of women, by means of those faintly embarrassing thoughts about sexuality, poetic metre, and C.P.R. techniques:

> Wife,
> mistress, sister, mother of my lives and lines,
>
> one after the other for these thirty years,
> now three days a week you visit
> the Red Cross on Jefferson and learn

techniques no prosodist dare dream of
or any *Karma Sutra* recommend. Oh, I know –
you've saved my life before, time

after time, life after life, each time
more difficult the life that's saved, more
difficult the act of saving it. This

cold heart of mind

The phrase 'cold heart of mind' gives pause, with the sudden thought that it might be a typo for 'heart of mine' – though perhaps not, because there is an internal rhyme two lines later with 'how unkind if I could not respond' (a use of 'kind' that puns on its etymological links with 'kith and kin'). Yet even if not a typo, the phrase's nearness to the more colloquially romantic collocation is strikingly suggestive, for it indicates that this poet in his life and art has also suffered from that split between what Dickstein called 'the analytic side' and 'the affective side'. After all, 'heart of mind' might indicate an un-dissociated sensibility, were it not for the fact that it seems to be un-dissociated on the 'atrophied' side by means of the adjective 'cold'. If a typo, it's a fortuitously interesting slip, and if decided upon by the poet, it's no less personal a touch:

                        – now you'd pound it back
        to beating for you if you had to.
        And how unkind if I could not respond!

        A letter from my cousin says her husband
        'died peacefully in his sleep.' He wasn't even sick!
        If I must die, I'd rather die awake

        and staring in amazement while you filled my lungs
        with all the air your lungs could gasp
        and pounding on my chest

        in just and utter outrage over what I'd done.

'C.P.R.' is one of those poems addressed to long-suffering poets' wives, in which the things they may legitimately complain about are perhaps

being re-enacted in the poem that is apologizing for them. But there's
no way out of that double bind, and recidivism is the poet's natural
vice. But let's not forget that the second-person address in the poem
is its greatest fiction, a necessary one in which the poem pretends to
be addressed solely to the wife, in order to dramatise feelings for her,
but so as to articulate a sense of relationship that may, it is hoped, be
of value for anyone other than her. As so often with poems located
between the first and second person pronouns, poems which imply the
presence of a 'you' who is not the interlocutor but the reader (and this
is its way of acting by osmosis between private and public), 'C.P.R.' is
written to make something happen. It affirms a bond, one that includes
the inevitability of the embarrassing – a kind of material pioneered
by Allen Ginsberg, laureate of personal embarrassment as political
fulcrum, in poems such as 'Aunt Rose' and *Kaddish*. The deployment of
the embarrassing affirms the value of such implicit bonds with readers,
by analogy, because it depends upon a trustful interpretation of these
matters that is implied and evoked by writing and publishing material
which is not just vulnerable because calibrated, but at the same time
not invulnerably defended against human frailty and embarrassment.
'C.P.R.' is an exemplary poem that manages to have the strength of
its weaknesses, and to occasion osmosis through the membrane that it
must also acknowledge.

My assumption was that the same could be said for the more
recent poem 'Missing Cynouai'. This piece, occasioned by the loss of
contact between the family and one of the Matthiases' two daughters,
might also seem to be trying to make something happen, in that if the
daughter were to get back in touch it would have served its purpose of
calling out to her. Yet 'Missing Cynouai' is not located in that complexly
triangulated ground between the first and second person pronouns in
poems. It appears raw and unguarded in its address to readers:

> My daughter hasn't spoken to me now for years.
> I don't know why. I'm sure there's a good reason.
> She must be angry about something, but she doesn't say.
> No letters and no calls. She's nearly thirty-three.

It too enlarges upon relations between both the sexes and the
generations, introducing thoughts of death as the fact that renders such
matters urgent at any time:

My mother won't speak any more at all, but I know why.
And I'm surprised I think about her almost every day.
I'm over sixty. She is – what does one say?
My father spoke up last when I was just my daughter's age.

I don't think he's angry any more.
He's very quiet though. What was it made him angry
For so so long? I'd like to ask him that.
And other things. I'm surprised that I think of him

Almost every day. I didn't used to think of him at all.
It seems to me I didn't think of him for thirty years.
I wish my daughter would pick up the phone and call.
Or write a letter. Or a card.

That his daughter hasn't spoken to him for years explains the impossibility of a first- and second-person relationship in the poem – though this should be acknowledged as a decision on the poet's part, an honest one, in that such a relationship could in theory be attempted by a composing poet. What interests me is whether the poem's first- and third-person relationship, with the address to readers unmediated via a known interlocutor, as in 'C.P.R.', nevertheless tries to make something happen, to re-establish contact (though more indirectly), or whether the poem's feeling comes from it being stranded, unable to make amends because there is no human relationship within which amends can be made. Then again, it could be both; it could be hoping for the former, while acknowledging the latter. In a poem about relationship, and, more specifically, about the poet's relations with his female family generations, 'Missing Cynouai' also makes use of the literary leverage in having others' writings coming to the rescue, occasioning the utterance of new matter, as, for a writer, it might be thought they should:

I saw her last at someone's funeral.
'At the funeral of tenderness,' said Mr. Berryman.
Who was my friend. A while ago!
My mother had an injury that would not mend.

He signed his poem about his daughter for my daughter.
That was 1969 when she was one.

> Some months later he himself was gone –
> But where? The daughter heavier, the father lighter there.

The relevant *Dream Song* is no. 385, the final poem cited in 'Missing Cynouai' as epigraph. Berryman's first verse, set, it would appear, in the autumn of 1962, when his first daughter, Martha, was still a baby, improvises on the themes of those busy being born and busy dying:

> My daughter's heavier. Light leaves are flying.
> Everywhere in enormous numbers turkeys will be dying
> and other birds, all their wings.
> They never greatly flew. Did they wish to?
> I should know. Off away somewhere once I knew
> such things.

The reason I can guess at the date of the poem's occasion is that in its second verse it suddenly sidles into the literary, referring to a long-time resident of John Matthias's state, Ohio: 'Or good Ralph Hodgson back then did, or does. / The man is dead whom Eliot praised.' After leaving his post as visiting professor at Tohoku University, Sendai, Japan, in 1938, with his American third-wife, Lydia Aurelia Bolliger (whom he had met when she was a missionary and teacher in Sendai), Hodgson settled in Minerva, Ohio, where he died, at the age of ninety-one, on 3 November 1962. Speaking personally, this makes Berryman's poem that bit more involving, for I also spent a decisive period of my life in the same town and the same job, managing to beat Hodgson's record as the English Department's most long serving visiting professor before leaving there in March 2005, after having held the post for fourteen years:

> Or good Ralph Hodgson back then did, or does.
> The man is dead whom Eliot praised. My praise
> follows and flows too late.
> Fall is grievy, brisk. Tears behind the eyes
> almost fall. Fall comes to us as a prize
> to rouse us toward our fate.

Such personal associations with Hodgson are the kinds of thought that cannot be factored out of responses to poems, or indeed poets' projections of what their poems might mean to others. They are inseparable from what may be involved in enjoying a poem and taking it to heart. This perhaps embarrassing fact is not a problem for poetry and the appreciation of poems, but it is for the academic study of poetry. My professional life has no intrinsic relevance to *Dream Song* no. 385, but its meaning for me cannot exclude that extraneous curriculum vitae, and poems of Matthias's find their fulcrums for imaginative leverage in just such intersections of the personal and the public, as indeed does Berryman in his knight's-moves from his daughter's weight, to turkeys at Thanksgiving, to Hodgson's affinity with birds and beasts, and so to his own death in Autumn. Poetry is also 'a form of life', in Wittgenstein's sense of the phrase, and one of the ways in which poets take part in it is by identifying themselves with other poets, by finding inspiration in the words of their seniors, as when the 'man is dead whom Eliot praised':

> My house is made of wood and it's made well,
> unlike us. My house is older than Henry;
> that's fairly old.
> If there were a middle   ground between things and the soul
> or if the sky resembled more the sea,
> I wouldn't have to scold
> my heavy daughter.

Berryman's daughter is so much heavier that she falls out of his eighteen-line, three-stanza template for the *Dream Songs* sections. Yet it seems a bit odd, aside from the improvising sound associations of rhyme words (from 'older' to 'old', and then via 'soul' to 'scold'), that Berryman should be having to scold his daughter when she can only have been a few months old, and it's hard to think that, while 'heavier' in Matthias's poem could include the idiomatic usage of 'difficult', in Berryman's it can mean anything other than Martha's weight. The daughter in the poem might be a baby, being sensed as growing because harder to lift – as is the Cynouai that Berryman signed his poem for. But John Matthias can't scold his daughter, whom he has told us is now thirty-three-years-old. If anything he fears that she is, in effect, doing the scolding, for which she has her reasons even if these remain unexpressed. His poem concludes:

> She must be angry with something, but she doesn't say.
> Daughters frequently are angry, but often

Only for a moment or a day. I think she knows her old address.
I'm not certain where she lives right now. I think she

May have married someone, but I'm not entirely sure.
I'd be glad to meet him if she has. And her.
I'm surprised that I think about her almost every day.
I'm over sixty. She is – what does one say?

People used to love the music of her name, say *Cynouai*
just to savor once or twice the pleasure of the sound.
I sing it silently and carry it, a heaviness,
Around, around…

Missing's neither having lost nor found.

Like many of Matthias's 'speaking personally' poems, it seems to me to
be trying to make something happen, attempting to have a transitive
relationship with the world (as I would argue all the best poetry does);
and this makes it especially vulnerable, because it can't guarantee that it
will function, and so can appear unusually powerless; yet, once again,
that's its strength and lasting value. Although 'Missing Cynouai' does this
even more 'weakly' by 'wishing' and 'hoping', rather than by deploying
one of those theatrically performative-like 'Dear ghost' gestures, as in the
second verse of 'In Memory of Eva Gore-Booth and Con Markiewicz',
that allows Yeats's poetry its unusual power. Matthias's, though, is
poetry strong enough to be able to mobilise the strength of is evident
weaknesses, in many respects a much more human, and, in the current
circumstances I would also suggest, a more valuable thing.

Berryman also makes a couple of appearances in *Swell*, a seven-part
poem first published separately in 2003. The first of these visitations
triangulates their ages, thinking of Matthias's sixty years, on a sabbatical
visit to Walloon Lake, Michigan, in 2001:

Who at ten or twenty sees himself in forty, fifty years?
Robert Lowell barely made it: Berryman,
who sat cross-legged in my Salt Lake City room
and recited every word verbatim of *A Clean, Well-Lighted Place*
only got to fifty-eight. He said that story was a poem, and

he was right. I'm older than my teacher was
when he died. I'm older than Lowell. About the age
when Hemingway, who, like his father, like crazy Mr. B,
knew he'd had enough.

In case I was worrying that this poem has turned to thoughts of self-murder, the poet reassures his readers that 'I haven't had enough. / I'm greedy and want more. I like it here on this swell lake'. *Swell* takes stock of things, bringing forward an unusually candid and personal note, so much so that the matter of Hemingway and friends disappears from sight, reduced to a device for occasioning this more intimate material, just as the poem's presenting idea of writing a piece about catching a fish is left behind. *Swell* thus appears to achieve a breakthrough to a differently open and personally self-explanatory style. The poet has acknowledged both its unusual vulnerability and the ease of its writing: 'It's in some ways a very risky and vulnerable poem… I wrote it very quickly, and with greater ease than is usual for me.' It was going to be a poem about catching a fish in boyhood, something Matthias didn't then continue to do, as the work ends by spelling out, again in a second person address to his wife, Diana:

This started out to be a poem about a bass I caught when
I was ten. And never once again.
You'll read to me tonight, I know. Whether Proust or
Mother Goose, it does its work. It's no big show
at the Chautauqua with a smell of gaslight, but it's exactly swell
enough, no more. It's great. In my life it's starting to get late.
We haven't yet found Windermere
and now the sun has set entirely on the lake.

Beautifully ambivalent, this close is also incitement to continue. The method in *Swell* may have been there from the start: 'After the Death of Chekhov' also has its 'red herring' in the seemingly irrelevant tale from Chekhov's biography which comes to express the friendship between Bob Hass and John Matthias. Yet there is a difference, for the early poem is entirely metaphorical in function, to the extent that I could use it as an illustration of Wittgenstein's praise of a poem by Uhland in his letter to Engelmann: 'if only you do not try to utter what is unutterable then nothing gets lost. But the unutterable will be –

unutterably – contained in what has been uttered.' In 'After the Death of Chekhov' there is no speaking personally of a direct kind, while, as the passage from *Swell* indicates, there's an unfolded expressiveness that the younger poet could evoke, on occasion, through implication and indirection alone.

Swell seems to be among the first poems to display a fully developed version of what was to be called the 'kedging' method of the later poems of memory and self-evaluation. If you compare it with works from *Pages*, the tone is different, and the division Archambeau notes in Matthias's oeuvre between the documentary historical poems and the more personal ones is easier to sustain. Yet, even then, the former was as personal as you could wish in its unique deployment of such material, though still guardedly impersonal in its implications – a paradox, though not a surprising one. The techniques for 'kedging' are there: the use of Hemingway's connection with Walloon Lake as the kedge anchor, as it were, for the heave of the personal themes. So, to give a small example, the allusion to 'A Clean, Well-Lighted Place' in *Swell*, a short story about the insomnia of one old man who doesn't want to leave a closing café, helps to drag on the climactic matter of the poem, which I would suggest is the poet's insomnia, and the method adopted by himself and his wife to combat it, namely, reading him to sleep. The 'kedging' image, of writing poetry in the manner of sailors moving a boat across sandy shallows by fixing the anchor forward of the boat, and then winching it in as a way of dragging the boat across the ground, suggests a great deal of resistance to overcome, and it is worth reflecting that this resistance in the metaphor must be the poet's equivocal reluctance to speak personally.

Where did this new openness come from? Was it a question of reaching the same decade of his life as Pound was when he composed his own bit of kedging, *The Pisan Cantos*, written in the early autumn of 1945, when the poet was just sixty? One suggestion I have is that co-translating Jesper Svenbro had something to do with it. *Three-Toed Gull: Selected Poems*, translated from the Swedish by John Matthias and Lars-Håkan Svensson, also appeared in 2003. The striking thing about John's later poems is their openly self-explanatory autobiographical narrative-memoir mode, an absence of lyrical obliquity that can be heard in their collaborative rendering of the opening lines to Svenbro's 'Frascati':

During a certain period our friend Valentino
was of the decided opinion
that a rational account could be made of life
except on one single point: wine
was something so extraordinary
that its existence must be due to divine
intervention in the world.

Lars-Håkan Svensson's 'Postscript' informs us that 'the Roman poet Valentino Zeichen' alerted Svenbro to developments in Italian poetry during the 1970s and the 'various ways in which linguistic material of a supposedly non-literary kind could be incorporated in poetry'. Zeichen's own poems show one strand of this development, in that he found a way of making ironic allegories out of fragments of history and cultural knowledge. Behind the developments in Zeichen's poetry that influenced Svenbro so usefully lie the experiments of the neo-avant-garde Gruppo 63, and behind them the influence via translation of American modernist models such as that of William Carlos Williams on Vittorio Sereni. The likely influence of Svenbro's poetry on his American translator is thus yet another happy instance in the realm of international poetic relations of what Samuel Taylor Coleridge, in a rather different context, exclaimed about when speaking personally: 'O Sara! we receive but what we give'.

Swell and its use of Hemingway as the 'kedge anchor' material return me to the theme of 'Survivors', the fate of a fictionalised American maleness and its relation to strong supportive women. Here's the moment when the 'kedging' material makes its appearance – and in a context of speaking distinctly personally. *Swell* switches between a first and second person location relationship, as in the quotation above, and a first and third one, as below, suggesting that the more intimately explanatory relation with a reader also to be found in Svenbro's poetry grows out of, or is founded upon, a reassuring relation with a second person interlocutor allowing for a shift to relations with the larger world and implying that these are figured in the intimate ones of family and private life. In *Swell* the reader is included as the tacit second person in the triangulation of poet, world, and reader. The inscribed interlocutor, Diana Adams, the poet's British wife, occasions an enactment of, and talk to us about, that intimate relation:

Nights when I'm afraid and cannot sleep, Diana often says
Then shall I read? She means of course 'out loud.'
She knows that way it lasts a longer time. I always ask
for something that's too young for me, more likely
Pathfinder than Proust. It's what we have invented to
shut down the fear, and sent me off onto some quiet lake of peace.
She'll say, Some boy's adventure maybe?
How about your macho friend E.H.?
And I'll say, Adams, that's not fair! But I end up with
what I liked the best when I was twelve, & that was Adams
fishing here in Michigan.

It's not difficult to imagine that the works read might be John Buchan's
Greenmantle (1916) or Erskine Childers' *The Riddle of the Sands* (1903).
Even if not favourites of the twelve-year-old Matthias, they are nonetheless not far from that 'Some boy's adventure' category, if also once
aimed at imperial 'men' or 'old boys'. The strategy that the Matthiases
invented to fend off fear and insomniac anxieties are works of a fictional
fearlessness, used in a situation, and reported in a poem, where not only
is the auditor not living up to the image of fearless and intrepid manhood
being projected, but is allowing some sort of residual relevance for them
in his life to be both acknowledged and simultaneously dismissed.
This projection of an adventurous and heroic masculinity, dramatised
by trafficking with imperialist assumptions, rivalries, racist prejudices
and such, has become, or we would have hoped it had become, more
'fictional' as time has passed since Buchan published *The Thirty-Nine
Steps* in 1915 with a precise propagandistic purpose, one that is addressed
in the poem 'Kedging in Time' itself:

Pamela is actually asleep by now,
her daughter reading downstairs by the fire. Once again
her husband rushes toward the lighthouse just like a hero
in some romance – *Good show and cushy job.*
I say, Adams, that was damned impressive
though your lads got rather rattled by machine gun fire.
If you ask next morning what the
celebration is, Mr. Memory will say Remembrance Day –
and poppies blooming red in every field.

Yet, significantly, this material once again brings forward Matthias's vulnerably dependent relations with his wife, Diana, and so to the importance for an ordinarily flawed man of a loved woman in such a man's life – and how frankly irrelevant, and perhaps repulsive, that old 'fiction' of masculinity is to such a real man in the present and to his crucially supportive relationships. At one point in the essay 'Kedging in *Kedging in Time*' the young Matthias, opposed to the Vietnam war, finds himself amid an English crowd of British sea power veterans, including his future father-in-law, and doesn't quite know where to put himself when encountering this throw-back: 'Almost the first thing he said to me was that he wished the Brits were fighting with us in Viet Nam. For a 1960s peace activist, that made things quite awkward.' 'Kedging in Time' is an elegy not for the world of *Greenmantle* and that history, which Matthias manages to remain strategically even-handed about, perhaps because he is able to treat the real past as a form of fiction, since he makes such a point of its being shaped by such fictions, Oscar Wilde having a point when asserting that 'Things are because we see them, and what we see, and how we see it, depends on the arts that have influenced us' – though he was only able to put it so because the reverse was assumed to be un-contentiously true:

> there's sailing on the Alde. The American is not much of
> a sailor, but does what he is told. The river's difficult to navigate
> and full of sands and bars that can catch you at low tide
> and keep you for the night. They sail slowly out from Aldeburgh,
> past the squat Martello tower at Sloughden, down
> past Orford Ness, the castle keep and early warning
> radar nets, the bird sanctuary, through the mouth of Orford Haven,
> to the sea. The Captain smokes his pipe and snoozes in
> the sun. His daughter is the helmsman and is much preoccupied,
> though quite familiar with these waters where she's sailed
> since early youth and imagined wooden soldiers popping up
> in marshmist reeds and tipping Bismark helmets to the girls.
> Her mother rather likes the young American,
> but she doubts her husband does. At dinner he'd been going
> on about Virginia Woolf, his back against a bookcase
> full of Kipling, Buchan, Hope…

'Memory is shot by spies': as Matthias notes. This happens in the 1935 Alfred Hitchcock film of *The Thirty-Nine Steps*, but not in the book; and the poet wittily puts it like this to equivocate between the death of a capacity to remember and that of the music-hall character with that name in the film. 'Quand vous serez bien vieille', Ezra Pound writes in Canto 80, 'remember that I have remembered'. Matthias's memory is by no means shot, and his poem continues with his evoking by remembering: 'No one / pays attention to the little boat sailing in a mild breeze / along the coast of Suffolk.' Nor does he ever loses sight of the fact that the fictions which believers in the 'great game' lived by issued in the deaths of non-believers – and, in this light, I can't help thinking that the real topic of the poem, with its passing mentions of 'early warning / radar nets' and Jihad, is the American inheritance, and its consequences for our time, of this 'great game' approach to world historical power and control. So just as 'After the Death of Chekhov' is about the friendship between Matthias and Hass, something not directly addressed at any point, so too 'Kedging in Time' can be understood as an exploration of manhood in relations between British history and literature, explored via personal association and collage, and American history and literature – only alluded to rarely in passing moments. The activity of making history into something both painfully distinct and real, and yet a form of speaking personally, is clearly the thing John Matthias can do with this material, and it is what he does: 'No one fires a warning shot across their bow' and 'They sight no ship on the horizon', and, decisively in conclusion, 'There's nothing flying in the sky except the gulls.'

Though our acquaintance goes back over thirty years, many things have meant that for much of that time I was isolated in northern Japan and John in South Bend, Indiana. Indeed, in those states of isolation, it was the invention of e-mail that brought us back in contact, and to exchanging signed copies of new publications, as some poets do. I had rather expected that we wouldn't meet again. But nor was that to be, for thanks to the good offices of John Welle at Notre Dame and Randolph Petilos of Chicago University Press I was able to visit South Bend in late November 2006, to spend an evening with a group of colleagues including John and Diana. 'Because of certain medical problems and an accompanying claustrophobia, I never go to England any more,' the poet states towards the close of his accompanying essay 'Kedging in *Kedging in Time*'. Happily, though, John's problems and claustrophobia had eased enough for us to meet (thanks also to my eventual repatriation) not far from Trafalgar Square, London, during May 2008. We would stroll around the National Portrait Gallery, a place John said he preferred to the National itself, and there, as we paused before, among others, the Chandos portrait of Shakespeare, hung by familiar likenesses of Ben Jonson and John Donne, we remarked upon how actual historical personages had been represented, speaking personally.

LOUISE GLÜCK
AND THE NOBEL PRIZE

The anecdote from her childhood that Louise Glück tells in her Nobel Prize acceptance speech is about winners and losers: 'When I was a small child of, I think, about five or six, I staged a competition in my head, a contest to decide the greatest poem in the world. There were two finalists: Blake's "The Little Black Boy" and Stephen Foster's "Swanee River"'. The Nobel laureate had grown up in an emotionally rivalrous environment and internalised it from her other reading: 'Competitions of this sort, for honor, for high reward, seemed natural to me; the myths that were my first reading were filled with them'. 'Blake', she tells us, 'was the winner of the competition', though she doesn't give reasons why. She is more taken with what the two have in common: 'I realised later how similar these two lyrics were'. Each poem, if poems they both are, is differently concerned with the fact and consequences of slavery; and this memory may have come to Glück's mind when pondering her speech as relevant for the case of a white American woman winning such a prize in the year of Black Lives Matter.

It's right that Blake's poem from *Songs of Innocence* (1789) came out on top. His quatrains are complexly lucid on the incompatibility of Christian teaching and white supremacy. It is clear-eyed about the damaging implications of the ethical assumptions in the words 'black' and 'white' as conventionally used, and yet, a song of innocence, his poem imagines transformative heavenly love and equality in its closing stanza. Moreover, for the author who would later conceive of building 'Jerusalem / In England's green and pleasant land', the contraries which foreshadow and enable this progress project the possibility of that equality and human love as thinkable in the space of the poem, and therefore on earth, as the English boy 'will then love me.' 'The Little Black Boy' was written at a moment when the British parliament was debating the country's involvement in the slave trade, and Blake's opposition to slavery can further be seen in his engravings for J. Stedman's *The Narrative of a Five Years Expedition against the Revolted Negroes of Surinam* (1796). By contrast, Stephen Foster's lyrics, with their lonely nostalgia for 'de ole plantation' and other minstrel-show diction, however popular down the years, would require to be edited into acceptability in 2008 for continued employment as the state song of Florida.

Both of the poets in the young Glück's competition were white. The awarding of the Nobel Prize for Literature to Rabindranath Tagore in 1913 might look like a crack in its founding sensibility, but the citation gives the game away by praising how the writer's 'poetic thought' in 'his own English words' has made it 'a part of the literature of the West'. More than half a century would pass before writers not from Europe or the USA would occasionally receive its bounty. The first woman winner was a novelist, Selma Lagerlöf from Sweden, in 1909, but it would not be until 1945, when the Chilean Gabriela Mistral won, that a woman writer whose reputation rested squarely on her poetry would be awarded the prize.

The majority of Nobel laureates have been men, and while some of the greatest twentieth-century poets have won, few have been women. Since Mistral and before 2020, only Nelly Sachs, who shared it in 1966, and Wisława Szymborska, thirty years later, are identified as being awarded it primarily for their verse. With the exception of the dual-national Czesław Miłosz, who won it in 1980, and the US citizen Josef Brodsky, 1986, Glück is the first poet (and certainly the first woman poet) from the United States to receive the prize, not counting Bob Dylan, 2016, of course, whose unsung poetry was not what he got it for. It is then to Glück's credit that in her acceptance speech she strongly alluded to another prominent minority in the list of the Nobel's overlooked. With the partial exception of Wole Soyinka, 1986, who is also cited for his poetry, not until Derek Walcott was awarded it in 1992 did a poet of African heritage win the prize.

People receiving awards might be divided into those who are enhanced by it and those who enhance the trophy by winning it. Louise Glück may well combine these categories, helping by means of a respectable decision to leave in their wake a number of missteps by the committee over the past few years. She is a prolific and dedicated poet with two slim volumes of short essays to place beside the dozen or so collections of verse which have been awarded many of America's prestigious prizes, perhaps the most prominent being the receipt of the National Humanities Medal from President Obama, filmed embracing her on 22 September 2016.

In the light of the subsequent presidency, coming to an end in her laureate year, two of Glück's essays take on significances that cannot have been quite intended when written. In 'Against Sincerity' from *Proofs and Theories* (1994), the poet summarises that 'the source of art is experience, the end product truth, and the artist, surveying the actual, constantly intervenes and manages, lies and deletes, all in the service of truth.' But recent experience has shown to what extent truth is not a product, and while English expects us to state the facts it requires us to tell the truth. Honesty and sincerity cannot be stripped out of truth-telling, even for aesthetic purposes. Nor can an artist survey the actual, because that implies a privileged position outside of life from which to view it, and Glück's personal viewpoint within her life aligns with a characteristic in recent writing by women to give experience reach through the reconfiguring of myth – in, for example, *The Triumph of Achilles* (1985) and the Penelope and Telemachus poems from *Meadowlands* (1996). Nor do artists intervene, manage, lie or delete, because none of them have access to the whole of actuality, only that part of it within their compass. Rather, they gather what they can from experience and, by forming what is thus gifted into a patterned shape, attempt to make their portion stretch beyond themselves to return an echo and, in doing so, sound true.

In 'American Narcissism' from *American Originality* (2017), Glück observes that 'Henry James was among the first to note, and dramatise, the relation between American independence and American narrowness. It is a great inheritance, that independence: the presumption, the energy, the stubborn self-sufficiency – these are all tools any artist will need, over time. But the vanity that attends these gifts, the sense that no one else is necessary, that the self is of limitless interest, makes American writers particularly prone to any version of the narcissistic.' She defends her national poetry's greatest parent figures against this charge. 'Contemporary art', she writes, 'prizes the fastidious aesthetic response; it also places high value on the exposure of the secret. And in the latter sense it has, I believe, an antecedent or stimulus not in Whitman but in Dickinson, though she is, herself, never guilty of narcissism's superficiality and self-aggrandisement.' As has been recently demonstrated at the highest levels of government, accusing others of crimes and misdemeanours that you yourself manifest is how narcissism refuses to acknowledge by denying the possibility of its appearance in others' eyes. Glück does the opposite, including herself in the indictment, as in 'The New Life' from *Vita Nuova* (1999):

'Swaggering as a tyrant swaggers; / for all my amorousness, / cold at heart, in the manner of the superficial.'

Over a half century Louise Glück has published poems which demonstrate the restless development of a poet writing to extend her stretch towards others, such as the infant on 'The Chicago Train' from her debut collection *Firstborn* (1968) with 'lice rooted in that baby's hair'. She has written to outgrow youthful damage to self-worth, and later threats to well-being, to put the shadow of Narcissus behind her. Though not always entirely managing to compose a body for Echo and activating her hapless returns, Glück's best collections, such as *Descending Figure* from 1980, discover in the informalities of American lyric utterance ways of occasioning such invitations to participate ('Let us go then, you and I') as she sees transcending the limits of the character in T. S. Eliot's most famous early poem. In 'Illuminations', for instance, from that same volume, she tells us 'Last winter he could barely speak. / I moved his crib to face the window', evoking her son as he traverses the space between world and word, for now

> He sits at the kitchen window
> with his cup of apple juice.
> Each tree forms where he left it,
> leafless trapped in his breath.
> How clear their edges are,
> no limb obscured by motion,
> as the sun rises
> cold and single over the map of language.

In 'Death and Absence', the poet comments on this same collection's struggles with the word 'mother': '"Descending Figure" is saturated with a mother's grief and fearfulness and a haunted child's compulsive compensation. It means, also, to study maternal love, which continued to seem to me appalling, though I felt it.' Her award might be a tacit stand from the Nobel committee against tendencies recently highlighted in American public life, but this too is why Glück asserts 'that in awarding me this prize, the Swedish Academy is choosing to honor the intimate, private voice, which public utterance can sometimes augment or extend, but never replace.'

The great danger of prizes, like explosives, is their capacity to divide and rule. 'What happens', Glück writes, 'when the collective, instead of apparently exiling or ignoring him or her, applauds and elevates? I would say such a poet would feel threatened, outmaneuvered.' This is perhaps why she uses her childhood anecdote about a private competition for greatest poem in the world to downplay awards even as she graciously accepts one. In this, too, she is paying tribute to that early winner of hers. For when it comes to prizes, the last word is surely William Blake's, whose 1826 marginalia beside Wordsworth's poem for Coleridge's son Hartley, 'To H.C. Six Years Old', reminds us: 'This is all in the highest degree Imaginative & equal to any Poet, but not Superior. I cannot think that Real Poets have any competition. None are greatest in the Kingdom of Heaven; it is so in Poetry.'

THREE

JOHN JAMES AND *THE WHITE STONES* p. 71: MUSIC, RHYME, AND HOME

1. Discarding *The White Stones*?

Lines 16 and 17 of John James's 'The Dragon House' self-command the speaker to 'discard *The White Stones* / open on the quilt at p. 71'. If you pull *The White Stones* by J. H. Prynne off a bookshelf and turn to p. 71, you find it contains the second and concluding page of 'Thoughts on the Esterhazy Court Uniform'. In later printings 'Esterházy' has its acute accent, as on p. 99 of *Poems* (Newcastle upon Tyne: Bloodaxe Books, 1999); but citing the poem's first edition, I won't use the form here. Do James's lines mean that he gives up on the book at that page (it continues to p. 96)? Does the page number suggest that something there prompts James to 'discard' the whole book, or at least tell himself to discard it? In the second two lines of the quatrain he goes on: 'finish the coffee / & sniff the smoky November day'. Is he opting for the sensory pleasures of breakfast and autumnal fires over the challenge to be met with on that page of J. H. Prynne's book? I had bought copy number 75 of *The White Stones* (Lincoln: Grosseteste Press, 1969) from Compendium in Camden Town during the spring of 1975, the same year 'The Dragon House' appeared on pp. 23-5 of *Striking the Pavilion of Zero* (London: Ian McKelvie). These and related questions have, on and off, continued to arise since I purchased James's book from Heffers, Cambridge, in 1976. What follows is the best I've managed by way of speculative responses to those questions.

'The Dragon House' contains passages that might echo, in specifics of a single day, reflections that exercise Prynne's poem. 'Thoughts on the Esterhazy Court Uniform' begins 'I walk up the hill, in the warm / sun and we do not return, the place is / entirely musical', while in the second line of 'The Dragon House' an unstated pronominal presence 'draws back the curtains to the sun & coffee in bed'. There's another allusive clue, perhaps, when James writes 'I think it's going to pour with rain, lunch / can't be very far away either as you have this pain / you think is hunger so you eat, you eat too much / & so you are "in pain again".' The insistent rhymes on 'rain ... pain ... pain again' may allude to passages about rhyme in Prynne's poem: 'The sun makes it easier & worse, like the / music late in the evening, but should it start / to rain – the world converges on the idea / of return' and '*Again* is the sacred / word, the profane sequence suddenly graced, by /coming back.' Prynne returns to these rhymes at the close when 'thinking about rain, we / trifle with rhyme and again is the / sound of immortality.'

James's poem is at times a puzzle because of its informal jump-cut techniques, adapted to an English situation from the 'lunch / can't be very far away' of Frank O'Hara and his *Lunch Poems* (San Francisco: City Lights Books, 1964), much imitated by American followers such as Ted Berrigan; and James acknowledges the issue when what's for lunch comes up: 'what is / Wendy doing in the orchard? She has cut / either a cauliflower / or a... ! ? "your English vegetables are so good, all you need / is to prepare them in an American way...".' 'The Dragon House' is such a serving of English Sunday *after* a weekend at 'excitement-prone Kenneth Koch's', as O'Hara calls him in 'Adieu to Norman, Bon Jour to Joan and Jean-Paul' (p. 34). Yet preparing English vegetables in an American way makes them taste differently, as 'The Dragon House' illustrates. James's suspension points, exclamation and question mark ('or a... ! ?') suggest that the poet Wendy Mulford may have uprooted a mandrake – though on p. 120 of *Collected Poems* (Cambridge: Salt Publishing, 2002) any such implication is lost with the disappeared exclamatory question. When James wrote 'The Dragon House', O'Hara's work was not widely known and hard to obtain. Knopf had published Don Allen's edition of *Collected Poems* in 1971, a book that, though reissued in paperback by California University Press (1995), has never had a British publisher.

'Thoughts on the Esterhazy Court Uniform' is more articulately sustained, with its ratiocinative enjambments reminiscent of Words-worthian meditation, however intimately surprised by a Blakean ampersand or idiolect syntax and punctuation – such as Prynne's distinctive semi-colon-separated clauses without main or subordinated verbs to anchor their immediate applications. Yet Charles Bainbridge, welcoming James's *Collected Poems* in the *Guardian* (16 Oct 2004, available online), saw a connection between 'The Dragon House' and the blank-verse conversation poem, calling James's 'an updated version of Coleridge's 'Frost at Midnight' or 'This Lime Tree Bower My Prison' with its 'openness, intimacy, the same long meditative lines.' Prynne's puzzle title is easier to crack now than James's when 'Esterhazy' is a Google away. But I did used to wonder if the Dreyfus Case was relevant to the subject of Prynne's poem. The culprit in that anti-Semitic scandal was not Alfred Dreyfus but Charles Marie Ferdinand Walsin Esterhazy (1847–1923), who also had his day in court (though the case against him was scandalously dropped on day two) and so, I supposed, he had a 'court uniform' that doubtless Jeremy Prynne could have had thoughts on. Oddly enough, it turns out, Esterhazy left the French army in 1898 and lived in the English village of Harpenden, Hertfordshire, until his death. He was, however, an indirect descendent of the Hungarian Ester-hazy family, and so remotely connected with Prince Nikolaus Esterházy (1714–1790), and a more immediately relevant 'Esterházy Court Uniform' explored in N. H. Reeve and Richard Kerridge, *Nearly Too Much: The Poetry of J. H. Prynne* (Liverpool: Liverpool University Press, 1995), pp. 60-66 and Robins Purves, 'A Commentary on J. H. Prynne's "Thoughts on the Esterhazy Court Uniform"', *Glossator* no. 2, 2010, pp. 79-88. Though turning now to the music of Franz Joseph Haydn (1732–1809) and his patron, I do glance back at the Dreyfus Case.

'The end cadence deferred like breathing, the / birthplace of the poet', Prynne writes, and adds: 'all put out the lights / and take their instruments away with them.' This describes what the musicians of the orchestra do when performing Haydn's Symphony No. 45 in F sharp minor, written it is said so that the homesick players, dressed in their court uniforms and isolated in Esterháza, could give their employer the hint by taking leave one after another. Prynne's poem collocates the obligation to continue producing music, and the counter desire to return home, conflated in returning to the 'home' key in music. He then thinks about that ambivalence in the art of poetry, with a return to the home key made analogous with the timing of a cadence and the returning echo of a rhyme, which figures both a loss of wholeness (except perhaps in the case of homophonic 'rime riche'), and its partial recovery by the similarity-in-difference of a rhyme. Purves suggests that 'The "birthplace of the poet" must be the moment where the heard music stops and we are in the land of silence and darkness' (p. 85), but it might equally be in 'the end cadence deferred', the birthplace of the poet resting in an ability to defer the end cadence, keep speech airborne, sustain music over an enjambment, only then to fall into silence: the 'end cadence' also suggests a 'dying fall' in mortality, with that end notionally overcome by rhyme – as in the rhymed quatrains of Samuel Johnson's 'On the Death of Dr Robert Levet', where, with no 'cold gradations of decay', death 'free'd his soul the nearest way.'

So technique turns teleological in the para-rhymed 'heaven-haven' of a Hopkins.

James's 'The Dragon House' finds him not going 'in at the back door', as Prynne's poem does in its final line, but inside and home already, producing what Bainbridge in the *Guardian* calls 'a marvellously judged encomium to the possibility of the good life'. The lyric figure ('I' in line five) wakes into a bedroom with gendered things and actions but no stated subject:

> her bright green leather high-heeled pumps
>
> draws back the curtains to the sun & coffee in bed
> on trays with legs this windscreen of a morning
> moving with beech & yew a stewpond full of goldfish

Seeming to discard thoughts of 'the sacred', 'immortality' or where it 'resides', James announces 'I would wish to attend to nothing more than that / which is the measure of a lack of prayer' and adds 'how could I be able to propose anything other?' An echoic divergence appears between the secular James lyric and Prynne's exploration of the 'sacral' in taking a constitutional. 'The Dragon House' stays close to lived moments of its day, such as in glimpses of a sexual 'dragon' warmed by the ordinary effects of daylight: 'the way the ice melts all along your back / that soft declivity near your tail'. Its developing focus is not the thinking mind, its 'thoughts on' a topic, but the subject in domestic space making sense from an apparently random, but, it turns out, unexpectedly pointed, series of perceptions and observations à la Frank O'Hara:

> the sun warms through the glass
> we drank last night
> little yellow cups of Prunelle Noyer & now
> what litters today?
> a pile of pastoral trousers & an old straw hat
> a pale blue notebook bought in Hannover…

Though informal in its accretion of detail, its use of capitals and punctuation, studied items in an improvisational aesthetic, James's lines feature those cadenced suspensions and energised enjambments of lyrical writing in English: 'the sun warms through the glass / we drank last night' is a pentameter with its caesura (written as a line-break) after the third foot, while 'little yellow cups of Prunelle Noyer' matches it with a similarly decasyllabic phrase – which is why, when '& now' stretches the line to an alexandrine, it does sound like an addition. By such arrangements of metre, rhythm and cadence, James's lines have a casual aspect and a sound formal armature: the two-foot line 'we drank last night' is echoed by the similar 'what litters today', while, borrowing the extra foot from the previous line, the question '& now / what litters today' matches the opening phrase of the stanza 'the sun warms through the glass'. Similarly, 'a pile of pastoral trousers & an old straw hat', with its thirteen syllables, balances 'little yellow cups of Prunelle Noyer & now' (two near alexandrines), while 'a pale blue notebook bought in Hannover' is yet another decasyllabic pentameter. Note too the near anaphora, or half rhyme, of 'a pile... a pale...'. This is simultaneously an Anglicisation of O'Hara's 'I do this, I do that' mode for evoking a life on the move in the material world, and a skilful deployment of metrical means at the disposal of the poet in English, whether Vaughan or Dylan Thomas, since the renaissance. James's poem, in discarding *The White Stones* and employing lyric cadence, dissociates the formal inheritances of poetry, reconfigured in modernist practice, from their entailment to a sacral vision of diurnal departures and returns.

2. The Home World, Music, Loss and Gain

Prynne writes in his second verse paragraph that 'my life slips into music & / increasingly I cannot take much more of this.' The analogy with Haydn's musicians suffering acute nostalgia is in play; but what, exactly, can the poet not take? Prynne's poem puns on the musical 'subject', as Reeve and Kerridge point out (pp. 61-2), also on the plural of the musical 'motif' (meaning 'theme') which can be 'motives', as also impulses for our actions. The poem adds that 'Each move / into the home world is that same loss; we / do mimic the return and the pulse very / slightly quickens, as our motives flare in / the warm hearth.' The Esterhazy allusion, then, invites the thought that the deferral of sustained musical cadence is what keeps the musicians from their home. They need to work to support that place of return, but by doing so they lose its recuperative space – an experience of the musicians' replicated, to different degrees, in a great many lives.

Devoting oneself to writing poetry at the level that Prynne has followed out, requiring an acutely focused thoughtfulness and vast knowledge fed by sustained research, might also keep you for lengths of time from hearth and home. The 134 pages of Prynne's *Field Notes: 'The Solitary Reaper' and Others* (Cambridge: [No Publisher], 2007) forms a meditation – relevant to 'Thoughts on the Esterhazy Court Uniform' – upon purposeful travel, physical labour, song, poetic form, and the sacred in subjectivity, painfully exercised too by the poet's divided and distanced responsibilities in encounters such as Wordsworth's. Similarly, Prynne's critical writing on 'Tintern Abbey, Once Again' (*The Glossator* vol. 1, Fall 2009, pp. 81-7) makes relevant observations about indwelling, returning, and finding spiritual significance in interactions of perception and memory. Of 'Thoughts on the Esterhazy Court Uniform', Birgitta Johansson in *The Engineering of Being: An Ontological Approach to J. H. Prynne* (Umeå: Umeå University, 1997) finds '*da-sein*' (indwelling) and 'patience as a key to a soulful austere life', concluding that its poet 'shares with Heidegger the resolution to cultivate patience in meditative thinking' (p. 124). But the poem dwells in thought, not in specified or experienced place.

Citing Simon Jarvis's Hegelian interpretation of rhyme as leading 'us back to ourselves' (though, excepting 'rime riche', never exactly to where we were), Purves suggests that 'Prynne's poem might go as far as proposing this as a price worth paying' (p. 82). By indicating that there may be a 'price' in rhyming or not rhyming, he does register predicament and ambivalence in the poem's account of musical form, poetic device, indwelling, homing, and the shape of life, as when its 'motives' pun returns to Prynne's quasi blank verse:

> How can we sustain such constant loss.
> I ask myself this, knowing that the world
> is my pretext for this return through it, and
> that we go more slowly as we come back
> more often to the feeling that rejoins the whole.
> Soon one would live in a sovereign point and
> *still* we don't return, not really, we look back
> and our motives have more courage in
> structure than in what we take them to be.

The world is 'my pretext for this return through it', because assumed
behind or before the thought processes that require it to have sense.
What the thoughts don't do, except with gestures in the first and last
lines, is give the reader continuous indication of a subject moving in
space. Even when Prynne writes 'I refer directly to my / own need, since
to advance in the now fresh & / sprouting world must take on some
musical / sense', the 'now fresh & / sprouting world' is only minimally
sketched to occasion further thought on life as having a musical form.
This form, we're told, involves the thought that our motives for actions
have more courage because we see them as formally shaped like motifs,
or motives, in music: with statements, variations, repetitions, and returns
to the home key. The close of the first verse paragraph asserts this as a
relationship between walking, musical structure, cadence and rhyme:

> Literally, the grace & hesitation of
> modal descent, the rhyme unbearable, the
> coming down through the prepared delay and
> once again we are there, beholding the
> complete elation of our end.

The technical self-consciousness of enjambment and caesura here has
been raised to the level of an all but wearisome device or trick, seeming
to figure the experience of a poet who has come to the end of his formal
tether too soon. It is as if the poem knows a little too well what its
deployed rhythmic techniques can do and must mean, and this explicit
knowing in the poem's meditative style relies on shifts between the first-
person singular and plural pronouns.

These thoughts are centred upon a singular consciousness in
solitude, imagining itself in one passage of the poem not away from
home but unanchored to any such place of return, new-born in every
moment, when, if music 'would only / level out into some complete
migration of / sound' then 'I myself would be the / complete stranger'.
This is an illusory wish, indicated by the 'if ... only' and the repeated
'complete'. It could also never happen because such a notion of being
a 'complete stranger' *is* so centred upon 'I myself'. In my experience,
being a complete stranger is brought home as others confirm it by their
presumptions concerning where you are from. You are not a complete
stranger in yourself, but in relation to others who conceive themselves
as different. Free of any such second- or third-person pronouns for

others, 'Thoughts on the Esterhazy Court Uniform' remains within an undifferentiated home world of its first personal shifting between 'I' and 'we', which figures general conditions individually experienced: 'Our chief / loss is ourselves; that's where I am, the /sacral link in a profane world'. This is what gives Prynne's poem an expansive claustrophobia, its voice countering threatened loss of self by syntactical control of first personal meditation.

'Thoughts on the Esterhazy Court Uniform' is, then, a type of meta-poem in which the structures of formal poetic thinking shadowed in the shapes of poems, especially those deploying sustained cadence and end-rhyme, is brought forward, while the perceptual stream encountered when out for a walk is barely indicated. Prynne's observation on the method of 'Tintern Abbey' when noting that 'the pleasures of instant diversity were what characterised, and weakened, the prospect-poem of earlier tradition' (p. 83) might form one justification for a similar absence of descriptive sketching here. Yet the poem's lack of 'instant diversity' heightens its self-preserving claustrophobia. Its occasioning action is noted at beginning, end, and in passing, to situate thought – as again with the idea of it starting to rain on a sunny day:

> The sun makes it easier & worse, like the
> music late in the evening, but should it start
> to rain – the world converges on the idea
> of return. To our unspeakable loss; we make
> sacred what we cannot see without coming
> back to where we were.
>   *Again* is the sacred
> word, the profane sequence suddenly graced, by
> coming back.

The self-conscious use of the enjambment to figure 'coming / back... by / coming back' is once more all but too much to bear, too painfully obvious, its lift from the quotidian domestic routine of going for a walk to the going out and coming back of a life-span, to birth and death, prompted by the pun on another musical term – 'grace notes'. This is, again, the higher home of heaven, the place we cannot see but to which believers hope to return. And this motif in the composition is the point to which we are returned in the poem's conclusion:

> With such
> patience maybe we can listen to the rain
> without always thinking about rain, we
> trifle with rhyme and again is the
> sound of immortality. We think we have
> it & we must, for the sacred resides in this;
> once more falling into the hour of my birth, going
> down the hill and then in at the back door.

This end expresses division in its obligation to accept a human need to project the immortality of the self (or soul) in the sound of poetic form by the verb 'trifle', as if we clung to and reiterated this need without taking it seriously enough. We are sentimental, it appears to suggest, in wanting the poetic forms of immortality without being willing to pay the price of full belief in what they embody. A level of self-accusation, perhaps, emerges in the allusion to T. S. Eliot's *Ash Wednesday* in Prynne's penultimate line. His 'falling into the hour of my birth' (the 'birthplace of the poet' in cadence, from 'cadere': to fall) reverses, in its return to an origin, 'now and at the hour of our death' – itself a citation from the *Ave Maria*. 'Thoughts on the Esterhazy Court Uniform' drops from sacral reflection to the simple fact of returning home with the turn into the last line ('in at the back door') and its full-stopped end.

3. The Home World's Foreign Detail

James's poem, discarding such a prayerful sense of daily life, goes about its business rather the other way around. Its procedure comes from a 'no ideas but in things' aesthetic – made from fleetingly separate actions, perceptions, and observations. It echoes to depart from Prynne's sacred and profane theme by happening to take place on a Sunday in November with its 'lack of prayer'. This poem won't reflect on being the 'sacral link in a profane world', though it performs a valued subjectivity ('I duck /out under the eaves again, hunting for postcards / & send one with love to' Barry MacSweeney, giving his address in Barnet, Herts – sending it, that's to say, to his 'home world'. The poem does celebrate, though, by attending to what's happening around its first-person singular. Divergent in this too from p. 71 of *The White Stones*, 'The Dragon House' is populated with others. Its lyrical subject names and implies degrees of relation with Diana, the locals, Wendy, Barry MacSweeney, Grandmama Daubeney Russell-Clarke, as well as Picabia and, implicitly, Jeremy Prynne. It cites the name of a town in Germany, Smarden (where there is a house with dragons carved along the roofline) and Bethersden in Kent, Appledore in North Devon, a French liqueur, American cooking, and classical music for piano practice. It populates its 'I do this, I do that' with a spacious extent of names for other places, people, and things.

Yet, as I say, preparing English vegetables in an American way makes them taste differently. Unlike O'Hara's *carpe diem* in NYC, which enthusiastically embraces the passing scene, James's poem embodies in its subjectivity some wry detachment from the life around:

> ahhh, quick, shut the curtains!
> this continuous sun! O rum
> bustuous machine, redolent of Picabia,
>   his *Parade Amoureuse*, rattle
>   the rafters, the wall & quietude of Grandmama
> Daubeney Russell-Clarke her grey eternal smile
> enthralls me working freely in the morning

Francis Picabia's *Parade amoureuse* c. 1917 is among his paintings of mechanised metaphors for sexual relations, and so, with the example of Apollinaire too in support now, early modernist machine art is employed to evoke, discreetly, another of the things couples do on Sundays, disturbing a well-heeled, polite-sounding English neighbour into the bargain. The poem's neo-modernist aestheticism appears to be deployed against an older way of dwelling, by which it is simultaneously enthralled, held captive, spellbound.

Its relation of meta-poetry to the experiential plane is then, as it were, the reverse of Prynne's, for where 'Thoughts on the Esterhazy Court Uniform' employs the thoughts occasioned by the action of going for a walk, but with the perceptual stream of that action blanked out by the thinking, James gives us something of the perceptual stream with the 'thoughts', or rationale linking them, blanked between the lines of the poem – or occasioned in the reader's mind by the rendered perceptual stream that constitutes its reading experience. Just as in Prynne's poem the 'sun makes it easier & worse, like the / music late in the evening', so in James's the old lady's 'grey eternal smile'

enthralls me working freely in the morning though the
easing of the light is also good before Britannia
pulls down her shades of a wintry evening, yes
the piano please Diana, *F minor Prelude* pushing it away
like pressing buttons
or small clear bells
that sphere out lighter than themselves
against the indolence of the loggy room

What to those fabulous flying creatures carved & white?

That's 'Britannia', by the way, in the Salt *Collected Poems* – meaning, I
imagine, the nation figured as a woman closing the curtains as the short
day ends. This could be Chopin's *Prelude* no. 18, *molto allegro*, in F minor
or, perhaps, Bach's F minor Prelude and Fugue, in that its description
of the music fits better with the *Well-Tempered Klavier* than a piece of
Romantic pianism. And are the 'carved & white' flying creatures in the
last line the moving piano keys? Or are they the musical notes made by
pressing them as they 'sphere out lighter than themselves'?

'The Dragon House' does then appear to be in a dialogue with
'Thoughts on the Esterhazy Court Uniform' and the instruction to
'discard *The White Stones* / open on the quilt at p. 71' must imply
different approaches to the contemporary situation for poets (at the
end of the 1960s and early 1970s) focused around implications about
the traditional means for sustaining a poem (cadence and rhyme) and,
at the same time sustaining the mental and physiological attention of
the poem's reader – with the relations of such technical inheritances
to ideas of life's trajectories, selves and others, and the sense of home.
James may not be consciously deploying his techniques in this fashion
or taking specific aim at the thoughts in Prynne's poem. Rather, it is as
if the 'home world' theme of 'The Dragon House' and its own meta-
poetic implications are taking the earlier poem as a sounding board,
or thematic exposition, upon which James will play variations, ones
that also vary in their manifest beliefs about the relations of 'being'
and 'knowing' to the spiritual in poems, and the relations that these
different preferences bear to the pleasures and pains, the gains and
losses, again of cadence and rhyme.

But what of the other Esterhazy, the one who ended his days in
Harpenden, Herts? As James's 'Britannia' pulling 'down her shades

of a wintry evening' indicates, the home world, any particular home
world, and our indwelling in it has depended on identification with
specifically cultured places, countries, and nations – what Prynne's poem
calls 'watching jealously / over names', an idea James also comments
on following a line made up of place-names: 'Smarden   Bethersden
Appledore / foreign as white clapboard houses / windmills   a curious
zeitgeist never far away'. The Dreyfus case in France was reported on
for the *Neue Freie Presse* by Theodor Herzl, (1860–1904), a Hungarian
too, whose mind was decisively changed by his experiences of such
ingrained anti-Semitism, from a hope in emancipation and assimilation
for European Jewry to a Zionist belief in the recreation of a homeland
in Palestine to which the peoples of the Diaspora could return. Just as
I cannot definitively say why James's 'The Dragon House' includes the
command to 'discard *The White Stones* / open on the quilt at p. 71', so
I cannot be confident that 'Thoughts on the Esterhazy Court Uniform'
is also thinking about the application of wandering from home and
return to the fate of the Jewish people, and the consequences for the
modern world of its ideas about music and nostalgia. But given that *The
White Stones* was published some two years following the Six Day War
of June 1967 between Israel and her surrounding Arab neighbours, I
would be quite surprised if it didn't.

JOHN JAMES:
IN ROMSEY TOWN

Writing to Thomas McGreevy on 8 Sept 1935, Samuel Beckett described old men's kite flying in Kensington Gardens as 'So absolutely disinterested, like a poem, or useful in the depths where demand and supply coincide'. Lines are controlled to keep both kites and poems airborne. This requires a managing of the point where external circumstance touches human desire. The coinciding of wish and its embodiment in action down below is achieved through the balance of external force and human will up in the air. Re-reading Beckett's remark recalled a stanza of poetic theory from John James' 'Pimlico', a poem occasioned by revisiting the gallery now called Tate Britain and recalling the performance art of Richard Long:

> Richard walking in the grass
> Andrew walking on the grass
>
> & I took flatness as my starting point
> the line made quicker in its shorter pulse
> & slower in its flooded length
> the line a slinger to the surface from the depths of things
> where a breath touches the slightest branch
> & bends the stuff of accident to your will

James' technical wit might be working almost out of sight in the 'shorter pulse' line being longer than the 'flooded length' one. Depths and breeze are there too, and the point where circumstance, in this case 'accident', and 'your will' coincide. I'm not so sure about that bending the contingent world 'to your will' – pushing its balance towards the wilful, though without desire, will, and the need to express there would be nothing urging the poem into existence and achieving an equipoise between depth and surface, accident and will, an equipoise heard in the coincident implication of 'breath' which catches the wind in the trees and the poem as speech.

In Romsey Town includes work from the last years of James' sixth decade through to the beginning of his eighth. These are stages in life when time turns poets into senior figures, whether they feel like ones or not. The working world expects such persons to retire and fate turns them into survivors when their 'social comforts drop away' as Samuel Johnson so finely put it, as do the editorial allies and fellow poets of their starting out. Though none of the poems are marked in traditional fashion as elegies, 'Early Doors' reveals itself at its close as one for Barry MacSweeney (1948–2000), while the mention of 'Andrew' above suggests that 'Pimlico' contains similar feeling for Andrew Crozier (1943–2008) with its memory of his 1969 collection *Walking on Grass*. Geoffrey Hill had grimly alluded to generational change and survival in his poem 'After Reading *Children of Albion* (1969)' which cites then mishears as if at a public reading James' poem 'Bathampton Morrismen at the Rose & Crown': '*The dancers, faces oblivious & grave, –* / testing testing / the dancers face oblivion and the grave.' But death is so great a leveller its bell tolls for the poetically immortal and mortal alike.

James' book has its own reflections on poetry and poets, as in the three-line poem 'En Sevrage': 'in the barn the lambs were bleating all night long / but beloved have no fear / at least they will not do so in their poetry'. Similarly, in 'April 25 1998' he goes 'along to the CCCP / to check out the fatal strategy of the poets' and encounters some young people perhaps failing to appreciate the 'soft voice of the senior English poet' which 'murmurs gently'. This is Roy Fisher, reading at the Cambridge Conference of Contemporary Poetry for that year. James wonders if the cover of his 1961 first edition of *City* was 'the first punk cover' and asks himself 'who did it anyway was it Michael Shayer'. The incident then evoked is glossed by a report on the event by Bernardo Soares – a heteronym of Fernando Pessoa, so pseudonym for the reporter – in *Jacket* no. 4, its near contempt for older poets and resentment about an absence of reciprocal interest ('Fisher did not stay to hear what the young poets in Cambridge are up to these days, but he never did') perhaps prompting:

> with that a lunatic appears at the backlit door
> like Marlon Brando in Cambodia
> he denies your name
> claiming to be an accordion

Again, the poem is enlivened by a second-personal address, this time speaking to Shayer himself. James' lines sardonically allude, via *Apocalypse*

Now, to Conrad's *Heart of Darkness*, which comes to its conclusion by having Marlow lie about Mr. Kurtz's name to his betrothed. James' poem evokes 'time's perpetual motion' that is 'young & ticking onwards / inevitably hazardous'. A pointedly dated work, 'April 25 1998' then concludes by describing those younger poets present as 'blundering hamsters / flinching & confused' with their 'fatal strategies'.

In Romsey Town observes and comprehends the in-fighting of various generations of linguistically innovative poets, and does so by staying close to its best plain style of economically loaded, lyric cadence able to register such 'stuff of accident' and push back against it with equal and opposite pressure along the poems' lines. As is clear in the following passage from 'At Château-Chinon', James has not abandoned any of his punk-period stance against the injustices of contemporary English culture, though now those 'manners and liberty lost to abandon' indicates a less than enthusiastic view of cool Britannia's *mœurs contemporaine*:

> so why in this moment of well-being should we want to see
>   England again
> that overcrowded space become a fen of half-occult corruption
> in state academy & civic hall
> all trust eroded failing system & due process
> manners & liberty lost to abandon
> more windows soon to close again in claustrophobic places
> soon to be shivering under sleet & snow & hail
> each word of art as a good in itself an irritation to the mighty
> what hope of greater joy for those at the base of this monstrous
>   tower
> as the rich get richer with parental choice

James' new collection represents 'art as a good in itself' by exemplifying how poetry is put to the service of life, being useful in the depths and on the surface in poems such as 'Today', which is 'a kind of routine day' until he receives a postcard from Tübingen, setting off thoughts on Hölderlin and the vulnerability of lyric song, or 'A Benediction' where notation turns to prayer: 'the blinds are down / in the house across the way // you need a shave / a little sun breaks through // be well / & blessed be the day'. As if to underline the point of that turn, 'Nocturne with Baudelaire', alluding to his series of poems on wine, concludes:

'pour again hope / la primeur // & pride / the virtue of the work // restore to us an inkling / of the sacred'. In their sparse articulations of experience – interactions of consciousness and circumstance – James finely extends his evanescent materials and delicately twitches them into the equipoise of poems that stay aloft like flying kites.

VERONICA FORREST-THOMSON:
ON THE PERIPHERY

Veronica Forrest-Thomson published *Language Games* in 1971. Later she published *Cordelia*. Her death, after the 1975 Cambridge Poetry Festival, left Street Editions with a manuscript that constitutes her final volume. *On the Periphery* is a cycle of pieces, followed by 'Last Poems'. The book will also include a memoir by J. H. Prynne. Her poetry is pre-eminently concerned with the problematic relationship between language, non-verbal phenomena and consciousness. In the preface to the book she writes:

> I have argued elsewhere that this awfulness [the awfulness of the modern world] cannot be overcome with entire reference to the non-verbal world for the non-verbal world, like other deities, helps only those who help themselves. And what poetry gains from that world is gained through language, through the very languages that give us the world.

By such an account, consciousness is constituted in language and to transform the functional references in language is to transform consciousness, and hence the world. Any reference to a world outside consciousness or language is an appeal to the unthinkable, a mystifying abstraction.

In 'L'effet du Réel', she articulates in a highly conscious manner the interaction of such concepts as those mentioned above:

> We construct an event out of, behind these shutters 'people'
>   are sleeping.
> and from an intersection between 'the most perfect château of the transition period'
> and 'a cricket on a ball of dung'. Our capacity
> for indifference is truly astounding

If we are indifferent to the sources of consciousness and knowledge, the world is fixed in a number of dead metaphors or unsatisfactory attitudes:

> So would you mind just standing in the café doorway
> for a minute longer against the sun because I'm
> writing a poem about intersections

The inference of this passage feels uncertain. Irony hovers in the request to a person like that of a painter to her model. To feel at ease in the world is to commandeer it, only to find it an uncooperative presence:

> Such savage triumph returns us to Maillezais.
> The abbey stands still, without quotation marks.

Such intelligence prevents any recourse to the pathetic fallacy. The intelligence itself conveys us into a mesh of linguistic sleights-of-hand whose purpose is to disrupt the too easy and casual identification in the reader of 'human interest' or 'the touchingly picturesque'. But since the interrelation of consciousness and world in language is rendered so disjunctive as to disengage the easy response, generosity and the unpremeditated seem also impossible in 'An Arbitrary Leaf':

> Printed in natural colours, we find a way always
> to deny the world; even its 'aerial view' from
> 'the tower itself'

The travesties committed upon human experience by casual mortification of perception in language are so overwhelming; the learned credulity of the eye is too indifferent, itself a denial. Following poems develop a manner of writing which relies heavily on language as a palimpsest of attitudes and learned response so as to undermine these as 'Approaching the Library' puts it:

> Poetic diction performed for me two outstanding services:
> in confirming that the subject I proposed treating
> was a worthy one; and in feeding and clothing me
> after I had, in a moment of abstraction, fallen
> into Holme Fen Engine Ditch...

And the most successful technique for subterranean mining is humour. It has the insistence of a bad joke brilliantly told so as to point up the serious underlying purpose in 'Strike':

Hail to thee blithe horse, bird thou never wert!
And breaking into a canter, I set off on the long road south
Which was to take me to so many strange places,
That room in Cambridge, that room in Cambridge, that room
                                                    in Cambridge,
That room in Cambridge, this room in Cambridge,
The top of a castle in Provence and an aeroplane in mid-Atlantic.
Strange people, that lover, that lover, that lover, that lover.
Eyes that last I saw in lecture-rooms...

But such writing is clearly a strategy for the avoidance of one manner, though in itself another manner, and not the creation of a style. In the preface, Forrest-Thomson indicates the limitedness of such obliqueness:

> Thus also, the last poem 'Sonnet' is the love poem I have tried throughout to write straight and have been held back from by these technical and sociological difficulties. For, as to theme, this book is the chart of three quests. The quest for a style already discussed, the quest for a subject other than the difficulty of writing, and the quest for another human being.

But here difficulty does arise for what she regards as writing straight is itself an acknowledgement of the hopelessness of the poem's premise. And its quiet, delicate statement in the poem is summarised in her preface: 'And, of course, being caught as a poetic fiction, as a real person he is gone.' 'Sonnet' concludes:

> So, accept the wish for the deed my dear.
> Words were made to prevent us near.

If we do not accept the wish for the deed it is because her attitudes to the knowledge of reality and language seem incompatible with the wish itself. And it feels anti-climactic to find that the purpose of such determined interruption of discourse is simply this. But it also feels sad. The world is not affirmed, but its absence is apologised for and ghosts of biography haunt the text.

It may have been acknowledgement of this impasse that produced the energy to be felt in many of the 'Last Poems'. In 'The Garden of Proserpine' and 'Cordelia', the humour that had been effectively used to disrupt easy responses is uppermost, and its insistence is combined with a self-generating manner reacting continuously to previous statement as in the former poem:

> The moon is sinking, and the Pleiades,
> Mid Night; and time runs on she said.
> I lie alone. I am aweary, aweary,
> I would that I were dead.
> Be my partner and you'll never regret it.
> Gods and poets ought to stick together;
> They make a strong combination.

Also present is a good deal of direct statement of a kind that balances precariously between the effectively anguished and the embarrassing. But this precariousness only seems to add to the power of the poems, as does the nerve of some of her jokes in, for instance, 'Cordelia':

> March is the cruellest station
> Taking on bullying men
> And were you really afraid they would rape you?

For here the echo of T. S. Eliot allows access for her direct questioning of the relationship between real events linguistically implied and the consciousness of feelings that may or may not be in error, but which operate distinct from the assumed events. This mixture of humour and anxiety is finally very moving and I cannot but recommend it:

> Spring surprised us, running through the market square
> And we stopped in Prynne's room in a shower of pain
> And went on in sunlight into the University Library
> And ate yogurt and talked for an hour.
> You, You, grab the reins.
> Drink as much as you can and love as much as you can
> And work as much as you can
> For you can't do anything when you are dead.

Here you will not find perfectly wrought 'artifices for eternity'. The need to disrupt language makes many of these works fragmentary or consciously flawed, seen from a more synthesizing and craftsmanly aspect. The whole volume constitutes an effort to resolve a problem that must confront anyone who finds the world a deeply affecting yet intangible chimera. And the rest is literature.

THOMAS A. CLARK:
POET AS HERBALIST

Thomas A. Clark's work is offered to its reader as a cure for the common cold, a masterwork of serendipity, as the ideal herbal remedy. It combines providence, the herb found wild, with an attitude of knowledgeable attention and reverence – necessary for the collection and preparation of the remedy.

He acknowledges Francis Bacon's essay 'Of Gardens' as a source and an inspiration and, indeed, Clark's work seems a reinvestigation of the Elizabethan dialogue between Art and Nature; a pruning, a pruning and cutting back of disused and overgrown arbours. In this light 'An Epitaph' from *A Still Life* would appear a compression of the *ver perpetuum* listed in Bacon's opening paragraph.

For Clark, Art is the cultivation of language's nuances in context, of the readability of writing – not what language can be made to mean in the lonely forcing house of an exacerbated consciousness, but what it may be found to mean by arrangement with an author:

from A Thesaurus of Summer

Great, imperial, goodly,
majestic, conspicuous, prominent
distinguished, *august*, exalted,
dignified, grand, sublime.

Nature finds its way into his work by the double attention to the countryside as a given source of plenty, of food for thought, and by analogy to the potentialities of a given or discovered, a readymade piece of writing. Thomas A. Clark is a Marcel Duchamp addicted to seed catalogues: he adopts the once outrageous gesture of making art by simply naming random materials so, but to his own purposes, which would seem to be largely contrary to Duchamp's – the production of an art which celebrates life as ordered, attentive and happy, an art without alienation.

Thus, in 'Scotch Thistle', it is possible to read the piece as medicinal for those suffering from elephantiasis of the once outrageous:

The juice of this medicinal
plant is said to be good for a
crick in the neck. Perhaps this
is fortunate, for a flexible neck
is needed when studying this
grey-leaved giant, which may
reach heights of 10 feet or more.
With its mauve flowers it makes
a splendid summer wind-break.

His work is the antidote to afflatus. However, his integration of the
forms of language and Nature is not achieved without some loss.
Perhaps this can be intimated by noting the relative absence of verbs
in his poems, and the great emphasis placed on the name, the noun
and its singular adjective. In *A Still Life* the section 'Petits Fours'
suppresses all use of verbal action. The poetry of delicate stasis and
of unarticulated variation which results from this strategy succeeds in
avoiding any violation of the object by the attribution of an unfounded
volition, which would force it into a relationship of expressiveness or
correspondence to the poetic consciousness. The problem is that the
exclusion of the verb does not go unnoticed; some few of the poems,
rather than small, appear residual.

The poem 'Windows', which is potentially more rewarding, in its
emphasis on the window's multiplicity of roles and effects, than the
more often encountered use of the window as a transparency which can
merely 'show' the view, nonetheless stays as a potential by rendering
these implied verbal conditions as participles, as verbal adjectives:

Light reflected,
branches framed,
storm deflected,
change contained.

Clark's debt to objectivism – the volume includes a fine elegy for Lorine
Niedecker – entails a belief that the thing itself, independent of the
poet, but to which the poet may relate, produces a more honourable,
because balanced, interdependence of man and world. However, this
belief does beg the question of the interdependence of the object
when embodied in language and may be thus sublimed into a belief in

the poetic text as an object, whose fullest expression is present in the readymade, or found poem.

The problem of verbal status for nouns, as things, is better accommodated in the found and arranged pieces where functional verbs occur, than in the smallest poems where they have been excluded. *Pebbles from a Japanese Garden* exemplifies this, as does this piece from *Pointing Still*:

> Greenock – A most daring robbery was
> committed here between Saturday night
> and Sunday morning. A shop was entered
> into by picking the locks, and property
> mostly consisted of gold and silver
> watches to the amount of several hundred
> pounds carried off.

The supposedly non-poetic function of the verbs in this passage, which are of course presented with a poetic status by the act of the finder, do, however, avoid the problem of the interference of a poetic consciousness by their pseudo-function as the articulators of a message, a newspaper message in this case, I imagine, which is no longer informative, or, better, is absurdly informative, functional without a purpose.

Thus, Clark's work is also a lesson in reading; it encourages its reader to adopt a relationship to the writing which embodies those qualities of oblique attention, reverence and humour, which have been engaged in the work's production or discovery:

> *from the french*
>
> le vert paradis
> the green parody
> *
> l'arc en ciel
> lark in the clear air
> *
> le pain de la vie
> the pain of life

This oblique attention reads in the disparities between the intent of the informational writing and its readings as mis-translation, errata, unsuspected *double-entendre* or whatever. In so un-emphatically inducing an awareness of what language can do, of potential meaning, in more senses than one, it provides the chance of positively misinterpreting our reading of the tangible, visible and changeable world. Or there is generosity in fine misunderstanding, offering to the writer the gift of living beyond his meanings.

END OF HARM:
DOUGLAS OLIVER

It's curious that to praise Douglas Oliver's work by describing it as 'harmless', borrowing an adjective from the title of his 1973 novel *The Harmless Building*, would seem to denigrate it in the direction of the namby-pamby. This is presumably because the second meaning of 'harmless' given in my *Webster's* is 'lacking capacity or intent to injure: INNOCUOUS'. The offered synonym too, though its Latin root is *nocere* (to wound), seems to have little positive charge, and rather indicates a lack of capacity. The word 'innocence', which shares that root, has also engaged the poet's sustained attention, as in his description of a Tupamaros guerrilla in the first of the 'Diagram Poems' (1979) as 'Already bereaved of innocence and late'. The use of 'bereaved' in that phrase grazes one of the founding harms behind his writings, the loss of a Down's Syndrome son, Tom, who died in a cot accident in 1969. Then to call Oliver's work 'harmless' would be to say it doesn't wound or harm because it can't, and that as a consequence its value as art (which is where the embedded cultural assumption comes into play) is significantly reduced, perhaps to irrelevance. While oozing a capacity to harm may well taint the virtue in not doing it, there can only be such a virtue present if the power to hurt is also implicit. Douglas Oliver's work is alive with this recognition. So where's the harm in it?

The Harmless Building contains a world of harms. There is physical and psychological cruelty, reactionary political indifference, the abduction and murder of a mongol child, a railway accident with fatalities, Pinter-like threatening dialogue, gun-point transvestism, masochism and sadism; but, as if in explanation, the narrative voice at one point tells us that 'we have entered vicious passages of this book where the weakest go to the wall.' A more pervasive and disturbing harm in the novel, one that the put-upon reader undergoing the work can squirm at, is thus manifested by the fearful omnipotence of its author-narrator. The book's opening paragraphs attempt to steer this structural disturbance towards a positive end: 'Loving that real baby as I tried and still try to do, failing to love him as I failed – once crucially – and still fail to do, I have an index of how vanity mars my good intentions and of how, proudly shunning my own mental inadequacy, I so often cause harm.' These disarming riders do manage to curb the novel's picaresque-surreal action and its obtrudingly managerial voice within the enclosure of a moral project – though one which risks sentimentality because the unequivocally good is split from the harm by the plot's dislocated pile-up of horrid incidents. What's more, the remarks are themselves opening instances of that authorial obtrusiveness which combines with the jump-cut story-line to prompt occasional flashes of a readerly protective resentment.

Such sensations do not tend to occur with much of Oliver's poetry from the 1960s and '70s. Poems like 'The Furnaces' and 'Mongol in the Woods' collected in his first book *Oppo Hectic* (1969), those such as 'Going Away to Utter Pradesh' or 'Babeuf Enters the Cambodian War' associated with *The Harmless Building*, the 'Introit' to his eccentric oracle prose *The Cave of Suicession* (1974), and, above all, the remarkable 'Diagram Poems' are exercises in turning the improvised informalities of that moment to pressing personal and cultural ends, and they have worn well. Seeing and hearing Oliver reading the last of these, as the diagrams were leafed over on a large board, produced the odd impression (as the diagrams were displayed on a large board) of attending a briefing session for some mad military venture, and, simultaneously, a debriefing – since the burden of the narrative being interpretively related had already grimly soured:

> We know Tom's voice, we now know this, we see
> the magnets sunder in half, induced repulsion
> in every sense of order, and soon, my children
> in the warned world, the street awakes to shots
> and enemies and wounds and chivalries
> and carelessness, and showdowns, and innocent bystanders
> left to bleed behind an arrow pointing to an unseen cemetery.

On the supporting diagrams may be seen the magnets with their directions of attraction and repulsion, an arrow pointing towards a sign of turmoil, various dotted lines, circles, brackets, copious annotations – and the entire thing looking like a schoolboy's plan of battle for his toy soldiers. The 'Diagram Poems' act out just such a context of childish innocence and a dawning sense of collusive culpability.

In his Judith E. Wilson lecture, 'Poetry's Subject', Oliver describes his responses to two passages of highly wrought verse. Dryden's description of the 'false Achitophel' uses 'the speech apparatus when you perform it' to mime Shaftesbury's 'turbulence'. 'Performing Dryden's lines', Oliver adds, 'I intensely realise that some of their scorn could be directed against myself, for – to my shame or credit – I have something of a Shaftesburyan restlessness with my country's present politics.' Of two stanzas sceptically caressing a Christian patriotism of blood and soil in Geoffrey Hill's 'The Mystery of the Charity of Charles Péguy', Oliver remarks that 'I remain uneasy whenever response to violence is seen as the final test of a person', but also underlines how 'performing the poem, I can't distance myself as I just have from the very words that distress me'. The act of creative reading, of performing, is rightly felt here to be a process of taking into an attending body and mind the difficult matter of the world's turbulences, its woundings, harms, its damage and their damaging consequences. Oliver recognises that works of art have to begin by embodying this harm if they are to do anything positive with it. Among the roles for artistic technique, though, is to mitigate its representation so as to make our endurance of it bearable, and, thus, to disarm.

However, as already implied, 'disarm' is another word with a complex life, because while my dictionary gives as meaning 1c 'to make harmless', meaning 2b is 'to win over', and, in the adjective 'disarming', this sense can extend to 'allaying criticism or hostility: INGRATIATING'. In his accounts of performing Dryden's lines and Hill's, Oliver makes clear that their languages and structures necessarily win over the engaged reader, however temporarily, to the beliefs and convictions that are being dramatised. He admits that in the case of the former he is made to undergo a self-scrutiny which 'leads me to desire that my restlessness be fully responsible, that is, to use a dubious word, patriotic', while in the latter, he comments that 'I am briefly forced to live through this religious politics' and 'It rather flusters me, frankly.' Here, the suggestion that he is 'forced' to do it, like Pound's remark that in a poem sounds are 'forced onto the voice' of the reader by the nature of the verse, momentarily loses sight of the fact that no one's forcing you to read it. The performing reader, flashes of resentment or fluster and all, is necessarily the one taking responsibility for the embodiment of these senses.

Oliver's important poem of 1980s Britain, 'The Infant and the Pearl', is energised by that 'Shaftesburyan restlessness with my country's present politics':

'We must make a start
somewhere,' he said. 'The prosperous have first part
in the likely prosperity. Let the lower ranks
labour for it; and let *them* live apart
from the idle, the dull, the deprived, the drunks.

Liverpool's slums, Lambeth's… the dull haunt
our labour markets; they must live monastic
lives until the industrious, the investors, the brilliant
and expert haul us on stretchy elastic
towards wealth.' We whisked by the scant
foliage; finally the faint tick
of the Bentley puttered through a gap; the pennant
waved in an autoroute's wind; then as quick
as changing channels, we chased in fantastic
acceleration along the high banks
of the motorway, meditating our majestic
escape from the dull, the deprived, the drunks.

Here, the poem's author character, while being whisked around the country in a symbolic blue Bentley is given a lecture on the monetarist 'trickle-down' theory of distributive justice by Sir Pretentious Privilege, Bart. The rhymed stanza with its chorus-like echoic final line demands a restlessly energetic enjambment. Of the 17 lines above, only the stanza's final lines are end-stopped. This run-on syntax mimes the careering motion of the stockbroker's cultural ideas and the car's get-away speed. It's as if the patriotic poet's whiggish restlessness is distortedly mirrored by the market-led, deregulating anarchism of the then new right's ideology. And yet the poem benefits from these headlong cadences, for, among Oliver's writings, it is the work with the most unrelentingly sustained narrative drive.

Satire thrives on what it loves to hate, and though 'The Infant and the Pearl' draws attention to its indebtedness to the mediaeval dream-poem *Pearl*, much of its local vigour derives from Oliver's engrafting onto its stanza, the Byronic rhyming bravura of linking, for example, as if they were natural bedfellows, 'Churchillian' with 'the sillion / reeked', 'making a million', and 'crowing at each minion'. In the Preface to his *Selected Poems* (1996), the poet tells us: 'I've tried to show that any political flaws in the public arena also reside in the 'self' – in 'myself' –

and therefore inside the area of the poem-as-art too.' So there is a further level at which the affinity between the rhythms and rhymes of a poet's politics and his enemies' might register – in the tacit acknowledgement of a more pervasive cultural complicity, one which 'The Infant and the Pearl' later makes manifest in criticizing the gamut of political attitudes readily available during that unhappy Thatcherite decade.

Such complicity also forms one main thread in *A Salvo for Africa*, the collection of poems and prose commentaries Oliver published with Bloodaxe Books on 31 March 2000, less than a month before his death. The first poem, 'Our Family Is Full of Problems', announces that 'We're in England, / descending the house-combed hillsides of Coventry, / early seventies, when the idea for these poems was born'. There's no reason to doubt him, but other works indicate a longer implicit gestation for the idea. *Oppo Hectic* contains 'Remember Stortford, Birthplace of Rhodes' which obscurely cuts together erotic memories and allusions to African history likely prompted by the show-down between Ian Smith and the Wilson government during the previous decade. The poem ends by taking its stand:

> My forefinger dabbles at the sweet crumbs.
> They diminish resistance to rancid blood and I must
> try to keep ideas clear of it. Which is why
> I think of Bishop's Stortford and
> damn Rhodes.

That 'rancid blood' may also be coursing through the poet's veins – as some of the autobiographical prose and poetry in 'An Island that is All the World' (1990) makes clear. Oliver grew up in an 'area of cliffside detached homes' built on the estate of Shelley Manor, its mansion providing the original for 'The Harmless Building' in the poet's secret mythology: 'I sometimes dream of the park now as if it were the whole of Africa and I flying over in a light plane looking for lions.' The entire passage makes this middle-class boy growing up in a retired colonial atmosphere complicit with its ethos via an *Out of Africa* fantasy life.

The formal principle for *A Salvo* is adapted from 'An Island that is All the World', in which brief prose passages of a candidly confessional kind are intercut with poems that appear to embody and yet rise away from the circumstances sketched. Discussing a phase in mid-life of shuttling across-Channel between Paris and his family in England,

Oliver convincingly states: 'lacking comfortable continuity of feeling, the moral rhythm of my life was broken.' Oliver's researches into the corporeal registers of rhythm and how they help to 'fill the instant with content from thought and conceptualised emotion' can be followed in *Poetry and Narrative in Performance* (1989). Oliver's work as a poet and writer is crucially valuable primarily because of his intimately apprehended and technically elaborated attention to what could be meant by 'moral rhythm' in life and art. 'An Island that is All the World' is one of the best places to start if you are coming fresh to the poet's 'three linked stories' (autobiographical, political, and prosodic), stories told in outline, as his Preface also informs us, by Oliver's choices for the Talisman House *Selected Poems*.

'The Borrowed Bow' from *A Salvo* would not appear amiss in 'An Island that is All the World', recounting as it does a childhood 'vanishing point on a post-war seacoast, / the pier blown up in case of German invasion' where the boy poet plays with a retired colonial's souvenir:

> I borrowed the bow of black hardwood,
> took it and a bamboo stick into the garden.
> Couldn't pull the leather string back;
> the magic of the bow-spar wouldn't bend for me.
> I knew I was just meddling. So I went indoors
> to fiddle with the wireless innards:
> electronic emotions and jerky excitements
> in the village of valves, which cracked like gunfire,
> a tracer arc streaked across dusty connections,
> as if before the snap of it, the coil of smoke,
> a tiny bow had shot a brilliant arrow.

The role of poems like 'The Borrowed Bow' is to situate the poet's concern for what was once called the dark continent in his own and his culture's history – the purpose of which might be to accept the burden of that history so as to leave it behind in present acts that point towards an African future, one indicated by the arrow that contributes to the salvo fired by these poems. The book's title, by the way, includes an awareness that 'salvo' is cognate with the Latin greeting 'Salve!' and thus has 'salvation' as one of its linguistic relatives. Oliver's opening prose section 'The Dumb Barter' speaks of 'Compassion fatigue' and 'colonial guilt fatigue' as if these media effects excused a lack of attention; it claims for poetry a role in re-imagining a 'dulled-over political issue'. Oliver had also realised since at least *The Cave of Suicession* that being 'an addict of your own guilt' can mean being saved from 'having to take action'.

However, much of *A Salvo* rightly ignores Oliver's autobiography, and is energised not so much by memory (the poet had not visited Africa, as he readily admits) but research work in newspapers and acknowledged sources. The results can sometimes be less gripping, because the instants are less thoroughly filled, than when the writing is vivified with perceptions guided by the author's inscribed presence. On a number of occasions the poems go so far as to confess their shortcomings. The close of 'Protection from the Heat', for example, tells us that 'I know the poem has a weak foundation', little more than 'some mere coincidence in words', and ends by announcing that 'I am still going, still somewhat a fool.' Here Oliver's self-denigrating reference back to himself as a rookie local journalist in his first job suit is perhaps too self-denigrating, and it may be that poems (however well researched their information) cannot be built on foundations stronger than coincidences of words. On the whole, though, the poems, especially those which bring together the poet's life and his African concerns, stand up to repeated rereading far more sure-footedly than the interleaved prose passages.

In 'The Dumb Barter', the book's introductory prose, the poet makes a number of admissions, saying, for instance, that since the book was drafted in 1993 he has had to make changes to the prose because of altered circumstances, 'but the poems, by their nature, haven't needed more than slight stylistic revision.' This may have been the case, but a consequence implicit in the statement can be felt by the reader performing the work. The prose has us marshalling asserted facts, opinions and attitudes to which even those sympathetic to the project may occasionally feel the urge to quarrel. Being frequently replete instants of moral rhythm, the poetry, by its nature, disarms such responses. At one point in 'The Dumb Barter', for example, Oliver asserts that 'the rich, just by being rich, are always in debt to the poor'. While I don't doubt that many would not hold this belief, even those sensitive to the responsibilities of the world's rich nations to its poor ones might not hold it in quite these terms. All the rich? Always? To all the poor? Always? It's too sweeping a remark to bear much thinking about beyond its function as a rallying cry for the like-minded. Oliver understandably comments that, rather than 'debt rescheduling', the move by creditor nations and banks towards 'debt forgiveness' is 'the most exciting prospect of all.' But is 'exciting' quite the right word for a matter so urgent, in which, should I believe as Oliver did that the rich are always in debt to the poor, then this 'forgiveness' is no more than the proper response from apparent creditors who are, notwithstanding, categorically the debtors both in material and spiritual currencies.

The poet also advises us that 'So grave are the issues that I use a direct, undissembling voice, though one that exposes its deficiencies: my more avant-garde poetic styles are not appropriate here.' Despite mocking and exploiting in 'Walnut and Lily' the idea that poetic styles are just fashions in clothes ('not the old romantic tweed but middle-age black / and Celanian gloom'), Oliver surely knew that literary styles aren't suits to be chosen from the possible wardrobe; his remark in 'The Dumb Barter' must mean that he didn't find himself inclined to employ such styles, rather than that he was tempted to wear the Bauhaus cravat but, on second thoughts, donned the bicycle clips. Unfortunately, his statement betrays the unwanted implication that avant-garde styles are suitable for lighter subjects: not something that would have cut much crystal with the authors of *The Cantos* or *Four Quartets*, let alone the Celan of *Von Schwelle zu Schwelle* and his subsequent collections.

During the last decade of his life, Oliver was also deeply engaged with the condition of contemporary poetry, going so far as to announce at the end of the first stanza from 'Light in Back' that 'I can't hand on poetry while it's in / this state, widowed by words I married.' That line-ending contributes by doubling the states that poetry might be in to both those of its own constituency and of the political culture which it is obliged to inhabit. The poet married himself to the words as he joined them together; he was widowed by words from poetry as poetry was widowed by words from itself – and this state, perhaps of a widow-hood in which the 'better half' of poetry is somehow lost, sounds like one in which the various dominating literary exclusivities of the moment haplessly consort with the political condition of our present state to divorce us from poetry, poetry from itself, and poetry from us.

In 'Poetry's Subject', Oliver addressed such issues by speaking up for the art's 'bedrock qualities':

Without intense experimental inquiry poetry becomes com-placent, especially politically complacent; without popular outreach, poetry risks becoming driven in upon itself, another kind of complacency. Only by somehow encompassing both tradition and novelty will it achieve its bedrock qualities: beauty, truthfulness, wisdom, prescience.

His essay also provides a 'principal aphorism' about why an openness to an inclusively wide repertoire of poetry's possibilities is not merely important, but essential: '*Each narrowing of what contemporary poetry is supposed to do bears with it an equivalent narrowing in the definition of a human being.*' Oliver's best late work is plainly attempting to demonstrate what would be involved in living and working according to this manifesto of no more manifestos. In the selection from 'Shattered Crystal' that appeared in *Penguin Modern Poets 10* (1996), Oliver's Paris poems addressing matters of literary heroism (Celan, Heine) and ordinary neighbourliness manage to combine 'intense experimental enquiry' with a 'popular outreach' by adapting the 'I do this, I do that' approach of the old New York School to a candidly meditative style. 'Cirque d'hiver', a related piece in *Selected Poems*, recounts in a harsh and tender light how during his days working for Agence France-Presse (the 'Diagram Poems' period), in which the life of the journalists reporting the world's harms was itself a bit of a circus, the company had paid for his daughters to have a seasonal treat:

> Suddenly I noticed the animal trainer, half out of control, was
> > sweating with fear.
> I wondered if AFP was treating my girls
> to the spectacle of someone being eaten for Christmas dinner.
> My girls kept chewing their candy floss, not especially concerned.
> I didn't then know Kenneth Koch's two poems, The Circus,
> in which life's parade keeps passing on by without too much justice
> and people keep dropping out of the parade.

– which is how 'Cirque d'hiver' ends, generously describing and acknowledging the help that Koch's first whimsical then nostalgic poems were in occasioning Oliver's engaging work.

In 'Trink', alluding to the poet's '*Ich trink Wein aus zwei Gläsern*', Oliver affirms: 'In even deeper homage to Celan's integrity / I pour his two glasses away.' This hail is evidently also a farewell, as 'A Little Night' even more plainly states – Celan being 'the only poet I have to struggle against / because none wrote more beautifully post-war / of the perfection and terror of crystal.' Where Celan's integrity took his later styles into an ever more intricately difficult minimalism, Oliver's moral rhythm led him to longer texts that narrate pointedly moral stories, either fictional or autobiographical – ones which lay themselves open to a reader's performative attention with little of the searching after purity and authenticity that may be found in the attenuated styles of some atrophied experiment. This is not to say that Oliver ended by wanting to 'épater les avant-gardistes'; in 'Poetry's Subject' he notes that 'the avant-garde is ignored at peril', but also that 'Identifying the avant-garde is fortunately difficult'. Prescriptive aesthetics attempt a pre-emptive strike on the future before it has had time to find its own way; they can consequently wheel-clamp poets' responsivenesses by reductions of their repertoires.

In 'The Weekend Curfew' Oliver points out that the imitation of Celan's minimalism is no longer likely to be rewarding:

> And we, we'd emulate this,
> letting our lyrics croak
> the throat
> into broken music
> as if mere self-unease
> were our righteousness
> smashing the lyric vessel
> in darkness
> so to be as smart as he was
> oh to be as smart as he was
> our words nowhere near bursting
> with such a lesser weight of light,
> as we flip through
> the fragments
> of our cheque book stubs.

The moral here is plain enough: if you want to pay homage to Celan's integrity both in his life and work, the last thing you should do is try to hitch a ride for your well-heeled angst on his formal procedures driven so ruthlessly against silence by a repeatedly re-enacted historical burden. It's as if one end of harm were to coax out the best repertoire of constructively human responses we can manage. The Acknowledgements to *A Salvo for Africa* note that the volume is 'Book I of *Arrondissements*, a series of books on themes arising from life in the arrondissements of Paris.' Other parts of the series can perhaps be glimpsed in the 'Shattered Crystal' and 'New York/ Paris Poems' sections of *Penguin Modern Poets 10*. Unhappily, it rather seems that Oliver's death in his early sixties has rendered the project definitively unfinished. Four years ago, in the Preface to his *Selected Poems*, Oliver expressed once more the hope that a poet's work might reflect 'real variousness and avoid government by any persuasive definition of human consciousness or by any faddish narrowing of genres, forms or subject-matter.' He properly concluded by not 'claiming a cent for the results', just stating that this is 'what my own work tries to do.' Yet this is what Douglas Oliver's 'various life-work including genres as different as may be necessary' has indeed done and what his meditative poems, novels, satires, burlesques, and lyrics will surely continue to do.

ON *UNTITLED SEQUENCE*
BY PETER RILEY

First, some literary history: at the April 1977 Cambridge Poetry Festival, Peter Riley read from a sequence of poems that began –

> And then we…
> No.
> Not 'we'.
> I.

It was later broadcast on the BBC Radio 3 programme devoted to the event. I attended the reading and heard the poem again on the radio. The same sequence was published in *Perfect Bound* 4, the Autumn 1977 volume. This was a little magazine based in Cambridge, England, which ran for seven issues between Summer 1976 and June 1979. Poetry (and in one case a review) by Peter Riley appeared in four issues. Perhaps the sequence he read at the festival was published in *Perfect Bound* because I requested it, or maybe it was offered to us. Twenty-one years later, asked to contribute to this special issue on the poet's work, I remembered the sequence and thought it a possible text to discuss. Had it been reprinted in a separate volume during the intervening years? It must have been. However, when I contacted the poet, it seemed that after its magazine appearance, he had all but forgotten the work. Parts 3 and 10 had been taken out, lightly revised, and given separate titles with the idea that they be included in a projected selected poems. Peter Riley sent me 'In a German Car-Park' and 'Is this Düsseldorf or Kiel?'

I was surprised he hadn't put the entire group into a more visible publication, and said that perhaps I'd write on the sequence in its magazine form anyway. Some time later a further message arrived, which included the following:

> Concerning that sequence which you 'discovered' in *Perfect Bound*. I've tested it on a few connoisseurs and it seems to go down rather well. I might include it in the 'big book' I'm preparing – I had provisionally selected the 3rd and 10th poems. Anyway I've tinkered with it a little and below is the text as I have it now.

The main problem with my proposed contribution seemed to be that, with the exception of those few people who had filed away copies of *Perfect Bound*, no one would have read the work (in either unrevised or 'tinkered with' forms). What if it were republished in my contribution? Back I went to ask for permission. Here is part of the reply:

> The only thing about the *Untitled Sequence* and *The Gig*, is that I've now agreed with a small press to produce a separate edition of it (revised version of course) – Wild Honey Press in Ireland. … Perhaps it would be profligate to print it again in *The Gig*, or might interfere with Wild Honey's sales? But on the other hand this means it will be in print, so if you wrote on it you wouldn't be addressing a vacuum, as it were.

In what follows, aside from a few observations about the changes made between the magazine text and the one provided by its poet, or when history dictates that the earlier one be quoted, I cite from the revised version of *Untitled Sequence* – so the following comments can double as a review of the forthcoming Wild Honey pamphlet publication.

1

Untitled Sequence is, as its author's note states, a remnant of a larger project. Written in 1970, abandoned two years later, it was taken up again, revised and made public in 1977. The work was then described as a 'set of poems worked from materials formerly the fifth and last section of *The Linear Journal*, subtitled "Germany".' The *Perfect Bound* text also includes the information that 'This is likely to be no longer that fifth section', making it an outtake of sorts. An end of line bargain, or *disjecta membra*, this title-less or untitled sequence carries with it an unentitled air of dejection, of unpropitious circumstances borne over from the unpromising situation which it intermittently narrates and out of which it came:

> What happened was the hiking schoolboys got older
> and became a college dramatic society taking *Macbeth*
> round Germany on a coach, playing in gymnasia halls

and cinemas before large but almost entirely
compulsory audiences. I played Seton.

The opening poem in *The Linear Journal* (1973) announces: 'My
regard, of you, takes the form / of a band of adolescents in shorts /
setting out on an alpine ramble'. *Untitled Sequence* marks a continuity
in the narrative gesture with 'What happened', but it may have proved
the indication of a rupture, one in which the enclosed coherence of the
later sequence's story and the graver tenor of its concerns made it not
seem fitting as the earlier work's fifth part.

Nevertheless, *Untitled Sequence* signals its ancestry with a series of
echoing quotations from the book. Part 6 of the later sequence, for
example, echoes a phrase from the opening of *The Linear Journal*: 'the /
Central Gardens of your presence, your / image, that I hardly know' –

> Suffice it to say,
> here I have you in mind,
> the calm and fearless
> Central Gardens of your presence
> asleep or at the other end
> of the continent gives me
> some chance of weathering
> the obscurity, even if it denies
> most of what I think I know.

This calmly dependent second-person invocation of a loved presence in
absence imagines emotional security as a city park. It's a vivid touch to
bring the casual phrase 'have you in mind' alive in this way. The theme
is further drawn out at the start of the following section to *Untitled
Sequence*: 'Wind seeps through cracks in the park / and woos the inner
female.' This strikes a chillier, grimmer note than the playfully aware
manner of *The Linear Journal*, section 1, where 'your presence' appears
to be glossed as:

> a fixed-term loan of variegated parklands
> known as 'continuing to exist'
> or all of the past and all of the present
> 'Have fun,' they say, 'Goodbye.'

Despite its echoing recollections of the earlier book, *Untitled Sequence* developed away from its sponsoring occasion in an apparently ongoing work – only to be left aside for decades in one back issue of a small magazine.

Riley's recent tinkerings with the *Perfect Bound* text can be improvements: 'I played Seton' is better than the original 'I was Seton'. Both are repetitions of previously used verbs, but in the revised versions the play on 'played' is more resonant and suggestive about the predicament of the bit-part student actor, because the poem tells us that he wasn't at all, in a Stanislavskian sense, Seton. However, the older poet's modesty in saying he has 'tinkered with' the text may also inadvertently express a weakening of the original impulse, 'large but largely' is better, I think, because more crushing in the collapse (an important word in both this sequence and its sponsoring book) of 'large' into 'largely / compulsory', while the avoided repetition in 'large but almost entirely' is efficient prose, but no more. Similarly, 'a troupe of students' (felicitously echoing 'a band of adolescents') has become 'a college dramatic society' – which is not far short of authorial vandalism.

Untitled Sequence includes at least one allusion to the play these students are taking around Germany. Part 8 begins:

> The tour is not going well or badly,
> the tour is just going. We have not
> whistled in the wings. We have spoken
> a language we barely comprehend but in
> fits and starts, but we have spoken it
> as it stands. We have murdered it.

'Macbeth does murther Sleep', of course, but one of them has helped murder the play by saying it in act II scene ii. Seton (Seyton in the Arden edition) is one of Macbeth's attendant lords. He has about five lines to speak during his two appearances in the play's last act, his great moment is when he announces 'The Queen, my Lord, is dead' – the line that cues Macbeth's 'all our yesterdays' speech:

> Life's but a walking shadow; a poor player,
> That struts and frets his hour upon the stage,
> And then is heard no more: it is a tale

> Told by an idiot, full of sound and fury,
> Signifying nothing.

Seyton is on stage while Macbeth, night after night, repeats one of Shakespeare's most quoted and borrowed pieces of dramatic verse. Even the 'poor player' who has to stand there reacting is likely to know it off by heart. The narrator's role in *Untitled Sequence*, not surprisingly, borrows from its gloom and insight into a flawed life's meaninglessness:

> I played Seton.
> I
> had very little to say. And the scenery,
> the scenery was quite different: it was
> a set of collapsible platforms of hardboard sheets
> and perforated steel struts which towards the end
> of the run began to buckle, and swayed
> like reeds in the wind
> when Duncan leapt on his prey.

Here, an imperfect rhyme on verb and noun sounds a close to the stanza which the play's denouement and the floppy scenery figures as a series of collapsing structures – the flopping play itself, the narrator's sense of himself, the idea of the players as a coherent group, and on to more inclusive structures such as Europe, humanity, or that one noted in section two: 'we are divided, and reach across / by magic, which in schools is called / sympathy, and in universities, structure.' But what sustains the poet's claim here to give the authentic, yet more mysterious, explanation for what allows us to reach across division while other explanations are denigrated as (to exaggerate for salience) humanistic clap-tap in schools and theoretical clap-trap in universities? Here lies a key issue that the sequence tours around.

The makeshift scenery of the student players also has an echo in the collapsed and temporary-seeming landscape of a bombed Germany – the Germany that was a key ideological battleground for the Cold War world through which the student players are travelling. One of the original footers to the sections ran: 'a British officers' mess in a small town somewhere in the Rhine valley' –

Is there a war on? No.

But there has been. A photograph on
the hall-stand shows it, a sweep of the arm:
all these was rebuild, he was flat.

Riley's poem even-handedly acknowledges both the disorientation of
hearing your language garbled by non-native speakers, and of mangling
someone else's language when abroad, as here in 8:

So now I feel the need for a particular drink.
It's called something like flughaven mit schlosen
no, that's ridiculous, so I don't get one, and
the local bearer of Hölderlin's language looks at me
in blank dismay.

It *is* ridiculous: 'flughaven' means 'airport', 'mit' is 'with' and 'schlosen'
sounds like a badly defective participle of the verb 'to close': 'geschlossen'.
So is this attempt at ordering a drink, in which only the 'mit' might
be correct, a hopelessly garbled version of 'The airport is closed'? Re-
revising 'schlosen' to 'schmaltz' on the Wild Honey proofs looks like
a misjudgment; the Yiddish-derived loan word for sentimental art
is worse than ridiculous: it's impossible, as the student player would
surely have known. That lost echo of a sense in 'Schloss' or 'geschlossen'
had added to the serious air of entrapment in *Untitled Sequence*, as
more sardonically here in 9:

It's also quite exciting
staying in a hotel without windows.
You could really work here: you could
steer the whole bunker into victory.
The varieties of reflected light
suddenly seem a paltry affair to this
concrete corridor and threadbare carpet,
the tiny, empty bar, the porter in his
alcove with his accounts.

The ghastly hotel momentarily conjures up a memory of Hitler in
the Berlin Führerbunker, or of the winners in their blastproof shelters

after a nuclear exchange. 'You could really work here' away from the distractions of the natural world, but would you really want to, and for how long? Riley's choice of German poet to register his implicit point about art and language-competence is hardly accidental. Hölderlin (rather than the obvious candidate for the role of language representative, Goethe) has been a favourite of some English poets since David Gascoyne translated from his work. Though Michael Hamburger had also published a large volume of his poems in English translation by this date, Riley is probably making acknowledgement of the interest in the disturbed visionary's writings shown by Tim Longville and John Riley of the Grosseteste Press, publishers of *The Linear Journal.*

   However, having evoked the shadow of the pathetic fallacy so as to figure a relationship between the poor players and their collapsible scenery, or of the students when not called upon to strut and fret, and their disorientated experiences of knocked-about cities, the poet distinguishes the two by concentrating, perhaps a little melodramatically, on the dejection of the young theatre company in 8:

> But all that was really damaged
> was the fiction of ourselves,
> shattered. The ruins of empire strewn
> around us were works of art compared
> to what we knew we weren't qualified
> to be. The buildings are now all razed and
> grass grows in their spaces, for a time.
>
> Ruins of a war, ruins
> of a reconstruction scheme, the vast
> acreage of wonderful rubbish lying
> still in the day, meeting the light

Thus in 'I played Seton./ I / had very little to say' the lineation plays up the romantically isolated vulnerability of that 'collapsing structure' ('the fiction of ourselves') by detaching the subject pronoun from its verb and allowing it a line all of its own. The task of the poem will be to give validity to this 'I', distinguished from an inflated and presumptuous 'we', by finding means for bringing it into relation with those others and things from which it feels separated – its main implement for achieving this validation being the stylistic flexibility of the phrasing, lineation, and diction.

Such a task, in such unpropitious circumstances, is in need of permission. Riley ends the first section of his sequence by finding this in the heart of pointlessness and indifference:

> Knowing at last how little it mattered
> whether this show was on. Making it possible
> to continue.

Coming at the end of part 1 this is inevitably reflexive, expressing the poem's sense, at that moment, of how a poet may also be able to continue – one which acknowledges the reality of attempting to do something substantial when you are very much unacknowledged. And no legislator either. The benefit of that minimal self-permission is that if you can find it there, you can find it anywhere. A reader might also notice how much the poem denigrates and minimises the language competences of its protagonist, and yet in this unpropitious situation he will try to rise to some memorable speech and significant utterance.

2

This unpropitious situation registers for us as an unpropitious subject, overtly vulnerable, but not appealing for sympathy, intent on registering the subjectivity of the view, its singularity:

> Walking this bright boulevard which really
> could be anywhere, any big place,
> I seem made of insubstantial elements
> like a leaf in the wind, an unsteered ship,
> small bird lost in the sky roads:
> weightless, of no authority, moving
> on the stream of my, or someone else's
> wakefulness

The figures for the self here ('leaf … unsteered ship … small bird') sound like much-circulated lyrical tender, and 'I seem made of insubstantial elements / like a leaf in the wind' (a phrase worked into John James's poem 'Sister Midnight') draws on the mediaeval Latin of the Archpoet; but the phrase 'or someone else's / wakefulness' asks what is staked by this literary subjectivity. How important is it that this is happening to this person? Is the subject a blank counter for what anyone might feel, but someone specific will have to if it is to be part of a lyric sequence? If the collapsed sense of self that the sequence writes from signals a crisis of purpose for the poet, it is not a crisis unique to those composing poetry. Riley's 'I' character in these poems shares some of the cultural characteristics of the classic Cold War figures 'waiting' in theatrical settings like Beckett's most famous play, or Stoppard's Shakespearean one. Section 26 of *The Linear Journal* announces this theme too: 'waiting also, for the next phase of waiting' and 'waiting for what you say, what you bring / into the air'.

Untitled Sequence, though, has the spiritual condition of waiting in history, waiting in an individual life, built into its narrative situation. Riley's 'I' is someone –

> Waiting
> for a 5-minute cue in Act IV. But we become
> contracted, there's a strength in it, we drag
> the most collapsed notions of our stature
> around with us for years regardless and then
> we behave like people after all.

Here's the phrase 'collapsing structure' from 1, transmogrified into 'collapsed … stature'. This word 'collapse' and its variants had echoed throughout *The Linear Journal*: 'people's legs collapse, habitually, it's alright / everyone is sub-standard, artistically speaking'; 'the development section collapsing on me in the night'; 'and maybe an entire life / is waiting to be collapsed in the next phase'. Part 7 of *Untitled Sequence* narrates just such a fall:

> Sometimes I like myself very much
> and think I'd make a first-rate detective.
> Except for the bits that involve courage.
> and expertise. and enthusiasm for the whole thing.

The Marlowe-like detective, *in* a nasty situation but not *of* it, is a familiar role model for the junior poet. Riley makes skilful mockery both of liking 'myself very much' (a sure sign something is wrong) and of this poet-as-detective idea – for 'courage' and 'expertise' and 'enthusiasm' are required of someone engaged on a case, whereas the poet-detective is usually just an isolated waiter and watcher. By the end of that sequence of marked sentence-close revisions, there's little left to speak of in the 'first-rate' gumshoe musing.

A person who sometimes likes 'myself very much' is concerned about whether others share the same opinion. Hence the problems of group identities and subjectivities in *Untitled Sequence*, a note struck by the sequence's opening, its isolated 'I' and the problem of a relation with pluralities:

> And then we ... / No,
> Not 'we'.
> I.
> (Can't I get rid of that inflated pronoun?)
> What was I going to say?

What's telling about this is that while others were wondering about how to reclaim poetry's cultural centrality by abandoning the limited, lyrical subject in search of a communal voice, or by effecting an absence of pronoun-marked subjectivity, Riley writes with the specified aim of reinstating the singular subject, anxieties and all:

> All this is a method
> of avoiding looking you in the face
> because I'm shy or nervous or I'm
> a latent homosexual (ouch) or something
> distracted me, a crash or two outside,
> something one of us dropped in the grass a
> collapsing structure

In the *Perfect Bound* text '(ouch)' had been '(oh)': the surprise of a recognition has been turned into the twinge of a revelation. And who is the 'you' here? It must indefinitely include the reader, the audiences of the play, other actors in the troupe. The same could be asked for 'one of us', where that first person plural raises its head again. The sensed problem of whether the players are a group or a collection of isolated individuals is directly addressed at the opening of 5:

> Evenings off we drift and scatter,
> wandering round a foreign city,
> we re-certify small agreements.

If you specify who 'we' are then you make no necessary claim to speak for others, merely to report on the behaviour of a limited group. However, if you don't specify, then the pronoun will likely balloon out in its reference to include any readers and even humanity at large. Part of the rhetorical device of Riley's sequence is to keep both 'we' and 'you' pronouns hesitant between specified and unspecified options. So his narrative dramatises the post-romantic/modernist problem of the relationship between the poetic subject locked in a private life, and putative willing readers (a public), for the student actors are 'playing in gymnasia halls / and cinemas before large but almost entirely / compulsory audiences.'

Riley's 'I' character is practically obsessed with what can or may join us together. The use of intimate-milieu detail, à la Frank O'Hara, is here put to a more overtly moralised purpose:

> At times like this questions such as
> I wonder what John's doing now?
> assume a hitherto unrealised importance
> and tenacity, as a matter of, oh – survival
> even.

In the light of a work like *Untitled Sequence*, Riley, far from being an explorer of marginal possibilities, seems intent on performing culturally central tasks:

> The wonder is what does survive here
> of the eye-light
>
> in a metropolis meaning
> we are divided, and reach across
> by magic, which in schools is called
> sympathy, and in universities, structure.

In this passage already referred to, the poem grows sourly smart about the cultural role of English Literature, Shakespeare's *Macbeth* being a prime recruit, and how it has been moralised to function, often implausibly, as a substitute for religion in the inculcation and maintenance of social relations. But if Riley seems sardonic about an 'only connect' liberalism, it may be so as to smuggle a more mysterious version of it back as ... magic? Shakespeare's play, its weird sisters and their prophecies, gives little positive timbre to that word.

Riley is not one of those writers drawn to a desiccating of the human subject in poetry, not one who assumes it must be expunged so as to rid culture of that pasteboard enemy, the bourgeois subject. Rather, he attempts to sustain the poetic subject on other grounds. He is able to approach the issue of our relatedness only and precisely because he includes himself in as a vulnerable and damaged part of the material which can find itself in or out of relations with others and things. The sequence follows that crushed self, the student actor; but tracking him across Germany there is an ambitious poetic subject embedded in the writing who takes his all-but-rhapsodic chances when they are suitably prepared in the casually sketched circumstances.

What's underplayed is the notion of a guiding consciousness other than the inscribed subject, but this can be heard as present in the sound of the lyrical flights:

> Ruins of a war, ruins
> of a reconstruction scheme, the vast
> acreage of wonderful rubbish lying
> still in the day, meeting the light
> where the mind stops urging itself
>
> O the bright world is harder than horn.

The seeming address turns into an exclamation. The 'bright' turns into the 'harder': lyricism both evokes a surface pleasure and recognises an obdurate resistance. The obduracy is a thing equally to confront and be grateful for. The poetic voice in its ambivalences can render both for our benefit. The last line of this section is remarkable in its change of register and pitch. It manifests the poet's true self-image as distinct from that of the student actor who is its stand-in within the narrative.

Our being divided and the possibilities for connectedness ('we... reach across / by magic') is a drama played out in the poem at a level some way above the mimetic fallacy, in the terms of the poem's

lineation, as in the line-break above, and its sustained syntax. For this
sequence, the idiom that Riley develops takes the text a distance from
the 'fracturing' gestures of *The Linear Journal* (such as this from section
30: 'a littered field / beautiful refuse of the mind / O / the possibilities!')
towards a style distinctly more continuous and declarative, as here once
more in the hotel with no windows of part 9:

> To speak of love and point
> to the nearest blank wall
> and the rest is extra,
> deserved, and won, but extra,
> my own love of you, and you and you…
>
> When all that was damaged was the map itself
> of what lies between us.

In its self-correcting mannerism ('love of you, and you and you…') the
passage does break off and take up again with a syntactic disjuncture,
but barely a semantic one. Once again, what Riley brings to that
stuttering way of proceeding is a fairly articulated, founding moral
urgency. We can interpolate it across the gaps – by magic, or, if you
prefer, by sympathy, or, again, by implicitly construable structure.

So the personal feeling of collapse is made to bear the sense of a
more general collapse and the 'I's vulnerability comes to represent a
condition of the social and human fabric. The poem instances a desire to
do repairs to this, and attempts what it can at the level of its structured
voicing, but is wide enough awake not to think that this effort can be
made to register on the hard world by an act of afflatus, or aesthetic fiat.
Untitled Sequence is awake in its casual registering of circumstance on
a map of Europe during the Cold War, in its sense of Germany: 'It is a
country turned against its own borders, / falling in double light across
the streets.' And a few lines later –

> It is very much Europe, this,
> very much a tattered bar off-centre to
> a sense of realised spaciousness now inhabited
> mainly by retail chains.
> Where in the lower stratum
> of a converted warehouse a horizontally

> elongated structure dimly glows in the
> night of dereliction.

What is the 'structure' that 'dimly glows' here? De-centredness, far from being a state to aim for (so as to throw off the spectre of collusion with a theoretically constructed notion of the hegemonic subject), is represented in the sequence as a condition of disempowerment. Its opposite, a 'realised spaciousness' like those 'Central Gardens' or parkland, has been bought up by the 'retail chains' – with their quiet pun from the slogan at the end of *The Communist Manifesto*. Unsurprisingly, the sequence articulates a predicament that it can't begin to transform, not least because of the terms in which the problem is set. But what it can do is to mitigate the consequences of the problem with its style, that elongated structure (linear journal) dimly glowing 'in the / night of dereliction' – and with this the strategies of the *Untitled Sequence* come into sharper outline.

3

Roy Fisher's sketch of Riley's poetic in the later *Lines on the Liver* from a recent interview with John Kerrigan ('Come the Think of It, the Imagination' in *News for the Ear: A Homage to Roy Fisher*) praises its contrariness:

> I think Peter's hard/soft/hard, straight/twisted/straight poetic
> is a valiant attempt to duck out from under the Impossible
> Poetics plastic sheet, and he's good enough to have something
> to show.

What this indicates is that Riley has been attentive to the siren calls of 'Impossible Poetics' – the risk being that you reduce your creative options to zero by imbibing too much from the prevailing theory-driven accounts of what, if you dare to go that way, will make you fatally incorrect, politically speaking. Yet Riley has cut them with some shamelessly flexible methods and obdurate materials from his own history and sensibility. The results, as Fisher's sequence of slashed concepts implies, can be heterogeneous and at odds with themselves.

Riley's poetry, at this point and later, has been composed from far-fetched allegiances whose implications can run to conflict and contradiction within the textures of the poems. Yet this is as it should be, since it both testifies to his poetry's restless ambitiousness and to the crisis in the 1960s which supposed that the old models would no longer work, but left the new models somewhat short of a broadly acknowledged cultural role. Looking back, it may have been that the sense of a cultural purpose was too readily assumed, while the poetic means to that supposed end were never sufficiently appreciated in their consequences and, as a result, never widely absorbed. Riley's sequence exemplifies both the benefits and problems of its pluralism, not least in the attempt to get a modest and historically beaten-up English sensibility ('This would never have happened / if I'd stayed in Stockport' as section 25 of *The Linear Journal* notes) to take on the brashly enthusiastic and culturally engagé tones of the American models that the author followed and championed back then. The 1970 Cape Goliard edition of Charles Olson's *The Archaeologist of Morning*, for example, acknowledges and thanks 'Mr Peter Riley, who gathered early.'

A reader may hear the tensions and conflicts of allegiance in the uneasily self-dramatizing behaviour of the seemingly improvised, thinking-on-your-feet lines in part 2, when Riley writes how

> questions such as
> I wonder what John's doing now?
> assume a hitherto unrealised importance
> and tenacity, as a matter of, oh – survival
> even.

That 'oh – survival / even' attempts, quite effectively, to have its flip cake and profoundly eat it too; and it's with the inherent precariousness of such a literary 'collapsing structure' that I want to conclude:

> So you see there is no solution, this web
> of tensions is what we are going to live in,
> into the future; to talk of breaking it
> is to damage more than us; it is what
> also we act by, and with, raising
> messages to the ends of the earth holding

> intact each working space. A spreading
> light moves to the land's edge.
>
> Where a ship is always waiting.

This 'web / of tensions' and 'to talk of breaking it / is to damage more than us' carry, in their syntax and enjambments an improvisationally structured sense of our separations and connectednesses in the style itself. There is a certain lack of attunement in the breath-driven iterativeness – suggesting the benefits and drawbacks of a jamming manner, the sense of the poem as preferring (with its 'better to travel than arrive' poetic) to seem more a performed 'gesture' than a finally made structure.

Yet the sequence has brought to articulation a dilemma about the grounds and sources of poetic authority – to which Riley brings a native charm and wit, self-deprecating and modest, but with an ambitious lyrical impulse concealed, Trojan-horse fashion, within it. His poem avoids the occasionally fatal self-importance of the late modernist high moral style through its informality, and the included subject's recognitions of itself as a seemingly collapsed source of insight that, nevertheless, proves thematically up to its task of articulating both its dilemma and a poetic context for the larger cultural consideration of that material. Thus, in *Untitled Sequence*, a complex of aesthetic, moral and cultural problems related to the role of the individual subject in life provides the terms for its provisional amelioration in coming to see the world as necessarily more benignly structured, a 'web / of tensions' not to 'talk of breaking' or that 'waiting' ship which, unlike the 'waiting' student actor but in concert with the poet whom he partially represents, is about to reach across geographically separated pieces of terrain. *Untitled Sequence*, like that ship, has, to borrow words from W. H. Auden and Roy Fisher, somewhere to get to and will arrive with itself.

AN ASOCIAL ART

The writers who are interviewed for *Prospect into Breath: Interviews with* North and South *Writers* have all found places in British society where they can write their poems. They have also found others willing to publish their work. They will have given readings from time to time, received occasional prizes, perhaps, and small fees. A number of the interviewees refer to making poetry as a craft. As Richard Caddel (b. 1949) puts it: 'Surrounded by all these great architects of our craft, I feel I'm just a jobbing builder: I undertake each thing as a separate entity – patio; double-glazing; new front door – that sort of thing.' It is the 'poet' as a member of a guild, a profession, or person with a recognised vocation within an institution that probably does not have a place in contemporary society. There are many reasons for this, and they are not all bad. 'Art', the Italian poet Umberto Saba observed, 'is profoundly asocial' and the professions, society itself even, is to some poets like a club to Groucho Marx: you wouldn't want to belong to one that would have you as a member.

Yet, despite Margaret Thatcher's observation that there is 'no such thing as society – only individuals and families', people can barely exist outside it. Poets, it seems from the testimony here, are people who make notes on it, as if at a distance, but from within. Elaine Randell (b. 1951) writes 'endless notes that get consolidated.' For Caddel, too, making poems involves 'a process of note-taking and note-editing', while Catherine Walsh (b. 1964) 'could over a week produce – for example, in off moments, you know, travelling by train or on the bus, when I get the chance – two sides of foolscap which look like a complete mess'. Making notes is a way of projecting yourself through time: you do something now which will, some day, become something else. It is one reason why writing poems is not like keeping a diary. This process of projecting yourself into the future may involve believing that you are becoming, have become, or just *are* a poet. However, this form of private self-credence should be distinguished from the public event of being called a poet. I think the name 'poet' is best understood as a appellation which may be given by others to people who have written poems and one which can as easily be used with envious sarcasm or barely veiled contempt as with respect or admiration.

Thus, it seems sensible to try to write poems, but nonsense to try to become a poet. This distinction, between the activity and the self in a role, is also worth maintaining as a defence against pretence and imposture. Lee Harwood (b. 1939), when asked to 'talk a little about your family background, early life and education', replied: 'My first reaction to that question is that my personal history really doesn't matter that much.' Elaine Randell only appears to contradict him when she says 'the question about a writer's early life and family is the most important and holds the key to all the other questions.' After all, a reader's desire to understand better a writer's urge to give off-the-cuff versions of significant milestones, and different again from the complex and partly subliminal ways in which, like it or not, a writer's life shapes the writing produced in it. Lee Harwood doesn't presume to think that even his life in writing is necessarily of interest to a reader. He talks about 'writing and books and possibilities'. The emphasis is on the interest of the activity in itself, and not on Lee Harwood performing the activity. My interest in the latter springs from the former in the Harwood interview, as not always or sustainedly everywhere else in this collection. Richard Caddel warns people against 'writing poetry for their ego', because 'they think they are projecting themselves and invariably ... invariably there's nothing to project and no-one to project it at.' I would add that what goes for 'writing poetry' here is even more true of becoming a poet.

The interviewees are all asked to respond to a quotation from Larkin ('You've seen this sight, felt this feeling, had this vision and have got to find a combination of words that will preserve it by setting it off in other people') and Ashbery ('I think every poem before it's written is something unknown, and the poem that isn't wouldn't be worth writing'). Jonathan Williams (b. 1929) deflects the question, and Frances Presley (b. 1952) more or less refuses: 'I don't want to comment much more on their words ... because they were written very much out of their experience, and I'd have to think about them in context.' Larkin, the popular figurehead of the British poetry establishment, comes in for some stick. Kelvin Corcoran (b. 1956): 'Well I think we'd all be very surprised if I went for Philip Larkin in this case.' Eric Mottram (b. 1924): 'Larkin's command is characteristic of the autobiographic poet under the illusion that poetry is a direct transference of bits of experience – however, and usually, trite – into words with therefore as little interference from imaginative invention of syntax and measure as possible.' None of those asked observes that Larkin (who once joked that, asked to give his opinion about Ashbery, he would reply 'I'd prefer strawberry') is giving a popularised version of his writing for public consumption, or that his poems could not have been written according to the stated policy.

Catherine Walsh, however, notes that Larkin's remark is inconsistent: 'And "preserve"; surely if you manage to "set it off" in other people it's not static. So how can "it" be the same?' Lee Harwood, who prefers Ashbery, is right to note that 'the Larkin quote, if you take it in a very vague way, could be said to be true', though Elaine Randell has, for me, the best response: 'I have to say straight off I admire both those writers very much.' She remarks that 'the Larkin quote, well, is right' and she adds 'the Ashbery one is also true'. Asked, almost in disbelief, 'So you don't see a contradiction between the two?' she replies, 'Not at all.' Why her response seems fair is implied in Caddel's criticism of the second statement, also framed for the occasion: 'Ashbery is probably being a little ingenuous in suggesting that he's writing with this totally Joe Simple approach to what he's producing.' David Annwn (b. 1953) correctly observes that 'the distinction between what is known and isn't known in the writing of a poem is not so clear as those people seem to imply.' Just as Ashbery's view about writing as discovery is a *sine qua non* of poetry as a process for understanding the world, a process which cannot begin in a vacuum, so Larkin's inspiration in ordinary experience and his compulsion to communicate require him to discover what the nature of the inspiring occasion was, for him, in writing, and to make a shape of it which will inevitably reverberate differently in the minds of those who find his shape helpful to them. The composition, for example, of Larkin's poem 'Here' in four sentences, each with the word 'here' used once and without recourse to the first-person pronoun, indicates the activity of a more subtle and, indeed, experimental writer than either his own remark, or most of these interviewees' responses, would suggest.

Saba, noting art's profoundly asocial nature, added that it was just this that allowed it to serve social life: 'all the poets are in this sense, and in this sense alone, civil poets.' Thus poets, in Sam Goldwyn's phrase, need to be 'included out', so that their made objects may have something troubling and refreshing to offer, and, I might add, excluded in, so that these objects can, to at least the necessary minimal extent, be received. However, because of its asocial, marginal character, poetry attracts the socially ill adjusted. Catherine Walsh, who admits to being 'extremely intolerant', has noticed that a 'lot of people involved in that kind of scene … are quite crazy. I don't mean strange or eccentric or anything, I mean genuine cases.' Elaine Randell mentions that one of her advertised volumes never materialised because the publisher 'unfortunately had a sort of breakdown just at the time that he produced it'. Yet mental problems are not the preserve of artists. Harwood makes the point that in any community there are 'quiet ones, aggressive ones, good people, bad people', but also calls the 'idea of a community of writers … a completely false one', adding that 'Experience within the world of literary politics shook that nonsense out of me.'

Literary politics, that kind of scene, the place Vittorio Sereni called 'the fenced-off zoo which has become the writer's and the poet's world' is the only context in which becoming or being a poet has any substantial social meaning, and it is a cage not worth finding yourself locked inside, for, self-enclosed in this literary pound, a poet's ability to view the world from various distances within it has been drastically curtailed. What remains? Lee Harwood wants writing which can 'make you intensely aware of being alive, of the world around you. Which is what art is meant to do, I thought!' Elaine Randell is involved with 'indicators of loss, of all sorts of losses that we deal with every day' and concerned with what can be done 'with reparation'. There are some people who write because it helps them to live and who hope that what they write will encourage others, in their own ways, to do likewise.

'GENEROSITY OF SPIRIT':
LEE HARWOOD

Re-reading Lee Harwood's poems, I found myself recalling that Frank and Nancy Sinatra hit from the sixties: 'and then I go and spoil it all by saying something stupid like "I love you".' Harwood frequently writes it: 'When I say "I love you" – that means / something' ('When the Geography was Fixed'), or '"You're great! and very wise" we laugh as / we reach the top of the rock outcrop / "and I love you for it"' ('Central Park Zoo'), or 'I do like oil slicks, but I love you.' ('Sea Coves') Yet he also writes that 'For some reason the word "LOVE" does not suggest / a strength, or grace, only a mild ineffectuality.' ('Plato was Right Though'). This is a characteristically honest reflection on his compulsion to include frank avowals in poems whose erogenous *paysages moralisés* already contain such unutterables in their uttered.

Harwood was born in 1939 and didn't see anything of his father for the first six or so years of his life. He was, as he notes in a 1990 interview, 'brought up in a household of strong women.' Writing about the same years from the perspective of a boy nine years older, Roy Fisher observed that 'there was, with the prolongation of stoicism, a deadening of areas of feeling.' The presence of such avowals in Harwood's work may then be a historically understandable method, not unlike Allen Ginsberg's, for engaging with reader embarrassment in a post-war culture that would benefit from the renewed expression and acknowledgement of ordinary emotion.

'It's in the reader's hands', Harwood remarks in the Foreword to this welcome collected edition of work that, since the mid-sixties, has appeared from small and fugitive presses – like the dedicated Shearsman Books. Such emphases on the reader's role have been repeatedly made by the poet, and by supporters such as Robert Sheppard. A snatch from his review published in this journal appears on the cover: 'Harwood's aim is to leave the text open, to enable his readers to participate in its creation of meaning, to force them to make connections between disparate fragments.' In his Foreword, the poet seems generosity itself – though he isn't always: 'I need to write this for whatever reason / but you don't need to read it. (goodbye)' ('Summer 1993'). Still, Sheppard sees Harwood's aim as to 'force' readers. But is there any relation between what Adrian Stokes called the invitation in art, and that oddly bullying word? Every book while being read is in the reader's hands, and all poems require an active and enactive performance – a very different thing from forced labour.

In any case, Harwood's strengths don't derive from his espousal of open-plan or DIY poetics. Of his various 'mannerisms', he has said he uses them 'without thinking "I'm writing this way because I believe in this theory of unfinished matter and openness for the reader".' Some of Harwood's 1970s work, bewitched by Charles Olson's geographic self-projection (which he attempts to domesticate with warm feeling), has a thin insistence from the exercise of too much will: 'to not   lose / sight / of / what's held dear / the line of hills / that edge / (the) coast' ('Chên'). Rather, his poetry thrives when an ear for sustained cadence, spare prose syntax, and narrative economy is allowed space in which a generosity of spirit can flow. 'The building is very large that you see / across the fields, dear reader,' he writes in 'Air Clamps', and then asks 'can you see, above the green the white / of its walls and red of the tiles?' Though his shorter lyrics – such as 'The White and Blue Liner…' – can be evocative and pointed ('just fold it up and pack away / a tangle of circumstances'), he's best with larger canvases on which to build up broad areas of mood, texture, and associated idea. The poet has characterised such work from his Fulcrum Press volumes *The White Room* (1968) and *Landscapes* (1969) as '60s baroque'; but that's what he's most famous for, and not without reason.

In the same interview, Harwood winningly evokes his favourite fiction writers: 'in a good piece of prose, like say Elizabeth Bowen's, you read a sentence and it just works, it's so right. It's just perfect communication. And why shouldn't a poetry have that clarity?' Elizabeth Bishop, though, spotted a thing to watch for in Bowen, seeing her in a 1960 letter to Robert Lowell as belonging to 'what I think of as the "our beautiful old silver" school of female writing, which is really boasting about how "nice" *we* are.' Harwood may not be boasting, but there's plenty of fine feeling worked into the weave of his poetic textures: 'At dusk – coral pink clouds / lined up along the horizon / like mysterious monuments symbolizing "Hope"' ('Late Journeys'). Such tenderness, affection, and vulnerability are his keynotes throughout. Though the results can be unusually attractive, readers are rarely allowed to forget they're in the company of someone trying to do the right thing – even when acknowledging failure. In 'African Violets', an elegy for his grandmother, he notes that 'we both love(d) love and were, are natural liars, / easy with the "truth", turning facts to meet the story'.

This is where Harwood's work, for all its commitment to reader collaboration, manifests what Keats saw as Wordsworth's 'palpable design upon us'. Presenting himself as a nice person and not afraid or ashamed of weakness, Harwood is frequently candid about the ironies and contradictions that have arisen with his projects. In 'Plato was Right Though', whatever it adds to the ancient quarrel between philosophers and poets, his problem with aesthetic effects and moral purposes is pointedly addressed:

> And what the words and poems attempt degenerates into this –
> a clumsy manifesto in which the words used
> appear emptier than ever before and the atmosphere
> more that of an intense but bad Sunday School.

This poem, important in his development, concludes that 'PLATO was right to banish / poets from the Republic' because when they 'go beyond the / colours and shapes', they 'fail, miserably – / some more gracefully than others.' Plato declared that the poets would, regrettably, have to be banished because their representations of the behaviour of gods and men taught bad lessons. They succeeded in ways that the philosopher thought socially dangerous.

Harwood's work found a defining direction in alarmingly insouciant poems such as 'The Recent Past' from John Ashbery's *Rivers and Mountains* (1966). His earliest masters, though, were the Dadaist Tristan Tzara (whom Harwood has extensively translated) and Ezra Pound – a poet whose political utterances might well lead you to think Plato was right. Elaine Feinstein's poem 'A Quiet War in Leicester' recalls how in their bomb-shelter 'erotic with the / might-be of disaster' she was 'carried into / dreaming with delight'. Born in the same town, Harwood similarly breathes a self-delighting dream life back into modernist and Dadaist aggression by rendering history as a far away adventure in which the author is nevertheless oddly involved. 'It was not caused by famine or war – / "It was all my fault"' is how 'The Doomed Fleet' puts it. In the absence of fully-fledged dramatic monologue, Harwood's frayed patches of late imperial narrative can't entirely avoid construal as authorial projections. Here a problem with reader-collaboration theory in vanguard poetics haunts the text, for if only fragmentary grammatical guidance is given, readers must fall back on prior resources for understanding. Violence or cruelty may be disarmed, but only because poem and reader acquiesce in exchanges of genial familiarities.

There have been various realisations and changes of direction in Harwood's oeuvre. In the 1990 interview he announced that at one point 'I tried not to make more carbon copies of, for example, romanticism about colonial days and elegance in Paris and New York'. He recalls how 'F. T. Prince gently chided me for pattering on'. The phrase 'We patter on' occurs in 'Pullman' from *The Sinking Colony* (1970), a poem that ends '("Forgive me"?)'. His comment about Bowen's prose emphasises clarity in communication – tried and tested notions of the writer-reader relationship. Harwood also admits that he 'came a cropper' in *Boston-Brighton* (1977) through temporarily abandoning the need to be selective about materials. The *Wine Tales* (1979–81) collaboration with Richard Caddel and the *Dream Quilt* (1983–4) pieces are just the opposite: there we see how much can be imaginatively conjured from minimal starting points.

Harwood has also decided, as have numerous British poets associated with linguistic innovation, that there are limits to the textual 'dérèglement de tous les sens' beyond which he need not go. Attachment to special landscape and living space appears to set one such limit. His recent writing shows no lessening in sensitivity to landscape and art. That early devotion to the stating of how 'I love you' has modulated into a sustained meditation on the nature of secure and protective topography. Where 'The Words' from *The Sinking Colony* includes 'but "home" is so long ago' and adds 'don't cry', 'The Artful', from about twenty years later, ends with 'Obscure silhouettes / that act as possible guides to get home, / to touch familiar things, never taken for granted.' Harwood's work returns to local habitations and names, the lives of family, elegies for friends, to direct communication among intimates. These vividly rendered, plain-style evocations, inter-cut with speculation and emotion, construct improvised holding environments where the home world and the safety of loved ones is primary. Despite the conclusion to 'Plato was Right Though', he has experienced how the aesthetic and the ethical cannot be disentangled, how poetic value will not exist without a leavening of social fact. Lee Harwood's *Collected Poems* documents a strategically ingenuous exploration of such issues – which is one of the reasons why much of the work gathered here is so distinctly good.

DAVID CONSTANTINE:
ROMANTICS AND FOREIGNERS

David Constantine's three lectures *A Living Language* are a pleasure to read, and must have been as enjoyable to hear. They lean a little near a tour of received pairings ('mechanical' and 'organic' form, for instance) to be especially enlightening; but the tour is well guided for the most part. What follows is the thought his first lecture, on the benefits of translating, provoked in me – and for which I'm particularly grateful. Constantine offers his portrait of a translator's relation with the original adapted from a Keatsian creative psychology as explored in the young poet's own letters: 'Using the terms I have borrowed and applied from Keats, we may say that Hölderlin allowed the identity of Pindar's Greek to press upon him almost to the point of his own annihilation; but came through the ordeal, into his own vernacular, by an equal act of self-assertion.' Hölderlin would count as an extreme case in any one's terms; and Keats's idea of his self-annihilation in a room full of people was not so total as to prevent him from being highly conscious of what might have been happening. Constantine's account of translating sounds like total war. The foreign language threatens to annihilate, and then the receiver language – in danger of being overrun – valiantly reasserts itself. If the translation has, at first, to be evacuated from Corunna with Sir John Moore, don't worry; soon the original will meet its Waterloo.

Perhaps Constantine, if pressed, wouldn't actually recommend Hölderlin's translation method. But why are such or similar struggles to be undergone? He adds that 'for the nation, especially if that nation is English-speaking, the continual shock of the foreign is absolutely indispensable.' Doubtless true; but why does the 'nation' have to raise its ugly head at such a moment? Why do texts in other languages have to be called 'foreign' – and even by so distinguished a translator, one who is now co-editor of *Modern Poetry in Translation*? According to this line of talk, my wife is a foreigner; my children are half-foreigners. We live in foreign or half-foreign countries – where I'm a foreigner myself. Which is perhaps why I would prefer a sense of translation that emphasised the degree of attention to differences required to effect an understanding, for readers without the relevant language, of writing from another culture more or less related to their own. That might be helpful for them as people. Nations, in my experience, are only too able to look after themselves. What's more, for Welsh, Scots, and Irish poets it's perfectly possible to make translations from one of your languages into another one. So it would seem that 'foreignness' is not a necessary condition when thinking about rendering a work of art in a different tongue. Poets, I believe, should be leading the way in encouraging the disappearance of 'foreign' as a translation category, if not as a category as such.

Given that Keats is a constant and practically un-criticised point of reference, it's a pity Constantine refers to his 'Ode to Autumn' when he means the poem entitled 'To Autumn'. But there is a more substantial slip and slide during his discussion of Keith Douglas's 'Vergissmein-nicht' towards the end of the second lecture 'Use and Ornament' (another conventional pairing). Constantine writes of how in the last two verses 'Douglas shifts perspective to that of the bereaved and in her picture of the girl herself'. The relevant lines state: 'Look. Here in the gunpit spoil / the dishonoured picture of his girl'. The lecturer is urging us to see the poetic value of Douglas's supposed pitilessness. Yet to take the 'dishonoured' picture as a picture of a girl 'dishonoured' is a false move. Douglas's poem keeps the details of the scene fairly sanitised. If the photo had been in the German soldier's pocket, perhaps it was crumpled, torn, and spattered with dried gore and other body parts. The girl herself is not dishonoured at all. It's the glimpse of her photograph – from another place and time – that allows the British poet to identify, in sporting fashion, with the enemy whose 88-gun would have 'dishonoured' him if given the chance.

In his poetry too, Constantine is admirably a man of feeling. There's much to admire: his language can be descriptively vivid and precise, grounded in convincing observation; he has a humane interest in the natural world, in unusual social happenings, and the predicaments of outsiders; his heart is in the right place. His is also a neo-romantic mode that favours energy and vitality at all costs. The results can be strikingly urgent, at once highly wrought and slightly slap-dash. Constantine is a technician, but one who believes his poems should be written in a fine frenzy. So his lines are half crafted and half inspired, with, in worst cases, each side letting the other down. Sometimes – as when he begins 'The Saint observed at his Vigil' with the one-line sentence 'It was a strange sight' – an editor's blue pencil, or a better-employed critical sense in the poet might have helped. That piece properly begins with its strong second line: 'He entered the North Sea like a candle'. At its best,

Constantine's mix delivers telling pieces about unusual people, natural processes, moments of joy, excitement, pathos and grief. 'A man like that' – says his poem 'Under that bag of soot', working up its image of flattened grass into an emblem for suppressed human energies –

> Released into the community with a shaved head
> And the marks of fangs on his temples stands
> Every day at the lights and when the green man shows
> And everybody hurries he stands still, through red
> And the next green he stands there like
>
> Caspar on the asphalt with his wounded feet…

This exemplifies Constantine's writing at its vigorous and pointed best. The flow of syntax and lineation is both assembled and headlong (as in the triple deployment of the verb 'to stand'). Sometimes, though, it can appear as if a Dr. Frankenstein had body-snatched odds and ends of poem-parts, then galvanised them into some desperately busy life: 'Man called Teddy had a garden in / The ruins of Mary Magdalen / By Baxter's scrap. Grew leeks. What leeks need is / Plenty of shite and sunshine' ('The Pitman's Garden'). Constantine's reader is being nudged and jostled here into attending to whatever it may be, but allowed rather less of a rhythmic experience that deploys these urgencies so they can be lived with and digested. Some of his poems might be more satisfying, at least to me, if they were less hectic.

This is, as Constantine's vitalism would suggest, a tirelessly varied and ambitious *Collected Poems* with, at its heart, the long *Caspar Hauser* in nine cantos. Its extended second sentence runs like this:

> He stood there swaying on his sticky feet,
>
> His head was bowed, the light had hurt his eyes,
> The pigeons ran between his feet like toys
> And he was mithered by the scissoring swifts,
>
> Their screams and shadows, then the hour
> Rolled off an iron tongue in an iron tower
> And clouted him, like ferrets sound

Screwed the discovered burrows of his ears
And through the cobblestones
Another massive novelty of pains

Entered his fork.

Once more, a mimetic bluster is borrowed from the natural world, though jazzed up too with some Martian in those 'scissoring swifts'. There's a touch of idiom in the two bits of northern dialect. I was born in the same town as Constantine and like the sounds – in themselves – of both 'mithered' and 'clouted'. Yet his effort to express the impact of a great strangeness on a non-acculturated eighteenth-century German curiously matches how it felt to live in south Lancashire during the early 1960s. Similarly, 'like ferrets sound / Screwed the discovered burrows of his ears' is at once elaborately calculated and syntactically tricky to construe, both consciously worked out and thrown off. What's more, if you don't happen to know how ferrets sound, you're worse placed than Hauser at that moment in the poem.

Constantine's writings about outsiders do suggest that his heart is in the right place; and his valuable involvement in the poetry of Hölderlin, as both translator and commentator, is one of the places where he found an enormously significant outsider's fate to explore. Yet there's a conventionality about his treatment of these themes, as if the artistic payload from such a position were a given – as if being a mad poet, a foreigner, being a down-and-out, or brought up with no human contact would make for literary interest in itself. What's more, this assumption tends to reinforce the 'outsider' status at the very moment that it draws emotive sustenance from the excluded one. Here, outsiders provide insights only and precisely because we are not like them. Thus, as in Constantine's valuing the 'foreignness' of the texts from which he is translating, so too his commitment to the excluded can lack the conceptual flexibility to get beyond a world split, however well-meaning in its partitioning, between 'us' and 'them'. Sliding scales tend to be more subtly responsive than divide-and-rules – and the danger in set patterns of feeling is that they harbour sentimentally assumed responses.

At the close of his lectures, Constantine aligns himself conventionally with the ability of poetry to be that Audenesque 'way of happening' and asserts that 'We are, when we read poetry, during the reading of the poem and lingeringly for some while after, more wakeful, alert and various in our humanity than in our practical lives we are mostly allowed to be.' Much as, in the terms of a shared humanity, I sympathise with his hopes, I fear that reading, and reading poetry in particular, has to have a more lasting and identity-shaping transformative influence on the mind, the body, and the nervous system. Otherwise, it's a form of ethical or aesthetic caffeine – one which fades only too soon when we cross another conventional divide, and return to our 'practical lives'. Not from mine it doesn't; and I bet it doesn't from Constantine's either. His final two sentences bring him back to what Pound's *Mauberley* called the 'relation / of the state to the individual': 'Any further stage, any conversion of this alerted present state into action, into behaviour, is the responsibility of the citizen. And the poet, like the reader, is always a citizen.' But a citizen of what? Now it seems ever more pressing that if we are actually to be 'wakeful, alert and various', whether as poets or readers, and necessarily as people, then we will have to become not merely citizens of some nation and its national language, but (to borrow a title of Oliver Goldsmith's) citizens of the world – a place in which, since we are all foreigners to somebody somewhere, that word might be encouraged to drop from the equation.

ON MATTHEW MEAD
AND JOHN WELCH

Having followed the work of the poets under review for over thirty years, it's a distinct pleasure to revisit them in these collections of their writings. Born in 1924, Matthew Mead mentions in *Word for Word*, that in 1962 he was 'an unknown poet trying to learn German.' His first collection, *Identities and other poems*, didn't appear until five years later, making him just one year younger than Wallace Stevens when his first book *Harmonium* appeared the year before Mead was born. *Identities* was published by Rapp and Carroll, in time for its poet to benefit from the first round of thee-in-one Penguin Modern Poets volumes, his work selected alongside poetry by Jack Beeching and Harry Guest in 1970. Mead emerged among poets who had adapted the lessons of modernism, noting the inheritance of Pound in a sequence called 'Render unto Ezra', allowing one part of it into print in his first collection, and again here. 'If we have homes / he has instructed the architect', it equivocally begins, concluding on a note of praise for his evocative powers: 'Lost ages are the early wind / and the feel of it.'

Mead is preeminently a poet of the post-war; he had served with the armed forces from 1942 to 1947. It's a period that didn't end with the ending of the Cold War, and may not have ended quite yet. Indeed, it's not so much a period in Mead's work, more a condition:

> No age but this,
> Shaped by the dead;
> What they destroyed
>   rebuilt as what they built,
> A future traced in palms like parchment.
> The silence mine, as if a dead man spoke
> Or pondered in a sunlit interval
> The dark from which he came.

This passage from the title sequence to his 1970 collection *The Administration of Things* shows Mead's abilities in the careful structuring of an unrhymed free verse. The passage begins in matched two stress lines, extends to three (making a concealed pentameter with a line break at the caesura). This is followed by a tetrameter, and then there's a pentameter in which it is 'as if a dead man spoke', like the past of English poetry; and this is then matched with another before the passage closes with a ballad-stanza trimeter. The relevance of this expertise in metre and cadence to the matter in hand is thematically deployed around the contrast of speech and silence, while that contrast is located in the grief-strewn lands of the post-war with the presence of the dead among the living. The title of the sequence contextualises its muttering lines in issues of political management, the Cold War division of Europe, and how that is written upon the skin of those who must endure it. The varying lines of verse figure the lifelines of the survivors, including the poet's own, and his paradoxically broken silence.

By contrast with this style of addressing a poem, Mead has also sustained throughout his writing life an interest in the possibilities remaining in traditional forms built around repetition and reiteration. The more recent hey-days of the ballade, the sestina, the villanelle, and the triolet were the pre-Raphaelite, Decadent, and early Modernist decades. Mead reconfigures these forms for sardonic political comment, a line of development that might have been suggested by William Empson's villanelles. 'Ballade of an Unforeseen Nostalgia' rhymes on paradoxes in the evolution of Eastern Block political power-broking:

> You knew just who the villains were
> Because you had them on your list.
> The ritual gun butt on the door,
> A handcuff round the waiting wrist,
> Then off in early morning mist;
> It seemed as though it couldn't fail
> And no one bothered to resist –
> Even Gomulka was in gaol.

Władysław Gomulka (1905–1982), a Polish Communist leader of a particularly unpleasant order, would order the things that take place in the first seven lines of the stanza only to find himself done unto as he had done to others. The poem grimly articulates an unforeseen nostalgia for a divided world when it appeared that things made sense (it appeared in *The Midday Muse* in 1979, the year Lady Thatcher came to power). These poems arise from a ground of silence and the requirement to generate repeating lines, producing a sense of verbal rationing, the poem eked out from the interplay of a formal compulsion and a reluctance to speak about the unspeakable.

Mead also has poems that deploy the odd functioning of the negative in English, as in Larkin's 'Nothing shows why' from 'Talking in Bed'. His blankly joking 'Minusland', from the same 1979 collection, identifies its humour's target (perfidious 'Albion') in the closing lines – 'Looking like dawn defining day / To call it by its proper name':

> I know it well – the coast recedes
> Past nothing into doom and debt,
> And once ashore a low road leads
> Through four days walking in the wet
>
> To nowhere much and then turns back
> Past lesser places long since gone.
> Dead end dies out in cul de sac
> With a sackgasse further on.

The genial rhyming cushions the sourness, discovering a fondness for the place in its revisiting of the English disease of complaining. Mead has a version of Beckettian minimalism, as in 'Skeleton Speech': 'Ha worm. You strip the bone / but leave the bone.' With age, as might be expected, this note has become more insistent, as in the sequence 'The Sentences of Death', the second one of which is 'Death as a Foreign Language, Lesson One' that concludes: 'An easy language to learn. / Simple to translate.' This is the kind of joke the best comedians tell without smiling. I wouldn't know, of course, but suspect it can't be true. And can it be easy to translate? I'm still looking for the third full rhyme with 'death' in English. Keats rhymed the word with 'breath' at the end of his 'Bright Star' sonnet, probably because he didn't have a choice.

The translations collected in *Word for Word* are not 'word for word', although they do offer English words for German ones. I looked at some of the originals (not included in this monolingual gathering) and found little of the creative writers' 'versions' about the way they have gone about delivering their sparsely traumatised originals into respectfully cadenced English poems. Coming across on every page is belief in, and admiration for, their originals; and (far from disabling the translators) these qualities tighten the microscope on their attention to detail. Where Nelly Sachs writes 'In der blaue ferne / wo die rote Apfelbaumallee wandert', the Meads have 'In the blue distance / where the red row of apple trees wanders'; or in response to Johannes Bobrowski's 'lieb ich dich mit dem Stroh in der Kammer, / mit dem Landwind über dem Dach, / mit der Hecke vor deinem Haus' in 'Fischerhafen', they write in 'Fishing Port' that 'I love you with straw in the chamber, / with the land-wind over the roof, / with the hedge before your house'. These are well-formed poetic translations that, if you have some German, can be used as guides to their originals. *The Autumn-Born in Autumn* includes Mead's 'Translator to Translated', dedicated to Bobrowski, which first appeared in *Identities*:

> Love
> translates
> as love.
> Her song sung
> in a strange land.
>
> An air that kills.

It's a reassuring belief that human values, though called differently in other languages, translate tautologically (and one that I don't myself hold). The last line conjures up the fortieth poem in Housman's *A Shropshire Lad*, though the 'land of lost content' will be post-war Eastern Germany. The middle ones recall Psalm 137 and so suggest that love is enduring a Babylonian captivity. Thanks to Anvil Press and their high production values, Mead has been able to achieve a well-presented laconic oeuvre in splendidly reluctant-sounding isolation.

Living and working in London, an active member of the small press poetry scene since the 1960s, John Welch's isolation has been of a more gregarious kind. He writes a poetry whose terrain is the shifting ground of projection and introjection, of what Adrian Stokes in his autobiographical meditation called *Inside Out*. Welch's poetry also includes the outside in: the outside world populated with psychologised shapes of the inner life, and the inner life structured by its resemblances to forms of material space. His prose memoir, *Dreaming Arrival*, fills out some of the life contexts for his poetry's location in the ambit of the capital's psychoanalytical community, and its overlap with the literary and visual arts. On a visit to Rome, the city that provided Freud with his image of psychological development in *Civilisation and its Discontents*, Welch finds himself reflecting that 'Writing is a try at restoring the balance, the balance between the inside-me and out there, half-tamed and half-wild. "I" can only be propped up like this, a sort of membrane that needs all these words to strengthen it, or it will be taken over, like the ruins taken over by the grass.' Welch's longer poems can at times seem not so much that 'momentary stay against confusion', which Robert Frost identified with achieved closes, as a continuous background hum without which balance might be lost. Yet sustained poems of this kind are also fed by a sense inflecting psychoanalytic writings that practically nothing is meaningless, as when he writes of a family visit to the Downland Museum in Sussex: 'The sense of close lived life the house conveyed was moving and reassuring. There was a pool too, which my son Simon recalled from a previous visit as being "absolutely full of fish".'

Though Welch began writing in 1957, at the age of twelve, the earliest poetry he has chosen to preserve in his *Collected Poems* is from the 1970s. 'Clearway' from *Out Walking* (1984) keeps the inside and the out interacting by means of lightly allusive, appealingly oblique gestures:

> The undefended
> Roads went quiet and corn slumbered
>
> And the same sky as in childhood
> Rose behind, like a curtain,
> But always changing. We are here
> Days, hours, minutes without number –
>
> Outcrops of flesh, that keep reappearing.

Characteristically, in the short 1970s poem 'Mourning' we find 'A flat in North London carpeting the silence / Traffic grumbles in the distance'. Loss shows in the appearance of the visible world around: 'Crossing the air / His departure is in the trees / But not human', including the dispersal of the dead person into the world through cremation, a material inter-relation of inside and out: 'The feet going over the air / And everything burning.' Feeling is projected into space, the cremated person returning to the world's matter as smoke drifting off into the ocean in the mysterious close: 'Atlantic achieved. Scarcely a sound.' The poem's minimal story occasions the registration of sensibility in the low-key twists and turns of the syntax linking body contexts with spatial ones. The medium of transition is language, as in the opening of 'Dreams Dreams', also from *Out Walking*, when the poet begins by asking 'How to convey the dictionary home / Across streets of bruised wordage?'

Welch's poetry turns around the theme of a protective home and, beyond it, of feeling welcome in the world. A poem from *Greeting Want* (1997) responds to one of the book's two epigraphs, this from W. D. Winnicott: 'It is delightful to be hidden but a disaster not to be found.' 'Found' reverses the process of 'Mourning', dramatizing the introjection of the outside world into the body space with 'Again the owl's call floating in' and 'It's in me but it / Speaks to me from somewhere else'. An incipient sadness of the poetry scene comes perhaps from the identification of psychological well being with visibility, with arrival – only too likely to be crushed in the scrum at the institutional entrance. One criticism of the institutional theory of art, though, is that if we are justified in thinking the institutions (publishers, review editors, reviewers, and the like) have good reasons for their decisions, then the fact they are institutions is not what's determining the recognition of art: it's their reasons. Yet at the entrances stand the taciturn authorities, like persecutory parent figures, as in Welch's 'Collected' from *The Eastern Boroughs* (2004), a poem on his father's copy of T. S. Eliot's *Collected Poems*, and Eliot recurs in a recent meditation, 'Visiting Silence', upon the Faber editor's first wife Vivien's grave.

So the themes of a life in art and an individual's psychological balance loop round to the vivifying spirit of domestic wellbeing. 'Found' concludes:

> And so it was I came back, found you
> Stupid with sleep, the light still on,
> And the curtains not quite shut
> But parted like blank lips
> Half open onto the hot street –
>
> One day I said I'll tell you all about it.

If you want to be found, like children playing dead, you must go back and find someone yourself. In the hinterland of both their oeuvres is the figure of love as a ground for continuance. Some poets are lucky enough to stay hidden and be found; others have to go out and discover who will find them. Both Welch and Mead have had sufficient tenacity and resilience to prevent these contrasting fates from damaging the work that they have been able to produce, and to find ways of bringing into print. Among Welch's later work, a favourite of mine is 'Bungalow: "La-Mer"' from *The Eastern Boroughs* – a poem of puzzlement about the daft French of the house's given name, and prompting implications in what it might express:

> For the time being it simply lifts
> Its puzzling hyphen.
>
> Today we're heading for the shore, but this?
> It brings us close but still it holds us off,
>
> Feather of air, a dying breath
> Confronting ocean fronted by a word.

Welch's poetry at its best fills everyday existence with the intense interplay of a sensitised, verbally alive consciousness. Mead, by contrast, brings the ramifications of an inhuman *Weltanschauung* into the intimate spaces of a private life, where it is resisted by whatever we have at hand, as in 'For You, Ruth' from *A Sestina at the End of Socialism* (1996), with its post-mortem projection of loving behaviour:

> I shall be up that instant from the shade
> finding a track that will not fade from view
> racing along to be a man remade
> blinking bright light way outstripping fear
> and coming to see you and only you.

Where Mead's work comes out of the fates and human consequences of Nazi and Stalinist social engineering, trapped into a darkening vale by the apparent disappearance of alternatives to capital's selectively destructive benefits, Welch's poetry has been worked out under the shadow of psychoanalysis's own fate. It has been suggested that the post-modern was the imaginative space made available by the demise of explain-all theories, their socialised ramifications in political institutions, with a hoped-for mitigating of the cruelty in exclusive world-views. These bodies of poetry by Matthew Mead and John Welch explore what it's like to live with the structures of such imposed forms, cognizant of their flaws, alive to the desolate consolations of living without them, and to the intermittent sustenance in being able to find a form of life in poetry that resists being straight jacketed by ideologies at all.

IAN HAMILTON:
'ONE WAS TORN'

Ian Hamilton, we're told in Alan Jenkins's informative introduction to this *Collected Poems*, thought poetry might 'make things better' and 'bring back the dead.' He could write of a poem whose subject is 'the suffering of another person' that 'by writing the poem, there might be some mitigation of the suffering.' He explained this hope by distinguishing 'ordinary speech' in life which 'made little difference, couldn't save the other person' from poetic speech which 'might work differently'. While 'writing a poem, one could have the illusion that one was talking in a magic way to the subject of the poem. One might even think that this was doing some good.' The idea is being set up for a fall, one that quickly comes: 'you know it isn't. You wake up and it hasn't.' Yet Jenkins then adds: 'this was one dream Hamilton never relinquished'. The dream that he woke to find untrue, but clung to nonetheless, is related to a collapse in the position of the poet in general culture: 'if he has any sense of his own importance, it's a huge sense, of being the central figure of the tribe, the seer, the wise man... Yet the facts tell him that he's of no consequence at all.' This structure of thought is not dissimilar to that in W. H. Auden's 'poetry makes nothing happen': you pitch the claim for what poetry might do unrealistically high, and, disillusioned, find yourself precipitated into a position that is unrealistically low. For it is possible to have importance without hugeness. Poems might then achieve what you had hoped, might 'make things better' or 'bring back the dead' – even though you were now too personally disappointed to sense that they could or had.

One weakness of the collapsing ambition is its distinction between 'ordinary' and 'poetic' speech, for if someone speaking cannot 'save a person from death or from illness', why expect that the words of a poem could do so? While there must be workers in psychotherapy and counselling services who believe that human speech may help save people from death and illness, so too there is no reason to abandon the practical idea that reading poems can be good for the coordination of beneficial mental and physical focus through the joint action in structured patterns of cognition and rhythmic affect-embodiment. No dream, this is one subliminal but practical consequence of reading poetry. Yet Hamilton's two examples of what poems might do were not random ones. The work in this scrupulously edited *Collected Poems* is largely about two subjects, the death of his father from cancer and the mental illness of his wife. They set the pattern for his entire output, the latter evolving into poems on difficulties of other relationships and the former into the gathering shadows of his own mortality.

'Epitaph' is one of the poems that touches on the consequences of Hamilton's attendance at his dying father's bedside when a teenager:

> The scent of old roses and tobacco
> Takes me back.
> It's almost twenty years
> Since I last saw you
> And our half-hearted love affair goes on.
>
> You left me this:
> A hand, half-open, motionless
> On a green counterpane.
> Enough to build
> A few melancholy poems on.
>
> If I had touched you then
> One of us might have survived.

This is a poem characteristically placed between the first-person singular of the poetic speaker, and the suffering second-person subject of his speech. The doubled occasion conjoins a teenager and a man in his thirties. It is painfully modest, those 'few melancholy poems'; fleetingly confessional in psychoanalytic mode, that 'half-hearted love affair' between son and father; and yet grandiose in its similarly doubled finale – that a laying on of hands might have cured the man dying of cancer, or, equally, saved the teenager and now adult poet from the emotional death that appears as his poem's real hinted-at subject. Yet the problem with the concluding two lines is that because I don't believe the first sense (that touching his dad's hand could have cured his cancer) so I don't credit the second (because the son *has* literally survived to write the 'melancholy poems'). So the latter is an undemonstrated sentimentality, the former an omnipotent fantasy. This is not meant to impugn the reality of the experience from which the poem derives, or to underestimate the psychic damage that 'Epitaph' indicates, but to suggest that this poem denies itself the scope and scale plausibly to inhabit and explore its occasion. The concluding two lines betray the poem's true feeling in the double sense that they allow it to show, and they don't show it properly. An air of persecutory critical judgment hangs over the 'melancholy poems' of 'Epitaph', as it does over the 'There was no hiding it. / Your poems wouldn't do' of 'Critique'. Hamilton's last and posthumously published book, *Against Oblivion: Some Lives of the Twentieth-Century Poets* (2002), addresses one more thing poetry might do: grant immortality to some of its practitioners. Jenkins's edition has done all possible to give Hamilton's work a chance of that – for countering oblivion, an irrelevance to the dead 'I' and deceased 'you', is rather a side-effect of continued reader availability and use.

In his classic book on Vermeer, Lawrence Gowing notes in passing that 'sensitiveness may not only qualify but disable.' This might help understand the fact admirers of Hamilton's poetry readily acknowledge: that there are so few of his poems, and most of them are very short. In a passage by the poet on this issue, again candidly cited by his editor, Hamilton decides to 'wait for poetry to happen rather than force myself to go in search of it. After all, the poems I *had* written arrived more or less out of the blue, prompted by circumstance rather than by any subject-seeking impulse on my part.' Yet it doesn't follow that because you 'wait for poetry to happen' you will only get it at a rate of about a lyric a year. 'Newscast' is a rare Hamilton poem occasioned beyond the haunted limits of his and his relations' personal grief:

> The Vietnam war drags on
> In one corner of our living-room.
> The conversation turns
> To take it in.
> Our smoking heads
> Drift back to us
> From the grey fires of South-east Asia.

The explanation for why Hamilton didn't write more cannot be that he waited for circumstance to prompt. It would have to explain why circumstances didn't prompt him more often, more variously, and why the promptings didn't issue in more substantially fleshed out poems. Here, I suspect, is where his sensitivity comes in.

Al Alvarez famously criticised the 'gentility principle' in English verse of the 1950s and offered in its place what Marjorie Perloff has referred to as 'the *poètes maudits* of the genteel tradition': Robert Lowell, Sylvia Plath, John Berryman, and Anne Sexton. Hamilton, who would go on to publish the influential *Robert Lowell: A Biography* in 1983, recognised the cost of their open cast mining of the self in verse. Hamilton's 'Birthday Poem' shows the *Life Studies* influence in its triad of adjectives and syntax of performance and foreboding:

> Tonight,
> Half-suffocated, cancerous,
> Deceived,
> You bite against its gilded china mouth
> And wait for an attack.

The adjectival knowingness of the style has devastating feedback effects on the ability of the lyric speech to make a difference. In an interview with Peter Dale, Hamilton locates himself in 1962 between the mighty opposites of that moment: 'There was something very attractive about the Larkin-Amis debunking but there was also something it missed out on, something one prized but could not name – not without embarrassment, not without some Movement-inspired fear of sounding arty and pretentious. One was torn. So one stuck to what felt genuine – poems about personal experience, poems that made no great emotional gestures but were "feelingful".' But there were too many injunctions, too many not necessarily compatible formulae that would produce self-cancelling effects. This can be seen in the poems about his wife's mental illness. The lyric subject, in the presence of another's suffering, tries not to put itself forward, tries to avoid drawing attention to its presence. At the same time, it will try not to prey upon the feelings of others as a rich vein of subject matter. For a poem that is circumstanced between a lyrical 'I' and a suffering 'you', this can be nearly fatal because there is an almost complete negation of subject matter. You mustn't talk about yourself, and you mustn't trespass on the other person's experience. The third point of the poetic triangle, the reader, suffers an acute undernourishment.

With some of the poems from *The Visit* (1970), occasioned by visiting the patient in a mental hospital, it can be difficult at first to get more than a glimpse of what is taking place. Though happening from the blue of the circumstances, the poem doesn't allow its reader much of an access to the lyric subject's feelings, or the suffering other's, or to the surroundings that might stand in, like transferred epithets or the painted objects in a Vermeer, for those unstated feelings. Here is the whole of that collection's title poem:

> They've let me walk with you
> As far as this high wall. The placid smiles
> Of our new friends, the old incurables,
> Pursue us lovingly.
> Their boyish, suntanned heads,
> Their ancient arms
> Outstretched, belong to you.
>
> Although your head still burns
> Your hands remember me.

The penultimate line is probably a reference to ECT (electro-convulsive therapy). Once patients came round after their shakings, they were asked questions by a psychologist to ascertain how much memory loss they'd suffered as a result of the current fired across their temples. That's where the poetry of Hamilton's final line takes its bearings. Yet 'The Visit' is equally stunned, numbed, and un-remembering. The lyric subject has himself been made helplessly passive. He never gets as far as a first-person singular, kept firmly as a third-person 'me.' It's rhythms are finely attuned but under-energised, refraining from the creation of emotional transfer, as if this too would be an offence to the life experience that the poem minimally records. The pronominal danger is that all the poem's reparative attention goes into the precarious joining of the 'me ... with you' while this action is not sufficiently presented to those other new friends and old incurables, the readers, for them to take any help from it. Hamilton's critical injunctions, motivated by the best and highest of moral-aesthetic reasons, are more or less ruling out the possibility both of art's invitation and its benefit to others.

If you are going to make something better, you need to articulate as clearly as you can what the damage is, and you have to help readers experience, at a safe remove, both the damage, and the effort of repair. The effort is in the poet's technique, and the burden of material it can shape. Jenkins's exemplary edition provides instances of the poet at work, of his post-publication revisions, and, in an appendix, of his adjustments to an unpublished poem called 'Letter to the Editor'. This may have evolved into the last lyric in *Collected Poems*, one called 'Prayer', printed in the main text with the 'day … OK' rhyme deleted below in a version cited from the editor's note:

> Look sir, my hands are steady now,
> My brain a cloudless [~~day~~] sky.
> Is that the sound of breakfast down below?
> To eat again seems possible.
> To breathe?
> No problem, Lord, [~~I promise.~~] [~~I'm OK.~~] [~~I'll try~~]. But why?

I prefer the undeleted readings here, their attuning a rhyme that substitutes for a weather report a synonym for heaven, and ends on a rising note by the pitch of that third question to the divinity. Feeling a preference suggests that there is no saying how much good a technical felicity may do, and that poetry is – no less than football according to Bill Shankly – much more important than life and death. After citing a flurry of praise from Andrew Motion, Douglas Dunn, Michael Hofmann, Peter Porter, David Harsent and Craig Raine, Jenkins observes: 'Yet not one of these poets, with the possible exception of Hofmann, shows much trace of Hamilton's influence in his own work, and I can't think of a single poet who does – or does any longer.' Even Hofmann in poems about his father is displaying traces of Lowellese, shared with Hamilton, rather than something unique to the editor of *the Review*. Hamilton's poetry attempted to deploy the occasioned reality of the confessionals without their high-risk, hurt-laden flurry. Ian Hamilton 'was torn' in many ways. The best of his lyrics delicately register that rending.

FOUR

HERE COMES (ALMOST) EVERYBODY

Perhaps I'm not the only reader who, on receiving a new issue of *Poetry Ireland Review*, turns immediately to Dennis O'Driscoll's 'Pickings and Choosings' to see what poetry's great and good (and the others too) have had to say for themselves in recent months. Doubtless I'd be a better person if the new poetry were my first resort; but reading poetry requires an investment of energy and understanding that isn't always on tap at the end of a tricky working day, and I wouldn't like to approach new poems as Helen Vendler appears to do: 'It's like being a talent scout for an opera company, when all you can say about the voice you hear is, "No, it has no carrying power, it hasn't any capacity to stay on pitch, it hasn't any sense of innate rhythm, it hasn't any expressive colour, it hasn't interpretive power … it's just no, no, no." Before we all despair of pleasing the impresario, let's not forget that if 'no, no, no' is all you can say, then you're probably not usefully managing your time. Her presumption of perfect pitch and judgment is equally hard to credit or take; and, after all, it's so much more courageous to risk a 'yes, maybe', now and then, with some struggling young hopeful. Vendler has a reasonable reputation for explaining why long-established poets are worth reading; she's not so famous for spotting who among the complete unknowns may prove good in the longer run.

The assurance is not only contradicted by the history of poetry and the full contents of many a remembered poet's complete works, it's put in its place by Charles Simic, whose quotations – some penned as aphorisms – are usually on the money: 'It is absolutely amazing how many great poets started as seemingly talentless half-wits.' Vendler similarly appears to be keeping up standards when she writes: 'When one remembers how many separate talents go to make a formidable poet – talents musical, imaginative, psychological, visual, intellectual, metaphysical, temperamental – one wonders that the thing is done at all.' She should raise her expectations of obscurely unlikely people with their 1% inspiration and 99% perspiration. Her own colloquial slide could also use some attuning: like the king in *Hamlet*, poets have doubtless been called 'thing' before, and many probably wouldn't mind being 'done' by the right person if occasion arose – as the formidable Joseph Brodsky notes: 'You can spend a lifetime, twenty-five years, in a concentration camp or you can survive a bombardment of Hiroshima and yet not produce a single line, whereas a one-night stand gives birth to an immortal lyric.' Maybe it does. Yet just as it isn't the camp or the bomb, so it isn't the stand that produced the poem. If it were, red-light districts would surely have more stationery shops in their vicinities.

O'Driscoll's anthology is packed with such stuff as quarrels are picked on – and that's one of its virtues. Another is that if you don't like what one writer claims, you can always rummage the book for its antidote. In many cases there's no need to contradict, debunk, or gainsay – because another quotation has already done that for you. Sometimes there's no need even to rummage: the editor has thoughtfully placed them next to each other. Don Paterson's 'Poetry is like solving a crossword puzzle in which you are also the compiler' hardly catches the excitement and unexpectedness that poets report feeling when new work comes along and comes right; as if in reply, Paul Muldoon immediately asserts: 'I don't believe in poetry as crossword puzzle, as being necessarily difficult.' In response to Gregory Orr's 'In order to write well, a poet needs to go to that place where energy and intensity concentrate, that place just beyond which chaos and randomness reign,' you might find yourself imagining a tiny space between the piles of unmarked homework and the sink full of greasy washing up, or recall André Breton's *mot* about how poetry like love is made in bed; but, don't bother, Michael Longley's riposte is better: 'If I knew where poems came from, I'd go there.' Mind you, the thought of Breton's remark does make me wonder what an anthology of poetry quotations that took the ages as its fishing grounds would read like.

In his Introduction, O'Driscoll evokes and fends off the analogy between his collection and media opinion-feed when he notes that 'The best of these quotations are "sound bites" only in the sense that they sound out ideas memorably – encapsulating larger debates in bonsai form – and that the adjective "sound" means "judicious".' Fair enough, but 'The relation of statements about poetry to the poem itself,' Dave Smith suggests, 'is approximately the relationship of sexual instruction handbooks to sexual intercourse.' These snippets from innumerable poetic equivalents to the advertising blurbs on the back of *The Joys of Sex* must then have an even more tenuous relationship with what Smith also calls the poem's 'felt reality' – something I prefer to think is the equivalent of making love, not sexual intercourse. This isn't, after all, a collection of crafted aphorisms by different hands, although some of the quotations are, and on the page they all look like it. Most of these pronouncements are excerpted from newspaper prose, interview talk, from lunges into generalisation in mid-review, or when writing a preface or introduction. O'Driscoll's range of sources is extraordinarily capacious – from *Harpers and Queen* to the *Irish Farmers Journal...* unless that's the journalistic equivalent of Dorothy Parker's 'the gamut of emotion from A to B'.

But could it also be that anthologising these bite-size chunks from people's writings has altered their meaning? In issues of the magazine their selection may perform a role like the lines of lesser events scrolling across the screen below the newscaster's talking head. You can skim them to see what people are sounding off about, and then go back to the big story in the body of the magazine. Sequenced together here in just under two hundred and forty pages, they can't help accumulating broad cultural significance. Reading them can, for instance, start to feel faintly tiresome, as in the section called 'What is it anyway?' where most of the entries begin 'Poetry is...'. That was when the thought crossed my mind that this book might be a sight more valuable if the same intelligences were sounding out a wider range of subjects – 'beyond all this fiddle', as it were. Speaking of which, here's Robert Crawford: 'As far as politics is concerned, the poet's most important work is to fiddle while Rome burns.' Most of the poets I know are too worked off their anapaestic feet to loll around in a palace doing that; and the man capable of dedicating one of his books 'To Scotland' would presumably be less inclined to fiddle while Edinburgh burned. Willy-nilly, this anthology – not dipped into, but read from cover to cover – does start to look like a mirror held up to the nature of the current poetry scene.

O'Driscoll has also caught a lot of people with their guard momentarily down. Here's Hugo Williams from his *TLS* column: 'If a thing isn't commercial it has a kind of holiness about it which exempts it from responsibility. Poems are chits that get you off work.' Nice work if you can get it, but most poets can't get it even if they try; and, more importantly, what sort of holiness is it that has no responsibility? Not the salvation through good works kind, that's for sure. Donald Davie shows himself suffering in the valley of the shadow of salvation by election when he observes: 'Many are called but few, very few, are chosen; it is a lesson that we are happy to learn about everybody's lifetime except our own.' Sure it is; but perhaps the real lesson is to write poetry because you like doing it, not because you long to be accommodated into some anthological heaven or hell of posterity. Jorie Graham is cited in *Newsweek* (maybe she didn't say it then) as announcing that 'For every lie we're told by advertisers and politicians, we need one poem to balance it.' Ah, so that's what's been keeping the creative writing programmes busy over there. But then again, what was it Plato said about poets and liars? Whole swathes of this compulsive reading feel like a combination of Karl Kraus's samplings from the then current journalism to demonstrate his language's corruption, and Gustave Flaubert's *Dictionnaire des idées reçues*.

Michael Hofmann tries to keep his head when all around are losing theirs: 'I am hostile to the very idea of poetry, so to speak, in the plural, as a collective mass or enterprise' (which might be a misprint for 'collective or mass enterprise'); he's hostile to 'Poetry as a certain good.' This is true of all abstractions from activities. Nothing human is a *certain* good; examples of it have to be evaluated. Seamus Heaney, the writer granted the most quotations here by a long chalk, can usually be relied on to speak up for its benefits, as when on the facing page to Hofmann's hostility he asserts: 'If you've got one person responding to poetry, you have an autobiography; if you have 20 people, you have the beginning of a culture.' Hofmann's prescription for avoiding writing 'bilge' from mere 'ambition' is also a bit rich: 'You need a pure heart, a good ear, and a wicked vocabulary.' It won't be long before that modish and self-defining use of 'wicked', if read, will require a footnote; and, while no one would quarrel with 'a good ear' (one for Flaubert's dictionary), if Hofmann has a pure heart he should be put in the imaginary museum: he must be the first poet in the history of the world who hasn't got one that's a Dante's comedy of ambivalence, contradiction, conflict, intolerance, obsession, envy, resentment, and worse. After all, that's what poets use as a help to understanding the other people who also have hearts but may or may not be poets. Perhaps the mystery of making a poem rests in people, who feel themselves especially alive when trying to do it, permitting themselves to engage an ordinary heart and a practiced ear in judging what are the proper words in the right order for that particular creative occasion at that specific cultural moment; and it has to be done at a run with trained instincts, not by consciously deploying concepts, however retrospectively relevant. Vendler can hardly be faulted for attempting to remark that very good poems are not easily written. Hofmann has probably been distracted by the superficial wit of balancing 'pure' of the heart with 'wicked' of the vocabulary. But then, not only does 'wicked' cancel out (because, in case you didn't know, it means 'good' in teen-talk), but also the heart of a poem is the words.

Though O'Driscoll wouldn't perhaps relish the role, in his anthologising he appears like the walking conscience in Browning's 'How it Strikes a Contemporary'. The thought of him alighting on your unguarded utterances might help save you from the mockery of the ages; but for some of us, alas, it's too late, as when the current British poet laureate announces that 'Poetry ... is a hot line to the emotions.' Hey, that sounds exciting. Mind you, he also says that 'Poetic manifestos invariably say "yes" and "no", but poetry itself "maybe" and "perhaps".' This is not what Ezra Pound thought when he damned the use of 'perhaps' in his marginalia to *The Waste Land* manuscript. Haplessly characterising various English predicaments, Motion's notions have poetry urgently shouting uncertainties down the phone to a crowd of prosopopoeia – 'the emotions' – like those in Gray's 'Ode on a Distant Prospect of Eton College'. Other comments immortalised here have the air of graffiti, or prompt the desire to scrawl ones like the legendary and true 'Ginsberg revises!' said to have graced the New York subway. John Kinsella's one entry (perhaps consciously echoing Marianne Moore's 'Poetry') reads: 'To write poetry you don't have to like it' – to which this defacer felt tempted to add 'but it helps.' To other quotes my bosom returned the instinctive echo of laughing out loud, as when Liz Lochhead answers the interviewer's question 'Does it make any difference to you being a woman poet?' with 'I don't know. I've never tried being a man poet!' Maybe the odder are the better: 'Nobody writes poems about parsnips' (Anna Pavord); 'Poetry: three mismatched shoes at the entrance of a dark alley' (Charles Simic); 'Writing poetry is like trying to catch a black cat in a dark room' (Robert Greacen). They have the marked advantage of provoking thought without necessarily inviting rebuttal.

There are, needless to say, many observations worth further pondering. Caitriona O'Reilly truly notes: 'The problem with sentimentality is that if it is not risked then the poem can entirely lose emotional register.' Perhaps this is a variation on T. S. Eliot's view that poetry isn't made from original emotions, but from fresh combinations of ordinary ones. I also like the torque in her describing this thought-provoking advice as both a 'risk' to be run and a 'problem' to be addressed. Equally the thought that sentimentality means wanting to have an emotion without being

willing to pay for it also applies to writing poetry. Tom Lubbock's one
entry goes some way to explaining why poetry readings are punctuated
with what Michael Hamburger glumly calls 'the titter of recognition'
when he writes that 'While an audience can laugh if amused, there are
no conventional noises for being moved or provoked to thought.' True;
but there is a noise which audiences make when they realise they should
have been moved or provoked to thought, but have been wrong-footed
because they were expecting another laugh. It's a sort of 'hum' sound
with a lengthened vowel; it means the poet had better put a funny one
in right now before he or she loses them altogether while preferably
recalling that, as Marie Heaney is cited as saying, 'There's no such thing
as a short poetry reading.'

In the end, though, perhaps it's Paul Farley's comment that sounds
the sorriest and most telling of the complaints against this sound bite
age: 'Poets of my generation – born in the early 60s onwards – …
haven't had criticism; they've had marketing.' Very true; but poets
of my generation, born about ten years earlier, have seen the age of
criticism go into perhaps permanent hibernation; we've seen the age of
marketing make a farce of practically everything we hold dear; and we've
had to head for higher ground so as to let the tsunami of promo and
all it takes with it sweep by. As Heaney, whose volumes also sport plea-
bargaining quotes, properly remarks: 'There is a disgraceful abdication
from truth in the words that are wrapped around books' – and he's not
even referring to the laughably attention-seeking titles that get put on
contemporary poetry about to go down in our flood of publication.
Taking the longer view, Brodsky at least allows us to hope that we
may be able to evolve beyond this market-driven phase: 'The charge
frequently levelled against poetry nowadays of being difficult, obscure,
hermetic, and whatnot indicates not the state of poetry but, frankly,
the rung of the evolutionary ladder on which society got stuck.' Since
it's also true of unregulated market forces that they don't necessarily
produce the best results for the consumer (the classic example being
the supply of donated blood), who could ever have thought the market
place alone would deliver the best poetry to the people who might
most want and need it? Equally, you could be forgiven for thinking
that the minuscule amounts of money to be made from this art would
have inoculated it against our present culture-wide malaise. Not so,
Gresham's Law applies to poets too.

Dennis O'Driscoll has, over the last twenty years and more, performed the Herculean task of picking through a vast morass of secondary and ancillary material about poets and poetry – a great deal of which, I have to confess, had passed me by. Whether he and his publisher Neil Astley meant it or no, *The Bloodaxe Book of Poetry Quotations* is an economically packaged tour round the horizon of the state we find ourselves in now. Somebody should give its editor a medal.

THE WAY WE DIE NOW:
DENNIS O'DRISCOLL

Dennis O'Driscoll's poetry is vivid and fresh, with a down-to-earth pitch and a morbid streak. His *New and Selected Poems* is a pleasure to read. The publishers have designed a book that gives the texts space to breathe, and there's a cheerful bit of abstract art by Albert Irvin on the cover. One of the attractive things about O'Driscoll's poetry is that he's mastered a great many ways of presenting insights and observations. The varieties of form and shape are continuously intriguing – and are, for the most part, also apt to their different occasions. He's particularly good at the sequence assembled from lightly built lyrics: 'Rose Windows', 'Delegates', and 'Before', for example. There's a vein of humour throughout, which, again for the most part, doesn't sell the poems out cheap to the poetry-circuit light entertainment industry.

My first thought about a title for this review was that it might allude to Wordsworth's sonnet in which the 'world is too much with us', helping us lay waste our powers with its 'Getting and spending'. Certainly his poetry is frequently drawn to the most day-in and day-out of subjects: like the one about a couple trying to meet each other when they're in different supermarkets ('Misunderstanding and Muzak'). He has an attractively direct way with his preferred materials; but they can threaten sometimes to get their revenge. His later and longer poems are occasionally clogged with so much dross and junk from our contemporary culture. That's where the morbid streak comes in, as exemplified by the stunt poem 'Towards a Cesare Pavese Title' – made up of 14 variant joke translations of 'Verrà la morte e avrà i tuoi occhi'. The presence of death in, to recall a phrase, every third poem (see 'Reader's Digest *Family Medical Adviser*', 'What She Does Not Know Is', and 'Nor' with their traditional *carpe diem* or *memento mori* motifs) both invigorates the treatment of the everyday and puts it in its place. 'Churchyard View: The New Estate' is the sort of O'Driscoll title where you can't help seeing what's on its way: 'Days when death comes so close, / you say No to life. / Days when you should show death / how to live.'

The early loss of his father ('Two Silences'), his need to begin work at sixteen ('*Man Going to the Office*'), his becoming guardian to his younger sister ('Siblings United'), and the sense that the literary life is a long way off figure sharply and vividly in his early poems. 'Porlock', for instance, is an anaphora-driven list: 'this is a poem of distractions, interruptions, clamouring telephones / this is a poem that reveals how incompatible with verse my life is'. The piece appears within the first twenty pages of his book; but by the time we're at page 265, I can only admire the way he's managed to get that life to be compatible with his inspiration and need to make such telling works. Whether intentionally or not, 'Porlock' deploys something of the silent irony in Coleridge's famous note. After all, if 'Kubla Khan' is the kind of poem he could write when interrupted by that perhaps mythical 'Person', then I for one can only wish the chap had knocked more often. O'Driscoll's piece sounds like a manifesto for the way his poems will be firmly located in the world of work, and the world of people who don't usually read poems – but who might well do worse than start with his.

Early on I was taken aback to notice in 'Serving Time' the phrase 'summoned by bells', three words indelibly marked with their use as a poetry book title – but then later, in 'England', their author gets a name check: 'Goodly, portly Sir John Betjeman'. When 'the great, / supposedly fouled-up Larkin' got alluded to in 'Love Life', I had to accepted that there must be more than an accidental affinity. O'Driscoll's poems don't read or sound much like either of theirs, mind you. He's far too adept at the more informal ways of putting together poems that, even beyond linguistically experimental territories, have now become one sort of norm. Nevertheless, the empirical subject matter and the way death functions as an omnipresent means for delivering point and urgency suggest underlying affinities:

> Death is moving into newly-constructed suburbs,
> through semi-detached houses, ugly identical twins.
> Hired cars will call for widows who have come as brides ...

In the final section of 'Home Affairs' we discover 'It is an ordinary morning without pain.' But the sense of relief doesn't last long. Soon we must 'fortify ourselves with its light, our house's silence, / against the trouble, bustle, pain / which other mornings will, irrevocably, bring.' Though this is doubtless true, it's not necessarily how to make the best of some morning sunshine. Such melancholy is infectious, and 'we' (a pronoun O'Driscoll uses with a genial lack of self-consciousness) might also feel the need to wean ourselves off it. The aim of such death-haunted poetry is, presumably, to attach us more to life. It would be a pity if its melancholy strains were to encourage the opposite.

His poems have a distinctively strong and sustained rhythm that is only occasionally thrown off-stride by an adjective-noun clutter piled up to deliver that feeling of inescapable contemporaneity. After reading a swathe of his poems, though, I began to sense that the strong, steady rhythm was a little too much of a catch-all effectively designed to lift such inert material off the ground – as here in 'Exemplary Damages':

And can we go on satisfying orders for baseball caps, chicken nuggets, body toning pads, camomile salve for chapped lips? And what quantity of dolphin-friendly skipjack tuna meets a sushi bar's demands?

The steady rhythmic beat and flow isn't so much used to point and turn individual phrases as to allow the poet to load every rift with whatever up-to-the-minute stuff comes to hand. This all-purpose utility rhythm can allow the poems' themes to stay slightly out of focus, to avoid self-questioning, or over-generalise the view.

Reading '*from* Full Flight', I found myself wondering why I needed lines that hardly did more than enumerate an only too familiar routine: 'The in-flight magazine is yanked from its / elasticated pocket; newspaper readers settle / on sports; business-class curtains close ranks; / a mix-up in a seat allotment is resolved.' It hardly needs adding that before the piece's end we must be reminded of 'the risks of law-defying / hijackers, of pilot error, radar failure, lightning storms, / metal fatigue…' Oh God, spare us all. This is a danger his poems will inevitably face if they must be so squarely set on foreseeing the way we die now. O'Driscoll is a distinctly talented poet; but perhaps there's an even better one in there – if only he were allowed to exchange his general surveys for a detail-particular vision, and to give himself more of his own unique say.

DEREK MAHON:
RETURNING AN ECHO

Derek Mahon's 'Echo' in *Echo's Grove*, subtitled '*from the Latin of* Ovid, *Metamorphoses* III, 356-402', begins by explaining how she 'can't speak first but answers back' and concludes: 'the voice survives. Where? In a hollow cave, / in a valley, a forest clearing, a silent grove.' Naturally, this invites thoughts about the symbiosis of a possibly narcissistic original text and a helplessly echoing (and self-defeating) translation, which it is forever haunted by. Mahon's translation effectively imitates the ways her echoing phrases are haplessly ambiguous: "Anyone here?' said he; she answered, 'Here'. / He paused, surprised, gazing about, and cried, / 'Oh come on!', hearing the echo cry, 'Come on!" The original might be offering good advice about how self-love and other-worship can prevent or ruin relationship, for, just as a translation is not metamorphosis (because the original stays the same), so good poems are not narcissistic, because dependent upon relationship with languages, cultures, and readerships, and good translations are not caught in a passively echoic dependency either.

Echo is thus tortured in Ovid and Mahon because her repetitions of the endings of phrases seem always to be interpretable with a sense she doesn't intend, while the object of her obsession remains uninterested in her. Even this may not be like the original and translation relationship, because an original, secure in its existence, can usefully be compared with a translation, for a rendering in another language is, in effect, a commentary on its source. What's more, the translation can't haplessly echo the original, since it inevitably changes it into the timbres of another language, and, in best cases, another poetic idiom, though not necessarily another's signature style. Mahon is careful in his Foreword to draw a distinction between his *Adaptations* (the title to his 2006 gathering, of which *Echo's Grove* is a substantial enlargement) and Robert Lowell's 'imitations' – one difference lying in Mahon's actually *being* adaptations, while what he calls the 'very uneven quality' of Lowell's renderings derives from their not being sufficiently imitative to be appreciable accounts of the sources.

Echo's Grove is subtitled *Translations*. Mahon's Foreword also contradicts it by affirming that 'These aren't translations, in the strict sense, but *versions* of their originals devised, as often as not, from cribs of one kind or another.' Yet there is no strict nomenclature for these distinctions: 'translation' means any attempted carrying over of one text into another language. So these 'adaptations' or 'versions' are translations too, even if Mahon can graciously note that the 'real translator' of his Propertius 'exercise' is Gilbert Highet. Mahon confesses that Propertius 'gets some rough treatment' from him, though not as rough as in Ezra Pound's *Homage* with its shameless anachronisms: 'a fridgidaire patent' or 'the ancient, respected, / Wordsworthian'. Not sounding like rough treatments at all, the great pleasure of his gathered versions is that you can hear on practically every page the sound of Mahon's metrical and stanzaic intelligence, his tact and taste as regards linguistic choices, cadences, and rhymes.

He can be freely adaptive, calling his version of Rimbaud's 'Ma Bohème', for instance, 'Hitch Hiker', and Baudelaire's 'Je n'ai pas oublié, voisine de la ville' he calls 'Antrim Road'. While his renderings from Li Po, Rilke, Pasternak, Guillén, Neruda, Metastasio, Michelangelo, Petrarch and Luzi all recommend themselves, I do feel his versions from such as Baudelaire, Corbière, Rimbaud, Laforgue, Jaccottet, and Houellebecq benefit from his greater knowledge of French, because their detail of invention and variation is more closely in touch with what prompts it. Take the fifteenth stanza from Valéry's 'Le cimetière marin', Mahon's 'The Seaside Cemetery':

> Mixed in a thick solution underground
> the white clay is drunk by the crimson kind;
> its vigour circulates in the veined flowers.
> Where now are the colloquial turns of phrase,
> the individual gifts and singular souls?
> Where once a tear gathered a grub crawls.

Well, where indeed? Valéry's 'L'art personnel' has been replaced by Mahon's 'individual gifts', and in the dead's 'colloquial turns of phrase, / the individual gifts and singular souls', Valéry's 'Où sont des morts les phrases familières, / L'art personnel, les âmes singulières?' are dust, but resurrected, as another metaphor for translation would have it, in the Irish poet's colloquialism, giftedness, and singularity. Its rhythms are firm, the late-twentieth-century part-rhyming audible, alluding to the rhyme scheme, rather than fully following it. This too is an echoing effect, not of the original but its own linguistic patterning. There are, inevitably enough, moments when memories of the original in this English-only edition register as regrettable losses, not least for me when in Rimbaud's 'Romance', 'le cœur fou Robinsonne' is done as 'The daft heart drifts to popular romance'. Where Rimbaud's allusion to *Robinson Crusoe* fills his line with a hollowed out heroism, Mahon's paraphrasing simply re-echoes Rimbaud's and his own title.

Among many high points here is the sequence 'Alexandria', from five poems by Cavafy. 'Voices', the third, takes after 'Phonès', which, as commentators note, echoes Shelley's 'Music', Tennyson's 'Break, Break, Break' and Verlaine's 'Mon Rêve Familier':

> Definitive voices of the loved dead
> or the loved lost, as good as dead,
> speak to us in our dreams
> or at odd moments.
>
> Listening, we hear again,
> like music at night,
> the original poetry of our lives.

Mahon's delicate play on 'original poetry' sets the living in relation to past voices from both life and literature. His techniques, in his own work too, are keyed to a sound of poetry, like a longed for original, drawn from traditions and resources beyond the competence of any single linguist. Reaching for the sky in versions, for instance, of Lucretius' 'On Clouds', Pushkin's 'The Cloud', and Brecht's 'White Cloud', they aspire to the condition of poetry and, like the aspirant in Collins' 'Ode on the Poetical Character', boldly hunt it as if by sonar. The very least I can say for them is that they achieve this for us too. Inviting readers' bosoms to return 'an echo', the phrase Dr. Johnson used to grant Gray's 'Elegy' its due, this is what they approximately do.

LOVING HIS FOOD:
HARRY CLIFTON

Harry Clifton started publishing early. His first collection, *The Walls of Carthage*, appeared from Gallery Press in 1977, when its author was just 25. Over the subsequent fifteen years he published another three books and capped them with a selected. *The Desert Route* (1992) included a Foreword by Derek Mahon – Clifton's most immediate forebear. The poet followed it with a thematic collection about living in Italy, *Night Train through the Brenner*, in 1994. Since then things have slowed. Over the last decade, admirers have had to look out for his name in such places as the little magazine *Metre*, run by Justin Quinn and David Wheatley. Now they have helped bridge the gap to his next book with eleven poems set in the city where, after many years of exilic bulletins, Harry Clifton appears to have settled.

Just three things produce a mild indigestion. The first is Clifton's recourse to enjambed phrases that place an 'of' at the beginning of the new line. The second verse to 'Investiture', from *The Desert Route*, has six lines of which half begin with that word. A problem of the device is that the line-ending closes down a sense-phrase on the noun, but then the next line has to re-energise itself like a car stalled when the lights change. The second qualm is about the way that, accompanying a night-walking Giacometti in 'Reductio', he sees:

> Not Paris now, but infinities
> Of disconnected people, faces, times,
> Humanity dissolving into shapes
> At the ends of avenues, at the ends of rhymes.

It's not 'times' and 'rhymes' that upset me; but 'shapes' here chimes with the earlier adjective 'agape'. No, he's not like the mythical Muldoon who might rhyme 'cat' and 'dog'. Clifton will rhyme 'Pyrenees' with 'me'; he will accept even more approximate collocations like 'revelation' and 'unconditional'. The third, more general one is the relation in his poems between the narrative voice and knowledge or information. His skilful sonnet, 'Descartes at the Court of Sweden', suffers (as such 'history revisited' poems tend to) from its air of an insightfulness about fates that your average well-informed poetry reader already knows.

'Rabbits at Orly Airport' is a lyric of just three quatrains:

And the last shall be first, and the first shall be last –
Herbivorous, nibbling at the runway's edge,
The rabbits quivering in our turbo blast,
The lower forms, across the broken bridge

Of evolution, have us in their sights
And look beyond us, through the fuselage
Of a 747 trembling before flight,
A batman's signals, to their own Golden Age

Of wind and heavenly grass, already achieved.
Their race is over. Patiently they wait
As we lumber towards take-off, to receive us
At the infinite point where both our lines meet.

The poem illustrates all three bits of indigestion. It's made by fusing the sight of the rabbits with a speculation about us. Of its twelve lines, three begin with 'Of'. The rhyming in the first stanza is finely turned: a full rhyme on the odd lines, and a stylish off rhyme of near vowels and same consonants on the even ones. In the second, the even rhymes do the same, but the odd ones have a singular rhymed with a plural. In the third, the odd rhymes are a participle and an infinitive with pronoun, and the even rhymes repeat the pattern – faintly disappointingly – of off-rhymed vowels. This produces, at the end of the poem, a curious relation between sound and sense. Parallel lines meet at infinity, we learn at school; but, since we never get to infinity, they don't. The rabbits 'wait' for the lines to 'meet' – and we hear that they never quite will. So the unravelling of the rhyme scheme in the final verse doesn't produce a powerful poetic turn that upsets expectations; it seems to capitulate to them.

These three stomach grumbles coincide, of course, because the narrative in a Clifton poem is carried by resourceful prose syntax through usually rhymed stanzas. The 'broken bridge / Of evolution' (nice line-break), or 'their own Golden Age / Of wind and heavenly grass' (less so), makes the other one 'the fuselage / Of a 747' sound flat in its bare factuality. Yet all three phrases facilitate the rhyme, string out the syntax, and sustain the authoritative-sounding register of the narrative. The poet's knowledge claim is inserted with the Biblical text in line one, then, less resoundingly, with the information that rabbits are herbivorous. The poem, not content to report the nature note, pulls together its reflection on the world's fauna, observed as it lumbers towards take-off. Its critical pathos comes in the hint that, with the closing off-rhyme, neither the poem, nor the 747, nor the human race, ever quite make it. We'd be better off – it seems to say – imitating the rabbits.

Clifton has put in a lot of flying time constructing his oeuvre. One of the many pleasures of his poetry is that you never knew where he would write from next. While in previous books he has filed reports from Asia, Africa, Europe, and North America, the poems brought together here find the poet settled in a cosmopolitan city where the world may come to him. The opening piece, 'White Russians', scouts this theme with an epigraph from Simone Weil, whom Clifton later seems to imply, rather harshly, was among his catalogue of 'Double agents, poets and impostors'. 'Reductio' and 'The Zone' explore other districts of the 'Fourmillante cité, cité pleine de rêves', as does a fine elegy for Seane Dunne, 'Mont Saint Geneviève'. In the final piece, as only seems appropriate, we wind up at a café table:

> No, instead I would sit here, I would wait –
>   A dinner, a *café crème*,
> A chaser of grog. Whatever else, there was time –
> Let Judgement take care of itself. To celebrate –
> That was the one imperative. Randomness, flux,
> Drew themselves about me as I ate,
> Protected by the nearnesses of women, their sex
> Blown sheer through summer dresses, loving my food,
> My freedom, as they say a man should.

The donnée for 'God in Paris' is the Jewish proverb that should the deity come to live in this city, where no one believes in him, he would have plenty of free time to enjoy. So God, alias the poet, can sit back and, superficially like the rabbits at the airport, 'wait' in post-prandial appreciation of his good-bad luck.

This last verse of Clifton's title poem shows none of my three quibbles. There's only 'the nearnesses of women' to start a rumble, and the phrase is not strung over a line ending. All of the rhymes are either full, or their vowel sounds just – significantly – miss. The syntax begins with three short, off-hand notations. Then a four-and-a-half-line sentence builds to its artfully shrugging close. Clifton's God is '*l'homme moyen sensuel* / Adrift on the everyday' and, as you might expect from the author of 'Monsoon Girl', women and their sex are never far. So his poem closes by evoking the Rilkean imperative to 'celebrate'. Pulling together those three or four qualities of a comfortable life in exile, Clifton lets them slide towards the recognition of an amoral paradise ('Let Judgement take care of itself'). Only then, with great skill, he reinstates a shadow of the justified life for even a God being human with that final modal verb. 'God in Paris', the poet at his very best, is one to add to his clutch of classics – 'Monsoon Girl', 'Death of Thomas Merton', 'Euclid Avenue' – already gracing anthologies. On the showing of this chapbook and the poems that have been appearing in magazines and newspapers, Harry Clifton's next full collection promises to be well worth the wait.

BRICK UPON BRICK:
PETER SIRR

Peter Sirr began early, winning the Patrick Kavanagh award in 1982 when he was just 22. The poems in his first collection, *Marginal Zones* (1984), are located in the wide wake of Derek Mahon. There's even one in short three-line stanzas called 'In a Japanese Garden'. This 'Snow Party' revisited doesn't make it into Sirr's *Selected Poems*, but then neither do a great many of his more distinctive pieces. At less than a hundred generously spaced pages (Gallery's production values are as good as ever), the book is little more than a sampler. My one complaint is that its last four poems are also in the new collection, *Nonetheless*, while many of my favourites – from *Ways of Falling* (1991) in particular – have had to be de-selected. Nonetheless, this *Selected* makes a perfectly fine introduction to Sirr's ways and means, whetting an appetite that would only be satisfied, in my case at least, by further recourse to the six collections he has now published.

Inhabiting a space cleared by Mahon and already occupied by the slightly older Harry Clifton, Sirr's early poems tend to be in poised stanzas with a cultured and cosmopolitan flavour. One of the best is 'Guido Cavalcanti to his Father', a poem inspired by a reading of *Inferno* X – where Dante encounters Guido's dad, who looks around as if expecting to see his son with their fellow Florentine. In Sirr's poem: 'I would endure again each silent storm, / words like provisions under sand / or maps of lands we strained to find // and each attempt at reparation / that proved a shyer kind of failure.' It's a well-built device to address indirectly the relationship between a contemporary father and son. This is a much-worked topos, but Sirr brings to it an evolving obliquity that will occasion a number of distinctive poems: 'Through the Window' from *Ways of Falling*, and 'Peter Street' from *Bring Everything* (2000), for example.

In 'Legacies' he extends the temporal perspective through Dublin pub generations:

> more talk,
> more drink, more noise
> till neither they nor you nor I can tell

whose head is starting to spin,
whose voice is telling the story,
whose life it happens in.

Sirr's mature connectedness is by steady accretion. In 'Hunting the Bricks and Mortar' from *The Ledger of Fruitful Exchange* (1995) he sets off from 'my books on architecture' to picture 'unbuilt / but not unimagined, my own / shelter, Home'. In 'the book, / the notebook', he 'can hear the sound // they make, brick lowered upon / brick, stem upon stem and name / upon name'. Though made of five six-line verses, this poem's syntax flows on over each stanza-break and down to the final full stop. The connectedness is in the enumeration of his capaciously open-ended sentences, while his rhythmic poise combines this need to range with a continuous, though momentary, need to rest before the slightly more sustained terminal repose. That's the sound of home his poems make.

Sirr's mature poetry is both about and proceeds by means of accretion and change. His forms grow by responding to their own leads and suggestions, to their lineation and enjambment. These often turn the sense in a fresh direction, one that can take in a wry comedy and understated pathos. The intriguing turns frequently lead to an unexpectedly apt close, as in the lines from 'Legacies' above. The risks in his way of proceeding can perhaps be counted in some of the longer sequences, such as 'Death of a Travel Writer' or 'A Journal', only one of which – 'Trade Songs' – is given intact in *Selected Poems*. The space he allows himself doesn't necessarily warrant the discoveries; and this may be because he doesn't bring each individual section to the same degree of focus as he does with single pieces.

To get this evolving sound, Sirr had more or less to abandon the stanza as a self-contained apartment, and to strike out into blocks of responsively improvised verse. At first this had a slightly showy informal look, seeded with wit and cultural reference, all issuing from a self-dramatised persona. 'A Guide to Holland' tells of a 'Land without secrets, heart worn / on the sleeve of Europe' and of how 'near the zoo / a cardboard tiger aims his leap / at an apartment block, and here three months / I borrow the posture, sink my teeth / into the interior life'. This poem is from section two in his second collection, *Talk Talk* (1987), a sequence intermittently about the break-up of a relationship. That's where he begins to hit both his own note, and his stride. There was one more thing to abandon first, though, before his self-arrival would be complete. He would need to drop that projected poet's persona, the world-weary wised-up lad whose innocence is signalled by just those signs and tokens.

Sirr's early interest in Italian poetry didn't prevent him also writing 'Translations', in which we 'behold the lovely sketches published / immediately our mapmaker returned / and know in our hearts his hatchings lie / since everything here depends // on our having no way of expressing it'. That sounds within the territory of Frost's notion that the poetry is what gets lost in translation. Sirr can be found now, though, very much more in translation. Here in the title poem to his new collection, he's 'remembering / the verb you sent me last winter / for feeling low in a new place' or 'the one for waking / in a panic of loss / three February mornings / in a row'. He's inclined to celebrate 'the endless / promise of language', and, though 'the world swells / with avid grammars / and hardly a thing that happens / survives our greedy mouths', as the poem and his book title reminds us: '*Nonetheless*'. 'Desire', from *Bring Everything*, asserts that if you 'Sniff the air in poetry', then 'the sun wakes up in Persian'. As if to underline this multilingualism, his new book ends with 'Edge Songs', a sequence imitated from Irish originals.

The collection also contains a bold rendering of Giorgio Caproni's 'Congedo del viaggiatore cerimonioso'. Caproni's poetry isn't informal; it's intricately and highly audibly rhymed. This has either to be mimicked, letting the sense look after itself, or abandoned. In 'The Leavetaking of the Ceremonious Traveller' Sirr opts for the latter, while producing rhythmic compensations on the way: 'I have been happy among you / since we left, and am much / in your debt, believe me, / for your excellent company.' This is far closer to its original than 'After Tasso' (not included in *Selected Poems*) is to 'A la Signora Duchessa di Ferrara'. The O'Shaughnessy Award citation described Sirr as one of 'a new generation of Irish poets whose urbanities have a clearly European aspect'. He was already making fun of this in 'At the Cultural Centre' with its 'short speech on Europe's / fascinating diversity', a poem from *Ways of Falling* that also didn't make the *Selected* cut. His internationalism extends way out beyond the Euro-zone.

Sirr's distinction may indeed not lie in following Joyce from Dublin to the continent without setting foot in Liverpool. 'James Joyce Homeloans', also from the new collection, is a genial mockery of the unholy alliance between Bloomsday and Irishry. After all, Joyce was the exception that proved a rule. Sirr, if his award citation may be believed, is the new rule. What's more, his work becomes that much more thoroughly European when he let go of that inherited poet persona, and focused more microscopically on the theme being explored: 'There's a moment the air will thicken and the light shifts, as if / another country has poured itself in, another life / lent its corona   and suddenly the stars are here, milk spills / across the heavens; whoever you are ripples' ('China'). This is especially so when he is writing in more recent collections about Dublin.

'The Writer's Studio', one of the new ones in both *Selected Poems* and *Nonetheless*, is about what happens to his preferred *modus scribendi* with the arrival of fame, death, and cultural memorialisation. He teases the Francis Bacon studio now at the Hugh Lane Gallery in the city where the painter was born: 'They've been worrying for ages / how best to show your chaos.' Fortunately, a *Selected* is just an interim report. You pick the ones you like from the mass of what you've done, and postpone the definitive representation of a *Collected* or *Complete* – something to attract the dust where infinity goes up on trial. In his two new publications, as in 'The Writer's Studio', Sirr displays an array of skills 'to show your chaos' in such characteristic detail as 'a smashed cloud' that floats in and out at a line ending. Doing so, he escapes from the museum of past performances with his vitality intact, his directions home open, and still more bricks to add.

SO GOOD SO FAR:
SINÉAD MORRISSEY

Sinéad Morrissey, the youngest poet ever to be given the Patrick Kavanagh award, published *There was Fire in Vancouver* in 1996. It's a promising debut, containing memorable pieces such as 'Losing a Diary', 'A Visitor', and the title poem – many of them written in lines that average somewhere between six and twelve syllables. There are, though, poems like 'Leaving Flensburg' where her line suddenly reaches out to the right margin. These moments feel not quite integrated, like hasty dashes for needed spaciousness that the inherited mid-length modes didn't provide. The great step forward of her second collection is the exfoliated sense that such reaches for spaciousness are now the norm. They have also found apt occasions for the larger explorations of complex experiences gathered from the poet's travelling all over the place.

Yet there may be an air of fended-off chaos in these reaches, as if the poems and their emotional materials had to risk being all over the place too. In the second verse of her title poem, about a Japanese graveyard for children, one of its long lines moves with an emblematic self-description:

> Like oriental soldiers contained by a wall, they would go
>   walking –
> spill over with all of the energy for life that fell out of
>   them too soon.

I suppose you could say that the word 'oriental' here – one I'd walk all round the dictionary to avoid – does at least indicate the kind of poem that 'Between Here and There' has to be. The 'oriental soldiers', who presumably reminded the poet of the Chinese terracotta armies, are little stone statues representing miscarried children: 'Except that even in stone some bodies have opened – / loose balls in the basin where heads have rolled.' So the Morrissey line is a headlong expression of ways that the world's energies can disastrously miscarry. Her book is divided into two sections, the first containing poems from various places, the second including only ones about Japan. If at first it looks like the title refers to the 'here' and 'there' of home and abroad, or west and east, her title poem indicates that it also refers to the journey 'between here and Ogaki to paradise.'

The preposition in the title suggests that the poems might be situated in the interstices between settled states of existence. If so, this is an area that rather than inhabiting, they point towards by describing one or other, or both, of the separated locations. 'Before and After' is another impressive piece about the experience of teaching in a Japanese agricultural high school. The 'before' part of the poem, entirely in inverted commas, is a sustained warning about all the dangerous and dreadful things that the poet is likely to encounter:

> The children who fall through the sieve of the system
>
> stop falling here for three years. Though if they rape,
> or get arrested more than twice, they leave –
> a free fall to the bottom, the Yakuza or the sex trade –

Once again, rolling long lines of mostly monosyllables are drawn to dramatizing the helpless tumble of these social misfits. The 'after' part is spoken in a lyrical first-person singular:

> At the Agricultural High School near Ogaki City, kindness
> falls over me
> more than anywhere. Like the persimmons in your garden
> by Yoro Hill –
> enough colour in the mouth of winter to stop the cold.

Here too, the long lines are drawn to a sense of falling. Yet, despite the skill with which the poem's warm contrast is handled, this is a classic piece about *not* understanding life in Japan. After all, the long account of what goes wrong for the kids in the poor school can't be all negativity and cynicism. Similarly, the poet's fondly expressed sense of gratitude is unlikely to be the only thing to say about such experiences. The poem splits between the bad version and the good one – the first too bad, and the second too good. I wouldn't begin to blame the poet for this. Her poem is also an accurate expression of the slightly schizoid attitude to life in the country that everyone, and maybe not only an alien, experiences. If 'Before and After' does offer a rounded picture, it must be in the work the reader performs integrating the two parts. The danger of 'Before and After' is that readers are merely cheered by the poet's second section – in a shift that risks a sentimentalizing contrast.

This danger is ever present in poems that veer and fall between starkly contrasted positions. Nevertheless, they give a raw strength to Morrissey's work in her second book. 'Sea Stones', for example, is a striking poem about being struck across the face in public:

> You turned away as the sun disappeared like a ship. And I,
> suddenly wanting to be struck again, to keep the fire of your anger lit,
> I bit my lip.

It's almost a rewrite of T. S. Eliot's 'La Figlia che Piange' with the pronominal relation revised, the gender direction of address swapped, and with his pre-Raphaelite cadences replaced, again, by Morrissey's lines reeling across the page. The cross-rhymes of 'ship' with 'lip' and 'lit' with 'bit', plus the subtly rhetorical stutter in the repetition of the pronoun, 'And I … I bit', produce a close that draws a line under the experience and yet also leaves the torn shreds of emotion reverberating in the air.

Finally, there's the curiously abandoned shape of 'In Need of a Funeral'. It's a poem that might have been made of four six-line stanzas in which the first two end with a line that plays a variation on the title. Then, in the third, this refrain-like variation appears as the third line, while in the fourth verse, it disappears altogether. And, in fact, so does the stanza – divided at its fourth line, making a quatrain and a couplet:

> …which is why we eat flesh and drink blood. *Kirie.*
> I took flowers, an Oxfam veil, a bottle of Scotch, a speech
> and made it to the sprawl of Milltown Cemetery
> where I littered a hill with old shoes and milk teeth.
>
> There was a pattern to the pattern my breath made on the air
> as it extended towards the motorway.

Sticking with the pattern set up by the title and the first two refrain-closed verses would be to set the speaker, as in a villanelle or a sestina, stuck in a felt lack. Instead, Morrissey allows the thought that this need of a funeral 'came to me the day I stole the communion in the cathedral' to get her out of the house, over to the cemetery, where she can stage her home-made version of a funeral with no death. Then, aptly enough, the poem ends by alluding to the replacement of the poem's abandoned pattern with a pattern in her breath – another structure to the structure. This is the way the poem responds to, by acting out, the need it sketches. Yet, as she says, there is another pattern behind this one: the poem with the refrains at the ends of the verses. To produce such a stereo effect in a reader certainly gives the poem a vital dimension. But are the two shapes coordinated with each other? It will be interesting indeed to trace the patterns that Sinéad Morrissey's future writings make on the air.

BORROWED ARMOUR:
CIARAN CARSON

Ciaron Carson cites a Yosa Buson haiku as one of the section dividers at the start of the third part in *Belfast Confetti* (1989): 'I've just put on this / borrowed armour: second-hand / cold freezes my bones.' The poet revisits a variant of this borrowed-armour idea in a passage about a samurai sword from the later sonnet sequence in alexandrines, *The Twelfth of Never* (1998). In 'Wolf Hill', a reworking of the little-red-riding-hood narrative in which our hero frees his country, it would appear, from the stomach of a greedy wolf, he's 'Protected by my sword and shield of samurai / Which gleam beneath the wintry skies' and he will 'gird my loins that I might suffer no assault', then:

> The haughty moon maintains her foreign silver coin,
> And I have tracked the rough beast to his last retreat.
> I slit him open from the gullet to the groin:
>
> Therein lay little Erin, like one of the Undead,
> A pair of bloody dancing shoes upon her feet,
> Her gown a shamrock green, her cloak a poppy red.

Yeats's horrific image out of *Spiritus Mundi* has become a Disney-like mix and match retelling. The firmness of the twelve-syllable lines in this sonnet's sestet, the iambic drive, the absence of enjambed cadences, the mere pair of lightly comma'd caesuras in lines twelve and fourteen, and the firm full rhymes all point to the poem's armoury of strong defences. Such features are Carson's sword and shield, the techniques in which he girds himself and his poetry so as to 'suffer no assault'. The course of his work, though, might be thought an exemplification of the idea that, however much we win the battles with our enemies, we're always in danger of a sudden counter-attack from our need for them, whether they be inner demons or actual opponents. What's more, behind such defences, undermining us there, are the reasons for putting them up in the first place. Carson's extraordinarily fluent and inventive poetry, using those rhymes to discover its meanings, might be said to have been wounded not only by the conditions in which much of it had to be written, but by the defences it constructed to protect itself from those conditions.

The techniques in the first collection, *New Estate and Other Poems* (1976 and 1988), might come as a surprise to readers who had first encountered him in his breakthrough second and third collections, *The Irish for No* (1987) and *Belfast Confetti*. Though seeming to take a freshness-signalling hint from Paul Muldoon, who had published *New Weather* in 1973, *New Estate* establishes its repertoire in the lyrical verse writing of the previous generation. The book's style registers vulnerabilities, hesitations, and uncertainties at the line endings and with sharp caesuras – as here, for example, in the title poem's second and final verse:

> A shiver now runs through the laurel hedge,
> And washing flutters like the swaying lines
> Of a new verse. The high fidelity
> Music of the newly-wed obscures your
> Dedication to a life of loving
> Money. What could they be for, those marble
> Toilet fixtures, the silence of the waterbeds,
> That book of poems you bought yesterday?

This lyric, which turns into its second line with 'Rusty / Iambics that escaped your discipline / Of shorn lawns' confirms a dissatisfaction with its own conventions in the ironies and rhythmic instability of its second verse. The idea of the well-made poem is compromised beyond repair, or so it would appear, by its association with self-betterment and the indicators of suburban self-esteem. The 'shiver' that 'runs through the laurel hedge' and the 'washing' that 'flutters like the swaying lines / Of a new verse' is brought to bear on the reader through the vulnerability of enjambments, the cutting dead of samurai caesuras, and the syntactical surprise, like running round the corner straight into a lamppost, in 'a life of loving / Money.' It's a bit too youthfully embittered, perhaps: after all, your 'life of loving' will come to grief if there's no money, and your loving money won't mean a thing if you don't also have something resembling 'a life of love' for it to fund. Yet, even if the poet were aware of such qualifications, the poem's lineation trashes that proffered first idea by having it collide with the second. Far from being a marker of its tough realism, this is a sign (in both lineation and thought) of hinterland weaknesses against which it is attractively failing either to armour itself or quite come to terms.

The New Estate is a first book in the classic sense that it is the place from which the poet departs, and Carson has never again ventured near articulating such shivering senses through the tremors of an equivocal lineation. With *The Irish for No* and *Belfast Confetti* a wholesale change of direction both of formal resources, range of materials, and confident voicing is established. Yet this confidence is achieved by desensitizing line ends and caesuras, and then associating this new firmness with the raw threat, the achieved violence, but not the elegiac aftermath (a genre already definitively worked by Carson's seniors, Heaney and Longley) of conflict in the North of Ireland. The second part of 'Bloody Hand' from *Belfast Confetti*, laid out as it appears on the page with turned over lines that emphasise the newly expressive de-lineation, exemplifies a drawing of strength from your adversary:

> I snuffed out the candle between finger and thumb. Was
>   it the left hand
> Hacked off at the wrist and thrown to the shores of Ulster?
>   Did Ulster
> Exist? Or the Right Hand of God, saying *Stop* to this and
>   *No* to that?
> My thumb is the hammer of a gun. The thumb goes up. The
>   thumb goes down.

The firmness of the voice is attuned to the enactment of the threat, to the aggression it abhors. There's a syllable count, and so a measure, but barely any cadence, and the poem's technique has been relieved of a monitoring role for the work's ethical sensibility. It goes without saying that these poems take upon themselves the dangers in the political situation and have developed a loquacious strategy for outflanking the 'whatever you say, say nothing' issue. They say a vast amount in a 'don't quote me, but' style of story telling.

This strategy involved quoting everybody else, throwing the dictionary at the problem, again a form of borrowed armour manifested in the cunning deployment of detail in a tale-telling frame. With Carson's mature poetry, Belfast finally found its Arcades-project *bricoleur* and became a post-modernist city, as in the opening of 'The Irish for No', a poem that takes off from Keats's 'Ode to a Nightingale', an emblem of 'the English lyric', and, via the Bard of Avon, finds itself confronted in a variously embattled cultural heterogeneity:

> *Was it a vision, or a waking dream?* I heard her voice before I saw
> What looked like the balcony scene in *Romeo and Juliet*, except Romeo
> Seemed to have shinned up a pipe and was inside arguing with her.
>   The casements
> Were wide open and I could see some Japanese-style wall-hangings,
>   the dangling
> Quotation marks of a yin-yang mobile. *It's got nothing*, she was
>   snarling, *nothing*
> *To do with politics*, and, before the bamboo curtain came down,
>   *That goes for you too!*

Of all the significant poetry to have come out of the Troubles, it is Carson's work that has incorporated as so much bone-chilling borrowed armour the human damage of those years. The other important poets, whether his seniors or contemporaries, differently developed both personal and poetic methods for preserving themselves from it by adapting to their own purposes the technical inheritance of the much-maligned and so-called English lyric, grafting themselves onto that stem in both their writing and their publishing strategies, while Carson, even when writing a sonnet, has established the modernist convention that traditional means are set in 'dangling /Quotation marks'. The chill air of a carapace-like defence in Carson's oeuvre is the index of its inner vulnerability, an appealing quality allowed to show in his first book, and then skilfully redacted. Here is the closing movement of 'Yes' from *Belfast Confetti*:

> I'm about to quote from Basho's *The Narrow Road to the Deep North* –
> *Blossoming mushroom: from some unknown tree a leaf has stuck to it* –
> When it goes off and we're thrown out of kilter. My mouth is full
> Of broken glass and quinine as everything reverses South.

If 'The Bloody Hand' brings home the haplessly prophetic phrase in Heaney's early 'Digging' about his dad's spade being 'snug as a gun' in his hand, so 'Yes' might be a close-up illustration of the gracefully implicit metaphor and implication in Mahon's 'The Snow Party'.

Since the end of the 1980s, the sequence of Carson's collections, arriving at regular intervals, books such as *First Language* (1993) and

Opera Et Cetera (1996), document the work of a folk musician in performance, or a visual artist deciding to work on projects in series. There are the 'Letters from the Alphabet' poems, sequences of sonnets, free or regular, the experiments with long lines or very short ones, the use of bravura rhyming all in a form of stylised quotation that means the poet appears never to be wholly committed to the style being given a work-out. This part of the *Collected Poems* offers a cornucopia of text, writing like the version of Baudelaire's 'L'albatros', for example, recast in 18-syllable rhymed couplets, more or less, concluding with that famous simile of bird and writer whose original outsoars translation:

> The Poet's like that Prince of Clouds, who soars above the
>   archer and the hurricane: Great Auk
> Brought down to earth, his gawky, gorgeous wings impede
>   his walking.

This self-consciously stylish exercise brings us down to earth with a staged bump in that 'Auk' / 'walking' close. Here, then, is the stubborn paradox of a non-lyrical style that is all his own, a uniqueness characteristically achieved since Rimbaud, if not the English Romantics, by playing up a single aspect of poetry at the expense of other technical features. The one that has tended to get played up in English now, because of its vast and bolt-on vocabulary, is diction. Carson has taken part in the recent compulsion to rummage the dictionaries, the dialects, and idiolect. As a result, his language outruns the person, coming to substitute for convincing lived experience, even while life-resembling events are refracted through it – as in sonnets jazzing around a 'Lost in Translation' Tokyo, 'The Rising Sun' for example: 'The Professor took me to a bonsai garden / To imbibe some thimblefuls of Japanese poteen. / We wandered through the forest of the books of Arden. / The number of their syllables was seventeen.' The rhyming here doesn't exactly work to make discoveries of what the poem will say. It occasions a tour of the snatched-at known.

Carson's way with warfare returns in some of his short-lined poems, as by a Louis Zukofsky *redivivus*, such as 'Trap' from *Breaking News* (2003) about an army patrol being ambushed:

> backpack radio
> antenna

twitching
rifle

headphones
cocked

I don't
read you

what the

over

Just as the British Army updated and refined its tactics in the districts
of Belfast, only to be ordered to redeploy them in Iraq and Afghanistan,
so Carson reprises the theme of 'Army' from *The Irish for No* where the
'private at the rear' of a street patrol is 'trying not to think of a third eye
/ Being drilled in the back of his head.' But the problem with 'Trap', for
me at least, is that its cadence-free form has no feeling. Is there protest,
and if so, against what? The last word is ambiguous between inviting
someone else to communicate on a walkie-talkie, and that life being cut
short. Why is the lineation not merely cruelly clever? This is one fateful
risk if poetry takes on the lineaments of the terrifying materials it evokes,
and one of the ways that Carson's work most bears the scars of our times
in its textures. His borrowed armour doesn't in the end protect him; just
as in Buson's haiku, it gives him and us the second-hand chills.

Though inexhaustibly large and various, this 592-page *Collected
Poems* nonetheless intimates a sense that while Carson's subjects and
techniques have grown, and grown more various, the work has suffered
a loss of focus and point. The self-wounding defensiveness of a poetry
that uses diction, confidence, and borrowed armour as a symptomatic
protection can leave it at a loss to connect with themes that move and
matter. This poet, inspired by and involved in music, has produced work
that may be stiffly unmusical, and is rarely melodious. He has, of course,
addressed the sectarian-inflected ambivalences in Irish poetry about a
heritage that includes Tom Moore's *Irish Melodies* in 'The Lily Rally':

The Papists stole me then and tried to make me play
Their Fenian music, but my loyal embouchure

Resisted them, and all the Melodies of Moore.
I threw their Roman legions into disarray.

His poems also face, in this fashion, a problem of the post-modern
(inherited from the modernists, the neo- and late-), namely that
traditional lyric poetry feels dissatisfying because it doesn't appear to
include enough of modern life's complexities in its melodiousness, while
a borrowed-armour allusiveness isolates itself in verbalism and cannot
integrate within a protected self what its opportunities deploy from the
flow and flux of image overload. Such project-based facility balkanises
poetry's repertoire of techniques for opportune thematic purposes,
appearing to dispose of each with a scorched-earth policy as it goes along.

Reading Carson *in extenso* the skill is everywhere to hear, but these
are performances in which the renditions don't finally feel as if they
have delivered the definitive work. The startling thing about Carson's
extraordinary fluency is that its productivity gives the impression of a
writer who has abandoned the idea that individual poems could be fully
satisfying, answering to all that a reader might go to poetry for. The second
poem called 'Le Mot Juste' from *For All We Know* (2008), a sequence of
obliquely playful paired love poems, is made of casual distichs riffing
across variants on the modern writer's dilemmas from Flaubert's famous
phrase, via Joyce's 'The Dead', to Eliot's 'East Coker' – the third alluded
to by the slightly mangled 'interminable' for 'intolerable' 'wrestle with
words and meanings' at the start of both poems with this title, the first
continuing: 'I'd an idea you were quoting from something. / But from
what?' Now there's a transparently *faux* device for a bit of indirection.
Naturally, it would be inept for such a pair of poems to be, or even aspire
to be, word-perfect examples of high modernist art; yet their tactically
wearied air of going through the syntactic motions ends in a further not
quite satisfying page, at least to this ear:

Your widow aunts discussing the quilt at their quilting bee
following the dips and gradients of its staggered repeats.

The way the bread is full of unrepeatable bubbles
when you pull it apart and fathom its interior.

Snow falling interminably, irrevocably on
the little village in a song your mother used to sing.

> Still the interminable struggle with words and meanings.
> These words foundering for now over a single sentence.

The paired love poems in *For All We Know* repeatedly give the impression of a poet whose bravura assemblage techniques are hindering him from being able to mean even the things that he evidently wants to mean. 'These words foundering for now' leave me wondering if, as the poet enters his seventh decade, assured of a position as one of the key figures working in either Ireland, Ciaran Carson will not find it in himself to allow vulnerabilities to rediscover formal devices in which they may reach a more complex articulation. If his prolific work is freaked with the bone-cold weakness of its ironclad strength, might readers hope that in future poems he can show the strengths that are inherent in his armour-plated weaknesses?

QUESTIONS OF BALANCE:
ENDA WYLEY

The cover of Enda Wyley's new collection reproduces 'Grafton Street Cloud', a colour photograph by Mark Granier, in which the precipitously sloping brownish rooflines of both sides of the street form a frame for the deepening blue of the sky. Across it a single white cloud is caught, poised mid-way, on its travel probably from left to right. Above the little cloud, printed in white, is the collection's title, underlined in a more turquoise blue, with the author's name immediately beneath it – associating, thus, the cycling painter and composing poet with the cloud in transit. This presentation of Enda Wyley's latest collection couldn't but remind me of works by two Trieste-based writers, both relevant, but one more happily suggestive than the other: James Joyce's story 'A Little Cloud' of 1906, and Umberto Saba's 1920 collection *Cose leggere e vaganti* (Light and Roaming Things).

Little Chandler's dream of literary fame – doubtless mocking Joyce's own aspirations to recognition, indicated, for instance, by his printing up a sheaf of review snippets for *Chamber Music* – has been a haunting caution: 'The English critics, perhaps, would recognise him as one of the Celtic school by reason of the melancholy tone of his poems; besides that, he would put in allusions.' As, indeed, would T. Malone Chandler's creator. What Joyce and Saba had in common, aside from taking inspiration from the city of Trieste, is that they both drew overwhelmingly upon their own family and city for materials. I've often wondered if either knew of the other, but found no evidence to suggest that Joyce ever read *Trieste e una donna* (1910–12) or that, at that time, the Italian poet knew of his Irish fellow citizen.

Yet Joyce would write the fragile lyric 'A Flower Given to my Daughter', dated *Trieste 1913*, only a few years before Saba published 'Ritratto della mia bambina' (Portrait of my Little Girl), in which he thinks of things with which to compare his own daughter:

> Certainly to foam, to the seaside foam
> whitening waves, to that blue wake
> which emerges from roofs and the wind disperses;
> likewise to the clouds, the indifferent clouds

> being made and unmade in clear sky
> and to other light and roaming things.

The Painter on his Bike is dedicated to Enda Wyley's daughter, Freya, and her husband, the poet Peter Sirr. The collection contains poems for both of them, and, sociably, many other people, including the beautifully crafted 'Home' for her parents, and others for friends. 'Tree House', for their daughter on her birthday, is one of a number written in paired lines, one of the most casual of poetry's formal structures, which allows for the collaging of such light and roaming things as a 'Day of bluebells and wild garlic, / of the willow heart nailed to the red door.'

Catching at such fleeting things in a moment of poise between dispersals requires an intuitive sense of rhythmic poise, as dramatised in the distichs of Wyley's title poem:

> He stops at the kerb,
> tugs at the twine, frees it
>
> from the spokes, sets off
> again, the bike wobbling,
>
> bumping over
> potholes and tramlines,
>
> the picture beating
> against his knee.

Taking a portrait home, the painter is 'balancing his father – / sketched in pencil –'. It's wrapped in paper, but the twine securing it catches in the spokes, accidently unwrapping it, and 'the painter's breath' is 'caught too' by 'the sudden sight / of his dead father's eyes.' The lines displayed above give an account of what the painter does to rescue the situation, but they also aptly illustrate how the poet finds a responsive form in acknowledging irregularities and instabilities. It is done by alternating lines with a fairly secure metrical shape (the iamb and anapaest of 'He stops at the kerb', for instance) with more rhythmically disjunctive lines that have stresses butted against each other, ('the twine, frees it' and 'the bike wobbling'), so that the poem's movement through the central sentence above takes account both of what Hopkins might have called 'the achieve of it' while also noting the 'potholes and tramlines' and other inconveniences with which the painter on his bike must struggle to be 'cycling / the portrait home.'

Elsewhere, the questions of balance can be addressed through a revealed semantic ambiguity, as in 'Safe', for the artist Jenny Murphy, where the poem first reinforces an assumption that the title is an adjective ('That you be safe'), only to reveal it as a noun in the poem's quietly bravura close:

> that we remain
> secure
>
> as the post office safe
> robbed years ago
>
> ransacked and dumped
> beyond in the ditch
>
> far away from that chase
> still enduring there.

The safe may have been stolen and emptied, but it too remains safe, a symbol perhaps of survival from and resistance to the sorts of human experiences that might turn you into a 'summer ghost', as the poet describes 'Hannah' who they should see 'ramble down / from her cottage again'. Notice too how this turn towards the poem's climax is itself made secure by a run of casually interwoven rhymes: 'lane … again … remain'. Once more, the poet is deploying the lightest of technical devices to apply pressure of an almost prayer-like weightlessness to the unstated threat symbolised by that ransacked post office safe.

In 'Euridice Speaks', though, the story that has to be told is of an emotional disaster caused by the impatience of the poet Orpheus; and that her rebalancing point of view is given form by a woman further multiplies the allusively implied conflicts that her forms must go back and resolve:

> The light ahead will make me woman again.
> But you haven't changed. The warning's ignored;
> your impatience takes over. You turn around your face

and I can't help it, cry out, immediately become shadow,
a ghost of a song you'll sing forever. You can't return twice
to where you found me. One look from you and I know this.

Given that her poem is in the 'speaking back' genre, and that the poet
is herself singing the 'ghost of a song', the possible ironies in poetry's
thwarting of this rescue mission through impatient love, and that itself
being recognised and responded to in poetry are what ruffle and engage
this resonant change of perspective on the story. Eurydice, being given
a voice by Wyley, takes the burden of poetry upon herself, internalises
the emblem of her abandonment in versions such as Rilke's, narrated
more from the Orpheus point of view; and it is the recognition of
responsibility which comes with this transfer of power that provides the
frisson in the poem's final sentence and just audible couplet half-rhyme
on 'twice': 'One look from you and I know this.'

'Ledger', dedicated to her husband, author of *The Ledger of Fruitful
Exchange* (1995), is a standing rebuke to that slightly too prompt idea
of Auden's that 'poetry makes nothing happen'. Though about the effect
of encountering Sirr's book and reading its second section, a journal of
lost love whose epigraph is the first line to Montale's 'Mottetti', 'Ledger'
is not so much a poem about poetry (that discredited 'meta' mode), but
about the ever-urgent relationship between reading and acting:

> this ledger of lost love I'd never read before
> that thrilled, made me stand up in the bookshop,
>
> then make for the door, our future racing out onto
> Dawson Street and into the city's expanse,
> Larkin raising his hands to me, the gulls cawing
>
> encouragement as I sought you out, your face staring
> from a high window over Parnell Square, the life
> you'd described becoming ours, the door unlatched.

What poetry makes happen here might be represented by the implied
transformation into affirmatives of those familiar sights and sounds, the
statue of Jim Larkin, his hands raised to the skies in O'Connell Street,
which might be indifferently passed by on an ordinary day, and those
seagulls, whose caws might as easily have been mocking. 'The Ledger'

can also be thought of as a pendant to 'Eurydice Speaks', for where in that one it is the permanent separation of Orpheus and Eurydice that prompts the flow of song, in this one it is poetry that overcomes lost love and separation by unlatching a door.

An inspiration, and a style to match, which is drawn to light and roaming things should not be expected to employ closes like John Donne's coiner minting the metal with his final blow, or that comes 'right with a click like a closing box' as Yeats put it. There are some here, such as the attractive 'Portobello Bridge Revisited', a memory of Pearse Hutchinson, which build with all the delicacy and touch of these poems at their best, but then, to my ear, don't quite clinch their discoveries. 'At Rosses Point, Yeats's Cat' is not one of those, though, while equally not being so showy about learning the trade as to click at its close:

> Queen Méabh's nipple was absent in cloud,
> and night came upon us fast while our camera
>
> caught you, Minnaloushe, slinking against
> our backs and now suddenly alive, dancing
>
> in the yellow light, lifting to the shifting
> moon your changing eyes, burning, wise –
>
> while we stayed put, transfixed, vowing
> not to climb Knocknarea that night.

On a first reading, I found this quietly matter-of-factual ending to be entirely satisfying, and, wondering why that might be, noticed how the lines tauten with a pair of internal rhymes in the penultimate distich, and then how the final word 'night' rounds in a concealed rhyme with the earlier 'yellow light', itself marked by a firm caesura in being buttressed against the initial stress on 'lifting'. Thus the seemingly inconsequential decision that closes the poem is subtly braided into the immediately preceding lines, while eschewing anything quite so overt as the claim to 'come right'. It is this combination of subjects taken from the experiences of a life presented with a deftness and lightness of touch that actually delivers a serious weight of implication while shunning overt claims to attention that I found so captivating, and a further balancing act that enables Enda Wyley's *The Painter on his Bike*.

JOHN TRANTER AND TRADITION

'Il faut être absolument moderne' Rimbaud wrote on the last page of *Une saison en enfer*. John Tranter begins his review of Charles Nicholl's *Somebody Else – Arthur Rimbaud in Africa* (Jonathan Cape, 1997) by telling us that at seventeen he fell in love with 'a sodomite' whose 'eyes were a dazzling blue' and who 'had the face of an angel'. It was clearly for him as important a romance (with or without words) as it was for Paul Verlaine – though evidently a good deal less personally devastating. Tranter alludes to the phrase in his 'Having Completed my Fortieth Year' collected in both *Under Berlin* and *Late Night Radio*. The poet's note tells us that his poem is a response to Peter Porter's work of the same name; but Byron is, of course, also completing his thirty-sixth year in the background. In the same poem Tranter writes that 'squabbling over Modernism won't help, / England needs liberating but not by me' and earlier: 'yet in the end it is our fault, i.e. my fault / not to be born Frank O'Hara'. The cross-currents of a nostalgic relationship with the modern now generations deep, of a glancing allusion to the political argument about how English poetry failed to learn the lessons of modernism, and of the modern's own fraught relationship with a repudiated past it depends upon even to be 'modern' are thickening the texture of Tranter's play with this arriving-at-a-certain-age occasion.

He also quotes Rimbaud's slogan, using Oliver Bernard's rendering, in 'The Alphabet Murders' reprinted in *Heart Print*. Part 21 ('U' being the twenty-first letter of the alphabet) begins: 'Undo the past. "One must be absolutely / modern." Sure.' 'Il faut' is difficult to translate – and though Jeremy Harding and John Sturrock modernised Rimbaud's English in their new Penguin versions they didn't see the need to change the slogan from Bernard's way of putting it. Unfortunately that 'One must' makes the 'homme aux semelles de vent' sound like he's being played by Trevor Howard in *Brief Encounter*, while it's James Dean who replies: 'Sure'. Tranter's poetry usually displays such skills at deploying styles, as it equally performs his complexly mixed idiomatic situation. In an interview with John Kinsella, the poet comments on a British caricature of Australia, one that the old country has used so as to feel superior to 'a society with a future, rather than a past.'

Yet, as readers attuned to idiom might expect, the concessive 'Sure' in that section of 'The Alphabet Murders' signals an account of how we could of course be 'absolutely modern':

> like a wicked boy punching in a stained glass knight,
> we can be witty partly because of our vodka slingshots
> and that's enough to kick the European jukebox in and
> get a laugh.

This promises through its dystopic characterisation of that '*dérèglement de tous les sens*' (the 'vodka slingshots') a qualification soon in coming: 'But this "building" thing, this Bildungs- / roman-à-clef, and forests foaming with the puppy love / of seasons ... this is architecture, friend, and masterful'. Vocative uses of the word 'friend' (c.f. Bob Dylan's chorus to 'Blowing in the Wind') don't necessarily sound that friendly, and Tranter goes on to build quite a case for 'the European jukebox' – which sounds like an up-beat American way of talking about the Old World's poetic traditions: 'we gape to find the cathedral of words so large / that everyone can find in it the works of his favourite / period'. Tranter's would seem to be the '70s – the 1870s, that is – when his mentor wrote 'Les Reparties de Nina', whose last line he lifted about a century later for his 'Poem Ending with a Line by Rimbaud' in *Selected Poems*. He has evidently taken to heart that famous phrase 'JE est un autre'. Though in his note to *Trio*, Tranter states that 'In a very few cases some minor revisions have been made', this may not be quite the case for the longer sequence entitled 'Waiting for Myself to Appear' also in *Selected Poems*. In its most recent printing the poem is called 'The Raft', and its ending has been substantially recast to remove the final two first-person pronouns. The older version's last line and a half, 'It is late at night. / I am waiting for myself to appear', have become 'waiting for the morning / to stamp my flesh with motion and regret.' Tranter's mature work has characters and voices, of which the poet's may be among them, but it doesn't usually have an inscribed lyric subject.

Now Rimbaud, Tranter writes in his review, 'was a poet, and I thought – and I still think, in my middle age – that he was one of the most brilliant poets the human race has ever seen'. Still, by the age of 19 according to Bernard (or 21 in the light of more recent research) Rimbaud had not only given up poetry, but had also stopped frequenting a Parisian Bohemia for whose ways he had little but contempt. Tranter can appear to put poets in their place too, as in his interview with Ted Slade for *The Poetry Kit* when he rather sentimentally says that 'Other people – doctors, garage mechanics, nurses, petty criminals, aircraft pilots – generally have much richer lives than poets do.' Still, the man who gives his present profession as 'company director' (meaning, I think, that he and his wife own a literary agency) and who edits the prize-winning Internet magazine *Jacket* has hardly 'done a Rimbaud'. The title of his book review, 'Odi et Amo', from Catullus, might equally be a starting point for thinking about Tranter's relations with the interwoven poetic traditions of Europe, the Americas, and, indeed, the world. His poetry is nothing if not studiedly literary, and it would be far from impossible to see him as ambivalently working at a set of styles that point towards an English-language version of that 'nostalgia for world culture' which Mandelstam offered as a definition of Acmeism, echoing even as he did the Goethe who is credited with having coined the term '*Weltkultur*'. And the literariness of Tranter's work is at its most evident in his inventive writing procedures.

Take, for example, his 1997 pamphlet from Equipage called *Gasoline Kisses*. The title has a 'beat' and 'pop art' pedigree: it doesn't so much take part in those movements as allude to them so as to deploy their modes with self-conscious panache. Indeed, as is often the case with epigone styles, the manner is even more thoroughly wrought and completed than that of the works upon which it's modelled. As it says on the jacket, these are versions of the 'haibun' – passages of prose followed by a haiku. Tranter collected four straight imitations of the form called 'The Seasons' in *Studio Moon*. *Gasoline Kisses* reconfigures it as twenty lines of free verse then a prose ending of varying lengths. The results combine vivid renditions of cosmopolitan styles and lifestyles in a variation on a form from classical Japan – an emblem, if you like, of quotidian Metro Tokyo:

> In a foreign country late at night, fine rain,
> you have an urge to talk about your childhood,
> alone on the railway station under the arc lamps.
> The specialists weave the fabric of the voice,
>
> he says gently, and turns to his cocktail.

Like a corresponding member of the Oulipo group in Paris, Tranter likes to set himself arbitrary or abstract constraints through which he funnels his material. He writes sets of poems that are exactly the same length; or, as in the 'Alphabet Murders', he writes twenty-six poems each of whose first letters is the one you would expect. Most unusual of all, perhaps, are his seven short stories, *Different Hands* created by rewriting wildly raw first drafts produced by doing computer analyses of 'letter groups' in two pieces of writing. 'Lonely Chaps' is mysteriously based on *The Well of Loneliness* and *Biggles Defies the Swastika*. It ends: 'Oh, but ardent, she remembered, drifting in the sky above her, the only loving mass, as the British fleet floated above the landed Ginger.' A well-written literariness playing with muffled allusions is one source for the pleasure these works provide.

Much of Tranter's most intriguing writing is characterised by its relation to a prior text, form, or style. These relations are significantly flagged in subtitles, notes, and blurbs. His chapbook, *Borrowed Voices*, is a series of poems that are described as 'suggested by' or 'a version of' works in other languages: Laforgue, Rimbaud, Rilke, Hölderlin, Schiller, Baudelaire, Jacob, Callimachus, and Huidobro. The poem sponsored by Hölderlin's 'Da ich ein Knabe war…' shadows its original nearly enough to suggest an outline of Tranter's project here. Where Hölderlin's original tells of the child's blessed upbringing far from human words, never understood, and 'Im Arme der Götter', Tranter's substitutes for the heavenly bodies of 'Vater Helios' and 'Heilige Luna', some cut flowers that 'still seem to hanker for the sun' in a beer garden, and 'a movie theatre's satisfying gloom / where a little moon followed the usherette / up and down the blue carpeted stairs.' These are now the poet's teachers, as he wryly concludes by lifting part of a plain translation of Hölderlin's final line for his own ending: 'and I learned the language of love / among the light and shadow / in the arms of the gods.' Tranter thus uses a 'free indirect style' of transposition whereby he can move in and out of the source text, allowing its detail by turns to prompt composition or provide bits of phrasing, while aiming, it would appear, simultaneously to mock and pay tribute to the evocative power of the quaint-sounding original.

'Invitation to America' is 'a version of Baudelaire's Invitation to the Voyage'. Reprinted in *Studio Moon*, seven of these poems are there called 'extremely free versions … versions too loose to call translations'. The only part of 'Invitation to America' that recalled 'L'invitation au voyage' for me were the phrases 'Along the canals … the traffic lights are only ever green or amber, / and the big orange moon rises on cue', which seems to have been suggested by '– Les soleils couchant

/ Revêtent les champs, / Les canaux, la ville entière'. More nuanced, given its source, are the lines earlier in Tranter's poem: 'Like a paint job on a new convertible / the talk is brilliant and skin-deep. / No history – who needs it?' Well, he clearly does, as his allusion to Baudelaire confesses. However, the title of his Shoestring pamphlet seems slightly off the point. All these poems sound like Tranter, especially his version of Rimbaud's 'Brussels' that glancingly grazes the original in a number places. In the light of their obscurely relevant originals, these poems profess the need for a reader's knowing where they're from, what it is they're 'after'. The acknowledgement under each title seems a promise that isn't anything like kept, and Tranter's note then makes a genial apology for this disappointment – or non-disappointment, since we're enjoying the practically faithless but characteristically lively renditions of takes on the way we live now.

Even more unusual than his 'not-translations' are the poems he calls 'terminals'. These are constructed, as Tranter explains, by taking the end-words of someone else's poem, arranging them down the right side of the page in the order that they come, then writing a different poem with the same number of lines and words at the end of each line. Where James Schuyler's elegy for Frank O'Hara, 'Buried at Springs', begins 'There is a hornet in the room / and one of us will have to go / out the window into the late / August midafternoon sun. I / won', Tranter's 'Elegy, after James Schuyler' begins: 'It's just an empty room / in a beach house. You go / somewhere for drinks, stay out late, / get lost coming home. It's the awful page I / choose to look at in the diary'. O'Hara's own '3 Poems about Kenneth Koch' is a very wired performance:

> May I tell you how much I love your poems?
> It's as if a great pipeline had been illicitly tapped
> along which all personal characteristics
> are making a hasty departure. Tuba? gin?
> 'qu'importe où?' O Kenneth Koch!

Tranter's 'Three Poems about Kenneth Koch' is more relaxed, conversational, friendly – and an altogether curious way of compensating for the 'fault' of not being born Frank O'Hara: 'He never writes poems about writing poems, / this dog-eared wunderkind who's tapped / the unconscious of the race. His main characteristics: / in the fall he develops a fatal liking for stiff gin / martinis. He's not a disguised Mayor

Ed Koch –'. Something of the like happens with the shift from Auden's 'In Praise of Limestone' to Tranter's 'In Praise of Sandstone', a bravura performance that is in every sense a variation on the older man's theme. One of the ways in which Tranter's poems are 'terminals' is that it would be difficult for a third poet to take his 'Three Poems…' as the starting point for a third poem. How exactly would it not be merely also 'after' O'Hara?

When Tranter uses relatively unfamiliar sources that are in unrhymed free verse he gives himself a practically free run at his poem. In the revisiting of 'Buried at Springs' there seems barely any echo; with the O'Hara poem there is a more overtly shared theme and more comparison; in the Auden variation the two poems run in close parallel. However, when Tranter takes a very familiar rhymed poem to use as his base text the result can be truly spooky:

> And so the farm sleeps, waiting for a new
> owner, and Rover waits too in that yellow light
> that seems to paint the wet sand with pain
> so it resembles a watery plain
> where screaming seabirds dash their reflected flight
> over the glitter of the State Fair, Saturday night.

This is generated from the final six lines of Matthew Arnold's 'Dover Beach', the lines where 'the world, which seems'

> So various, so beautiful, so new,
> Hath really neither joy, nor love, nor light,
> Nor certitude, nor peace, nor help for pain;
> And we are here as on a darkling plain
> Swept with confused alarms of struggle and flight,
> Where ignorant armies clash by night.

What the comparison illustrates, if nothing else, is the extent to which a series of rhymed end-words will tend to determine far more indelibly the emotive contour and thematic trajectory of poetic lines. The 'pain … plain' and 'flight … night' sequence inflects Tranter's poem with Arnold's grim melancholy, even as his dog and seabirds and the State Fair on a Saturday night would seem to diffuse the mood. Whether intentionally or not, too, Tranter's two poems using the terminals of

'Dover Beach' can't quite keep away from Arnold's subjects. The other one ends in the territory of marital life and unhappiness: '…how we made light / of their marital troubles – bad dreams about the pain / our "friendship" caused them, and the plane / tickets Rover ate so they missed their flight / out of town that last, long, lonely night.' Would it be unfair to note that the 'plane / tickets' get into the poem by means of a cheating pun? Even so, the final rhyme can't escape – and indeed hams up – an Arnoldian plangency.

A further brush with Arnold's best-known poem occurs in Tranter's response to Veronica Forrest-Thomson's 'Address to the Reader, From Pevensey Sluice', a poem in her engagingly flippant academic collage manner which half-reveals and half-conceals its emotional burden:

> DANGER SUBMERGED STRUCTURES
> and all at once Transformational Grammar
> 'peoples' the 'emotional landscape'
> with refutation.
> You may hear its melancholy
> long withdrawing roar
> even on Dover Beach watching
> the undertow of all those trips
> across to France.

Here, and in the subsequent line 'for to be true to any other you must', the allusions are coming through loud and clear – expressive, it would seem, of a fairly raw love-hate relationship with the intrusively memorable ancestor. Tranter's re-write recesses and embeds the Arnold allusions soothing the poem's nerves: 'a melancholy murmur / heard even in France' and 'for to be true to your dreams'. Where she opens with 'If it were quicksand you could sink; / something needing a light touch / soon and so simply takes its revenge', he begins: 'In the art of sinking into a landscape / or falling through the sky, a light touch / moves you to sympathy, or a deeper knowledge / of a heroine's little faults.' So Tranter substitutes for Forrest-Thomson's jagged-edged assemblage a fluid eloquence, a knowing tribute, and one which implies a more digested sense of the individual poem's necessary negotiation with its cultural sources.

If his fifteen-part sequence 'Rimbaud and the Modernist Heresy' in *Selected Poems* and *Trio*, is the *nec plus ultra* of Tranter's wrestle with the angel-faced Mr. Hyde of French nineteenth-century poetry, 'Grover Leach', 'See Rover Reach', and 'The Great Artist Reconsiders the Homeric Simile' document a recurring *odi et amo* relationship with the Dr. Jekyll of British poetry from that same century. Rimbaud may have been the poet Tranter would have supremely liked to be (at least as regards the writing), but Arnold is the poet he seems most to dread discovering was, in fact, his natural great-grandfather:

> so Matthew Arnold brooded
> on his failing similes. His cup of tea
> grew cold as he stared out at the Autumn
> leaves; a change of air was what he needed,
> a holiday at Dover, or Torquay…
> and as he mused, the lounger at the gate –
> the Future – turned his back, and walked away.

What's striking about this is that Arnold's creative predicament, his seeming to be lumbered with an outmoded vehicle, if not a national endgame, produces a finely judged elegiac mood. Tranter's poem might at first seem to be putting Arnold in his place – the past; but then no one has the literary key to the future (and if Rimbaud did, he threw it away), while all are likely to have this sad trick played upon them by time. Yet when Arnold crops up in one of Tranter's notes to *Trio* it's not as a definitively passé exponent of a worn-out mode, but, intriguingly, as a harbinger of the future: "The Knowledge of our Buried Life': the alarmingly modern words of Matthew Arnold, seeming to presage Freud'.

Wandering like so many of us 'between two worlds, one dead / The other powerless to be born', Tranter's experiments with classic poems function like Arnold's 'buried life'. His poetry has found a way of tuning in to the subterranean streams by which traditions can make themselves relevantly felt even in the most unlikely of circumstances. There is no real art without ambivalence. In interview he can refer to 'the dead hand of the past', and also state that 'I try to stay open to new ideas. And I try to fill out my knowledge of old ideas, which is perhaps more important, seeing there are more of them.' His creative ambivalence may most reside in uncertainty about whether tradition is one way in which the future is prevented from being born, or a means by which the past can act as its mid-wife. Reading his poems we hear echoes bubbling up unexpectedly along our contemporary veins 'in the world's most crowded streets … in the din of strife', 'where ignorant armies clash by night' – and where, as Rimbaud too may have realised as he got older, there are more important things to be in life than 'absolument moderne'.

'THE MIXTURE'S MOMENT':
ALLEN CURNOW

Allen Curnow's latest and last collection, *The Bells of Saint Babel's*, contains just twelve poems, five of them sustained meditations composed in lines measuring from three to six syllables, four more being poems imitated from originals by Pushkin. The remaining three are a rhyming pantoum for Peter Porter's seventieth birthday, an opening sequence of free verse lyrics called 'Ten Steps to the Sea', and 'The Pocket Compass', an unrhymed sonnet. 'When and Where', one of the poems after Pushkin, speculates about the exact time and place of the poet's own death:

> And which day of which year
> to come will turn out to have been
> the anniversary, distant or near,
> of my death? Good question. The scene,
>
> will it be wartime, on a trip,
> or at home or in some nearby
> street, crashed coach or a ship-
> wreck that I'm to die?

Allen Curnow died of a heart attack in Auckland, New Zealand, on 23 September 2001, in his ninetieth year, the month he published *The Bells of Saint Babel's* with Carcanet Press. 'The Pocket Compass' both re-renders and re-obliterates ('I paint it over again') one of Curnow's local scenes. In it, the poet may be echoing the first lines of 'A Small Room with Large Windows' ('What would it look like if really there were only / One point of the compass not known illusory, / All other quarters proving nothing but quaint / Obsolete expressions of true north') with lines about how he once used the dedicatee's compass to chisel the four cardinal points on the top of a wooden rail long since rotted away and replaced: 'pencil or chisel can't replicate / the rose in the mind's eye, indelibly true / north by needle.'

'The Pocket Compass', in memory of someone identified by initials only, is inclined to be far more specific about the *when* and *where* of the context than the *who* that was present, or significantly not present, at its sponsoring occasion. Such questions have echoed down the years for New Zealand poetry, at least since the controversy that grew from a galley proof of Curnow's Introduction to *The Penguin Book of New Zealand Verse* in 1958 and delayed the book's publication until 1960. This 'here-anywhere' controversy, as it's been called, was still rumbling in the distance when Ian Wedde wrote his introduction to an anthology with the same name published in 1984:

> The *who* and the *where* are interdependent, yet at times one will be a more appropriate question than the other. The concern with *who* you are implies a sense of tenure … By the time you have got it straight about *where* you are (where *here* is), the *who* may follow more naturally…

Wedde is addressing the problem that the earliest poetry written out of New Zealand was too concerned to indicate an identity that found its self-esteem elsewhere, which staked a claim on the basis of ancestry, for instance, as against a more evolved sense of identity which would grows of attending to the immediate locality first. While is seems unlikely that Curnow could have disagreed with this, and Wedde recognises the importance of the older poet's 'own disenchanted occupancy of that *where*', a certain divergence may be being marked – for Curnow was nothing if not a New Zealander proud of his ancestry and concerned throughout to render in poetry the exact facts of that history too. Indeed, the last poem Curnow published in his lifetime, 'Fantasia and Fugue for Pan-pipe', is about the *who* in Ian Wedde's ancestral sense – being a rumination on two related love poems, by his father and father's fiancée, in a book called *New Zealand Verse*, whose publication details Curnow characteristically gives in the poem ('Walter / Scott Publishing. / London. New York. / 1906') and comments with a glance at a far-away country churchyard and its elegy '– Safe / distances, for / blushing unseen'.

In an e-interview with Andrew Johnston published in *Doubtful Sounds: Essays and Interviews*, Bill Manhire recently reported that

> There's an interesting tape recording which Allen Curnow made at the Library of Congress back in the '60s, where he makes it clear that the moa's egg in his famous sonnet, while he describes

it as being 'found in a thousand pieces', actually existed in just
over 700 pieces. Facts are sacred for Curnow – as you might
expect in someone who became a journalist after growing up in
a vicarage – so, of course, he makes a mild apology.

The famous sonnet, 'The Skeleton of the Great Moa in the Canterbury
Museum, Christchurch', is called 'Attitudes for a New Zealand Poet
(iii)' in Curnow's 1960 anthology – suggesting a further importance
in the matter of fact for this founding father of contemporary NZ
verse. Manhire's point is that Curnow made a decision 'on behalf of
the poem's music'. It would be interesting to know if the poet knew
the exact number of pieces when he wrote 'a thousand', or checked
up on his poem later. For if it were the latter, then he could be said
even more firmly to have decided for the fact of the poem over the fact
of the correct number. Moreover, Manhire's remark suggests a further
complexity to the matter of fact in Curnow's poetry – for it was in flight
from a mistaken vocation for the ministry that the poet switched to
working as a journalist.

The factual and its sacredness will have been, then, a context for the
uneasy accommodation of secular and spiritual concerns. After all, the
way that facts are sacred to a journalist involves a sense of responsibility
to the subjects treated, to the newspaper owners, and to the readership.
It involves exercising the etymological relationship between 'true' and
'trust' in the everyday conflictual contexts of producing copy. The
way facts might be sacred to someone brought up in a vicarage could
well involve a responsibility to created nature and, by way of nature,
to a creator. In 'Early Days Yet', the title poem to his 1997 new and
collected poems, Curnow remembers his father preparing for a round
of visiting his parishioners by car:

> Lift out front seat-
> cushion. Unscrew
> filler-cap. Insert
>
> large funnel. Spike,
> and up-end four gallon
> can of Big Tree

> Motor Spirit. Let
> flammable contents
> flow *pingle-pangle-*
>
> *pingle* through fine
> gauze filter. Your new
> 1919
>
> Model T is now
> fuelled for the week's
> pastoral mileage…

And it is exactly the fact of the petrol's antique name that mobilises the pun that fuses together the material life of the poet's father and the non-material vocation that, in another sense, set his car in motion. The poem's first section ends by comparing the clergyman's car with the one used by the local GP – quietly enriching the colloquialism 'miles better' by giving it a literal, factual underpinning in the miles per gallon of the economical Model T Ford:

> miles better than the doctor's
> barge-size guzzler,
> and the right image
>
> for the poor *The Lord be*
> *with* you the pews creak back
> *And with thy spirit.*

In the earlier 'A Raised Voice', Curnow calculates the height ('twelve feet "clothed in fine linen"') from the ground to his father's pulpit by conjuring up 'a voice / that says Jess to my mother, heightened / three steps, to which add the sanctuary / rise, the subdued pile of the Axminster / runner.' This poem too ponders on death and the afterlife: 'I'm looking up into my thought / of my father, my certainty, he'll / be safe, but what about me?'

Curnow is by no means the first poet to put minute particulars of measurement into his work, but two English instances that spring immediately to mind serve to show how different his use of them can be. 'I've measured it from side to side: / 'Tis three feet long, and two feet wide.' Wordsworth could use his supposedly bathetic line from 'The Thorn' to measure not only the grave but his narrator's character, and Philip Larkin could measure a gap to underline the non-poetic nature of Mr Bleaney's room: 'Flowered curtains, thin and frayed, / Fall to within five inches of the sill'. Yet, rather than marking a limit to the poetic, something somehow diminished by the pedantic details, Curnow deploys precisely measured facts of time and place as access to his vision. In 'A Nice Place on the Riviera', he recalls the precise circumstances ('Villa Isola / Bella, Menton, / 18 October') of Katherine Mansfield's writing 'No personal God / or any such / nonsense' to Middleton Murray, then links it to the life of Pascal 'to whom God / personally did / appear that day / "from about ten / thirty p.m. / till past midnight".' Such fascination with the exact moments when things happened, and the precise reporting of the circumstances when they did, is at one with Curnow's preferred modes of composition.

Talking to Peter Simpson in 1990, he responded thus to a question about how he structures his poems:

> Impossible to say. A good deal of the work involves moving the poem out of one measure into another – it can start in short lines with no special attention to length, and then be moved into nine-syllable measure, in stanzas of five or three lines – if this isn't adequate, I can try a different count of syllables.

So the poet counted syllables, though, as he later says 'I've never counted stresses.' Is he then following the rules of poetry in syllabics? Perhaps he is, and this might be a critical issue about his work, as it can be with Marianne Moore's. The line length appears to follow a stiff rule, one which challenges the reader's ear, as Auden noted in an essay on the poet in *The Dyer's Hand*: 'a syllabic verse, like Miss Moore's, in which accent and feet are ignored and only the number of syllables count, is very difficult for an English ear to grasp.' That there can be such a difficulty suggests a reluctance to find poetic value in the following of what appears an arbitrary, imposed rule. However, how arbitrary is Curnow's syllable count? He also says 'if it isn't adequate, I can try a different count'. Here, a highly-skilled practitioner is not merely 'following the rules', because his search for an adequate structure is described as one of trial and error ('moving the poem out of one measure into another') and, as he goes on to say, this process of recasting the lines discovers the poem's 'necessary form', though only after 'a good many versions' – and he adds:

> I do want to say that there's nothing mysterious about any of these matters, and they're not trade secrets, either. What is mysterious, or at least unexplainable, is the way every one of these decisions affects the whole eventual structure and character of the poem.

Curnow's account of writing a poem illustrates Richard Wollheim's point in the second edition of *Art and its Objects* that, for the artist, evaluation 'functions regulatively, and it controls how and whether the artist should go on.' The poet makes evaluative decisions about an aspect of the work that can be controlled (its shape), deciding that this is 'inadequate' or the other is 'necessary', but the ramifications of these decisions on the entire 'structure and character of the poem' is not wholly subject to the will or judgement of the poet, so results are produced that could not be intended.

Nevertheless, Wollheim's sense of evaluation would come in again, for the final decision to stop changing things involves registering at some level that all these effects have produced something to leave as it is and to offer as a candidate for the evaluation of others. And an extraordinary thing about Curnow's syllabics is that they allow his verse to sound at once almost fussily correct, and casually colloquial. What's more, because two four-syllable lines have the length of a standard tetrameter, one of the most common forms in English verse, Curnow's late meditations are able to gain formal complexities from the interplay of cross-cutting structural principles – as here in a later section from 'A Nice Place on the Riviera':

> That rabid wind
>
> bangs shutters, dis-
> colours the sea,
>
> dishevels the world
> outdoors. Beside

the demitasses
the Abdullahs in

their silver box,
the *Imitation*

waits to be read ...
The climate here's

her only hope,
some doctor said.

I hear the contour of the colloquial phrases, the unexpected and
occasionally arbitrary sounding line endings produced by the syllable
count, the ghosts of more standard iambic metres, and all this underlined
at times by internal or end rhymes that arrive with the assurance and
closure of stanzas that have been relineated according to a different
principle. The result is a unique mixture of inherited techniques and
an old dog's new tricks. They combine a flamboyant sprezzatura with a
doggedly puritanical sticking to the task.

Curnow's phrase 'the mixture's moment' comes from the first part
of 'Moro Assassinato', a sequence first published in *An Incorrigible
Music* (1979). His title might be revising Wordsworth's 'still sad music
of humanity' by crossing it with Tennyson's nature 'red in tooth and
claw' – though not with the vagueness of a generality but, as might be
expected, with painfully specific facts of violence and cruelty, whether
in life or in the representations of art. 'Dichtung und Wahrheit', from
the same book, caused controversy in the early 1980s with its fiercely
revolted account of 'A man I know' who 'wrote a book about a man
he knew / and this man, or so he the man I know said, fucked /
and murdered a girl to save her from the others...' Something of this
controversy involving M. K. Joseph's *A Soldier's Tale* (1976) can be
gathered from Curnow's "Dichtung und Wahrheit' a Letter to *Landfall*,
reprinted in *Look Back Harder: Critical Writings 1935–1984*, where he
describes himself as 'repelled by a new and much-praised novel', but not
'for its "blend of violence and sex": on the contrary, for what struck me
as a sentimentally fudged presentation of those very subjects.' The poet's
unadorned account of events the novel narrates functions thus to express
his repulsion and to avoid the least taint of sentimentality. The result,

an instance of disturbatory art (Arthur Danto's term), would not be my favourite work of Curnow's, but it earns its place in a vision of reality.

The poem I like best from *The Bells of Saint Babel's* is the first piece, 'Ten Steps to the Sea', which takes its bearings from the crucial issue in pain control clinics, that 'They can control / the pain till there's well really / no pain, but then there's no reality'; so, says the cancer sufferer talking in the poem's seventh part, 'I try to balance / the two, as little pain / as possible, as much reality / as possible.' The sequence concludes:

VII

The pain is the dog
not heeding the whistle, on account
of scenting a rabbit or an old
turd, his own possibly, or snuffing
ashes of a Sunday campfire because of
the slab and the grate provided there.
Will he follow?

IX

Up and over the sandhills? Not much
help in the sea's habitual heave,
sprawl, grumble, hiss.

X

In reality,
no. A step in the right direction.
The pain is in the wind, which blows the whole
time, uncontrollably.
In your face.

As in 'miles better', so with the colloquialism 'in your face'. By placing a stop at the end of the poem's penultimate line, and a capital letter at the beginning of the last, he brings together a probably passing bit of slang and the enduring, painful fact of the human position in nature. And as if to underline Curnow's stubborn determination to stick with the matter and trajectory of his art, this late poem might be exemplifying a key sentence from his 1960 anthology Introduction, reprinted in *Look Back Harder* too: 'Reality must be local and special at the point where we pick up the traces: as manifold as the signs we follow and the routes we take.' That dog 'snuffing / ashes' (deadly enjambment) among dunes seems, with whatever irony, to be following the programme of Curnow's old polemic. While his 'In your face' directness can be hard to stomach, as it is for me in 'Dichtung und Wahrheit', such intentness is also a part of the poet's respect for the sacredness of facts and his unflinching attention to what our manifold reality can contain. Looking up into my thought of Allen Curnow, I want to say that if there is an afterlife for poets then 'he'll / be safe' and, not least because of this acute attention to such mixtures, that his work is bound to live far and away beyond its moment.

BILL MANHIRE:
'HAVE YOU NO HOMES?'

Marianne Moore ends her poem 'Silence' with a comment on a quotation from Edmund Burke – which is being offered as something 'My father used to say': 'Nor was he insincere in saying, 'Make my house your inn.' / Inns are not residences.' These lines came back to mind as I was reading the latest book by Bill Manhire, New Zealand's inaugural poet laureate, sometime writer in residence in Antarctica, and holder of the Katherine Mansfield Fellowship at Menton, France. His father was a publican by trade: 'Southland, Green Roofs, Railway, Oak Tree Inn, Crown, St Kilda – they are somehow the same place. For example, each one was full of drunk people.' When it was time to clear the house – though as Manhire explains this would not usually coincide with 'closing time' – here is what *his* father really used to say:

> I still have in my head as resonant noises the Irish farewell (courtesy of First Corinthians), 'Have you no homes?', the Churchillian 'Our finest hour!', and – obscure of origin yet best of all – 'Home, little bastards, home!'

One of the reasons why the first of these may be a resonant noise in the poet's head is because, *pace* Miss Moore, if your father is a publican, then an inn is your residence. It is the home you have to go to, even when it's full of adults who 'swayed and staggered, or burst into unexpected song.'

Though it seems Jack Manhire had a vocation as a publican, he did make one venture into the concrete fence-post trade: 'if you leave Wallacetown in the direction of Riverton, then the second-last house on your right is where we lived after we left the Green Roofs. It was a proper house, so for a while we must have been a proper family.' But the venture failed, and soon they were back in hotels. Manhire published his *Collected Poems* in 2001 (available in the UK from Carcanet Press), and while his lines never helplessly sway and stagger, they do quite often 'burst' or perhaps switch 'into unexpected song.' 'Ain Folks', for instance, is a poem about his Scottish mother's father, a signal man on the Kings Cross to Edinburgh line:

keeping his eye on the time,
the pure slog of rails up the incline,
the two making their way together

*

till they pause at the level crossing there
and he quietly switches the points
from yon bonnie banks

to the likewise purple heather.

Under the Influence concludes with Manhire's translation of Baudelaire's
'Enivrez-vous', a prose-poem from *Le Spleen de Paris*: 'It is the hour to
be drunk! And so, not to be the martyred slave of Time, make yourself
drunk; be drunk without cease! On wine, on poetry, on virtue – as you
please!' Manhire's memoir invites thoughts about the similarities and
differences between being under the influence of drink and of poetry.
As for virtue, it's clear his upbringing gave him unusual insights into
the varieties of human weakness and some complex lessons in how to
judge both himself and others, and also how to forgive.

At about the age of ten, for instance, he was outraged by his father's
'desire to do the decent thing' because 'In practice, the decent thing
meant an extravagant generosity directed at everyone except his own
family.' In mid-teenage, the poet was 'outraged in a wiser way' when
one of his dad's drinking circle

made a sly sexual overture to me. I complained to my parents.
My father took Doug Green's side and told me not to be silly.
Somehow I had made a mistake; my behaviour was letting
everyone down.

In later life, the poet's father suffered from professional deformation
in the shape of a liver problem, one recorded in 'Magazin' as an organ
that 'looks like the map of Africa' traced by his doctor 'for the third-
year students'. After this period in hospital he is recommended to have
nothing ever again to do with Baudelaire's advice: 'There were solemn
warnings. He would have to knock off the grog for good.' Many years
after, Manhire asks his long-living mother why her husband started

drinking again – the poet's memory being that it had been caused by a quarrel between the parents. But she replies that 'it was that big argument he had with you, wasn't it?' 'What about?' asks Manhire. 'I don't remember any argument.' 'Who knows?' she says. 'I think you were doing your Honours at university.' The poet handles the matter of his various disagreements with his father in a laconic style with which readers of his poetry will already be familiar.

After Jack Manhire's funeral, the mourners are invited back to the hotel for drinks on the house: 'His last shout, though this time he wouldn't be drinking.' Those youthful quarrels with his father, and a hint of the posthumous reconciliation that *Under the Influence* more thoroughly floats, can be sensed in his gnomic six-line poem 'Doctor Zhivago':

> The big stage and golden curtain,
> stars high up in the ceiling, one of
> the few films I think he would have seen.
>
> The sound of violins, then darkness
> about the wide, white screen. I can hear
> the sound of my father coughing.

Manhire's is a tight-lipped art that speaks volumes. Here the question is what does that coughing mean? The largest hint the poem offers is in the parallelism of 'sound of violins' and 'sound of my father', and the implied contrast between the wide-screen technicolour score of David Lean's film and that cough. Films were evidently not Jack Manhire's thing. So what was he doing watching one about, of all things, a poet? Was it his wife who wanted to be taken? *Doctor Zhivago* is also a love story that can only thrive in conditions of extreme solitude and isolation involving travel over vast spaces. This is exactly what Manhire's mother took on when she agreed to marry a New Zealand sailor doing wartime service in Britain.

Quite a few of Manhire's poems take up the attenuated romance and exilic distances in his mother's life. 'The Scottish Bride' includes the lines '*You cannot imagine, halfway / across the world,* her father wrote, / *the sorrow of the undersigned*'. 'The English Teacher', about his mother's work before she met her husband, frankly admits its interest in family memory: '"Give me more detail," I say. / "You know, to put in the poem.'" 'Onlookers: A Story' ends with a moment in what looks as if it might be 'a proper family', though, ordinarily enough, one with a hint of troubles not being expressed. Winningly, though, the entire situation is transformed by the children and Manhire's poem's bursting once more into unexpected melody:

> ... a mother says quietly
> that she couldn't say,
>
> there's nothing wrong. Breakfast.
> The children chant *Headlands*
> *heartlands lowlands*
>
> *high!* and the lonely
> room records them
> like a song.

A concealed rhyme tells us what this poet will also do: put a brave face on the 'nothing' that's 'wrong' with a poem 'like a song'. Manhire quotes his mother as saying that, being driven for the first time from Wellington to Dunedin in 1946, 'Somewhere halfway down the West Coast, it crossed her mind that they could just drive and drive for ever yet never get to Scotland.' This memory also seems to float between the lines in 'South Island Companion', a poem that takes the reader on such a drive to Dunedin's 'roofs and that gray / documentary harbour. Twilight is there // and one wee sail, / and the car'. Am I just imagining that Tennyson's 'Crossing the Bar' is there too, there with a 'Twilight and evening bell,' a 'Sunset and evening star / And one clear call for me'? That poem, that bizarrely apt non-pun in its title, was one of the hymns at Jack Manhire's funeral.

Though superficially similar in their pitting a self-appointed cultural 'common sense' against the supposed 'nonsense' of the then current experimental poetry, the 'Wingatui' Incident and the Ern Malley Affair had consequences which point in different directions. The ultimate target for the authors of Ern Malley's hoax oeuvre may have been Herbert Read and the poetic climate in London during the previous decade. (Did J. G. MacLeod's *The Ecliptic*, published by Faber in 1930, help Ern to his title *The Darkening Ecliptic* thirteen years later?) Yet

McAuley and Stewart's sights were set to strike nearer home, on Max Harris and his magazine *Angry Penguins*. The immediate target of the Pseud's Corner's complier will more likely have been the choices made by the then poetry editor of the *Times Literary Supplement* than the New Zealand poet who happened to have perpetrated that 'bit of surrealistic waffle' (Bill Manhire's own words for what his poem 'Wingatui' must have been thought) which was awarded *Private Eye*'s ultimate accolade. I was reminded of this little episode in the protracted history of English philistinism by Gregory O'Brien's cover design for the poet's *Collected Poems*, 'Bill Manhire rides Phar Lap at Wingatui' – a title concisely alluding to two of the poet's works, his homage to the famous winner 'Phar Lap' and his five-line lyric set at the Wingatui race course:

> Sit in the car with the headlights off.
> Look out there now
> where the yellow moon floats silks across the birdcage.
> You might have touched that sky you lost.
> You might have split that azure violin in two.

Hard to believe anyone would have any trouble with this poem as far as the verb 'floats' in line three, but it's the second half of this third line that put the cultural cat among the pigeons, for a New Zealand reader would probably have known that 'the birdcage' is the place called 'the paddock' in the British Isles where the horses are paraded and viewed by the betting punters before the race. So 'birdcage' is not surreal at all, but the local name for an ordinary place, and in that context neither are those 'silks' which will be the colours of the jockeys. Nor is it difficult to see the point of the word 'lost' at the end of line four, or to catch the nuance of feeling in that 'might have' tense – the tense whose anaphoric repetition ties the final line with its more mysterious 'azure violin' to the rest of the lyric. Yet even this leap seems far from senseless with a moment's reflection: a 'birdcage' would secondarily but undeniably also be a place where singing birds are kept, and it's not a far leap, or lap, to associate that with the sky where you find birds flying free, or to take the metaphor of the yellow moon and late afternoon azure sky as competing jockeys, or to see the wires of the birdcage or the race track, or telephone lines overhead, for instance, as the strings of an instrument that produces a high and often sad-sounding tremulous note, a blue note that you might have thought to banish from your life if you'd come home with some long-odds winnings on a horse with a name like, who knows, 'azure violin'.

In 'Mutes & Earthquakes', a piece on his creative writing course at Victoria University, Wellington, collected in *Doubtful Sounds*, Manhire speaks up for 'cranky constraints' like writing 'a haiku using only the words you can find on the racing page of the *Evening Post*'. 'Wingatui' is a haunting air on a loser's feeling of what 'might have' happened if all had gone differently during a day at the races – and it's a resonant metaphor for more general feelings of disappointment in life. Thus, unlike the Ern Malley Affair, which had immediately serious repercussions for Max Harris and at the very least equivocal ones for a decade or two of Australian literature, the Wingatui Incident makes the metropolitan satirists look ignorant about the English spoken in a Commonwealth country, ill-equipped to take on trust a hardly taxing imagistic lyric, and presumptuously quick to rush to judgement. What's more, things seem to have worked out in this way because the non-hoax poem appears manifestly embedded in, and arising out of, possible experience, so that the presumption of 'nonsense' looks demonstrably wrong, and because equally the incident could be taken up by its apparent targets (Manhire and his poet colleagues) as a form of vindication – hence O'Brien's cover painting on the *Collected Poems*, or the remarks about what happened in *The Penguin Book of New Zealand Verse* (1985) edited by Ian Wedde and Harvey McQueen.

Commenting on the author's 'Statement' to his first book, *The Elaboration*, which he reprints in the note to his *Collected Poems*, Manhire now thinks it 'impossibly mannered' but is 'pleased to find' himself 'still comfortable with the sentiments'. The poems, as their writer put it in 1972,

> seem, more and more, to be fictions, elaborated out of the truth of this or that situation. At some point, hopefully, the elaboration ends and they come to be arbitrary facts, making their own way into the particular worlds of those people who cared to read them.

If this account might loosely fit a poem like 'Wingatui', it nevertheless (as is usually the case with poets' brief statements) leaves a number of issues far from decided and far from unequivocally articulated too. Does the elaborated fiction carry the truth of the situation with it so that the poem is both true and fictitious, or does elaborated 'out of' also mean 'away from', so that truth becomes fiction? What weight are you to give to the arbitrariness of the 'fact' that the poem hopefully becomes? So the passage seems likely to default back to the terms of that fact-fiction contrast – a pair of false opposites disarmed by noting, for instance, the many kinds of fact and innumerable degrees of fiction that there are in the world.

The hopeful idea seems to be that the 'arbitrary' is valuable, not least because it appears to grant the poems the power to make their own way into the particular worlds of other people. Though this is one of the ways writers have commonly talked about their works, it is revealed to be a conventional formula by the fact that the people have 'cared to read them' – for in practice this doesn't tend to mean citizens just happened to have given the things a moment, but people who care enough to put some effort into finding the books and devoting time to them. The poems don't make their own way, they are found a way by being cared about, and usually because their arbitrariness (if that's what it is) turns out to have meanings which can be appreciated by people not in particular worlds but in the one world where 'birdcage' can be understood to mean 'paddock' and 'paddock' can mean 'field'. Then again, if the truth of the fiction derives from the elaboration of the poem out of the situation, shouldn't this imply that the created fact is nothing like arbitrary, but complexly conditioned by its imaginative origins? The ways that 'Wingatui' can be understood, or pointedly not understood, might lead to such a conclusion.

To my ear, Manhire's poetry takes a great leap forward in the middle of his third book, *Good Looks* (1982). 'Loosen up chum' is how one poem around there begins, and no sooner said than the sequential reader encounters a run of longer, more situated poems, the most immediately attractive of which is 'Wellington'. There's still the characteristic lightness of touch, but the matter is harsher and the jokes, if that's what they are, pointedly not that funny:

> and the boys from Muldoon Real Estate
> are breaking someone's arm.
> They don't mean harm, really, it's
> nobody's business, mainly free
> instructive entertainment,
> especially if you don't get close

>   but keep well back like
>   all the distant figures in the crowd.

The word 'distance' makes its first appearance in the third of the poems collected here, and from then on it, and its cognates, are never far away. The 'you' experiencing this poem then pretends to be interested in the real estate in the estate agent's display, and this occasions the poem's closing lines: 'You haven't even got a window / and his is full of houses.' Hardly have you come out of this watching while someone gets beaten up, than you're into 'The Voyeur: An Imitation' and considering 'how pale the late Victorian girl is, sleeping / in her bed.' There's a new urgency and a thematic concentration to the poems, and the syntax is often sustained with a great fluency over long periods. The poems start to group themselves into pairs, or runs of pieces with similar concerns (the poem after 'The Voyeur...' is called 'The Late Victorian Girl').

Manhire himself notes that something was happening about that time when talking to Gregory O'Brien about his collaborations with Ralph Hotere:

>   The kind of poems I'd wanted to write had shifted a lot and I don't think they suited Ralph. They were busier, more aggressive poems... making a great noise about themselves... The series was going to be called 'Loss of the Forest' – and indeed there is a poem in *Good Looks* called that. Some of the titles of those poems would turn up later in Ralph's paintings, although I don't think any of the poems themselves made it. I think Ralph needs room to move that those poems simply don't allow.

I wouldn't, myself, be inclined to call the poems in that book 'busier... more aggressive... making a great noise...' They just seem to be more sure of themselves, their directions, and their purposes in existing. One of the biographical things that might have effected this change is that Manhire had evidently by this stage become a father. The last eight poems in the book are all either poems about children, or for them, or they respond to the thoughts of aging and obsolescence that becoming a parent can produce as one of its by-products. 'Children', for instance, opens: 'The likelihood is / the children will die / without you to help them do it.' It's a thought that seems to haunt Manhire.

The last poem in the book, a commissioned millennium poem called 'The Next Thousand', includes the lines: 'No one will remember our old blue shed. / Both of my children will be dead.' Yet so will his great-great grandchildren, and so will his great-grandparents, and so will he, and you and me. But it's the children his poem worries over, and you can't help liking him for it.

From here on Manhire is in his element. The next two full collections, *Milky Way Bar* (1991) and *My Sunshine* (1996), are his finest to date. In an interview with Iain Sharp, Manhire suggests that his early reading and the early poems with their imagistic oddities had been driven by the need to add mystery and complexity to an over-determined ordinary life:

> The American poets I read with most interest somehow used words to make the world a little more mysterious. I liked the enigmatic quality, to use your word. Living in Dunedin in the early sixties, which was really still the late fifties, you needed a bit of mystery in your life... I lived in a fairly predictable, secure world, and I was very happy in general to be there, but somewhere inside my head I also wanted a sense of mystery.

Yet the fairly recent, longish poem 'An Amazing Week in New Zealand', about attending a Billy Graham religious rally when a boy, fends off one kind of mystery with consummate skill:

> One thousand miles of miracle
> lead to where the ground is level
> at the foot of the cross
>
> and here we are on our knees
> inspecting the world of loss...

By this stage the poet can address that daily existence so as both to pay it a tribute ('broken twigs, a hair, / a scrap of food'), to express a resistance ('Lord, I am / not going forward'), and to transform it with technique ('the *pangka-bongka* of the banjo / the *zhing-sching* of the cymbals') – paying homage to Denis Glover's poem 'The Magpies' ('And *Quardle oodle ardle wardle doodle* / The magpies said') even as he does: '*whow-zeedle oodle-ee* / *whay-whonga* / *whaw... Lord*'. The difference between

Curnow's post-Christianity and Manhire's would seem to be that while the earlier poet experienced it as an impinging personal abandonment, the later takes it as read: 'But God is not here, / not in sunshine, not / in God's open air'.

Thus Manhire's concern with the themes of distance and loss speaks beyond anything that could be called an especially New Zealand experience. In the collection's last poem, 'Moonlight', an elegy for 'occasional Kate' Gray (1975–1991), the elements come together:

> I hear myself saying
> please and please and please;
> I want to go back
> to the start of the nineties.
>
> Sleepless night, big almond eyes,
> and a hand rocks a pram in the passage;
> from somewhere a long way
> outside our houses
>
> the moon sends its light to this page.

There is, perhaps, just a trace of a risk that because his poems are so taken with effects of sadness such as this, and that they are sometimes conveyed with a mild oddity that can be whimsical, moments of really irreplaceable loss are sentimentalised. But poems have to take all kinds of risks, and I find the directness, simplicity, and understatement of 'Moonlight', with its acceptance and measured recognition of the sentimental as one way people do manage grief, prevents it from succumbing to the pitfalls it knows are there and steers itself around.

Beginning to write during the decade whose opening had been marked by the publication of Allen Curnow's controversial *The Penguin Book of New Zealand Verse* (1960) with an introduction that rubbed various of the contributors up the wrong way, it's hardly surprising that Manhire's early collections should steer clear of the sorts of nation-founding themes that had exercised his seniors. Yet the other thing that starts to happen mid-career, especially in the new poems section from his *Zoetropes: Poems 1972–1982* (1984), is that he starts to draw upon his family background and its relation to his country. Reviewing *The Penguin Book of Contemporary British Poetry* (1982) at about this time, Manhire notes that, in an anthology out to promote the Martian metaphor school of 'ludic' writing, 'Jeffrey Wainwright... seems to have history, as a poetic territory, almost entirely to himself.' Manhire was simultaneously finding ways of combining his lightly playful touch with the painful matter of history – as in 'The Scottish Bride':

> *You cannot imagine, halfway*
> *across the world,* her father wrote,
> *the sorrow of the undersigned.* Was that her mother
>
> then, who made those numbers on a slate?
> Were those her children, almost finished eating,
> blowing upon their faces in the spoons?

He addresses the question of what it is to be a Kiwi in 'Zoetropes' (written in London, England), a poem which offers the most overt of cultural explanations for the poet's obsessions with distance and loss. 'Words which begin / with Z alarm the heart' not least because

> The land itself is only
> smoke at anchor, drifting above
> Antarctica's white flower,
>
> tied by a thin red line
> (5000 miles) to Valparaíso.

That loss should be one of Manhire's key concerns also shows in his delicate account of how poems by the gimmicky Craig Raine work:

the source of his sadness, it seems to me, has to do with the way in which each new piece of a poem effectively abandons the piece before it. That's to say, his poems build displacement into their structures: they move forward in discrete couplet and triplet units, they offer small bright pleasures and ask us to pass on quickly. Simile and metaphor insist on the links between things, but in a Raine poem the sheer number of them leaves you feeling that individual images have been brought into line only to be dismissed. It is a disconcerting effect for the reader, who is made to undergo a concentrated, slightly mannered, experience of loss.

What's so fair about this passage is that it takes note of precisely what can only too easily get up your nose about Raine's manner, and what can leave you with the sense that a poem had better be doing rather more. After all, living an ordinary life only too commonly feels like undergoing a concentrated experience of loss. What's more, the fact that Raine is putting you through this in 'slightly mannered' fashion may do no more than rub salt in the wound. Some readers may prefer poems to be working with loss, not just putting you through it in ways which make dismissal the characteristic note, and which seem to imply that the experience of loss is the price of the small bright pleasure. It sounds uncommonly like a means of mass-producing aesthetic intensities of the sort hymned at the close of Pater's *Renaissance*. After all, when you really lose people and important things, sadness is likely not to be quite the feeling. But then again, what this goes to show is not only Manhire's acute critical sense (his comments were published in 1984) but also his tact and generosity.

One of the poems that inspires his insightful passage is Raine's 'Flying to Belfast'. Still, if you compare it with Manhire's classic OE poem about the disorientations of long-haul flights, 'Breakfast', you can see how he ranges further in his methods for rendering losses, and how his liking for punctuational asterisks and spaces, far from producing discrete units, works both to disrupt and to reach across, composing stubbornly tenuous links. The poem is made up of nine passages, each separated from its neighbour by one of his signature asterisks, and yet in not a single case is there a coincidence of asterisk and completed syntactical unit. With one exception, the parts are also written in triplet units, yet here again, no three-line stanza ends with a full-stop. The poem touches on loss, and has its own moody tinge, but an unmitigated sadness is not the effect. Though it's difficult to sample a poem so jointed across is disjunctions, here's the last leg:

> everything's a possibility, or
> so thinks the mind that's (mind
> that's not yet quite
>
> *

at home – either we *are* the journey
or just the place through which
the journey passes. Goodbye

London! goodbye Europe! somewhere
between Sydney and Wellington,
somewhere above the Tasman,

*

breakfast is served again (breakfast

*

is served again by
Flight Steward François
Ferrari.

This ending comes off so well partly because 'goodbye Europe!' – which
looks like one of those slightly mannered losses which the poet admires
in Raine – turns out to be not goodbye at all, but hello once more to
breakfast and a memory of the continent left behind in that Flight
Steward's Franco-Italian name.

Like so much of Manhire's poetry, his Pseuds Corner poem 'Wingatui'
is imprinted with distance and loss. You could even see it ramifying in
the loss of meaning that 'birdcage' underwent when translated to the
London literary scene. The distance in the poem is there in the size of
the race course, the lengths of the races and the winning margins, and,
most overtly, the distance from the car with its headlights switched off
all the way up to the rising moon. The loss is there emblematically in
what might have been for the betting man at the races. Conveying all
this, the poet's work goes the distance, counts the loss, and, in so doing,
finds a series of curious links by way of compensation. If Bill Manhire's
poems have split that azure violin in two, he's equally gone a long way to
sticking it right back together again.

DEREK WALCOTT'S
QUIET REGRETS

'Another emblem there!' W. B. Yeats exclaims in 'Coole Park and Ballylee, 1931' of his mounting swan, a 'stormy white' that 'seems a concentration of the sky'. Derek Walcott remembers the Irish Nobel laureate's words when in this new book's title sequence he evokes 'with its gawky stride, erect, an egret-emblem!' An emblems of what? When at the close of the same poem 'the egrets soar together in noiseless flight / or tack, like a regatta, the sea-green grass, / they are seraphic souls'. As is natural in later-life poetry, Walcott elegises his friends and colleagues gone before, and the soul he has in mind here is probably Brodsky: 'seraphic souls, as Joseph was.' He and Walcott were great friends, and Brodsky was a great poet in that, like Walcott, he invested everything in his art. Yet was he a 'seraphic soul'? He could treat with dismissive contempt people not on his level, and few were assumed not to be. *White Egrets* essays the cost of seriousness, the price both poet and those around him may pay, and have paid, for the single-mindedness of his outlook and works.

Walcott rhymes the 'elegance of those white, orange-billed egrets' with 'that peace / beyond desires and beyond regrets' in the second section of his title sequence. The effect is subtly complex. Chiming the trochaic 'egrets' against the iambic 'regrets' already established a conceptual discrepancy or slight mismatching of ideas, the birds symbolizing both purity and freedom from care, an idea that the prepositional phrase 'beyond regrets' attempts to meet squarely. Yet the rhyme-sound and the placing of the word at the line end – consequentially after 'beyond desires' – momentarily pauses the reading mind on the foreground-rhymed concept of 'regrets'. The syntax and the lineation want to move the poem and the poet on to 'that peace', but the creative intelligence hooks the 'regrets' onto the 'egrets' and checks the desired advance 'beyond'. This pausing movement is what the entire book, *White Egrets*, performs. To say that its trajectory doesn't reach 'that peace' is no criticism, for the equilibrium gained by accepting that you could live it all again wouldn't be a state of grace if achieved by overlooking or forgetting those very regrets that make 'eternal recurrence' so unlikely a wish.

In the course of his book Walcott's techniques do quiet regrets in distinguished and peculiarly muted poems. The book is organised, as have been most of Walcott's collections since *Midsummer* (1984) as a numbered sequence of texts (bearing a resemblance to Robert Lowell's *Notebook* and later sonnet volumes), some of them forming sub-sequences, both with and without titles. The untitled number 18 addresses dissatisfactions with his oil painting technique, bringing together disappointment with your art-skills and regrets about your life:

> The angle at which the late afternoon light
> fell across both canvases revealed the coarse impasto
> of the paint, a crudity that now showed so late
> in life, when I had imagined I would master
> portrait and landscape by this time, I'd be seventy-eight
> and had done some more than tolerable, I thought,
> things, sold, exhibited them, but the scabrous surfaces
> were like some dread disease the paint had caught
> that suddenly in that hour raked scenes and faces
> to nothing, not a style, just a crass confidence –
> a thickness, not of skill as in van Gogh or Bacon,
> that showed the self revealed for what it is;
> the revelation came so quietly.

Not only does this passage give a sense of the reflective mode the poems are composed in, but also the relaxed, rhyming, formal confidence that shapes such a capacity to speak out over subtly enjambed syntactic stretches. Walcott is a distinctly competent painter – as can be seen from the Farrar, Straus & Giroux covers of *Collected Poems 1948–1984* (1986) and *The Bounty* (1997) for instance, reproducing a still life and a landscape by the poet. But there is a disequilibrium in the way failures in art are added to those of life, because dissatisfactions with your art take place 'in life', as, of course, do those with your behaviour, but successes in art take place 'in art' and are less readily cashed out in life. As Walcott puts it in his searching essay on Lowell collected in *What the Twilight Says* (1998): 'Poetry is not the redemption of conduct.'

Elsewhere, in number 35, Walcott writes mimetically of his supposedly faded powers:

> All of this happened when I turned away,
> the deliberate delight in incoherence, the whiff of chaos
> off the first page of some new book, the putrescent decay

of drawing which I had begun to smell, the coarse
exuberance that passed for wit, it's incredible the way
my gift abandoned me like a woman I was too old for...

Yeatsian again is Walcott's squarely facing an old man's infatuation with
young women, which appears early in the volume (as if the poem were
a response to the rumour-mongering that obliged him to withdraw his
candidacy for the Oxford Professorship of Poetry in 2009). In 'Sicilian
Suite' he reassures readers, in the first line of the seventh part, that
'There was no "affair," it was all one-sided', and goes on to explicate his
passion in an 'ombre des jeunes filles': 'By the open-air table where I sat
alone / a flock of chattering girls passed, premature sirens / fleeing like
pipers from the sudden thought of a stone.' So that –

> I wondered in the inching sun how it was known
> to the ferry's horn, the pines, the Bay's azure hills
> and the jeering screaming girls that I would lose her
> or an accordion's meandering sob and moan
> through the coiled, serpentine alleys of Siracusa.

Once again, as in 'lose her' / 'Siracusa', we hear how fluency of speech
is driven by rhyme. The entire book, as if by Victor Hugo, finds in
the repertoire of traditional prosody, ample vocabulary, and applied
narrative techniques sufficient structure for an enthusiastic personal
turning of phrase, one which allows him to address, with a controlled
frankness, this matter of an old man overwhelmed by sexual desires for
a young woman – and a range of other issues.

So, despite the passages in which Walcott laments his declining
artistic powers, in 'Sicilian Suite' his reflectively elaborated syntax
impressively homes in on the issue of his continuing and felt-to-be
inappropriate attraction to the opposite sex:

> I'll tell you what they think: you're too old to be
> shaken by such a lissome young woman, to need her
> in spite of your scarred trunk and trembling hand,
> your head rustles with thoughts of her like the cedar
> in March, you blaze in her praise like a sea-almond,
> the crab scrawls your letters then hides them,
> certain that she would never understand.

The section closes with an even more risk-taking turn: 'How boring the love of others is, isn't it, Reader? / This page, touched by the sun's declining arc, / sighs with the same whinge, the Sonnets and Petrarch.' Something is wrong here, in that public obsession with celebrities could incline us to think readers can't get enough of 'the love of others', so long as they have a modicum of fame, and while 'whinge' might be an appropriately self-denigrating way to refer to passion in these late poems, you could wonder if Shakespeare's Sonnets are boring because about 'his' loves, or that Petrarch's lifelong transformation of brief acquaintance with Laura into a spiritual quest is either the same thing as Walcott is talking about, or that Shakespeare was exploring in his sequence, or, for that matter, 'boring' – in the sense that we probably don't go to the *Canzoniere* for the distraction or prurient interest that the word implies.

But, to be fair, the evocation of the Sonnets and Petrarch is tactically designed to focus a perhaps inevitable fact of love poetry and its ingrained egoism, namely the mismatch, in Shakespeare and Proust, for instance, between the self-awareness of passionate attachment and the simultaneous known social or cultural evaluation of its inspiring figure:

> What if all this passion is out of proportion to its subject?
> An average beauty, magnified to deific, demonic
> stature by the fury of intellect,
> a flat-faced girl with slanted eyes and a narrow
> waist, and a country lilt to her voice,
> that she should infect your day to the very marrow,
> to hate the common light and its simple joys?
> Where does this sickness come from, because it is
> sickness, this conversion of the simplest action
> to an ordeal, this hatred of simple delight
> in others, of benches in the empty park?

At the end of this section he associates the rhythm of poetry and that of the sea with the regularity and repetitiveness, as it might be, of his life-skill failures: 'I watch them accumulating my errors / steadily repeated as the waves as the sea's / decline'. Walcott has a sure, a reassuring, rhythmic touch and skill with rhymes, both the unusually inventive and unobtrusively routine, that carries the pulses of sensory experience to the reader like the waves breaking on his beaches – a simile repeatedly drawn on both by the poet and his admirers.

So the book's thematic rhyme is that of 'egrets' with 'regrets', as in this admission from 'Sicilian Suite': 'All of those people and their lucky lives. / I know what I've done, I cannot look beyond. /I treated all of them badly, my three wives.' Yet the overarching matter of *White Egrets*, with age-old old-age romantic obsession as a sub-theme, its refrains of 'the quiet ravages of diabetes' and of failing artistic powers, is the inescapable natural world of breakers and island flora and fauna, vivid in Walcott's poetry from the first, as here again in number 32, remaining intensely present, simultaneously underlining the temporariness of the sensibility that they fed:

> If it is true
> that my gift has withered, that there's little left of it,
> if this man is right then there's nothing else to do
> but abandon poetry like a woman because you love it
> and would not see her hurt, least of all by me;
> so walk to the cliff's edge and soar above it,
> the jealousy, the spite, the nastiness with the grace
> of a frigate over Barrel of Beef, its rock;
> be grateful that you wrote well in this place,
> let the torn poems sail from you like a flock
> of white egrets in a long last sigh of release.

Walcott's work is extraordinarily fluent and copious, and this is fed by his historic ambivalences, his straddling of categories, and his ability to evoke the appeal in what he also recognises as well and truly lost. He revisits complex allegiances with London, New York, Italy, Holland and Spain, with the end of the imperial, and returns to the scenes of his home in St Lucia.

Walcott's eloquently hybrid synthesis of traditions, and the multiple contradictions it contains, is addressed in the two-part 'A London Afternoon' when he asks:

> What have these narrow streets, begrimed with age
> and greasy with tradition, their knobbly names,
> their pizza joints, their betting shops, that black garage,
> the ping and rattle of mesmerizing games
> on slot machines, to do with England on each page
> of my fifth-form anthology, now that my mind's

> an ageing sea remembering its lines,
> the scent and symmetry of Wyatt, Surrey?

The passage skilfully answers its own question, though, by, for instance, that rhyming of an iambic 'with age' against the trochaic (depending on your pronunciation) half-rhyme 'garage', and the spondaic 'each page'. The streets 'begrimed with age / and greasy with tradition' can still be vividly evoked by redeploying the repertoire of poetic devices pioneered in English by those very Petrarch-influenced love poets that he recalls. Passionate attachment and remorse, self-belief and creative doubt: his embraced traditions have goaded him on and they judge him.

Not all the sections here are equally well written or finely imagined. Number 46, for example, is a brittle face-off between two views of Caribbean vegetation and culture. One is 'what that bastard calls "the emptiness" – / that blue-green ridge with plunging slopes, the blossoms / like drooping chalices, of the African tulip' and, Walcott continues, 'the phrase applies / to our pathetic, pompous cities, their fretwork balconies, / their retail stores blasting reggae'. Whoever 'that bastard' may be, he is nailed to the image from Conrad's *Heart of Darkness* with its 'warship pointlessly firing / into the huge empty jungle'. Walcott sides with Chinua Achebe, then, in thus castigating the old seadog for his cruelly well-observed account of European racism. His poem almost certainly has some unidentified other 'bastard' as its target, though Conrad inevitably catches some of its flak. Then it all turns to staging an act of solidarity: 'This verse / is part of the emptiness, as is the valley of Santa Cruz, / a genuine benediction as his is a genuine curse.' Which is finally where Walcott takes his stand, in benediction, and the inspiring materiality of his home world, as here in the close to poem 51:

> and yet there are the days
> when every street corner rounds itself into
> a sunlit surprise, a painting or a phrase,
> canoes drawn up by the market, the harbour's blue,
> the barracks. So much to do still, all of it praise.

Well, not quite 'all of it', as his raging against 'that bastard' in 46 has shown. If Walcott is drawn towards Rilke's answer in 'O say, Poet, what you do' ('*I praise*'), his book as a whole shows him more than aware that a blanket celebration of life can be a form of valetudinarian withdrawal from the battles of reality. If this volume does prove to be Derek Walcott's last book of poetry, then, despite its occasional momentary lapses, the sense of a horizon tour around his themes, it is nonetheless a remarkable swansong – or, no, make that an egret-song.

VAHNI CAPILDEO AND ETYMOLOGY

Geoffrey Hill, current Oxford Professor of Poetry, illustrates beliefs about poetic technique as a drama of sin and redemption in his essay 'Poetry and Value' by referring to 'supporting evidence' that is 'preserved in and by the *Oxford English Dictionary*'. W. H. Auden, though no less a believer, suggested that 'a dictionary is absolutely passive and may legitimately be read in an infinite number of ways', while Ralph Waldo Emerson thought dictionaries worth reading because they contain 'the raw material of possible poems'. Harry Guest's *Some Times* (Anvil Press Poetry, 2010) contains just such a poem, one called 'Divans', which riffs on a related bundle of meanings:

> Lounging on one
> in Persia or
> leafing through one
> to please or bore…
> Yes, *couch* or *set*
> *of poems* – yet
> it seems you call
> that *Customs-Hall*
> we scurry through
> in ones and twos
> with fags and booze
> a *divan* too.
>
> Poets can't claim
> immunity.
> The rule's the same –
> if duty-free
> that minimum
> demand's still fair:
> 'Have you got some-
> thing to declare?'

Recorded in English since 1586, meaning 'Oriental council of state', from Turkish *divan*, from Arabic *diwan*, a Middle-Persian loan-word in Arabic *dīvān*: 'bundle of written sheets, small book, collection of poems', the senses evolved through 'book of accounts' to 'office of accounts', 'custom house', 'council chamber', then to 'long, cushioned seat', such as found along the walls in Middle Eastern council chambers. Inspired by the *Divan-i Hafiz*, Goethe named his 1819 collection the *West-östlicher Divan*, and Edwin Morgan jokingly called one *The New Divan* (Carcanet Press, 1977). Guest's poem finesses its close – perhaps prompted by Wilde's answer ('Only my genius') to the US customs official who asked their standard question – by suggesting that crossing borders, living in different countries and languages produces occasions for poetic speech, while the word 'divan' illustrates how there's frequently nothing Anglophone about the English language, it being a hybrid pidgin. Guest's poem is dedicated to the Jamaican poet and broadcaster A. L. Hendricks (1922–1992) whose experience of 'translation' from the Caribbean to London may add to Guest's implications, for, until recently, if words crossed borders and were absorbed in other language areas, it was because people transported them, as happened to the Persian دیوان, *dīwān*.

The much-travelled Trinidadian Vahni Capildeo's third collection, *Dark and Unaccustomed Words* (Egg Box Publishing, 2011), takes its title from a passage in George Puttenham's *The Arte of Poesie* (1598) opposed to uses of 'all darke and vnaccustomed wordes, or rusticall and homely, and sentences that hold too much of the mery & light, or infamous & vnshamefast' because they 'become not Princes, or great estates, nor them that write of their doings to vtter or report and intermingle with the graue and weightie matters.' Her poetry will then use the 'dark and unaccustomed' to address 'grave and weighty matters', and frequently shifts between modes and codes within the course of a single work, the parts of a sequence, and poems in the sections of her collection. But the book contains more than one piece suggesting you can have enough of etymology. Capildeo was briefly employed as a researcher for the ongoing revision of the *Oxford English Dictionary*'s some 231,000 entries (spelling, pronunciation, etymology, definitions, and illustrative quotations). She addresses her subterranean working conditions in a poem called 'Sinking Lightwells', dedicated '*For the OED (Etymology)*':

> And what about those many operatives,
> those many office workers, well those people
> who clock in underground – can they be trusted
> to make good use of newly allocated,
> all-natural, mind-expander, mood-lifter
> no-excuse light?

Exploring the evolution of words might seem ideally suited to a poet; but she finds alienating both its working environment and the work itself. Far from stimulating a natural relation to the medium, it seems a Casaubon-like chimera in aspiring to a total knowledge of this now global language.

'Journal of Ordinary Days' begins by homing in on a verb aptly expressive of her frustrations:

> Do I look like the sort of person who's not fit
> to go out and buy a pen on her own? The phrase
> 'May I borrow a biro' is unspeakable
> for its vocalic ugliness. The task in hand,
> this third daze of work, is dis- and rearranging,
> suspecting, assessing, keying in and tagging
> all the historical spellings of the verb QUIT.
> 'That can't be a lot? QUIT is such a little verb?'
> But people have been quitting for centuries, and
> especially in Scotland, all in different ways.

As if 'daze' were a variant spelling of 'days', poets find their magpie inspirations in both cod-etymology and the real history that produces paradoxical words like the adverbial 'stand fast' and 'run fast' or the meanings of 'lie' so useful to jealous love poets. Yet the technical minutiae of etymology and the potentially endless task of sequencing variants is not an especially poetic prospect. Capildeo doesn't want to 'borrow' a 'biro' (a para-rhyme) because she needs to escape the office and 'quit', so goes and buys one, not caring how long it takes. After attempting to get an 'ethical biro' from a fair trade shop but failing, she falls into rap-like rhyming:

> I look elsewhere, and not far off the ordinary
> rewards the initiative: sell-it-all, old-fashioned,
> like nineteen fifty-three, nearly customer-free,
> a newsagent of the English variety.

This first part ends with a couplet made from an alexandrine and a pentameter: 'Anything is better than going back to QUIT. / I can buy a pen on my own. I'm fit' – where the current 'fit' in youth-speak, meaning *attractive*, consorts with more time-honoured senses. But as the poem implies, in the *OED*'s etymology section, she just don't fit and believes it's time to quit.

Capildeo's book addresses the vast hybridity of languages and an individual's interactions with their shifting terrains. 'Sometimes', she writes in the poem's last section, 'I dream in a language that is mine only in snatches', and explains how her sleep is populated by etymological shifts:

> Sometimes it is the actual people around me on a journey
> whose language drifts into another throughout my dreams,
> the prerequisite for transformation always being
> that both tunes already are familiar to my memory,
> so that the Irish have become Jamaican: the Spanish, Trinidadian...

The English-language 'subject' in speech whereby, grammatically, you are doing something, while, in experiments or the British state, you are the one to whom things are done, preserves agency within constraint. Thus the 'subjects' of verbs, the one qualifying the other (as in 'John loves you' and 'Mary loves you' – where John is your husband and Mary your mother), show how people are shaped by the words they speak, yet simultaneously shape the being shaped. Lexicographers understandably make a fetish of words, their object of study, as when Herbert Coleridge, first editor of the *OED*, wrote that 'every word should be made to tell its own story – the story of its birth and life, and in many cases of its death, and even occasionally of its resuscitation'. Here lexicographers sound like interrogators with ways of making words talk: but words don't have lives and deaths, and citations in dictionaries are the tips of titanic usage icebergs. Words are no more nor less than attempted transcriptions of noises made by people with their mouths and, as with 'quoof' in Paul Muldoon's family or 'glory' to Humpty-Dumpty, what we can mean by our oral and aural inventiveness is limitless. Capideo's poem has it that the poet is the person who goes to buy the writing implement, not the one who tags sampled, and inevitably partial, usages. Nevertheless, it's good to know that 'divan' may, felicitously, be related to the Persian *debir* meaning 'writer' – William Cowper for instance who began his long poem *The Task* with 'I sing the Sofa' to 'seek repose upon an humbler theme'.

FIVE

'LIVERPOOL … OF ALL PLACES'

I wasn't born in Liverpool, but came to live in the city at the age of three. My father's first parish was St Andrew's, Litherland, and the family moved into the vicarage behind the church in the year of Suez. We were to be there for six years. Liverpool, in the twilight of its hey-day, is the place I came to self-consciousness. It was still a thriving seaport, still a semblance of the gateway to empire it had been. We arrived just in time to take trams into the centre; I rode the length of the Overhead Railway before it was pulled down, and went for a river cruise on the *Royal Iris* or perhaps it was the *Daffodil*.

The terraces around Stanley Road in Bootle and Litherland were still interrupted in 1956 by bombed sites and pre-fabs. A bomb had exploded next to the church. There men would stand in tight huddles dropping coins on the cindery earth between them. What were they doing? Gambling?

There was a patch of waste ground behind our house. The upstairs landing airing cupboard was my grandstand seat while the men from Johnson's Dyeworks playing football in their lunch hour – until the hooter sounded and they disappeared.

Among my father's parishioners were the Veizeys. They became friends of the family, courtesy aunt and uncle for the next twenty-odd years. Aunty Gladys was the talker of the pair. 'Go to Bootle with your bother!' she'd say, and '*I want* never gets…'

My father's vocation took us away from Liverpool not long before the Beatles released 'I Wanna Hold Your Hand', and we spent the next five years in Wigan. My brother and I were called into our parents' bedroom and told that we'd be leaving St Andrew's. I didn't want to move. Why did we have to go to a place with holes in the ground called pits?

It was Aunty Glad, principally, who kept us in touch with the city during those years away. She would visit regularly to help my mother with her growing brood and the vast St Catherine's vicarage. Gladys also bought me my first record: 'Little Children' by Billy J. Kramer and the Dakotas. The choice is itself an example of her wit.

She also took us to see *A Hard Day's Night* when it first came out in 1964. The pride with which she did this must have conveyed to me something about what it meant to be a Liverpudlian. The city was a place to which I had become inseparably connected – yet without ever having the sense that it was somewhere I belonged.

During the spring of 1967 my father moved to his third and final parish: St Michael, Garston, in the south of the city. Once again, I didn't want to go. By then, puberty had occurred and brought with it the usual teen humiliations, a personal interest in pop song lyrics, and plenty to sublimate one way or another.

Regular bouts of tonsillitis had turned me into a reader in bed, though serious addiction to literary book worming didn't begin until encouraged by the English masters at school. By chance, or good fortune, we were to study Joyce's *A Portrait* for A-level. Just as I could read myself into that book, so *Dubliners* could resemble the city I lived in, and Alan Hodgkinson, the head of English retiring that year, presented me with a copy of the newly published Penguin *Ulysses*.

Penny Lane ran along the back of the school playing fields. I passed 'the shelter in the middle of the roundabout' whenever I took the 86 bus into town. It must have been about this time that a poem was read on John Peel's radio music show, a poem called 'The Entry of Christ into Liverpool' by the Mersey beat poet and painter Adrian Henri. There was something of a vogue for poetry taking place. One of my friends brought Michael Horowitz's anthology *The Children of Albion* into class and made his own versions of the jokey haiku to be found there. Later, Eliot's selection of Pound and a slim *Selected Poems* of Robert Lowell would challenge ideas about what could go into a poem. So, between the ages of fifteen and seventeen, writing poetry developed from a prank into an obsession.

I picked up from this reading and listening the conviction that art could be made out of what surrounded you, out of street names, 'blue suburban skies', and the details of people's lives. I had already written a now lost poem called 'From Long Lane to Russell Road' (both in the vicinity of Garston Park) before discovering Roy Fisher's *City*, Edwin Morgan's 'Glasgow Sonnets', or Charles Olson's *Maximus Poems* about Gloucester, Massachusetts – when reading English at York.

The spring 1974 issue of its student magazine contains a curious 'stanzaic section from a long poem' which attempts to combine the 'church monument' style of George Herbert with the leading Black Mountaineer's poetry:

St Michael's Parish Church is
The third edifice
   And stands near,
Since 1891, the gasworks
And the dock railway tracks.
   It was here…

And so it goes on, for thirty-odd more lines. Leaving Liverpool had meant encountering many different ways of seeing the relations between poetry and places. I would bring them all back home and try them out for size; though many, such as the above, would have to be discarded on the way.

'From Long Lane to Russell Road': but it wasn't only personal associations and alliteration that drew me to those places as a first serious subject for poems. My brother and I were day boys at Liverpool College – on the half-fees arranged for the 'genteel poor' children of the Anglican clergy. This raises the inescapable question of class and, more generally, a growing awareness of divisions. Some of this awareness comes from the social position of the vicarage. To his children, a vicar appears to be invested with a mysterious importance by those whom he meets. Yet an Anglican clergyman's family is, simultaneously, in an ambiguous relation to this cultural aura. There was also the equivocal privilege of the large houses we would live in; these were places my parents could barely furnish and heat, but which nevertheless marked us out in my father's working-class parishes at the very moment we were supposed to belong.

    At school the divisions were reversed: I became friends with the children of middle-class businessmen from Aigburth, Allerton, Woolton, and Harold Wilson's constituency, Huyton. These were more prosperous districts that surrounded the working-class, dockside village slum of Garston and, next door, the overspill estates of Speke. Sharp contrasts in wealth, social aspirations and possibilities, were laid out as the pattern of avenues and districts in South Liverpool's semi-rural urban sprawl.

    Growing up in Garston during the second half of the 1960s and first years of the next decade, I was not one of those who needed to be told by Asa Briggs in his *A Social History of England* that 'Liverpool went through economic, social and political crisis'. My father's necessarily polite, but distant, relations with Free Masonry, the Orange Lodge, and the far Left, or my own first encounters with middle-class anti-Semitism and racial tension are some of the ways in which these crises were brought home.

The old Garston dockside area 'under the bridge' was to be demolished as a means to upgrade the housing stock. My father became involved in efforts to preserve the street communities of his parish against the wholesale dumping of populations in high-rise estates miles from anywhere they knew as home.

The fact that he had an aura, a status, a place in society which meant he could perform so useful a role in the city, set me thinking about the absence of such a position for the participant-observer poet, a stance for which his five changes of parish, as first curate then vicar, had peculiarly prepared me.

At this time, too, a verbal awareness of differences had insinuated itself. During the five years in Wigan I lost whatever Liverpool accent I'd picked up in the schoolyard of Linacre Infants, Bootle, and adopted the altogether different tones of the mid-Lancs coalfield. In south Liverpool where the middle class speaks a more refined Liverpudlian, my Wigan sounds were a cause of some skitting, and for the only time in my life I consciously adjusted my accent.

Almost twenty years later, I would have imagined that extended contact with the world of universities in other parts of Britain had reduced the Liverpool echoes to a neutral inaudibility, but not so. Debating whether the rhyme of 'gone' and 'one' is a full chime or an ironic dissonance (for me the vowel sounds are exactly the same), I found myself out-manoeuvred by having my accent characterised by a professor of very close reading as 'post-Beatles'.

Shaped by the city that went from pre-fabs to post-Beatles in my childhood and youth, I wouldn't want to deny it. In Japan people occasionally wanted to know what my hometown is, and despite the doubt about birthplace, or where the most years have been spent, I always answer: Liverpool.

This would immediately produce a mention of the Fab Four, and sometimes I was asked which is my favourite. Many of the poems selected for *Liverpool Accents* are set in the city. Of the exceptions, 'For Different Friends' contains a concealed reference to one of their hits. It began as an elegy for the singer shot dead outside the Dakota Building in New York on 8 Dec 1980, and though the poem shed its original occasion, a trace of the starting point can be heard in the echo of lines from 'Help!' ('and I do appreciate you being round. / Help me get my feet back on the ground...'). After the 'indisputable ground' of the first verse, there are the 'frozen solid marks / of bicycles, feet – familiar things' in the second, and

> Walking then among the trees'
> angular, elongated
> branches' shadows cast like arteries,
> I appreciated
> the pausing, unemphatic breath
> of another speaking.

Almost exactly a hundred years before John Lennon's death, Gerard Manley Hopkins complained in a letter to R. W. Dixon (22 Dec 1880) that 'Liverpool is of all places the most museless.' But it hasn't been like that for me.

'HIT THE ROAD, JACK'

The first thing that comes to mind of those years as a pupil at Linacre Infants and Junior School is smooth red brick and rough grey asphalt, the tall windows, and a big thermometer on a wall by the entrance. Presumably the thermometer was there so that we wouldn't play out if the temperature dropped too low. But if these details are confused or mistaken, it's because we moved around in my childhood and they have been lumped together with things from different places.

There were two playgrounds, divided by a wall. The one on the left, if you were facing towards the Mersey, was for the Infants; the larger one on the right, for the Juniors. The sports day events were held in the larger one. We sat on thin rubber mats as we waited to take part in the races. That's me sitting on one in the class photograph taken in front of the Infants School, a black and white class photo that lay around unconsidered in my parents' houses for years and years. I'm the little chubby boy in the middle on the front row. You can tell from the clothes we're wearing that it's summer. I've got on some Clarks sandals with creamy-white crape soles. It used to upset me when, after wearing them for a while, the soles wore thin and turned black. If you look closely, you can see that this has happened to mine.

On my immediate left in the photograph is Barbara Penny. On the other side from her is Colin Wells. On the back row, three from the left is Billy Morrison. The school's centenary had been announced in Liverpool, with a call for memories and memorabilia. Billy had heard about it from his family, found me on the Internet, and sent a message from British Columbia in which he added some more names to the faces. On the third row, second from the left, is Paul Thompson, who when last heard of was in Australia. Leslie Beattie is just behind me and she may still live in Bootle. Phillip Stopford, back row, centre, is somewhere in Ontario. There is also a Billy Smith in the picture. He died a few years ago. Next to me on the other side is Sally McLeod. The girl on the back row nearest to the right is called Carol, I think. The boy with dark wavy hair in the centre of the middle row may be Glyn Hughes. There was also an Indian boy in our class at some point, though he must have arrived later. I can't exactly date the photograph, but perhaps it's from our first year – the late spring or summer of 1959.

There was a sand tray in the first-year classroom. It wasn't very big, and I can vaguely recall standing about in that room, or moving from one place to another, new to school life, not really understanding what I was supposed to be doing there. We sat around communal tables with maybe four children at each one for the lessons. There were also the usual big cards stuck high up on the walls, with 'A is for apple' and a picture of an apple – and so on. That's where we began to read, and I can still recall the *Janet and John* books, as well as the story about the hen that thinks the sky will fall down on her head. The teaching of reading was pretty successful in my case, because before leaving the school in 1962 I was borrowing big hardback books about fighter pilots and other war heroes from the local public library.

School must have started for me in September 1958, at 5 years and 8 months. I have a vividly painful memory of my first day at school. We are out in the playground, so it must be playtime, and it seems to be the morning. I'm standing around on my own, and that's because I don't know anyone yet. Up near the wall of the school is a small area fenced round with wooden sticks that are wired together. Because the playground has a hard floor, the fence doesn't stand up well, and has partly collapsed. Inside the fence there are some metal children's toys – a kind of rocking horse thing among them. Having nothing else to do, I climb over the fence and start to play on them. No sooner have I done this, than a teacher comes over and tells me to get out of there. Those are for the kindergarten children. So off I get, and go back to the schoolyard – feeling very ashamed of myself. Most of my strongest memories of these years are connected with being scolded, though I don't believe myself to have been a naughty boy.

In the second year class I didn't like the teacher so much. Yet this is likely to be only because we had a confrontation about reading. What Miss – I can't recall her name – used to do was to set us all to work on something. It comes back to me as I write that we learned how to tell the time in this class. Then she would call us up to her desk, one by one, and we would read things out loud to her. At the back of one of the reading books were some lists of words, written in very small print. As I was reading these out, she stopped me and corrected one of the words. But I kept insisting that what I had read was right – until finally she told me to look at it again more carefully. And I realised that I had been wrong. So there we are again: more feelings of shame, and another clear memory among the general blur.

The third class comes back as the one with the warmest glow. Maybe I had become the teacher's pet without knowing it. My only clear memories of this year also involve things that were to become among the most important in my life. I have a sharp sensation of puzzlement concerning a joke that involved play on words. It was something like 'Why did the cow slip?' 'Because it wanted...' But I can't remember the punch line. It was a pun on the name of the flower: a 'cowslip'. I didn't get it – but I did realise something was going on that I needed to understand.

The other memory is of doing a still-life drawing with coloured pencils of an apple, and taking special care over the different colours of peel around where the core came out. I think the teacher must have complimented me on this, otherwise why would I remember it? Is it possible that we used to write with pieces of chalk on little blackboards with a wooden frame around them? Is that how we practised our letters? I have a memory of ink wells in the desk with turquoise ink and dipping pens that used to get clogged and make nasty blots – but this must be from the Junior School, or even later at my next school.

The other thing we did that comes back clearly is 'Music and Movement'. This we did in a little gym. The music came from a radio. So there must have been some special programmes broadcast just for schools. The voice on the radio would tell you to pretend to be a tree, and there would be some tree-like music while you did it. Then the voice would say that a strong wind has started blowing and all the little trees will have been told to sway their branches – which we did to the special effects sounds. We also used to do dancing in this class. This certainly involved having partners, and I can recall that there was a certain amount of negotiating about who would dance with whom. Yes, we had our little favourites. So, now, looking at the class photograph, I can almost bring back some of the things that we said to each other. I certainly quarrelled with Colin Wells at one point, and I can remember saying something rather cruel to Barbara Penny as well – but this happened out of school.

If I did start at Linacre in September 1958, then we went up to junior school in autumn of 1961. I can only have done one year at the most, because my dad moved to St Catherine's, Wigan, sometime in 1962. In junior school the lessons got harder, of course. I can recall us sitting in rows of desks that were raised on shallow steps towards the back of the class. There we all are reciting our times-tables out loud.

One two's two, two two's are four ... twelve twelves are a hundred and forty-four.

Learning to write also got much more serious, because I can recall clearly noticing that it was very easy to make the mistake of writing 'baddy' instead of 'daddy'. We may have also learned how to sew and weave in this class. This is where I wove a rainbow tea cosy that we still use. There was certainly some teaching of Greek myths, about which I remain fairly perplexed. I also remember realizing that there was something wrong with all the drawings we did of some grass, with a house on top of it, and over the roof a sun with lines coming out for the rays, then a stripe of blue for the sky. After all, if you look at it, the sky touches the roofs of the houses. The business about who was my 'girlfriend' in the class also seems to have got slightly more fraught at this time.

Ray Charles' song 'Hit the Road, Jack' – I discover from the Internet – was a US number one and a UK number six hit in 1961. I can recall clearly standing on the asphalt of the playground of the Junior School at about home time thinking that it would certainly hurt if you hit the road, and wondering why Jack would want to do it anyway.

In those days we were never collected from school. I used to walk back home around the edge of the bombed-site where the men from Johnson's Dyeworks played football in their lunch hour, disappearing when the hooter from the works called them back. My parents certainly warned me not to talk to strangers, and never take any short cuts down back entries. Nothing frightening ever happened, mind you; and I don't actually recall any particularly violent experiences in the playground either. The only time I got hurt in the street was when I walked straight into a lamppost. There don't seem to have been any serious bullies. This was to change in Wigan, where the parish was poorer and the kids more violent. But maybe it was because we boys were getting older.

'Hit the road, Jack, and don't you come back no more, no more.' Perhaps the reason I remember thinking my painfully literal thoughts about the words of Ray Charles's song is that I was about to hit the road myself. Certainly, since leaving Linacre in 1962, I haven't met or spoken to any of the people in the photograph again.

BECOMING A READER

Somewhere there's a family photograph taken on a beach that may be at South Shields. My mother is sitting in the opening of a pup tent, looking after my baby sister. My brother has dug a deep hole in the sand and continues to work on it nearby. I'm in the hole, reading a book. Though I can't be sure what the book in the holiday snap is, something tells me it's a large hardback borrowed from the public library on Ocean Road. It is, or it might as well be, a history of the aeroplanes built before and during the First World War by Fokkers – one packed with barely comprehensible technical specifications for engines or guns, about how they invented the synchronizing gear which let them fire through the propeller without shooting themselves down. Why am I reading such a book? Why am I reading it with so much concentration as if oblivious to being there on the beach? This photo presents me with two problems: how did I come to be in that hole, and how would I get out of it?

The earliest book I remember reading, or being helped to read, was the tale of the chicken afraid that the sky would fall. I know he thinks it actually has, but he's mistaken, isn't he? Even at infants school I may have been something of a critical reader, for I recall that the story puzzled me. If you looked up, you could see that the sky didn't stop; it just went on and on. I'm a vicarage child who grew up where the words 'heaven' and 'the heavens' had assumed references. The sky wasn't like a lid or a ceiling, was it? So how could you think it might fall down? And if it couldn't, then what had the poor chicken been afraid of anyway? The wrong thing, I assume, if his and his friends' fate at the hands of the fox is the moral of the story.

My identity, it now seems, emerged from such puzzles about looking up and finding meaning. My mother's parents' house by the North Sea at the mouth of the Tyne was where we regularly spent holidays – such as the one that may have produced that photo of us on the beach. From the roof of the nave in a church we used to attend, a wooden model ship had been suspended. Gazing up at this beautifully crafted boat, I heard the congregation singing 'O worship the Lord all glorious above' and mistook the verb for 'warship'. My parents were much amused when I asked them what 'warship the Lord' meant.

But, then, wars and rumours of war were all around. Being born in 1953, a Coronation baby, meant also being born in the last year of the

Korean War, when wartime rationing finally ended, less than a decade after the atom bombs and the Japanese surrender. My father was thirty-three when he first became a parent, and my mother twenty-six. They had met at Durham University in about 1947 and were starting a family slightly late for people of their class and times – about six years late. My mother's father had been wounded in Palestine fighting Turkish forces in 1917 and, as a very small boy, I was told about the pieces of shrapnel still lodged somewhere inside him. But it wasn't only the wars in which members of the family fought that fuelled my reading habits.

In Liverpool around 1961 there was an exhibition at the City Museum commemorating the outbreak of the American Civil War a century before. My parents took us and that started a bout of devouring books about Stonewall Jackson and Robert E. Lee. Liverpool had sided, at least covertly, with the Confederacy. *The Alabama*, a blockade-runner, was built in Birkenhead. While not understanding anything about the Lancashire cotton industry and its links to the slave plantations, I caught this leaning towards the South – because the imagined heroics of the soldiers with grey uniforms were far more fatefully intriguing. Perhaps this temperamental habit of siding with the bound-to-lose stems from, or is at least illustrated by, that obsession – as by a somewhat later addiction to books on the American Indian Wars. It's a habit that must have been strengthened through being taught history from the Civil War to Bonnie Prince Charlie by a Catholic master at Wigan Grammar School.

Doubtless, there were innumerable boys my age who played with toy guns and refought the battles of parents' and grandparents' youths, but not all of them will have been inclined to plough through biographies and military histories to feed the imagination with pictures of what it may actually have been like. Two things probably encouraged the growth of this insatiable reading. My father moved from one parish to another when I was three, nine, and fourteen: that landed me in suddenly friendless phases at crucial moments. Then there were the regular bouts of tonsillitis and other childhood illnesses that were got through by going to bed with books.

A memory comes back from our Wigan years: I'm reading a series of flying doctor stories – aeroplanes again – which were set in Africa and involved missionary work. These must have been consumed during a fervently religious phase from about eight to twelve, during which I seriously contemplated following my father into the Ministry. I was a

choir boy and, of course, a regular church attender. My introduction to
English poetry came through *Hymns Ancient & Modern*: 'As o'er each
continent and island / Dawn leads on to another day'; 'In the bleak mid
winter / Frosty winds made moan. / Earth stood hard as iron, / Water
like a stone.' I'm quoting from memory. The repeated singing of songs
is still something I do, whether under my breath or aloud. A musician
friend recently described me as a walking songbook.

Another memory comes back sharp and clear: I'm standing on the
front row of the congregation in a church that isn't my father's. We're all
singing 'Jerusalem' – a song beginning intriguingly with a conjunction:
'And did those feet …' Of course, I didn't know who wrote it, but the
words seemed terribly relevant: 'those dark Satanic mills'. As far as I'm
concerned they're cotton mills. 'Bring me my arrows of desire', we sang.
This is the memory: though I'm singing too, my eyes are fixed on the
legs of a girl standing out in front with a group of others all wearing
their Sunday best. One leg is bent at the knee and the heel slightly
lifted. I'm fascinated by 'those feet', become conscious of looking, and
think I shouldn't, but don't want to stop. So that earliest awareness of
my being attracted to girls is inextricably entangled with those words by
William Blake.

The first poem I was conscious of hearing being quoted was
John Masefield's 'Cargoes'. Nobody required me to learn it off by
heart, as Paul Muldoon was – if that detail in his poem 'Profumo' is
autobiographical. No, it was my father who'd memorised it at school.
On the wall above the dining table in his mother's house at 472
Claremont Road, Rusholme, was a painting of an old cargo boat called
the S. S. Hardanger. I was obsessed with it and, as if to supply a text,
once dad reconstructed Masefield's third verse for us:

> Dirty British coaster with a salt-caked smoke stack
> Butting through the Channel in the mad March days,
> With a cargo of Tyne coal,
> Road-rail, pig-lead,
> Firewood, iron-ware, and cheap tin trays.

Many years later, when it will have come as a God-send, I would discover
in his study a book called *The Modern Poet: an Anthology*, edited by
someone called Gwendolen Murphy and published by Sidgwick &
Jackson in May 1938. It's a well-informed, up-to-date volume with

samples of work by Georgians, Modernists, the Auden group, and other new poets of the same decade, both famous and not so – from Robert Graves and Laura Riding to David Gascoyne, Kathleen J. Raine, Charles Madge, and even the Liverpool poet A. S. J. Tessimond. This book contains the inscription 'My Best Friend, / from / Lawrie / Christmas 1938'. Lawrie McAlpine was the vicar's son at Holy Trinity, Platt, in Manchester. Though a pacifist, he joined the Royal Engineers, convincing himself that peace would have to be fought for. He was crushed in 1944 when something fell off a transporter in Normandy.

The transition in reading habits from war to love took place, naturally enough, during teenage. I had a copy of a Biggles book set during the First World War where our hero is serving with the RFC on the Western Front. In it, there was a semi-romantic chapter where Biggles becomes involved with a Mata Hari enemy spy who he has reluctantly to leave when he discovers the truth. That story by W. E. Johns helped to fuel a good deal of vague sexual fantasy. The obsession with technicalities of early aeroplanes was about to metamorphose into a passion for other sorts of minute detail. So here you have me about thirteen, mainly interested in history and art, reading technical books about aeroplanes I can't fully understand, sliding from an obsession with war alone, to war and love, yet someone who doesn't have any real interest in literature. But I was volunteering to act in the annual school play.

At about this time I got the part of Denis, the bad-boy lead in a combined production with the local Girls High School of a musical about children being evacuated from London during the Blitz. Later parts included the White Rabbit in *Alice in Wonderland*, and Doctor Livesey in *Treasure Island*. But the highlight of all this was the musical – the occasion for my first 'relationships' at an age I now think woefully young. That I can still remember the names of the girls with whom I was involved, however briefly and superficially, suggests that they were coming to play a role in my imaginative life that would have astonished them had they known. While involved with the play about the Blitz and with Susan Fleming, the female lead, who happened to be our woodwork teacher's daughter, I came bottom of the class in English.

Literature began for me when we moved back to the Mersey in the spring of 1967. My brother and I started at Liverpool College, on half-fees granted to children of the impoverished clergy. There I was lucky to come into contact with two devoted English teachers, Peter Stott and Alan Hodgkinson. It was they who first noticed, then encouraged, the reader and writer. They made me the library prefect in the sixth form, which must have been the year I bought a *Selected Poems of William Blake* ed. F. W. Bateson – on the day the currency went decimal in 1971. This fact is noted in the front where my name is also scribbled with its three initials. Preserved in the book is part of the half-title page to Trevor Huddleston's *Naught for your Comfort*, about his experiences of Apartheid, on the back of which is written in my best hand:

from The Book of Thel.

Why cannot the ear be closed to its own destruction?
Or the glist'ning eye to the poison of a smile?
Why are the eyelids stored with arrows ready drawn,
Where a thousand fighting men in ambush lie?
Or an Eye of gifts & graces showring fruits & coined gold?
Why a tongue impressed with honey from every wind?
Why an ear, a whirlpool fierce to draw creations in?
Why a nostril wide inhaling terror, trembling and affright?
Why a tender curb upon the youthful burning boy?
Why a little curtain of flesh on the bed of our desire?

Bateson's selection includes nothing from the Prophetic Books. I'll have found this in the school library, and copied it down when on duty during a lunch break. My having done this, with a heavy symbolism on the back of that title page, suggests a partial emergence from the hole on the beach.

The first piece of writing I took at all seriously was a project set by Mr. Stott where we had to find something in a newspaper and write a summary. I produced a detailed account of the Six Day War from 5–10 June 1967. Mr Stott was complimentary about it, but with a tone of surprise. He may have been unprepared because I was simply hopeless at reading out loud in class. The occasions when it was my turn were agony. I couldn't pitch the phrases so that they sounded like sentences. My eyes would focus on one word at a time and I would be unable to pronounce it at all. The class just had to move on to the next boy, leaving me baffled and ashamed. How could someone who took such interest in books be so inept at reading them aloud? And how did this person once bottom in English, who couldn't sight-read to save his life, turn into a person who three or four times a year stands up in public to recite his own words, who reads texts to his students every week, who teaches the intonation patterns of English to second-language learners, and does Harry Potter for his children on a nightly basis?

Perhaps the explanation is that my difficulty with hearing and reproducing the cadences of English was what introduced me to its complexities, to the ways in which words and phrases can mean quite different things if said in ever so slightly altered ways. Whatever the explanation, fluency and assurance about the sounds of words has never been my hallmark. Not being able to foresee the pitch contours of sentences meant reading the words one by one, without projecting onto them a presupposed sense of the sentence's meaning. That's perhaps a useful thing for a poet, because you avoid the pre-formed and presumed. Everything has to be found as if from scratch with the individual words forming the meaning-structures. Not being adept at reading aloud may have meant not being too preconditioned to the sounds that English sentences were supposed to make. Even as a graduate student at Cambridge, I recall one contemporary expressing surprise that I read poems with such unexpected implications, but it was also he who noticed that some lines of mine asked to be intonated in two distinct ways to mean relevantly different things.

So it looks like my difficulty with reading was what kept me at it, what pushed me towards being this kind of reader and writer. Fiction has also proved a problem. The difficulty is that I'm conscious of a permanent commentary going on in my head as I'm reading. It can be critical, but it may also be simply associative. So there I am, reading novels for English homework, or for term-time essays, or later so as to teach them, or for pleasure even, and I'll get to the bottom of the page only to realise nothing of the plot has stuck. Don't get me wrong: I went though all James Joyce (aside from *Finnegans Wake*) about this time, and can recall soaking my way through *The Waves* in the bath. Just as I read poetry against the grain of my sensibility and taste, so I manage a fair number of novels a year.

Yet they probably take me longer than for real addicts who give themselves up to them. I have to keep stopping to think or dream, then go back to pick up the thread of the story. The fact that lyric poems have relatively few words and have all those technical devices to focus interpretive attention may be why I manage with them better. It may also be that poems often invite an associative reading – or that you can learn how they're meant to sound, so they are halfway to being songs. Since they're so much shorter, you can readily experience their formal wholeness, while that of novels must be constructed over time in memory.

Often in poems it's not just a matter of reading the words either. As with jokes, you have to 'get' them. For similar reasons, I'm fond of reading aphorisms and books of philosophy that are written in short sections – Lichtenberg's pennyworths of truth or Wittgenstein's *Tractatus*. With the latter, it goes without saying, my first reading had me fairly baffled. Yet, again, those years of ploughing through technical histories may have borne fruit. It's perhaps not such a large stride, after all, from a book on early aeroplanes to the work of a philosopher whose oeuvre includes a patent for 'Improvements in Propellers Applicable for Aerial Machines' drawn up in Manchester during Wittgenstein's studies there, a patent accepted on 17 August 1911.

My final move from obsession with war to engagement in art came at the end of the first term at York University, when I arranged to transfer from the joint English and History degree to one in English only. R. T. Jones asked in the brief interview why I wanted to change course. Whatever my answer, I won't have said that already writing and meaning to write more, I would have to read both intensively and extensively. There was a French Symbolists paper being offered by my tutor, Nicole Ward Jouve, and I wanted and needed to take it. My grasp of languages was, and still is, by no means secure. Here's another case of an attraction to the experience of deciphering something that you don't wholly grasp. So what does all this go to prove? I've recently come across a reference to 'that endangered species, the general reader.' Yet who is this? We all have a story behind why we read or what we choose to read. And when it comes to readers, I've always preferred the particular to the general.

A PERFORMING ART

If you were to ask a poet if poetry is a performing art, you might discover from the answer much about the kind of poet to whom you were talking. For some poets, whose poems are made of sounds but not words, their work exists solely to be performed; others, whose poems are visual arrangements of letters or words in attractive images, justly aspire to the silence of a gallery. Performance gives rhythmic life to the sometimes cleverly arresting lyrics of pop songs, and there are poets who have tried to emulate the enthusiasm and appeal of pop concerts. For poets who do not make sound poems or concrete poems, are not would-be pop stars or performance artists, the question may be harder to answer. Speaking is inherently ambiguous, often requiring interpolation or gesture to make the meaning clear, and when you read a text out loud close attention is needed from the listener to distinguish, for example, 'torque' from 'talk' by the context, or 'where, as' from 'whereas' by the stress and intonation. In a publicity statement for one concert of readings the organisers said that they aimed to bring the lyre back into poetry. Without a text to which listeners might refer, their statement could well be mistaken for a rephrasing of the old doctrine that poets are liars and should be excluded from the city.

Why go and listen to poets reading their own work if the meanings may be obscure without looking at a copy of the printed words? Critics have drawn attention to the literary significance of Keats's physical stature, T. S. Eliot's dental record, Byron's deformed foot, or his dieting … A corpus of work is created by a particular body, and in the first place I'd go to see a poet read as much as, if not more than, to listen. I can still quite clearly picture Hans Magnus Enzensberger at the third of the biennial Cambridge International Poetry Festivals in June 1979 on stage in the darkened Corn Exchange. He was reading from his poem *The Sinking of the Titanic* in German and his own English translation. Enzensberger's face was extremely mobile: ingenuousness, sarcasm, disgust and pity passed across his features as he read. He had been in Italy and was wearing a white summer suit that seemed slightly luminous under the spotlights. When he reached the end of the poem where imaginary and symbolic passengers are swimming away from the ship, Enzensberger seemed to have turned the darkness of the Corn Exchange into an Atlantic Ocean.

Just as it can be a pleasantly confusing surprise to see for the first time the face of a radio personality whose voice is a part of your domestic furniture, so too putting a physical presence and a vocal timbre to poems you've read aloud to yourself adds a new tone to their music. Poems and lines that have seemed shapeless or badly constructed may appear to have form in the poet's own mouth. It's for you to judge whether or not the poem's supposed form is an imaginary rhythm forced onto the words – a rhythm they do not inherently sustain. The same may be true of a poet who believes a poem to be awfully affecting and who therefore changes tone of voice to convey this as the poem's false climax approaches.

There will be productive conflict between the rhythm and intonation of a poem. This struggle of the stress pattern with the implied emphases exists as a variable equilibrium within good poems. At a memorial reading of work by Vittorio Sereni, who had died two months before he would have attended the 1983 festival, these different aspects of his poetry were drawn out by the contrasting styles of his near contemporary Franco Fortini and the younger Maurizio Cucchi. Sacrificing some of Sereni's rhythmic continuity, Franco Fortini read expressively in a staccato – sharply emphasizing both syntactic stops and line-endings. The approach implied an interpretation of every detail, and was one of the most effective attempts I have heard to convey one meaning of a poem in a language foreign to most of the audience. By contrast, Cucchi read with little insistence in a quiet, melodic voice that finely conveyed the through-composed cadences of Sereni's lines and stanzas.

The ancillary art of poetry translation was tried in performance at each Cambridge Poetry Festival starting with the founder Richard Burns' in 1975. Listening to readings of poetry in other languages followed by English versions, you are confronted with both the untranslatable and the translated. The applause that greets a poem in another language passionately delivered by its writer may sometimes be little more than well-meaning homage to a principle, but much is to be gained from paying attention to the sound of other poetries and glimpsing different assumptions about its power in the unfamiliar modes of reading, little from defensively imagining that ours is the only possible situation. Nor is it satisfactory to argue that because poetry cannot be fully translated you should not bother with partial achievements. It is important to reflect at intervals upon Britain's position in the world, and one of the instructive places to do this is in an international poetry reading where such contrasting outlooks are implicitly and sometimes directly aired.

Both the English language and its poetry in Britain are incalculably indebted to influxions of linguistic influence from abroad; the quality of British poetry now and to come will depend upon the character of this country's life and culture, yet also upon an openness to the importance of developments elsewhere. Translators engaged upon the inherently vulnerable task of bringing something of their original over into English will experience divided loyalties to the art of the other and that of their own language; they are nevertheless an indispensable part of a poetry festival and a living literature. Because the translators have the advantage of an audience that can more readily understand the language of their piece, they had better not exploit that familiarity to up-stage, and further distance, the more intractable original. Rosemarie Waldrop's renderings of work by Edmond Jabès in 1979 are an exemplary instance for me, and in 1981 you could compare, after Josef Brodsky had read poems by Osip Mandelstam, a bevy of translators' attempts to convey, honour, rival and even possess the great Russian poet's texts.

Much can be deduced about poets' relations to themselves, their poetry and its public by what they say to the audience between poems. Some poets over-prepare the event; they not only know what pages they will read, but exactly how they will introduce each piece. Often they feel bound or tempted to explain what the poem is about: it is certainly more disappointing when they appear correct than when they seem wrong. Sometimes the audience hears an anecdote about how the piece came to be written, or is given a brief tour of the formative events in the growth of the poet's mind. At others they will be informed of the writer's political tendency or literary allegiances. Then there are the pieces of indispensable information required to catch the next poem's drift, or acknowledgements of homage and indebtedness. Judging the ratio of talk to poetry may imply tact in the writer as a person, though not necessarily as an artist. Some poets have humorous stories that they intersperse with readings, or bits of lightly ironic crowd control. Roy Fisher dedicated a poem to his audience in 1977 by saying something like: 'This is also for you as you've been so good… so far.'

Though poets sometimes under-prepare or seem not to have prepared at all, it need not follow that their reading will be a disaster. Certainly in the attacks of nerves that poets undergo during performances they are capable of forgetting where the next poem they'd thought of reading comes in their own collected poems. The more traditionally bohemian, under the influence of excessive socializing, have been known to lapse into embarrassing anecdotage – yet I can only recall two or three such calamities in a decade of festivals. When W. S. Graham read at Heffers bookshop one lunch time in 1981, he appeared neither well nor well prepared. In the lengthy silences and mumblings between and sometimes within poems you wondered if he would be able to continue at all. His wife was close at hand encouraging him and mentioning titles of pieces he might read. Yet perhaps there was an element of play-acting in his performance, of putting on the helpless and difficult man: his late and oddly scatty elegies to painters or the poem addressed to his sleeping wife were very well served by precarious delivery, remotely resonant and secure within their author's apparent self-confusion.

Hearing a poem that I like the sound of will probably lead me to the Festival bookstall; for the composed work has an ambivalent existence which seems satisfied neither by its utterance nor indeed its text alone. Between text and utterance too the combinations of emphasis are extensive. You might learn something of what your poet thinks or assumes about these two states from the word used to describe the action of turning a poem from an arrangement of print into one of air. Some poets rant, others declaim, some intone, others speak; they recite, or read, and some just say the poem. These varieties of delivery involve, as I have implied, different compromises between the meaning introduced into a sentence by the way in which it is spoken and the meaning a sentence introduces into a voice by the way it is written. Ezra Pound was drawing attention to the latter when he wrote a postcard to Mary Barnard on 23 February 1934:

> Thing is to cut a shape in time. Sounds that stop the flow, and durations either of syllables, or implied between them, 'forced onto the voice' of the reader by nature of the 'verse'.

I think this is the right emphasis for a poet to bear in mind when composing, but what would it do to the reading style? And is 'forced onto the voice' an accurate account of the relation between speech and writing when the poet reads?

You sometimes hear it said that a certain poet doesn't know how to read his or her own work. This may be a fair description of the situation, but it might also suggest that the concern has been primarily to write and that the poet believes the poem's character is in its cadences, its form, its syntax and diction – not in the emphases of particular words and dramatic intonation added by a performing and overtly interpreting voice. The poet may seem to be reading in an uncertain tone because a voice filled with the conscious awareness of what the speaker understands the piece to mean takes pre-emptive possession of both the poem and its auditors.

When a dramatist writes a part with a particular actress in mind he is shaping her speeches with the imagined sound of her speech shaping his. Staging a drama requires the directorial introduction of interpretive layers that can evidently make or mar what the dramatist wrote. But if you say that a poet didn't read his or her poem very well, you may also be implying that this doesn't matter: the business of making or marring has already taken place elsewhere before the poet steps onto the stage. A poem may be enhanced, but not realised from the podium. I don't much enjoy hearing actors performing poems because, excepting the most subtle and subdued, they so often seem to be attempting artificial respiration on a body which was already breathing without their assistance.

Soundless private reading is a solitary occupation. Within such isolation readers are free to gain pleasure and instruction according to the dictates of their own self-accompanying thoughts. You can always put the book down. At a poetry reading the listener is rather less at liberty. It's true that people sometimes leave ostentatiously to show their preferences or imply criticism. Yet occasionally even a favourite poet will read a piece you do not like and you are obliged to sit through it – whereas in the powerful privacy of silent reading you might flick over a few pages or throw the thing aside.

Though this social obligation to endure parts of a reading may seem a drawback of poetry in performance, it does instance the direct nature of the relationship between audience and writer, a relation normally concealed behind the processes of publication, bookselling, reviewing and reading. It is useful occasionally for both poets and readers to have the opportunity of acknowledging each other's existences. In any decent relationship there will be moments to endure as well as those you enjoy. A poetry festival is a place where the poets and the readers come face to face with the evident yet occluded fact that, though made in separated privacy, culture is produced by and for a community. Like the society of which it is a part, the poetry community is at odds with itself. Its strengths and weaknesses are inextricably intertwined. Fellow feeling and friendship jostle with envious rivalry; wounded *amour-propre* is trying to take its revenge while colleagues are honouring each other's labours. The atmosphere itself is vital.

The ability to listen to others with imagination and understanding is a rarer quality than people think. The very best poets are more likely to be good listeners than impressive talkers. Perhaps sometimes poets write because they find it hard to speak, or find silence intimidating. There are poets whose work seems an invitation to experience vicariously the outpourings of words that went into the self-expression their poems display. I prefer to imagine that good poetry encourages constructive listening. The moment of inspiration for some poets, or, more accurately, what distracts them into the thought of a poem, comes with the impinging of an unforeseen noise: a door slamming, an outboard motor, English heard in another country, a car backfiring, a cuckoo clock ... And the process of composition can be an attending to the silence within your head from which the words slowly or suddenly emerge in mutual associations of sound and sense.

Listening to poetry being read may be an example of a Wordsworthian wise passiveness. You sit still, open to influences, actively engaged. The degrees of concentration required vary from poem to poem, poet to poet. Attention spans are short, but can be trained to let us hear more, more thoughtfully. Like awkward moments between acquaintances when you rack your brain for words to ease the tension, the mute instant between a poet's uttering a work's title and the first line is a vacuum that draws you into it. By the end, the poet reading to you will have tried to transform that emptiness into a hush replete with the senses of words – like the intimate quiet of friends where speech is no longer necessary. The poem will have succeeded if you hear, within the silence after its final line, a great relief in the feeling that now at last nothing further needs to be said.

IN A TIGHT CORNER

The social sciences library of Bradford University was, in the early 1970s, and may still be, above a skating rink. The muffled sounds of that decade's dance music would seep up to the few students at work on a Saturday morning, insidiously whispering that fun was to be had elsewhere. Though not attached to the university, I used to accompany my girlfriend there and take advantage of its contemporary poetry collection, the shelved slim volumes in mint condition. Among the many books that nobody wanted to read, I pulled out one with a sepia photograph of a pre-war street party on the jacket and decided to give it a try. I've never been able to ice skate.

In the early 1970s, the elders of Bradford, who would a few years later have David Hockney's *A Bigger Splash* banned from his home town's flea-pits, were arranging for its Victorian Gothic centre (attacked by Ruskin for aesthetic-moral hypocrisy) to be replaced by a then already dated style of cheapskate brutalism. Sitting in the social sciences library, reading for the first time works such as 'City', 'For Realism' and 'The Memorial Fountain', I had in my hands a key to begin understanding the processes which were substituting one grim environment for another in the town that I would visit with my own romantic notions every other weekend. Bradford could even boast a small estate of new box-like council houses, where, in a cold December 1974, I helped deliver the Christmas post, locally called – no, not 'Toyland', but 'Toytown'.

It's been suggested recently by another poet of about my age that Fisher's writings are important because they make us 'foreign to ourselves'. That is not how it felt to read him in a half-demolished Northern town just two years after *Collected Poems 1968* had been published. I'd been introduced to a little modernist poetry ('Prufrock' and the 'Exile's Letter' from *Cathay*) in the sixth form, and followed up the lead in the school library by trying *The Waste Land* and 'Mauberley'. So even then it was possible to catch 'What are the roots that clutch, what branches grow / Out of this stony rubbish?' behind 'What steps descend, what rails conduct?' And a not-so-distant relative of the woman who had asked: 'What are you thinking? What thinking? What?' could be heard wondering 'At least – why can't you have more walls?' in 'Experimenting'. 'What have you been reading, then?' asks the 'I' character in the same piece: modernist poems written by men of my grandfather's generation might have been one reply. Not only did Fisher's poetry indicate that there was a line linking me through a book published when I was sixteen to those famous works of about half a century before, it showed that such ways of writing could be directly relevant to the immediate environment. They seemed to be at work on the world where I had been born and grew.

Most of my 1970s was spent trying to teach myself how to write. The poems I published in little magazines and small press editions reveal the homage that is paid by indelible influence. Unlike the hapless student of one of the 'Paraphrases' who exclaims that 'It is / too late! for me to change / my subject to the work of a more / popular writer', I changed my doctoral dissertation topic to the work of three contemporary English poets, one of whom was the 'please Mr Fisher' of that burlesque. When I finally plucked up the courage to inform the poet of this fact (we had been in very occasional correspondence for a couple of years), he replied with a finely wrought minimalist postcard. The printed 'University of Keele, Department of American Studies', holding-note read 'Thank you very much for your letter concerning', but had been firmly cancelled with a diagonal black line, and the solitary word 'Judas!' inserted – a word whose initial shock effect was only slightly relieved by the '& best wishes, Roy.'

When crises come, they throw us back upon whatever reserves and resources we may have stored away – and so it was for me in the early years of the 1990s living in Japan where I couldn't really speak the language, going through the accelerating break-up of that same relationship (by then a marriage) which stretched back to Bradford's social sciences library, and on top of it all waiting to undergo major surgery for the removal of a brain tumour. The years spent compulsively reading Fisher's writings had left many echoes in the back of my head; so finally I let them act as a set of magnets for other words and phrases: 'A Well-Made Crisis', its title from the third of the 'Seven Attempted Moves', catches a moment of desolation outside the art department in Kyoto University where I was confronted by some dusty plaster casts of European sculpture; another poem, set back in England, travels down 'the old paths trouble knows' from 'Diversions'; while the sequence 'A Burning Head' recalls one more question asked in 'Experimenting' ('Perhaps you've had a child secretly sometime?') with 'You'd got pregnant once and lost it? / How come I never knew?'

That same sequence describes being allowed home to convalesce about a week after the operation:

> Become a favourite of the night shift
> I hardly take up any time,
> am moved to ease bed shortages
> from ward to ward to visitors' room
> with apologies, repeated goodbyes: had left
> as if going home by gentle stages.

A glance at the earlier version of this sestet, published in *Stand*, reveals only too plainly its source: 'as if going home in easy stages' had been provided by another poem with a hospital connection. After the subsequent funeral in 'As He Came Near Death', we mourners 'got out into our coloured cars and dispersed in easy stages.' It was one of those echoes that had slipped under my guard, but the shame-faced revision is no more than a fig leaf. 'Built for quoting in a tight corner – / *The power of dead imaginings to return*' is how the third of the 'Diversions' describes such haunting visitations by, for example, 'the ghost of a paper bag'. In his self-review, Roy Fisher describes himself as 'an effective phrase-maker, and he'd be eminently quotable, if only anybody could find a reason to quote him.' But it's been among my lots in life to find a host of them.

LOST AND FOUND

Japanese hospitals don't exactly have an appointments system. If you think there's something wrong with you, you try to get there as early as the admission opens, enter your name on a list and then just wait for as long as it takes. It can take the best part of a day. During 1992, living in Sendai, I began to hear a faint tinnitus in my right ear and thought I was becoming slightly deafer in that one than in the other. There's a poem made of four fragments about this from *Lost & Found* (1997) called 'Hearing Difficulties'. It begins:

> About the shell of my right ear
> it's true there's something ominous.
> Added to the chorus
>   of voices I can hear
> is a thin, continuous
> rushing noise like the sound of the sea
> or like an old valve record player
> left on through the night.

That autumn, while taking tablets for a supposed inner ear infection, I started to feel stabbing pains across my right cheek, and, unconvinced by the private clinic's diagnosis, booked myself in to have some more extensive checks at the City Hospital – well, not booked myself in, because I'm afraid my Japanese wasn't that good; I'd been in the country for just over three years, and the English department assistant had volunteered to act as a guide.

Visiting professors in Japan can find themselves treated royally by students and colleagues, and the social attitudes towards academics are far more respectful than in England. Such things can go to your head, and on one occasion, waiting and waiting, I complained to our assistant, Yasushi Saito, about the lack of a more personal treatment. He quietly rebuked me. 'When it comes to sickness, we're all of us equal,' is what he said.

My first two years in the country had been spent in Kyoto, living in traditional-style houses, being taken to famous temples and beauty spots, suffering acute loneliness: my marriage was disintegrating, the time I spent alone being interrupted by brief and difficult visits from a wife whom I had known for over twenty years, but whom I was beginning not to recognise. The feeling may well have been mutual. This, however, is not the occasion to go into that story.

Japan being a place to learn patience, it must have been the third or fourth time we went through the hospital process that the specialist in the ENT department tentatively uttered the one word 'diagnosis' in English – and handed me a piece of paper with the words 'acoustic neuroma' on it. When I asked the assistant to ask him what it meant, the doctor again reached into his English vocabulary and found the words: 'brain tumour.' Out in the waiting area, among all the other people and their illnesses, I felt as if I'd been punched in the stomach:

> In a hearing clinic's waiting room
> someone's worse off than yourself;
> putting up the CT scan
> he shows what lies beneath the skin
> and bad news after hours of patience
> arrives in the shape
> of a paler shape about the size of a coin.

That half-line, 'what lies beneath the skin', remembers T. S. Eliot's phrase about Webster, who 'saw the skull beneath the skin' and 'was much possessed by death' – as indeed was I, sitting there among the other patients and digesting the simple words 'brain tumour': a diagnosis that (not knowing any better) I took to be tantamount to a death sentence.

In our head of department's office with the junior professor, Hiroshi Ozawa, and the assistant one day later, I found myself with a choice of having the tumour removed at the University Hospital in Sendai, or going back to England and undergoing the operation there. My decision to return home, where I could have family and friends nearby, was accepted with equanimity. So, at the ENT department in Addenbrookes, Cambridge, that early December, it was explained to me that mine was a benign tumour, and that, not being a cancer secondary, there was little chance of death (they had only lost one patient in some 80 operations) – though the side effects and the convalescence would be serious: partial deafness, some facial paralysis, headaches, chronic tiredness ... Since my tumour had been there for seven or eight years already, and was growing at a very slow rate, there was no danger in

simply adding my name to the waiting list. They would let me know
some time in January when the operation could be performed:

> 'God help you' comes from overseas.
> It means *the very best of luck*
> in the English of a Japanese,
> and it's true you need it when
>
> a consultant pats you on the knee
> offering some courage,
> lays his hands on you and says,
> 'You'll be wondering soon: why me?'

No sooner had I arrived in England than I began to receive 'Get Well'
cards (and a tiny origami crane) from Japan – from Shoichiro Sakurai,
for instance, the Kyoto professor who had first arranged for me to take
up a one-year post there as a visiting lecturer. His knowledge of idiom
is not perfect; but he evidently intended the phrase 'God help you' to
be taken literally, which is how I took it.

However, it was not until some time in February that the hospital
finally informed me that my operation was booked for 12 May 1993.
Long before being told this, I reported the basic situation back to my
department in Sendai by fax. Earlier in the new year, a reply had come
from Japan which said that since I couldn't say when the operation
was going to be, and could not fulfil my duties, my contract would
be terminated at the end of March. This seemed the final blow: I was
facing major surgery, my wife was divorcing me, and my job was lost as
well. As the poem says, '…why me?'

> But I was thinking: Well, why not?
> What would they mean, the hours of boredom
> and jokes about a poet going deaf,
> all things being equal in sickness and in death,
> if not that here's just another of those people?
>
> So when you tell him we're getting a divorce
> (letting him know as a matter of course)
> he replies, 'It never rains but it pours.'

That's how 'Hearing Difficulties' ends, with no mention of the threatened job loss. Among the many reasons for its absence from this autobiographical collage is that only a day or two after getting the message terminating my contract, I received another which said something like: 'disregard previous fax'. What had happened?

From what I later gathered, it seems the head of department (a year or two away from retirement age) had gone to the dean and described my health predicament. Together, with the best interests of their faculty in mind, they had decided to replace me, so as to make sure that the visiting professorship post was not lost through falling vacant should I be unable to return by 31 March 1993 to re-sign the annual contract. The Ministry of Education had been making noises about abolishing such positions and its loss would mean a reduction in the faculty's standing in the Japanese academic world. It would mean the end of a tradition: the post I held had been occupied by, among others, Ralph Hodgson, George Barker and James Kirkup.

When he heard of this decision, the junior professor had telephoned the older Kyoto academic – in tears, as I was later told. During my first year in Japan, he had listened to a paper I gave on *The Rape of Lucrece* at a Shakespeare conference in Shikoku, and when, the following year, a vacancy in Sendai had arisen, he contacted me about the possibility that I might take up the position. He would also become the head of department in just a year or two and had expected that I would be his colleague during the interval when there might well be only himself and the foreign professor to run the English teaching. With or without the encouragement of my Kyoto sponsor, the junior professor confronted his senior and protested that terminating the contract in absentia was not the right course of action.

Such behaviour is (I understand) rather unusual in Japan; after all, a junior member of a hierarchy had opposed his direct senior in the faculty and, what's more, he had done it at least partly in the interests of a foreigner – someone categorically outside the hierarchy. At this point, the head of department, Zenzo Suzuki, also did an unusual thing: he suggested that, since there was a conflict between what he had done and what his junior felt should have been done, they would resolve the dilemma by asking the opinion of the only other member of the department on a salary from the Ministry of Education: the assistant, Yasushi, who had accompanied me on my hospital visits. He supported the younger man's point of view against his professor, the professor whose sponsorship would assist him in finding a post of his own while I was away. It was then that I received the second fax.

Once the decision had been reversed, the senior man put himself out to make sure that the new line of action would succeed. There followed complex bureaucratic processes for arranging that the post should be kept open over the course of one semester. A special intensive course was arranged with a visit by the foreign professor at the University of Tokyo, so half my credits could be granted to the students, the other half being covered by the department head's extra classes on Natsume Soseki. I would go off salary, but continue to rent my flat, and had to promise to be back in Japan again by 14 September 1993.

You don't just get up and walk away from brain surgery. The removal of the tumour required an eight-hour operation and a twenty-four hour anaesthetic. Modern hospital practice, however, puts the emphasis on rapid recovery by pushing patients to become autonomous again as soon as possible. I have a clear memory within a surrounding blur of coming to consciousness in the intensive care unit, finding myself attached to various machines with wires and tubes. The team, when they realised this, made a bold attempt to get me back on my feet. But the removal of the right inner ear had destroyed my ability to balance, and I immediately collapsed to the floor. The result of this total failure at the first hurdle was that I was moved out of intensive care, put into a separate room – where, among other things, I wouldn't scare the patients awaiting similar operations.

Just ten days after, having relearnt how to walk and other basic bodily skills, I was released into the community for convalescence – a process that was interrupted a month later when I suffered an infection of the right ear which produced newly unbearable headaches and was thought to be meningitis. Being back in hospital for two weeks of intravenous penicillin, and with the prospect of a second investigative operation to find out and put right whatever might be wrong, made me begin to doubt whether I would make that September deadline. However, by the end of August, and without need of a second operation, the ENT specialist at Addenbrookes felt confident enough of my improvement to allow me to take the twelve hour flight to Japan. That autumn I was just about able to get through my classes, and kindly encouraged to cancel anything I felt unable to manage. Fortunately, the occasion didn't arise.

When I later spoke on the telephone to Sakurai, my Kyoto sponsor, who mentioned the junior professor's tears, he gave me a piece of advice. 'Don't,' he said, 'hold it against your head of department that he'd agreed to terminate your contract; it was nothing personal: he would have done the same with anyone in that situation.' Here was another lesson to learn.

However, reflecting over the years on what happened, I suspect the lessons may be more various and complex. After all, the junior professor and the assistant had not done the expected thing. If the older man, born in 1930, had behaved in what he thought were the best interests of the institution (regardless of the individual concerned), the younger, born in 1954, had done what he thought best (by following his own judgement and considering the individual). Nor, by trying not to take it personally, did I feel inclined to discount the kindness that had been shown me by the junior professor and the assistant, born in 1963 – a kindness which meant that within a year of returning to Japan I was able to become a father for the first time, and, within 18 months (the no-fault divorce come through), was free to marry my first daughter's Italian mother. Being an unemployed semi-invalid would have made both of those events much less likely.

When I first came to Japan it was to take up a job. I didn't come to develop a prior interest in the country, its language or arts. That I still live in Japan isn't only because over the years I've come to admire and enjoy qualities in the culture, qualities that have helped me grow in unexpected ways, it is because at a crucial moment a few individuals particularly wanted me to be here. I am, and shall be, eternally grateful to them.

OTTERSPOOL PROM

'O cursed spite'
Hamlet

There's a dazzle of sunlight on the low-tide river
and our far shore
has a silver-grey blur, bright as never, never,
ever before.

You see it's enough to bring tears to the eyes
by silhouetting trees,
winter boughs spidery on mist-like white skies
twitched in a breeze.

But then down the promenade its flyers release
their dragon-tailed kite;
frost on the pitches is shrinking by degrees;

a student's words return, her going 'England's shite!'
and I'm like 'Please
yourself' in sunshine born as if to set it right.

'Otterspool Prom' was first published in the *Times Literary Supplement* on 5 June 2008. I had not taught creative writing on a regular basis until I returned to England and came to work at the University of Reading, after my eighteen years in Japan. It's been intriguing and enlightening to lead weekly two-hour seminars in which students present their work, and have it discussed by their fellow writers. What has also been pleasantly surprising is the extent to which the group members, who if discussing a canonical author might have been fairly tongue-tied, would loquaciously engage in minutely constructive criticism of their contemporaries' writing, making points ranging from the adequacy of the punctuation to lacunae in plotting, character inconsistencies, and many other things that I hope they will go on to apply not only to their own writing, but also to the work of those canonical writers who had appeared to overawe them in literature seminars.

Most of the conversations have tended to be amicable and temperate, but occasionally there have been quite heated and vociferous exchanges. My poem 'Otterspool Prom' would not have come to be written without some words from the latter. One student's chosen project for the term was to write a collage prose piece based on gun crime in a Los Angeles high school. Most of the material for it had been discovered on the web, and then cast into an attempted imitation of Californian speech among armed minors in a poor district of the city. As chance would have it, there had happened to be, that term, a number of stories set in simulacra of American metropolitan areas; and in each case I had delicately raised the question of whether the handling of the spoken idiom was sufficiently convincing to carry the themes that were being explored. The bee in my bonnet at the time will have also contributed to what I was saying to the students, it being that the landscapes and societies of our own country are themselves a terra incognita under our very noses. It's not a new idea. George Borrow wrote in *Lavengro* (1851) that 'there are no countries in the world less known by the British than these selfsame British Islands'.

So I suggested to them, in the gentlest possible terms, that it helps when attempting creative composition, especially starting out, to write about something that you know, using experiences that have made strong impressions on you, and, most of all, that you can only make discoveries about the matter you want to write about if you attempt it in a language coming out of yourself. That way the sounds and associations of words can interact in your mind to generate phrases and sentences, which, when you work on them and read them back to yourself may well illuminate what you are doing, may teach you things about yourself, and thus, whatever the outcome, the process, with luck, will have been a benefit anyway. So I suggested to the student of the Los Angeles high-school gun-crime story that she consider setting the work in one of the areas of Britain where, sadly, we also have teenage violence of an equivalent kind, even if not on an American scale. I will have mentioned a few such inner city areas, including parts of the place where I'd been raised – reminded of Liverpool by the shooting of the 11-year-old Rhys Jones in the car park of the Fir Tree pub in Croxteth on the evening of the 22 August 2007. I had imagined that my line of thought to the seminar group was practically a self-evident truth, but could sense some crowd feeling developing against the idea...

'I can't do that,' the student replied, 'England's shite!'

Well, her words did make me laugh, and out loud if I remember, given that I'd spent the last eighteen years on the other side of the planet, making the most of my economic migration, enjoying what I could in a country not my own, and wondering what the circumstances might have to be for my return. I lost the argument too: none of the students who were presenting works located in high-threat transatlantic environments relocated them in our own backstreets. And I would say, though it may sound mean, that in retrospect the student's sudden outburst seems the most creative bit of language use she came up with during the term. After all, her two-word phrase had identified the theme she should have been exploring in her work. What had made her reach the age of nineteen feeling that these words might be a true representation of the country in which she'd grown up, and, if they were, why? Her words got under my skin, if not on my nerves, interacting with snippets of usage and quotation filed away in the recesses of my mind. Back at the beginning of the 1970s, I had been taken through *Hamlet* in minute detail for A-level. Not long after that creative writing seminar, my thoughts somehow drifted to Marcellus's 'Something is rotten in the state of Denmark'; to Hamlet being sent to England where it is 'no great matter' if he doesn't recover his wits because 'there the men are as mad as he' (as if Shakespeare added that plot twist just to work in the joke); and to Hamlet's couplet from Act 1: 'The time is out of joint: O cursed spite / That ever I was born to set it right!' The student's word 'shite' might have helped me recall the rhyme words, and I made up a short version of Hamlet's predicament: 'O cursed spite / Denmark's shite.'

A week or two after this incident we drove up to Liverpool for an overnight with my parents and, as is our habit, went out for a Sunday pub lunch on Otterspool promenade with its view across the river Mersey towards the Wirral side. It was a day of bright diffused misty sunlight in mid-February, a day briefly evoked as best as I can in 'Otterspool Prom', an improvised sonnet which was not planned as such before the writing process. I had jotted down words and phrases about some of the phenomena that moved me and made my eyes water, along with the odd accidental detail, like those people flying their Chinese-style kite.

English is not a language especially rich in rhymes. If the phrases I'm noting down seem to point towards a poem whose materials don't demand to be extended very far, and contain phrases with three rhyming echoes, then my mind will turn to the Petrarchan sonnet, a form requiring triple rhymes in its sestet. But the key thing that had to take place for the poem to happen was the association of that stirring scene beyond the pub window with the words of the creative writing student. Maybe the sudden plethora of rhymes helped that happen too. Not only is there the 'spite / kite / shite / right', but also the other sestet rhyme, foreshadowed in the second quatrain: 'trees / breeze / release / degrees / Please'.

Contributing to this association, there could have been the background of Rhys Jones's shooting, though I don't recall it consciously impinging on the writing process. I was certainly aware of the evident emotional contradictions in the student's words, and my relief at having finally returned home, where the feeling of shame at your native land, which is unlikely to arise in an expatriate elsewhere, is natural. Relief and shame: so the problems of being away and of being at home were combined for me in the implications of that student's colloquial phrase. Then what will have made me think there was something apt about imitating the youth-speak of 'I'm like' followed by the more long-in-the-tooth colloquialism, 'Please / yourself', must have been that it exemplifies the process of her words getting under my skin to the extent of sounding like her, and then performs an attempt to recover a dialect equilibrium of my own. Maybe the hook-line to Ricky Nelson's 'Garden Party' was also coming to my rescue: 'You see, you can't please everyone, so you got to please yourself.'

'No! I am not Prince Hamlet, nor was meant to be', as T. S. Eliot has it. Behind the arras of 'Otterspool Prom' there may, I fear, be a tired old Polonius advising the young, prompted by an ingrained temptation to try and take responsibility for the state of things; and yet, in the poem's concluding transfer of Hamlet's words from the Prince's duty to the sunshine that Sunday lunchtime, there may also be a recognition of limits to what can be amended, along with an implicitly expressed need for things still to come right, and not just for me in my return home, but more widely – as subliminally articulated in the closing rhymes of the intuited sonnet form. My hope is that in reading the poem, preferably aloud, you hear echoing within you the working out of those contradictory feelings and that analogy for a state of things being wrong, and of things still needing to be set right.

NOTE ON 'SEIN UND ZEIT'

SEIN UND ZEIT
for Nadja Guggi

Light's going, going out over the houses,
built above a century ago;
yet what they saw of attrition's losses,
no, I wouldn't know.

But now this one long up for sale
is sold, is nearly emptied;
and by a wrought-iron area railing,
you appear to stand aside
from the few things offered us:
a bread bin with BREAD printed on it,
firewood and some kindling
set down like a Grecian temple ...

Bare feet on the grey pavement's grain,
toes curled to grip, you try and talk
with your faint German accent
today of all days, to explain
the choked tone's from torn vocal chords,
then rub a suntanned throat
hurt in that tourist route attack –
your own Moroccan incident...

You try to say the words,
and it's as if a hundred years
were summed up in the half-throttled sounds
of a woman speaking.

4 August 2014

'Sein und Zeit' is a poem that characterises some of the things that happen when I manage to write, and has the added benefit, for me at least, that it came fairly promptly and found a form I liked. Among my favourite poets is Umberto Saba, inventor, as far as I know, of lyrics shaped from a short opening stanza, then a longer development of the stated theme, and a concluding line, or couplet, or brief verse. I had first encountered it as borrowed by Vittorio Sereni for a number of his lyrics. Almost as soon as I'd drafted the first few lines in my notebook a day or two after 4 August 2014, it seemed the poem might evolve into such a form, though it was only during the revising that it achieved its chiastic shape, like an ABBA rhyme scheme, in which the opening quatrain and octave is then matched by a reversed octave and quatrain. As I say, it came quickly, and though I retained the date '4 August 2014' at its foot as part of the poem's meaning, there is a nearly completed draft with multiple layers of correction in different coloured pens dated Thursday 7th. The poem needed condensing by three lines; it needed to lose some overemphatic rhymes, and to have its middle eights adjusted; and it was all but done on the following day.

It is dedicated to Nadja Guggi, the typographer and designer for Two Rivers Press, with whom I have worked on a number of poetry books and anthologies. As the poem notes, she had recently been able to sell her terrace house, just around the corner from where we live, and we had been invited to go and collect some things that she was giving away – which we happened to do in the early evening on the one hundredth anniversary of Britain's declaration of war with Germany. Nadja is a native of that country, now permanently resident in this one, and the coincidence of my wife and I visiting her on that day, of all days, had already struck me as we walked along the east-west facing street leading up towards her house. The sun was beginning to set, the roofs of the east-facing terrace casting into shadow most of the west-facing façades, façades still caught by the sun's last rays.

'The lamps are going out all over Europe, we shall not see them lit again in our life-time,' Sir Edward Grey is reported to have said one hundred years before, and the sunset reminded me of his remark, while, despite the WW2 song 'When the Lights Go on Again (All Over the World)', it's possible to wonder whether, in the metaphorical sense that the British Foreign Secretary meant, we have seen them lit again yet. The terrace houses in the streets around where we live were built by the firm of Huntley & Palmers in the Edwardian era to house their workforce, and the nearby St Luke's church hall has a brass plaque inside which records that it was used as a clearing station for the wounded repatriated during the 1914–18 war, doubtless because the Royal

Berkshire Hospital is just a few hundred yards further on. Volunteers and recruits for the local regiments will have come from these terrace houses; but how many of them were the locations of family mourning, no, as the poem admits, I wouldn't know.

Although I have done little more than leaf over the pages of Martin Heidegger's *Sein und Zeit* (Being and Time), I happened to have recently re-read his essay entitled 'On the Origin of the Work of Art' for an aesthetics study group, and have a passing acquaintance with some of his more familiar concepts, such as that encapsulated in the expression 'Dasein', or 'being-there', and I'm aware too of his compromised associations with National Socialism. So I was to some extent primed, you might say, to be struck by a number of coincident things as Nadja stood on the pavement outside her house in a little black Greek-style summer tunic-dress and bare feet, with the useful objects we were taking away placed on the pavement, explaining to us why she had such a hoarse-sounding voice, and was finding it so difficult to speak.

In Heidegger's essay there's a homage to Greek temples and a discussion of Van Gogh's boots, the difference between the boots and the painting of them, prompting thoughts about the being of things in themselves, their having art-significance attributed to them, and their use function, as well as the relation between the usefulness of objects and the usefulness of the words that name them, the bread and the bread-bin and the word 'Bread' on the bin – and of words in speech acts, such as explaining (as Nadja was), and the same words in poems, that can explain too, but also 'condense', which, Ezra Pound's *ABC of Reading* first informed me, is the meaning of the German word 'Dichtung' (poetry). Hence the difference, too, between what I am doing now, and what I was doing when composing the poem. And, though I didn't know it at the time, there is, it appears, an expression used in their classical studies: 'griechischen Figurengedichte' (Greek figure-poems) – of which my 'Sein und Zeit' might be an unconscious imitation.

It turned out, as my poem does its best to catch in a compact and evocative way, that Nadja had been on holiday to Morocco and, while camping in the desert, had awoken to find someone attempting to strangle her. Another coincidence there – I will have thought – vaguely recalling the Agadir, or Second Moroccan Crisis, of July 1911, one of the many causes of the First World War, when the German government sent their gunboat, the *Panther*, in response to the massing of French troops in the interior. Again, the report of that violent incident, overlaid with the temporarily averted threat of war, seemed symbolic of individual experience under the shadow of public events, and especially for women over the last century (and before), when vulnerable subjectivities have endured many forms of suppression, a suppression that can render what isn't quite said even more expressive. And this might be an exemplary instance of when lyric poetry finds it has something to say, not least because it too occupies such a marginalised position in our commercial-technological world.

So the scene was set: a woman is standing before me, trying to speak, a victim of aggression and co-national of a country that has twice in the last century been concertedly aggressive towards my own, and, in retaliation, vice-versa. Her *being* and our *time* have been yoked by violence together. The lyrical subject, indicated as it appears only once, immediately to withdraw by means of that shrugging expression in the fourth line, has attempted to turn his poem, through its second-person address, and allow the other figure to speak in it; but she can't (it's a lyric poem, and she's half-strangled), so he has to write in such a way as to try and evoke her vocalisation – in which endeavour he is, strictly speaking, bound to fail. Then he has to show the poem to its dedicatee and hope that she isn't offended by its obliquely epideictic presumption. And the fact that you have read it here means, I'm relieved and grateful to report, that she wasn't.

BALKAN DIARY

As chance would have it, on 23 June 2016 at 10:15 in the continent of Europe, an hour earlier according to British summertime, I stood up before a small audience in the Faculty of Philology, University of Montenegro, Nikšić, to give a keynote lecture called 'At Home from Home: A Poet's Experience of Country and Migration'. This was to be my contribution to a conference with a very long subtitle called *Writing Places: The Conceptualisation and Representation of Space, Location and Environment in Literature*, in the course of which I illustrated, with a couple of poems each, three familiar points: the attempt to feel at home in a primal landscape that has failed to sustain a secured sense of belonging; the attempt to feel at home in a place to which you have migrated, but where you are treated by definition as a foreigner or alien; and the attempt to feel at home in a place where you are assumed or taken to be at home, but where you continue to feel isolated and displaced. In my case these happen to be growing up in the industrial and pre-post-industrial northwest of England, living for eighteen years in Japan as an economic migrant, and returning to live in the United Kingdom for the last nine years.

The day before had found me on a 6:15 am flight out of Bristol with two other contributors to the conference, Tom, one of its co-organisers, and Mary, a freelance sound recording archivist and curator. It was a rainy morning and the departure area was crowded with a great many people queuing to get through security, heading for easyJet destinations all across Europe. The initially anxiety-creating crush had been caused, it seemed, by an out-of-order escalator, and we were soon enough through into the departure lounge. Yet there did seem a very large number of travellers intent on escaping from an English June, though whether from the weather or political climate I didn't have a way of ascertaining – though it was an unhappy mixture of both for my travelling companions and me.

Dubrovnik was our flight's destination, and we arrived there safely some two and a half hours later. I had never been in the Balkans before. The entire region was experiencing a sudden heat wave, and a familiar wall of warmth met us at the door of the aircraft. The marble pavements and Venetian-style façades in its old town would dazzlingly gleam in eyes unprotected by sunglasses as we set off in search of lunch. Our leisurely seafood meal by the harbour-side over, we walked a little way around the outside of the old castle walls so that Mary could take a dip in the Adriatic. There we could scan the heights above the bay where the Serbian and Montenegrin artillery had shelled the town late in 1991, and we could pick out in the stonework where this historic jewel, named Ragusa by the Italians, had been artfully reconstructed, as a neater simulacrum of the place it once had been. Walking back towards our meeting point for the pre-arranged transport into Montenegro, we passed the shop of a local artist, Ivo Grbić, whose frontage is a memorial to the bombardment – emblematic of the not forgotten, even when the reconstruction of the town has, superficially, effaced its results.

At the latitude of Dubrovnik the Croatian state, which declared independence in 1991 and joined the EU in 2013, is little more than a coastal strip at the foot of mountainous terrain into which we were being driven towards the border with Bosnia-Herzegovina – which is not in the European Union. We would then be taken across the lower end of that country to enter Montenegro, also outside, in the course of a drive of less than two hours. Our return the following Sunday would see us travelling the short taxi-ride from Herceg Novi in Montenegro to Dubrovnik airport, crossing back into the EU. Since borders are not normally internationally collaborative, this brief tour around the Western Balkans would see us going through two passport controls for each of the three borders we would cross. Whether lonely mountain outposts with a mangy dog rummaging amongst debris, or the toll-booth-style highway checkpoint just south of Dubrovnik airport, there we experienced a stasis and routine that I had not encountered in continental travel, it crossed my mind, since the establishment of the Schengen area – where your mobile phone pings to let you know the country is no longer France but Belgium, not Belgium but Holland. Opposite the stamp in my passport when I entered the United States for a mini-book-tour in late 2006, there is now one to prove that Montenegro accepted me within its borders on 22 June 2016.

Outside Dubrovnik, and the Adriatic coastal strip, whether in Bosnia Herzegovina or Montenegro, the condition of the architecture that we encountered bore more than a passing resemblance to the seventies tower blocks in parts of my own primal landscape. In Nikšić, much of the domestic housing dates from the Tito era, and is still spattered, at ground level, with the remnants of conflict-marking graffiti. There was hardly any traffic in the part of town where we stayed, in a three-star hotel next to the Faculty of Philology. Global consumer capital, too, did not appear to have made many inroads into the lifestyle or superficial appearance of the place. Its executives must have made profit-and-loss calculations that suggested it wasn't worth the trouble. During lunch breaks or before dinner, we would regularly resort to a quiet bar with an outside terrace awning on a corner across the street. It was called *Casa Mia*, which, given my marital connections with the other side of the Adriatic, did provide a home from home of sorts.

The morning after giving my paper on country and migration, I headed down to breakfast in that Nikšić hotel. My instinct was to feel, though anxious and uncertain, that the bookies' odds, and upsurge of support for Remain in the wake of the MP Jo Cox's murder would mean, as Derek Mahon put it, that everything was going be all right. The approaching summer recess could then be spent mending the rips in the political and cultural fabric that the referendum campaign had made only too manifest. In the hotel dining room, the only one of the conference attendees to have already come down was Timothy, a Native American from the University of Central Oklahoma. He had Internet on his phone and was telling me the result when Tom and Mary arrived in a state of shocked disbelief, telling me that David Cameron had resigned. This moment of ashen-tasting breakfast, and the response of those voting to Remain to their defeat would manifestly reveal that the referendum for many had not fundamentally been about the complexly technical issue of sovereignty, or the economic benefits of being in a single market. It had been, you might say, about immigration – but not whether there was too much or not enough, but what it meant about our country and its mentality if we had voted (for the people have spoken, as we would be repeatedly reminded) to 'get back control of our borders'. The disorientation was palpable as I headed back to my room through the door marked EXIT.

The final stage of the conference, after all the papers had been given, would be a Saturday in Herceg Novi by the sea, the temperature a difficult 34 degrees centigrade. That evening the conference organiser, Marija, and her partner Neil, director of the film *Reel Injun* (2009), took Mary and Philippe, a Belgian professor of Spanish whom we had hooked up with at the conference, to a seafood restaurant in the old town called the *Tri Lipe* – its three trees' branches intertwined as in that song 'Cherry Pink and Apple-Blossom White'. Marija, it being the last night, told us the story of her life during the break up of Yugoslavia and the recent Balkan Wars. We heard of the familial interconnections between what are now separate countries, the accusations that she was a Croatian spy, the hiding of refuges from the other side, insults hurled in the street, acute food shortages, her escape to Sweden and return... and much more besides. I was particularly surprised to hear her say that the Italian occupation between 1940 and 1943 was less bad than now. The tensions between the different countries were everywhere to detect, while, at the same time, delegates at the conference from across the area had collaborated and listened to each other without any such conflict, and we had sat down to meals together. It reminded me of a conversation with a Leave campaigner outside our house a few weeks before. I had agreed with him about what the Euro-zone had done to employment in southern Europe (having seen signs of it myself in Elche at a poetry festival in April). I felt no hostility towards him at all. It was just that I didn't blame the EU, but the policies of the banking system and their government defenders, encouraged to act as they did, in many cases, by domestic voter pressure too.

Once located on the bus to the plane at Dubrovnik, we found ourselves in conversation with a couple from Bristol returning home from a holiday in the Balkans, one where they had enjoyed Internet and television access, so brought us up to date with the resignations of the Labour shadow cabinet. They too had postal-voted Remain. It was a relief at least to find we belonged to a large and sympathetically articulate minority – which had not been my experience when returning from Italy at Easter 1982, the Falklands/Malvinas conflict having broken out in my absence. After landing safely and returning to the rain and wind, we found that the taxi driver from Bristol airport, eager to talk about what had happened, was married to a French woman who had worked as a schoolteacher in the UK for several decades. The city had voted Remain, we already knew, but here was a Remain-voting taxi driver who told us that his wife felt outraged at the ingratitude the result implied. Back in Reading, my Italian wife had doctored the I'M of our window-poster by crossing out the apostrophe and inserting 'w-a-s' across the three white down-strokes of the letter M.

There was already a petition, we'd discovered over breakfast in Herceg Novi, for a second referendum set up by a Leave voter before the plebiscite, who, fearing they might lose, demanded that if there were not a sixty-per-cent vote one way or the other the result should not be allowed to stand. This has now, in the first days of July, garnered over four million signatures. In the days to come I would hear on radio and television of 'the decision of the British people' or that 'the UK has decided', and that we must abide by its decision. Here was an interesting instance of political synecdoche, where a part (the decisive 1 million or so, out of something more than 65 million inhabitants in total) was taken as the whole. Thus, though a raw majority from the turnout had voted Leave, this by no means meant that everyone else now accepted the decision as 'the will of the people' – even if politicians on both sides were understandably unable to say they would not respect the not-legally-binding result. What the UK had 'said' is that we disagree.

While still in Montenegro we had also become aware of the cultural-geographical fracturing that the referendum had laid bare, with London, Bristol, and other cities, a majority of Scotland and Northern Ireland (the latter divided on this question too along sectarian lines) voting to Remain, while, as my recent visits to seaboard and marginalised parts of the country had suggested, the rural areas and the coastlines had tended to leave. Some days later I was to be informed that Reading had voted firmly to Remain, as indeed had Wokingham, its sitting MP, John Redwood, a famously staunch Euro-sceptic Leaver. The news that a majority of young people had voted to remain was also upsetting, my daughters of 19 and 21 being among them (they discovered the result in Japan, while revisiting childhood haunts). It also appeared that those with university degrees had predominantly voted to Remain while those without had preferred Leave.

The sight of Wiltshire under heavy grey clouds and steady rain from the Great Western Railway as we sped towards Paddington, stopping at Reading on the way, was as good an instance of the pathetic fallacy as I could have wished for at such a moment. At this stage in my dawning realisations, the overwhelming feeling was one of loss – though not so much because the vote had been lost as what that loss implied. This is not something that can be readily got over, or moved on from. For if 'getting our country back' is one thing for a political elite who want to run the state, only to discover that they are constrained by many things, of which the EU turned out to be the most readily blamable – though our own faceless, unelected bureaucrats in the Civil Service have also been targets of politicians frustrations in the past, and will doubtless be again. It is another if your hometown or village has been impoverished by nearly four decades of government policy, and another again if by their very protesting that they want theirs back, you have further been stripped of the spirit and the fact of your own.

Just a week after that day on the Adriatic coast at Herceg Novi, I was perched on a bed, now located in his living room, belonging to the writer Roy Fisher, who, given Geoffrey Hill's death not forty-eight hours before, has an even fairer claim to be one of England's most important living poets, a poet much admired and supported by commissions for work from the current Laureate, Carol Ann Duffy. The presenting symptom of my visit was the need to correct the proofs of his latest collection, *Slakki: New and Neglected Poems*, due out from Bloodaxe Books this autumn, which I had edited in the light of his increasing physical frailty. Naturally enough, we also exchanged views on the current state of the nation (see Fisher's 'The National Poem'), the fracturing of the main political parties, the fearful difficulty of imagining what our fellow citizens were thinking, and what might follow from their divided and conflicted decisions.

Driving home so as to be in Reading when our daughters arrived back from their Japanese sojourn, we lost our way on the roads to the south of Earl Sterndale, and improvised with the help of only a dad-nav by heading south-west across the Derbyshire National Park and into north Staffordshire. We were following an unfamiliar, hilly road through little towns and villages towards Cheadle and Uttoxeter, so as eventually to reach Litchfield and the M6 Toll. The weather had been changeable all day, with heavy downpours, periods of sunshine, and great piles of cloud heaping up and collapsing, shine and cloud trailed across the turning windscreen. The greenery was lush and the light at times sublime.

Yet what I remember most from that journey south was the number of Union Jacks and Crosses of St George flying in the gardens of bungalows and semis, and a glorious double rainbow which happened to form across the carriageway of the M40 later that afternoon. But while those flags might have been celebrating the country's newfound 'independence', asserting the identity of a *Sinn Fein* England in a neo-nationalist UK, or still lamenting the exit of its football team from the Euros, there was no doubt that those banners were intent on meaning something; while the double rainbow, I had to remind myself, didn't herald the safe return of our two darling daughters to these shores (though that would gratefully occur some few hours later), no, it intended nothing – which was one reason why its 'coalition' colours could be the more happily enjoyed, at least by me. For those two rainbows were, as I put it in the last line of a poem written more than thirty years ago, 'the oldest illusion in the sky.'

PARMESE DAYS

Pairing the word Enigmas from various canvases by Giorgio De Chirico with one taken from the endless beginning of *Finnegans Wake*, 'Enigmas and Environs' is the title given to a set of twenty-five poems associated with the San Leonardo district of Parma, Italy. Facing north in the direction of the river Po, this suburb extends, at least for me, beyond the railway line on the edge of the city, from via Palermo as far as via Genova, and along via Venezia from via Trento to via Trieste. It's a compact quarter of small factories, mostly now repurposed, and post-war housing where my wife and her sister grew up, and where my mother-in-law still lives – not far from our apartment, with its slowly diminishing mortgage, a little fourth-floor flat which allows us to spend holidays with them when we are free of work obligations in England. We were there over the 2019 festive season, and on Christmas morning my elder daughter accompanied me on a constitutional stroll about the city.

Via Paradigna, which takes its name from the tiny hamlet towards which it leads, is the street with our address, and out towards the ring-road we went, passing by the villa – a portion of whose park was sold off for the construction of our building at number 11, built in a late-modernist style during the 1980s. We then turned left along via Corini and on into piazzale Salsi with its swings and slides where our daughters played in childhood. On via Genova we skirted the now largely demolished edges of the Bormioli Rocco & Figlio glass factory. Its remnants look like nothing so much as one of those portrayed on easels in metaphysical interiors from De Chirico's Ferrarese period. This is the route we would usually take to our favourite local restaurant, the Tirolese, which, despite its name, specialises in seafood.

My plan was to walk along the Lungoparma, the promenade-road parallel to the river – strictly a torrent, which can flood in winter, be dry in summer – and continue as far as viale Rustici 26. This was the first address I ever visited in the town, some thirty-five years ago. Its second floor flat facing the river was where the poet Vittorio Sereni's eldest daughter, Maria Teresa, who was sadly to die prematurely of cancer in 1991, then lived with her husband Nico and daughter Laura. I had gone there with Marcus Perryman to discuss our translations of her father's poems. Sereni had himself died not long before that first visit on 10 February 1983, just two months before he would have read at the

Cambridge International Poetry Festival. I had been reading European poetry since university, Italian increasingly since the later 1970s, and it was thanks to his poetry, then, and especially a late poem called 'In Parma with A. B.' that I was introduced to the town – the 'A. B.' being his friend Attilio Bertolucci, the poet and father of the film director Bernardo.

Marcus and I had driven down from Verona, parked the car, and wandered between Liberty-style mansions in that part of the city. We rang the bell and after some coffee and a little work, around lunchtime Maria Teresa led us past the ramparts of the Cittadella, where Fabrizio del Dongo is supposedly imprisoned in *The Charterhouse of Parma*, on to the old Pianetino restaurant where I ate, for the first time, tortelli made with pumpkin or with chard and ricotta – Parma specialties. As Sereni puts it in his 'Pre-War Letter' of 1938, it's good to be introduced to a town through the poetry it has inspired, and in that late poem he recalls the time before the Second World War when he'd 'have liked to be you / the poet of this city'. The poet's wife, Maria Luisa Bonfanti, was a native of Felino, a town famous for its cured pork products not far from Parma in the direction of the Apennines. Sereni's first collection, *Frontiera* (1941), includes 'Storm at Salsomaggiore' set in the spa town nearby and touching on a temporary setback in their courtship, while 'To M. L. Passing above her Town in an Express Train' finds the poet travelling along the raised railway line that marks, the length of via Palermo, one extremity to my wife's part of town.

The Serenis' first daughter, known as Pigòt in the family, was born in July 1941 and spent her earliest years in Felino with her mother's family. Meanwhile her father was surviving his disastrously anticlimactic military service that led to capture, on her second birthday, by an American airborne division near Trapani in western Sicily on 24 July 1943, the eve of Mussolini's fall from power, and his daughter's second birthday. There followed two years as a POW in Algeria and French Morocco. In light of having read 'Pre-War Letter' and Sereni's review of Bertolucci's early poetry collected in *La capanna indiana* (1951), I had stumblingly asked the poet himself about his Parmese friend's poetry when we met for the second and last time at the Mondadori offices in Segrate, Milan. That was at Easter 1982 in the lead-up to the Falklands War, a moment the poet later commented on in print by linking the experience of the Argentinian defenders of the island to his own war experiences in 'Port Stanley like Trapani'. He recommended me to look at Bertolucci's then most recent volume, *Viaggio d'inverno* (1971), a presumably Schubert-inspired title, which I immediately set out to do.

As chance would have it, I was to encounter a young woman from Parma in the year following Sereni's death. We met in an advanced-level language class in the Studio School of English, Cambridge, on 18 June 1984. The course I was teaching on lasted only two weeks, but by the end of those ten school days my meeting her had left me shaken and torn between attraction and resistance, calm and disturbance, gratitude and renunciation. I was at the very least infatuated, and imagining how, when I next went to Parma in aid of our Sereni translations that September, I would try and see her again. This would have been all very well, but for the fact that I had been married to an English woman since November 1979, to someone I had known since the summer of 1971. We had been through many things together, including the traumatic near-death experience some nine years before of witnessing in Italy her sexual assault at gunpoint, five months after which we had been at the Tribunale di Milano face to face with the accused at his trial for an act of 'violenza privata'. So it was that, after meeting this Italian girl, my heart and head were saying different things, and there was I not knowing which way to turn.

There followed some three years in which the city of Parma came to be the imagined site of fugitive temptations, followed by a further six in which it was as good as out of bounds, while I engaged in acts of attempted reparation towards my marriage, attempts that came to an end in February 1992, when it rapidly unravelled. During those years, I must have made three or four visits to viale Rustici so as to work on the Sereni translations. After the first, in September 1984, I did meet Ornella Trevisan, the language student from Cambridge, and then again, the following year, when I wrote the acrostic 'Aria di Parma'. The next to last visit to Maria Teresa was in April 1986, immediately after the notorious air attack on Tripoli, during a ten-day amorous fugue in Ornella's apartment at via Nazario Sauro 11. And 13 April 1986 was the first time that I visited the San Leonardo quarter, invited to her twenty-ninth birthday dinner in the family.

Six years later, my first marriage coming to pieces, I had been teaching at universities in Japan for nearly three years and had recently accepted a position as the foreign teacher in the English Department of the Faculty of Arts and Letters at Tohoku University in Sendai. With that marriage effectively at an end, I visited Parma again in March 1992 and talked about the possibility of our being able to have a life and family together. There would be further obstacles in our way, including the diagnosis of a benign brain tumour in November of that same year. Yet this also focused the mind as only extreme circumstances can, and it was in Parma I decided to spend my six months on the waiting list for the NHS operation, an operation that took place on 12 May 1993 – the day the town's football team won the European Cup Winner's Cup at Wembley. I already had all the reason in the world to clap our National Health Service long before it was called upon to cope with a pandemic.

But the fact is that we were only able to become a couple because I was in receipt of a salary from that national university in Japan, a position which I retained during the brain-tumour crisis thanks entirely to the generosity of colleagues in the department there. This alone made it possible for us to be together and raise a family. So my love for a Parmese woman could flourish on the condition that we both renounce the desire to live in her town, which did seem easier for her than me – but then she grew up there, and while you may take the girl out of Parma, you can't take Parma out of the girl. This was why as soon as the four-month spring semesters were over in Japan, and sometimes earlier for her and our two girls, the family would come back to Europe and spend the best part of two months in *la petite capitale d'autrefois*, as Stendhal's highly fictionalised setting for his novel is sometimes called in honour of the influence Napoleon's second wife Maria Luigia had on it in the aftermath of the Congress of Vienna. The dialect, for instance, is peppered with terms for everyday objects – potatoes (*pom da tera,*) tomatoes (*tomachi*), earrings (*boclèn*), money (*franch*), and corkscrews (*tirabusòn*) come to mind – all corrupted from the French.

It was during those hot summers in the Po valley that I became familiar with the local squares, the parks and playgrounds, swings and slides in the San Leonardo quarter of Parma. Those were also the years when I first got to know other expatriate writers who had made a home in the town, chief among them Wallis Wilde-Menozzi, author of *Mother Tongue: An American Life in Italy*. I was with Wallis and her local writing group on 11 September 2001 when news of the attack on the World Trade Center reached us. We were due to fly back to Japan and experience those new airport conditions just five days later. More recently I have come to know Alex Jones, who composed directly in Italian *Il traduttore* (The Translator), a detective novel set in

Parma; and now, even more recently, Tobias Jones, writer *inter alia* of *The Dark Heart of Italy* and *Ultra: The Underworld of Italian Football* – these Joneses-to-keep-up-with both introduced to me through the good offices of Carlo Ferrari, self-styled 'apprendista libraio' (apprentice bookseller), proprietor of a Mondadori bookshop in the commercial centre near via Paradigna, and a dedicatee in 'Enigmas and Environs'.

Five months before that Christmas constitutional around Parma, my elder daughter had returned home from a year living and working in Switzerland. Her relationship, of three years' standing, with a Swiss-German speaker had come to a sudden and calamitous end. In the course of that break-up, she had discussed the problems of settling in the Zurich area with an American who had also moved to the country for romantic reasons. He had remarked on the difficulties involved in 'importing love', as he called it, across language and cultural frontiers – and we took up that theme both in the light of her own recent experiences and those longer ones of the relationship that had brought her and her sister into the world some two decades before. For our daughters spent the first ten and twelve years of their lives in Japan, the offspring of a British father and an Italian mother, examples of what I believe are called 'third-culture kids', with multilingual upbringings, complex identities and complicated relationships to wherever they happen to find themselves. There was plenty of ground to cover, and our intensive conversation had taken us all the way to the vicinity of that flat in viale Rustici 26, Parma.

By now I was distinctly in need of a bathroom, so we stopped at the Bar Rustici to order a couple of drinks and pastries by way of respectability for the use of their facilities – only to realise as we sat down by the window looking out on the Lungoparma that neither of us had brought any money. My daughter's spoken Italian is much more fluently natural than mine, while her youthful stature and good looks command more attention. She explained to the proprietors that her old father had forgotten to bring his wallet and so we couldn't pay, but if they could let us go, we would come back and redeem the small debt. Well, it was Christmas Day, wasn't it, and a little good will was in order. Besides, the bar was very busy, so they waived those evidently foreign customers away with a wave of the hand and a barely raised eyebrow.

We were expected for lunch in the hills between Medesano and Sant'Andrea, where my wife's sister's family lives, and were to ferry my mother-in-law there too. Making a detour back to the Bar Rustici would require an inconvenient loop in the wrong direction, but, risking the mild domestic friction entailed, I insisted that we make it and duly presented the sum for the drinks and pastries to the owner. The bar was even busier by now and they gave the impression they'd quite forgotten that earlier incident with the foreign customers; but I was glad to have been able to pay back my way – an Irishman's proudest boast, as it says in *Ulysses* – and what writing poetry entails according to another poem of Sereni's. Despite that minor disagreement about priorities, we were only slightly late for the serving of the aperitifs, at which I was immediately engaged in conversation not about a mysterious virus which was already making its way through the population in Wuhan, China (for we knew nothing of it), but what my response was to the General Election result of just two weeks before, and to the fact that 'remaining' was now definitely over.

During the last few weeks, I have heard some writers say, whether on the radio or privately, that this lock-down has not radically disrupted their necessarily withdrawn working-from-home lives. This is mostly not true for me, though, since you can't write poetry all the time, and a lifetime devoted to it is not, in that sense, an occupation. So much of my work for about nine months of the year would normally include face-to-face meetings with colleagues and students. However, I do have to admit, to myself at least, that almost two decades of living in Japan for nine months of the year and spending most of the other three in Parma, Italy, has prepared me – as had returning to England after so long away – for the social distancing that we are all now expected to live by. My repatriation to this country on the eve of the Credit Crunch, to a decade of austerity and four protracted years hoping for the mitigation of a national change of direction for which I cannot find it in me to see the benefit or virtue, had in any case encouraged an increasing sense of inner emigration. The obligation now to take evasive action if I see a fellow citizen advancing towards me has only served to deepen the feeling of distance, even as I do my tiny bit to protect the National Health Service by not becoming a further burden on its evidently stretched resources.

'Enigmas and Environs', a sequence more of revision than vision, as befits a poet in his later years, was begun in January 2020 and put aside as the British academic year intensified into early February. The drafts were taken up again and completed under lock-down in the second half of March and early April. Two of the poems that comprise it, 'Toast Funèbre' (a response to the Bormioli factory's remnants) and 'This Other Lifetime' (a love poem placed as an afterword to the series), had already appeared in *The London Magazine*, while my earliest publications in the journal, still during the Alan Ross era, were, I fondly recall, translations of some poems and that prose piece, 'Port Stanley like Trapani', by Vittorio Sereni. The invitation to contribute some prose to this special supplement has provided the occasion for these contextualising reflections, an opportunity partly to repay it by acknowledging my indebtedness to Parma, which had the honour and misfortune of being elected as Italy's Capital of Culture for 2020, which has now been entirely postponed for a year.

Thanks to the friendship I still have with a student and a faculty member from my Sendai years, for this spring's semester, which was to have begun on 1 April, I had been awarded a four-month research professorship at Kwansei Gakuin University, Nishinomiya, a private institution where those two friends now teach. It was founded in 1926 by American protestant missionaries and, as if to ease their homesickness, the campus was built in a southern Californian Spanish-colonial style of architecture. The house we would have been living in now – No. 6 West, Uegahara-Ichibancho – is also constructed in the campus style with two numbered palm trees to the right of its front door. But I'm not there: first the Japanese Embassy suspended our entry visas, and then British Airways cancelled our flights. On our imagined return from Kwansei Gakuin at the end of July, we were planning to use some annual leave to visit my wife's family in Parma and accompany her eighty-seven-year-old mother on a holiday to the mountains or the sea. Instead, I find myself – like so many of my fellow 'citizens of the world', by no means 'citizens of nowhere' now, as Theresa May put it – confined in the garret or ivory tower that is our small family house in Reading, England. Here, in this new normal, I've been dreaming back across the distances to those two countries, and those familiar cities in them, where we couldn't and can't go, and where I've felt so inspiringly not at home and yet still home.

May 2020

SOURCES

'The Personal Art' in *PN Review* 108, vol. 22 no. 4 (1996)

'Basil Bunting: We'll Enamel Him!' in *Poetry London* no. 86 (Spring 2017)

'F. T. Prince: "Delivered up to fiction"' in *PN Review* 93, vol. 20 no. 1 (Sept-Oct 1993)

W. S. Graham: 'A changed other person' in *Poetry Review* vol. 94 no. 2 (Summer 2004)

'"As wallpaper peels from a wall": Donald Davie' in 'Donald Davie at 70: A Celebration', *PN Review* 88, vol. 19 no. 2 (1992)

'Thom Gunn's Sense of the Movement' in *Metre* no. 14 (Summer 2003)

'Geoffrey Hill: Toiling over Time' as 'Behind the Lines' in *Studies in English Literature*, English Edition (2003), as 'Toiling in a Pitch' in vol. 26 no. 3 (1997), as '*The Triumph of Love* by Geoffrey Hill' in *Notre Dame Review* no. 8 (Summer 1999) and as 'Laugh, damn you!' in *Tears in the Fence* no. 34 (Spring 2003)

'Charles Tomlinson in the Deep North' in *Raceme* no. 7 (Spring 2018)

'Gael Turnbull: Grace Abounding' in *Poetry Ireland Review* no. 89 (2007)

'Roy Fisher through the Years' in *Grosseteste Review* no. 13 (1981) and *Notre Dame Review* no. 22 (2006)

'Elizabeth Bishop: "Exact as horror"' in *Notre Dame Review* no. 24 (Summer-Fall 2007)

'Robinson's Reply to Weldon Kees' in *Notre Dame Review* no. 17 (Winter 2004)

'"The Spaces Between": Jean Valentine' in *Poetry Ireland Review* no. 85 (Winter 2006)

'"Friendly Exchanges": Anne Stevenson' in *Times Literary Supplement* no. 5229 (20 June 2003)

'"As my way is": John Ashbery's Gift' in 'John Ashbery in Britain: A Supplement', *PN Review* 99, vol. 21 no. 1 (1994)

'Ted Berrigan: No Apologies and no Prizes' in *Jacket* no. 34 (October 2007)

'"Big Ideas": Jorie Graham and Charles Simic' in *The Cambridge Quarterly* vol. 28 no. 4 (1999)

'James Lasdun: Early Retirement' in *Notre Dame Review* no. 14 (2002)

'Things as They Are: Rae Armantrout' in *Poetry Salzburg Review* no. 28 (Autumn 2015)

'John Matthias: Speaking Personally' in *The Salt Companion to John Matthias* ed. Joe Francis Doerr (Great Wilbraham: Salt Publishing, 2011)

'Louise Glück and the Nobel Prize' in *The Edition* (14 May 2021)

'John James and *The White Stones* p. 71' in *Poetry Wales* vol. 47 no. 2 (Autumn 2011)

'John James: *In Romsey Town*', *Poetry Wales* vol. 47 no. 3 (Winter 2011–12)

'Veronica Forrest-Thomson: *On the Periphery*' in *Perfect Bound* no. 1 (1976)

'Thomas A. Clark: Poet as Herbalist' in *Perfect Bound* no. 5 (1978)

'"End of Harm": Douglas Oliver' in *PN Review* 139, vol. 27 no. 5 (2001)

'On *Untitled Sequence* by Peter Riley' in *The Poetry of Peter Riley*, *The Gig*, nos. 4-5 (2000)

'An Asocial Art' in *Printed Matter* vol. 16 no. 2 (Summer 1992)

'"Generosity of Spirit": Lee Harwood' in *Times Literary Supplement* no. 5304 (26 Nov 2004)

'David Constantine: Romantics and Foreigners' in *Poetry Ireland Review* no. 85 (Winter 2006)

'On Matthew Mead and John Welch', *Poetry London* no. 62 (Spring 2009)

'Ian Hamilton: "One Was Torn"' in *Poetry London* no. 64 (Autumn 2009)

'Here Comes (Almost) Everybody' in *Poetry Ireland Review* no. 88 (Autumn 2006)

'"The Way We Die Now": Dennis O'Driscoll' in *Poetry Ireland Review* no. 83 (Summer 2005)

'Derek Mahon Returns an Echo' in *Poetry London*, no. 78 (Summer 2014)

'"Loving his Food": Harry Clifton' in *Agenda* vol. 40 nos. 1-3 (2004)

'"Brick upon Brick": Peter Sirr' in *Times Literary Supplement* no. 5340 (5 August 2005)

'"So Good so Far": Sinéad Morrissey' in *Agenda* vol. 40 nos. 1-3 (2004)

'A Question of Balance: Enda Wyley' in *The Dublin Review* (2019)

'John Tranter and Tradition' in *The Salt Companion to John Tranter* ed. Rod Mengham (Great Wilbraham: Salt Publishing, 2010)

'"The moment's mixture": Allen Curnow' in *Metre* no. 11 (2002)

'Bill Manhire: "Have you no homes?"' in *Jacket* no. 16 (2002) and *PN Review* 163, vol. 31 no. 3 (Jan–Feb 2005)

'Derek Walcott's Quiet Regrets' in *London Magazine* (Aug–Sept 2010)

'Vahni Capildeo and Etymology' in *Poetry Review* vol. 102 no. 2 (Summer 2012)

'Liverpool ... of all places' in *Liverpool Accents: Seven Poets and a City* ed. Peter Robinson (Liverpool: Liverpool University Press, 1996)

'Hit the road, Jack' in *The Draft Will* (London and Tokyo: Isobar Press, 2015)

'Becoming a Reader' in *The Reader* no. 13 (2003)

'A Performing Art' in *The Cambridge Review* vol. 106 no. 2287 (1985)

'In a Tight Corner' in *News for the Ear: A Homage to Roy Fisher* ed. Peter Robinson and Robert Sheppard (Exeter: Stride Publications, 2000)

'Lost and Found' in *Japan Experiences: Fifty Years, One Hundred Views* ed. Hugh Cortazzi (London: Japan Library Press, 2001)

'Behind "Otterspool Prom"' in *The Reader* No. 36 (2009)

'Note on "Sein und Zeit"' in *Prac Crit* no. 6 (March 2016)

'Balkan Diary' in *English after Brexit* ed. Adrian Barlow (Leicester: The English Association, 2016)

'Parmese Days' in *Untitled, 2020* ed. Matthew Scott (London: The London Magazine, 2020)

Seven of the memoirs were also published in *The Draft Will* (London and Tokyo: Isobar Press, 2015)